T0367278

Baby Boomer Lamentations

Metaphysical Essays to Die for

Lewis Tagliaferre

iUniverse, Inc.
Bloomington

Baby Boomer Lamentations
Metaphysical Essays to Die for

iUniverse books may be ordered through booksellers or by contacting:

iUniverse
1663 Liberty Drive
Bloomington, IN 47403
www.iuniverse.com
1-800-Authors (1-800-288-4677)

ISBN: 978-1-4620-1034-9 (sc)
ISBN: 978-1-4620-1035-6 (dj)
ISBN: 978-1-4620-1036-3 (ebk)

Printed in the United States of America

iUniverse rev. date: 4/13/2011

Preface

Many, if not most, of the aging baby boomers are going to be disappointed and possibly depressed to find their future is not as bright as their past. They will need spiritual preparation, else the shock will be too great. Most everyone wants to be healthy, wealthy, and happy and to live a long time and then to die comfortably in their beds. There is no end of books and new age teachers who claim you can have whatever you want, but they rarely deliver on the life that they promise. So, where do you turn when you feel abandoned and sick, and poor and depressed, and your traditional beliefs provide no comfort? How is it possible to feel good inside when your world is shaken and you realize it is God who is doing the shaking? That was the challenge for this grieving husband who questioned his faith after traumatic death of his wife at the untimely age of 52. You may not believe this, but I got some unusual and very powerful answers from teachers provided by the late Sedona M. Schnebly, (1877-1950) namesake of the famous scenic resort in northern Arizona.

Here is the way it happened. During metaphorical side trips to Sedona, AZ while on business travel seeking some comfort from loss of his wife, the writer "met" five spiritual teachers who described five universal principles of reality that have grown into a metaphysical system of Theofatalism ™, i.e., the belief that God is that which runs everything in the universe from the smallest subatomic particle to the largest interstellar galaxy. That would include the lives of baby boomers. Such principles cannot be created, only discovered. It is a vision of God with the blindfold removed presented in one little peak at a time in these essays so the shock will not be overwhelming. This is not a religion in the sense that it includes a tax-exempt hierarchical commercial organization, worship of a deity or dogma composed by some guru, rituals of worship and traditional sacraments, etc. It is a belief system that accommodates all of these plus the agnostics and atheists, because God the Almighty One made them too.

This special collection of metaphysical essays for baby boomers was excerpted and revised from the larger work in Lessons from Sedona by the author. That was in turn derived from the Principles of Theofatalism™ developed in Voices of Sedona, also by the author. They are available from Barnes & Noble book stores and online at www.amazon.com and www.iuniverse.com. You may either read these essays in the order they are presented or you may skip around however the spirit moves you. This work could be like eating a large pizza...you can only digest a small piece at a time. And, as with slices of pizza, you will find the same ingredients coming up again and again.

The word "sheeple" replaces the word "people" throughout because the relationship of the shepherd to his flock of sheep flows from Genesis to Revelation in the Bible and provides the basic voice for this work, that of a shepherd/Jesus tending and feeding his sheep. "The third time he said to him, Simon son of John, do you love me? Peter was hurt because Jesus asked him the third time, Do you love me? He said, Lord, you know all things; you know that I love you. Jesus said, Feed my sheep." (John 21:17) Sheeple are divided into two groups: 1) those who are living God's will 24/7 and know it and; 2) those who are living God's will 24/7 but do not know it.

Many sources unknowingly contributed to this work, often posthumously. For all of them I am very grateful. The miracle is how they were gifted to me by powers beyond my understanding. I could never have discovered them on my own. All sources and quotations are included for educational purposes with legal advice under the "fair use" doctrine of the U.S. laws on copyright in accordance with Title 17 U.S.Code, Section 107. Bible scriptures are from the New International Version, used by permission. Some of the quotes, data and statistics were obtained from internet sources and are not directly referenced because they may be temporary. No claim is made about their accuracy or validity. Sources of quotations are integrated with text wherever possible.

The Chicago Manual of Style does not apply as this is not presented as a scholarly work. It also is published without formal professional editing, so there are no doubt errors of commission and omission that could be improved. Iuniverse deserves much credit for enabling unknown authors to make their contributions to this publishing genre, because they may have something valuable to say worth reading. If you somehow find this book and think it worthwhile, please recommend it to others. The baby boomers and their families need it.

Caution: If the discussions about the reality of aging in this work make you feel scared and confused, that could be normal because all growth comes with suffering. But, if they make you feel panic and uncontrollable anxiety, please seek professional care immediately from a qualified counselor. Nothing in this work is intended to be a substitute for competent medical or mental health treatment.

Contents

Introduction

This work is for those baby boomers whose spiritual belief system no longer provides comfort or support for the life they must live, a challenge that often occurs during the second half of life when the awareness of human mortality becomes conscious. C. G. Jung (1875-1961) observed, "Death is psychologically as important as birth... Shrinking away from it is something unhealthy and abnormal which robs the second half of life of its purpose." Perhaps you are searching for some relief from existential anxiety, which Jung said "sets in during the middle of life and is actually a preparation for death. If viewed correctly in the psychological sense, death is not an end but a goal, and therefore life towards death begins as soon as the meridian is passed." If the student is ready, the teacher has come. A new belief system is needed to help this cohort called the baby boomers to transition to whatever comes next. It could be called Theofatalism™. And now may be its time.

You may not like this book, but if you are one of those 76 million sheeple born from 1946 to 1965, i.e., a baby boomer or a member of their family, you certainly will need it. This book is not about health, wealth, and happiness in old age like you see in models airbrushed onto those slick magazines about retirement. It is about the metaphysics of aging in America, something unpleasant to contemplate but inevitable. This culture is all about enjoying life as long as possible, but eventually it ends for everyone and dying can be quick or slow, but hardly ever is it easy for anyone to give up and let go. Lamentations is appropriate use of the word in this title because what is happening in America will cause much weeping and gnashing of teeth with remorse and regrets aplenty.

Soldiers, sailors, marines, and airmen returning from WWII brought pent up demands for weddings, houses, cars, and the good life they earned after four years of battle. The G.I. Bill of Rights enabled them to finance educations and lifestyles in stark contrast to their parents who struggled through the Great Depression. Naturally, they made a lot of babies. The parents of baby boomers, i.e., "The Greatest Generation," have reached their age of fulfillment, dying at the rate of 1500 per day, and their offspring are poorly prepared for what comes next because they brought a social revolution to America.

The aging baby boomers are causing major changes in the U.S. economy, in case you did not know. You can see them everywhere in restaurants, airports, shopping malls, theaters, and just walking around the streets of America. Their impact is being felt as a shift from irresponsible consumption and living on credit to saving more and paying off their bills to prepare for retirement. Resulting decline in demand for goods and services, houses and cars for examples, threatens to stifle economic growth for the coming century. On the other hand, their needs for medical services and retirement entitlements threaten to bankrupt the Federal and state budgets. To balance their budgets, republicans want to reduce public entitlements and democrats want to raise taxes on the rich, and neither side can compromise enough to make it happen. They could be fulfilling the prophecy lamented by British economist, Alexander Tytler, (1747-1813) "A democracy is always temporary in nature; it simply cannot exist as a permanent form of government. A democracy will continue to exist up until the time that voters discover that they can vote themselves generous gifts from the public treasury. From that moment on, the majority always votes for the candidates who promise the most benefits from the public treasury, with the result that every democracy will finally collapse due to loose fiscal policy, which is always followed by a dictatorship." [The founders attempted to avoid this prediction by setting up a Senate in the Constitution appointed by the states (later changed to popular vote in the seventeenth amendment adopted in 1913) and appointment of a judiciary for life not subject to whims of public elections. Whether they succeeded or not is indefinitely uncertain.]

According to one analyst, baby boomers control over 80% of personal financial assets and more than 50% of discretionary spending power. They are responsible for more than half of all consumer spending, buy 77% of all prescription drugs, and 80% of all leisure travel. Take them out of the economy and you can imagine the impact on jobs and overall consumer demand. The baby boomer economy ran on minimum monthly payments until their credit limits were hit, and then it stopped. They financed everything from autos to movie tickets to restaurant meals and treated houses like ATM machines, refinancing them for cash to pay off debts more than once so long as the bubble lasted. Although the financial crisis has impacted nearly everyone, those who are nearing retirement may have a special concern. Their retirement funds have lost a great deal of their value and there is too little time left to recover the loss. Some of them with jobs expect to work as long as possible, even until age 70 and beyond in some cases. But, if they lose a job beyond age 50 it will be impossible for many to find another employer. The baby boomers also may be needed by aging parents as well as their own dependent adult children, putting them in a sandwich not of their liking. When you consider that half of their adult children cannot care for themselves, much less their parents, the future looks bleak indeed. They have been having a party on a houseboat heading for a waterfall. Their life of ease may be over. Many of them still don't get it. But they will.

As they enter retirement, many baby boomers will be shocked to realize how poorly they are prepared for it, physically, intellectually, emotionally, and spiritually while they live longer to think about it. Beginning in 2010 at the rate of 7,000 - 10,000 per day, up to half of them will depend solely upon government support for several decades that will strain the Federal budget as they claim more entitlements from Social Security, Medicare, and Medicaid supplements. Many will have to work as long as possible to help ease the impact of their withdrawal from the producing ranks will bring. The U.S. economy will be hobbled for a generation as this cohort ages and shifts from production and consumption to dependency and withdrawal. Their reduction in demand for consumer goods also makes it more difficult for the young graduates who emerge every May-June to get jobs and become consumers, so the economic impact is multi-generational.

The average annual income of U.S. taxpayers has been flat at inflation adjusted $33,000 for thirty years while the top one percent has soared, leaving no chance for upward mobility. Overall softening of consumer demand forces corporations to go overseas where they can earn the increasing profits demanded by stockholders, further reducing jobs for Americans. The impact of this demographic tsunami caused by aging baby boomers also will stress the basic social establishments as the institutions they have fostered are bereft of the charity they have provided. More than that, their families face demands for personal care giving that scarcely anyone can anticipate until too late for the health challenges to overwhelm them. The traditional religious and other social institutions cannot help much because at the end of life they are impotent and irrelevant to the tasks that aging and terminal illness bring. Politicians are afraid to talk about their impact because government solutions all bring painful consequences including rationing of scarce resources. [The Obama medical reforms call for reducing payments for Medicare recipients and shifting Federal resources to younger patients who are uninsured.] Politicians tried to offset the declining consumer demand caused by retiring baby boomers by opening the southern border to unlimited immigration, and when that did not work they injected artificial demand with excess deficit government spending on wars and social entitlements. None of their schemes has worked to sustain the bubble in economic growth the baby boomers created which now is over.

This American baby boomer generation has been driven by motivation to achieve virtual health, wealth, and happiness. But, now those foundation principles of baby boomers are being stressed by reality with no solutions in sight. Politicians cannot openly debate the issues involved because the emotions raised are beyond control. The debate on medical reforms had to abandon any discussion of formalizing end of life counseling under Medicare because too many critics irrationally predicted it could lead to “death panels” which might ration care for the elderly and foster actual euthanasia. This idea was so repugnant that it could not even be openly debated. But, rationing of medical services for the elderly is here now and will only get moreso as diseases of aging bring a tsunami of chronic terminal illness including cancer, diabetes, Alzheimers, heart failure, Parkinsons, kidney failure and the many accidents that aging brings, among others.

T.S. Eliot (1888-1965) observed that "mankind cannot stand much reality" so they attempt to avoid it with all manner of diversions, including sporting events, travel, movies, and such. Or they may withdraw from social contacts and become reclusive in hopes that by hiding their fears and emotions they will not emerge and become troublesome. Family members who are uncomfortable with the symptoms of aging may encourage either of these responses in their relatives so they won't have to deal with them. Make no mistake, aging is life threatening. Celebrated author, Ernest Hemingway (1899-1961) observed that "life breaks everyone," and then he committed suicide at age 62. The fact is that aging baby boomers and their families who are not prepared for the changes that are coming will have to meet them anyway. So you better have a firm and reliable belief system to handle the impact of this new reality the aging baby boomers now are imposing on the American economy.

There are only three responses to overwhelming challenges; avoidance, denial, and vigilance. While avoidance and denial may postpone the inevitable, only vigilance offers any hope of managing the outcome. Since sheeple will not change until it hurts too much not to, this discussion is offered in hopes that it may reduce some of the pain from the social and psychological dislocations that are swooping over the country at warp speed. These matters are neither easy nor quick to resolve because it will take changing a lifetime of assumptions that no longer apply to the aging baby boomers. It is like walking a labyrinth where there is no choice but to take the pathway that is perhaps provided by God, the almighty One who is Generator, Operator and Destroyer in the ancient Hindu tradition. Hence, the symbol of an ancient labyrinth from the Cathedral of Our Lady of Chartres, France is used as the symbol for this work. In this form of labyrinth there is only one way in and one way out and as with life, the task is to begin and to continue. [You can buy a placemat size labyrinth for table use from www.labyrinthcompany.com] The human ego wants control and immortality above all else. When both are challenged beyond endurance, the demolition of human psyche can be devastating. Baby boomers may not find answers to their challenges in traditional beliefs or social institutions. They will have to come from within. So let the spiritual work begin.

1. EXPLORING THIS MIRACLE PLANET.

Most sheeple act as though their puny, pitiful lives were the most important on the planet. Many of humankind are given to think they were created "just a little lower than the angels." They not only want exclusive control of their lives, but they want control of their environment also. Some might say that God made them that way. Homo sapiens are not the only forms of life on this planet, but the only other ones they may encounter are household pets or animals seen in a zoo. They share it with many other life forms, all that must contend with the natural environment as well as their own species and others as well. Becoming more aware of the others in their natural habitat might help individual humans to see their lives in a different perspective. Moving from a self-centered to an Earth-centered perception also may help one tolerate the challenges of life that are inevitable towards the end of it.

We may not all be able to see Earth from a space ship with the astronauts, but most everyone now can see it as if from space on the computer application called "Google™ earth." This is a modern form of the older globe that used to be used in all school rooms for geography classes. One can explore the whole planet and zoom into any spot for closer observations, down to a street address, often with photographs of local area scenes included. Also, high definition views of Earth from space on videos published by NASA show the planet and its place in the cosmos like no product of artistic imagination ever could. [Photos compiled by a half century of space exploration are posted at http://

www.nasa.gov/multimedia/imagegallery/] Viewing the Earth from the perspective of space may help puny Homo sapiens to realize how insignificant each one really is, and yet seemingly indispensable to the sum of the whole.

One can only wonder what impact such views have upon the astronauts who have provided us with the fantastic photo images available from their international space station orbiting 250 miles above Earth. The visual impact he saw returning from the moon prompted astronaut Edgar Mitchell to organize the Institute of Noetic Science to help bridge the chasm between consciousness and its relationship to the physical world. From just a few miles beyond the atmosphere there can be seen the greens, browns, yellows, and whites of terrain very few can visit in person. The thin line of atmosphere surrounding Earth itself is a miracle of creation, existing as it does as a very thin band of life support that provides the oxygen, carbon dioxide, nitrogen and other gases that make life on the surface of the planet possible. The scientifically accepted dividing line between Earth's atmosphere and space is the Karman line, about 62 miles above the planet's surface. Actually, humans are sustained by only five miles of atmosphere, beyond which oxygen is too thin to support life on this planet.

Even more amazing is the vast area of blue marking the oceans that cover more than four fifths of the Earth's surface which interact with the atmosphere in mysterious ways. The oceans provide much of the food for humankind and habitat for countless species of life. The most popular catch is tuna; about seven million tons are harvested per year for human consumption making them the most widely consumed seafood in the human diet. They are considered one of the most efficient forms of life on the planet, having survived for millions of years. Researchers are discovering the vast stretches of underwater geology surpass anything seen on surface land above. The life forms that live below depths of 10,000 feet (where there is little available oxygen and no visible light and where the pressure would crush a nuclear submarine hull) are only now being discovered. More than 300 species have been identified in the "black smokers" that are streams of heavy metals and gases more than 700 degrees F from volcanic vents at the bottom limits of submersible robots. Seen from the distance in space, nowhere are there any visual indications of national boundaries or political jurisdictions, and language, ethnic, and social barriers that separate the various tribes of Homo sapiens that occupy the planet.

Explorers from space must first of all be baffled by the strange sight of lighted clusters that appear after dark all over the planet. As they approach closer they may see apparent contrasts between these areas and others that remain dark at night. Even closer, and they would see strange movements of apparent creatures that seem to be most active at certain times of day, streaming from one area of the lighted clusters to another while seeming to host some form of parasites that exit and board them again on recurring schedules. The parasites also seem to enter other more stationary objects during the day which they exit with approach of the evening sunset and then repeat the patterns of movement from the morning. Only after even closer inspection would space explorers eventually separate the parasites into forms of life that actually use the mobile creatures as vehicles of transportation as they move about their concentrations of habitat called cities. Why this should be so would be a total mystery to space aliens as it is a mystery to the ones exhibiting this strange behavior if they stop to think about it.

Paleontology is not an exact science, but some researchers think humanoids appeared about 30,000 – 300,000 years ago following evolution from the previous human species, called Neanderthals, which became extinct for some unknown reason – perhaps because some asteroid hit the planet and destroyed its climate. In Africa, early modern humans appeared as long as 195,000 years ago, if the carbon dating of remains uncovered in Omo Kibish, Ethiopia, is correct. The earliest sites outside of Africa with early modern humans are at Skhul and Qazfah caves in what is now Israel dating about 100,000 years ago. However, written history has existed only for about 4500 years, so the only evidence for early humans is found among buried artifacts. Some of these artifacts raise questions with no answers about the sheeple who created them. Among them are discoveries of the ancient city of Alexandria in Egypt buried under the Mediterranean Sea, the origin and purpose of the Great Pyramids of Giza, the strange rock structure called Stone Henge in England, and the remnants of civilizations found in Asia, the Sahara desert, and jungles of Meso-America. Obviously, civilizations have come and gone among Homo sapiens, one conquering another and another, so maybe the ones existing today will disappear to be uncovered by explorers centuries from now. But the Earth goes on, and each individual life appears to be a necessary, even if insignificant, part of it all.

The societies of Homo sapiens on Earth today range from those highly dependent upon technology for sustaining life for processed foods to those who still rely closely upon the planet for their survival. While "advanced" nations require electricity for their air conditioning and video cell phones and personal computers to survive, the least developed tribes in Amazon jungles and isolated islands of Indonesia and remote areas of South America and Africa along the equator still live in hunter-gatherer societies like their ancestors did for thousands of years. Many of them still have no written language. One such is the Zoe tribe found only a few decades ago by flying missionaries who live near the Amazon River in northern Brazil. The government has restricted visitors to their villages so little is known about them, except they live like hairless chimpanzees only one step removed from their genetic ancestors. They do not travel beyond their village limits and they know nothing of the outside world, not even modern villages along the Amazon.

Homo sapiens also occupied the harshest climates of the north in arctic regions where they lived in ice igloos and subsisted on raw seals for both food and clothing...until they moved into electrified houses, got cell phones, and learned to eat pizza. Which is the more advanced and sustainable, the primitive villages in the jungle and the arctic or New York City, is open for debate. An observer from space could not see the invisible but arbitrary lines of longitude and latitude that encircle the Earth to create accurate and dependable means of navigating around on its surface, now with the aid of the geo-positioning satellites aloft. The observer from space could not see the intentional boundaries between groups of Homo sapiens organized as nation/states either. Neither could an exploring observer from space see any of the wide varieties of other life forms that roam the dry land and saturate the ocean depths. But they are there. And nobody knows why.

If a celestial explorer were to see the Earth only from the perspective of the international space station, the reality of life in all its many forms would be totally missed. However, if the lens could zoom into the planet one section at a time the pictures that emerge would tell a much different story. The nature of life on Earth might be shown in the form of movements as complex as watching the traffic patterns during rush hours in major cities, while missing the complex subterranean metro rail systems buried underground, and as simple as the cattle grazing on a thousand hills. Before landing, a celestial explorer would pass through the fragile atmosphere that sustains life on Earth. It is composed of only a few gases including oxygen, hydrogen, carbon dioxide, and nitrogen, and extends but a few miles into space. Its composition is very fragile and now seems to be threatened by unlimited fossil fuel combustion that is eroding its ability to protect the planet from excessive heat. Explorers would probably not miss the weather patterns that change constantly as do the seasons of the year according to the position of Earth relative to its mother star, the Sun. Continually striking the Earth are lightning bolts that seem to be necessary to discharge gigantic charges of electricity constantly building up in the atmosphere for some unknown reason. What they might not see is the amount of radiant energy that interacts between the Earth and its atmosphere in a wide band of frequencies that bombard all living creatures on the planet.

Explorers also might overlook the miraculous way in which plants use energy from the Sun to convert carbon dioxide into oxygen to sustain mortal life, a process called photosynthesis. They may marvel at the visible lightning strikes that occur continually all over the planet, but they might miss the electromagnetic field of Earth and its pulsing resonance that some believe discloses its inner life to the molten iron at its core. If they looked carefully they might discover that the Earth is a dynamic planet with weather patterns swirling overhead and volcanic activity booming underneath. They might observe the changing seasons and connect them to the angle of tilt in the axis that is almost precisely 23 degrees from normal. They might even wonder why that angle was chosen because even a small deviation would make the seasonal shifts too extreme for life as we know it to survive. They might also note that the whole thing seems to be slipping and sliding around on a time table too slow for ease of detection in normal scale but more importantly when accelerated to geological time scales. In fact, the land masses are not stable and have been sliding about on the surface of the planet driven by gigantic forces from deep inside, called plate tectonics.

Periodically there are giant upheavals that inflict great damage to both the Earth and its inhabitants. Photos from space have disclosed evidence of rivers that once flowed over the Sahara desert when it was a verdant landscape full of villages and maybe even cities. Explorers have found cave drawings there of sheeple swimming in lakes where now there is only arid desolation. Scientists think the Sahara was a verdant plain around 7,000 years ago at the end of the last ice age. From cores of ice removed from glaciers around the world and other astronomical evidence, some scholars have concluded a giant asteroid exploded over northern Europe at 4:30AM on June 23, 3123 BCE that would have changed the climate of the Middle East permanently and caused a world-wide catastrophe that created the desert now covering all of North Africa. Dinosaur bones estimated to be more than 160 million years old have been found in Antarctica, indicating a much different climate on Earth way back then. And rocks at the bottom of the Grand Canyon appear to be two billion years old. Genetic histories among Homo sapiens seem to indicate that life on Earth could date back to 3.5 billion years in its most primitive form. Several vast areas are unexplored but seem to support life where Homo sapiens could not survive, such as the vast equatorial jungles of the Amazon forest, and the land arctic masses of Alaska and Siberia.

If the explorers could land and systematically visit the four corners of Earth they would find an infinite variety of life forms, each seemingly going about their business with unfailing determination, as though indispensable parts of a giant system of interconnected parts. Even the most informed sheeple on Earth probably are aware of only a small fraction of all the life forms they share with the planet. Researchers into such things have discovered many lifestyles among subhuman species on Earth that exhibit forms of intelligence, and social practices that are extremely complex. They occupy climates too harsh for humankind and flourish where no man has gone to explore. Many forms of life thrive in arctic climates such as Siberia that are too harsh for mankind. What man has learned about life species makes one wonder if Homo sapiens are mistaken in assuming the Earth was made for them only. Among them are mysteries without explanation. For example, the migratory patterns of whales, salmon, butterflies, geese and elephants show a remarkable level of skills in navigation and timing that seem beyond the ability of humans. There is a seagull that mates for life and shares the fishing and nesting in the rookery on shore with its mate. When the hunters return they find their mates by listening for a distinctive call from the cacophony among the thousands of birds in the rookery and land right at their sides. Prairie dogs on sentry duty are known to emit elaborate tonal language to warn their neighbors of intruders, humans as well as predators and prey. Look very closely and you may see a caterpillar go through metamorphosis to become a butterfly.

How can a Monarch butterfly species navigate each fall from Canada to Mexico to hibernate for the winter and then produce four new generations the following year on its way back north before repeating the same migration pattern year after year? Even though it is a small bird, the arctic tern is able to accomplish the remarkable feat of migrating over 22,000 miles each year, the longest migrating distance of any bird. When not nesting, the arctic tern almost never lands and is known to be in daylight more than dark because of its migration schedule. More mysteriously, why do they do it? Only the tern and the hummingbird can hover in midair. Humming birds' hearts beat 600-1200 beats per minute and their wings beat 200 times per second... except at night when they hibernate and heart rate drops to 30 times per minute...they need to eat half their weight every day in nectar and insects which they snatch in midair. Much smaller than any bird is the ubiquitous mosquito. They are known to carry several troublesome diseases including malaria and dengue fever. In addition, in Costa Rico mosquitoes carry eggs of a dangerous parasite that imbeds itself in human skin and proceeds to hatch and consume human flesh from the inside out if you become infected.

Here is some more trivia about life on planet Earth you probably never thought about. All sorts of unseen forms of life are moving about beneath our feet and under the concrete of our cities. A locust must consume its own weight in food every day during its short gestation. That may not seem like much because they are so small. But a swarm of them can contain billions of individuals and consume all the foliage in a 40 mile wide swath traveling as though under command of some common navigator. Sharks hatch while the eggs are still inside the mother, and the first hatchling eats its siblings before it is born, full grown and ready to catch its own prey. This macabre event has been photographed by researchers interested in learning such things. The jellyfish is thought to be one of the most primitive forms of life still surviving. Explorers have filmed it digesting live prey through its transparent organs. Its billions of tentacles possess lethal poisonous toxins so chemically complex that no antidote for humans has yet been developed. A certain species of jellyfish (turritopsis nutricula) which can reverse its own aging seems to be migrating and expanding all over the Earth posing threats to human ocean swimmers in all climate zones. Nevertheless, the jellyfish is prey food for other species, including a sea turtle, that are not bothered by its poisonous toxins. A species of harmless jellyfish found in salt water lakes hosts a form of algae under its hood that converts sunlight into sugars for its food.

Scientists study the marmot/groundhog, which hibernates for five months each winter, to see what may be learned to help treat cancer patients. The eight inch lizard-like "Geico" gecho that weighs only two ounces has billions of microscopic hairs on its feet that create an atomic magnetic bond with any surface, permitting it to tote heavy cargoes up sheer glass walls. The chameleon snatches its prey with a sticky muscular tongue that can lash out more than the length of its body. Scientists have discovered that all species of octopuses produce a toxic-packed poison that they use to paralyze their prey. They can even force a clam into opening its shell to be consumed. Fortunately, only the blue-ringed octopus is dangerous to humans.

Life on Earth is more diverse than imaginable, and also more deadly. There is a bird that lays its one egg in the nest of another species, which hatches first. The invading chick then pushes the other eggs out of the nest leaving the grieving parent to feed it to maturity while its own parent goes off to play. That may not seem to be just, but it is the will of God the Almighty One. Among the carnivorous predators on planet Earth, none are more vicious than the giant snakes, anaconda and python, which can grow to more than 30 feet long. They lurk in concealment and squeeze their prey do death and then swallow them whole, always head first. More deadly than these is a carnivorous plant found in jungles of Southeast Asia that lures small rodents and frogs into its inescapable trap and then digests them alive. The carnivorous plant (Nepenthes attenboroughii) can grow more than four feet tall and was found by researchers atop Mount Victoria, a remote mountain in Palawan, Philippines.

Experiments indicate that chimpanzees seem to have a short memory capability that far exceeds that of humans. And the loyal family structure detected among maternalistic elephants puts Homo sapiens to shame. With miniature video cameras, investigators have uncovered the complex societies of insects, including bees and ants, that are amazing. Each individual in hives and mounds seems to carry out its very specific role for its time and place. An estimated four million rats are born each day, ten times the rate of human births. They carry practically every disease known to mankind, but in some Hindu temples of India they are respected and even are invited to share the food eaten by sheeple at each meal with their hands. But, in poor areas of Asia they are eaten by humans as a good source of protein. Some Hindus think cows and monkeys should be treated with great respect as the dwelling temples of gods. Some sheeple prefer to eat cats and dogs that are embraced as intimate household pets by others. It must all be very confusing to the explorers from outer space.

On a more pleasant note, the fact that wheat flour rises when exposed to air was known for 5,000 years before Louis Pasteur discovered the unicellular yeast fungi organism in 1859 that was causing it. Wild yeast spores are constantly floating in the air and landing on uncovered foods and liquids. They cause the rotting of fruits and vegetables left uncovered. These wild varieties contributed some of the earliest kinds of sourdough bread mixes which did not depend on adding starter cultures. But it causes a common form of inconvenient infection in women. Vaginal yeast infection, which is the most common form of vaginitis, is often referred to as vaginal "Candidiasis." Moving on, humans have learned to use the copper laden blue blood of horseshoe crabs for testing antibiotics, while the fresh eggs of spawning crabs also provide a food source for migrating birds along the seashore. Whatever is involved, plant or animal, most of the life on Earth seems to live according to very specific plans and modalities. They even appear to grow through regular cycles of extinction and evolution from unknown causes. Why should it be any different among Homo sapiens? What makes them think they are so different from other forms of life? Earthquakes caused by gigantic rifts in the surface crust have devastated millions of sheeple as do floods, hurricanes and other disasters. One theory says that massive methane gas eruptions from the ocean floor have exploded to cause mass extinctions about every million years or so. We may be about due for another one.

One can only wonder why the Creator made habitat for creatures living in water four times as large as that for land-based creatures. One of the mysteries of this planet is the oceans of sea water that cover nearly seventy percent of its surface. Scientists still do not understand its salty composition after more than one hundred years of study. One theory says that ocean water is a weak solution of all the minerals on Earth, but its complexity is beyond measure and analysis. Water from the sea is transferred to the atmosphere where it is cleaned and stripped of its salt and then returned to the land as fresh water to nurture crops and surface creatures of all forms, plus the Homo sapiens. This process of recycling seems endless but is regularly impinged by weather conditions that often overload the system with events that seem out of control. The whole atmosphere, only 25 miles thick, seems like a gigantic electrical system continually striving to achieve some form of balance. Thousands of lightning strikes hit the Earth each hour discharging the immense energy stored for some unknowable reason.

Much of life on planet Earth occupies the ocean depths far below view from the surface. Located around the equator in shallow depths are curious living creatures called coral reefs. They conduct an elaborate and complex lifestyle that depends upon delicate balance between fish, plants, and sunlight. They seem to follow not only the sun but also seasons of the moon. Some of them reproduce by mass spawning and some of them reproduce by cloning themselves. Coral serves as a measure of global warming because it is very sensitive to slight changes in water temperature. Some forms of undersea life, called extremophiles, have been discovered living at volcanic rifts deep within the ocean at temperatures and pressures previously thought to be unable to support life. These organisms obviously have learned to use their habitat to support life while we as observers could not survive in their environment.

Miniature shrimp colonies, with individuals scarcely larger than a grain of rice, have been detected that live much like ant colonies, with workers and a queen perfectly molded for their roles in this life. A bizarre deep-water fish called the barreleye has a transparent head and tubular eyes. The barreleye (Macropinna microstoma) is adapted for life in a pitch-black environment of the deep sea, where sunlight does not reach. They use their ultra-sensitive tubular eyes to search for the faint silhouettes of prey overhead. Since the fish's discovery in 1939, biologists have known the eyes were very good at collecting light. But their shape seemed to leave the fish with tunnel vision. Its eyes are surrounded by a transparent, fluid filled shield that covers the top of the fish's head. Now scientists say the eyes rotate, allowing the barreleye to see directly forward or look upward through its transparent head.

Below depths of 10,000 feet ocean creatures have been seen by explorers in submersibles that survive without light or plants for food under pressure that would crush a nuclear submarine. How is unknown. We know more about the surface of the moon than we do about 95 percent of the ocean floor. There is a miniature worm living in the dense ice fields of Alaska that seems to thrive better the more cold that it gets, but they literally melt at 40F. From there, life in the sea ranges up to the giant whales that really are mammals and must breathe fresh air to live. The largest known animal on the planet is the Blue Whale, weighing up to 200 tons and large as two buses back to back. Science knows little of its lifestyle, although they migrate 2,000 miles to mate and feed upon schools of the most prolific miniature crill fish, consuming up to 7,000 pounds per day...each. And they seem to communicate over hundreds of thousands of square miles.

Whales and rhinoceros seem to have a common genetic ancestor now that DNA testing is possible that dates back some 25 million years. One current troubling surprise is how the snakehead fish that is native to rivers in Asia has found its way into rivers of North America. Since there are no local predators, their migration is driving many fisheries scientists to find a solution before the snakehead population becomes uncontrollable. The piranha fish found in 40 different species along waters of the Amazon cluster in schools that will turn into voracious predators when hungry at the drop of blood. They don't discriminate and will eat sheeple as well as their own kind when driven by a feeding frenzy. Thankfully, alligators like to consume them for lunch. Some one hundred new life species are discovered in the oceans each year. And yet, less than five percent of the ocean floor has been explored with remote controlled submersible vehicles.

Explorers visiting the planet would doubtless be amazed at one significant aspect of all life forms on Earth. Many species must kill and eat each other for food, often eating the prey while it is still alive. One can watch a preying mantis attack and consume a living butterfly close up on television if you watch the science channel. Did you know the chief competitor of mankind for harvesting lobsters actually is the octopus, with its eight tentacles and three hearts? Who said that man was the top of the food chain? Invade the shark habitat and you could be eaten alive. And remains of a human have been found inside the stomach of an alligator. Believe it, or not. Humans are not the only species that eats processed foods. The capuchin monkeys of South America have learned to harvest clams by waiting for them to be exposed in receding tides and then to open them by ritual banging upon a rock for several minutes. They also have learned to harvest pine nuts, first selecting them for ripeness, then pealing off the skin and drying them in sunlight, and then cracking them open with large rocks. How this behavior evolved is unknown. Actually, they eat a wide variety of plants also, some 5,000 species of apples for example. Some species of life on the planet are parasites that must depend upon a host in order to reproduce and survive. One such is the assassinator wasp that stings its victim and then lays its eggs inside it that hatch into pupae that consume the paralyzed host from the inside out before they emerge as adult wasps. Nice. Ants working in armies controlled by some unknown leadership can attack and consume much larger prey. For example, they have been observed cutting up a live scorpion by tearing apart the soft tissue that separates the armored sections and carting it off in pieces to the ant hill to feed the mass.

But, they often also attack each other to gain territory and control over their neighbors. A TV documentary showed one ant colony invading its neighbor, killing its queen and substituting its own to make the vanquished soldier ants serve her hatching eggs. First they send out scouts to find a potential enemy and then they organize to attack and take over the adjacent colony. Each ant seems to have an assigned task that it must complete or die trying. There was ant carnage all over the place. One is reminded watching it all unfold of a swarm of Homo sapiens that occupy a city-state or a nation attacking its neighbor for expansion in which each individual soldier ant has his assigned task but none of them realize how they fit into the bigger picture because it would not matter if they did. At the climax of battle, the opposing queens fight to the death and the survivor reigns over the new combined ant colony. Maybe that is where Homo sapiens get the idea for making wars. Only Homo sapiens have invented mighty weapons of mass destruction and no longer depend upon one-on-one combat as it were among the ants. They killed 55 million sheeple in WWII and apparently learned nothing to prevent it from happening again. They just rebuild the destructed land and repeat the same lifestyle over and over...just like ants in an ant hill. Invade a nest of hornets and you will find yourself under painful attack by thousands of worker insects dedicated to protecting the hive and the queens who lay the eggs for a new generation. Also, with night vision lenses researchers have observed a pride of hungry lions taking down a full grown elephant and consuming it alive. They have also photographed zebras attacked and consumed by crocodiles along the streams in Africa they use for drinking water. Modern research is amazing. So is life on Earth.

There is a small lizard with a tongue twice as long as its body with a sticky suction cup on the end that it uses to catch food. It can snatch its prey and consume it before the victim knows what happened. Some Homo sapiens kill animals for the sport of it or for money. For example, elephants are being killed illegally to harvest their tusks to make ivory jewelry and rhinoceros are harvested to sell their powdered horns as an aphrodisiac. [But not by Hindus who believe that all sentient beings possess a soul that is commonly connected as one in the universal spirit. Whether carnivores or herbivores and shedding blood or not, Hinduism would suggest that this is a necessary manifestation of the will of God the Almighty One to express their nature and to gather experience in realms of matter for growth through many reincarnations towards the spiritual goal of Nirvana. From this behavior they learn the joys and sorrows of transitory existence.] There is an orphanage in Kenya that has been run by a white woman for more than 50 years for baby elephants that are abandoned when their mothers are killed by poachers...amazing dedication and compassion. But, humans get their due with the two-foot parasitic Guinea worm that grows inside the body and eventually emerges, maybe through a nipple, or genitals, or a foot. The hardest to accept are the parasites that attack innocent children, like the tiny river worm that enters their eyes and causes blindness among the poorest in Africa who must bathe in polluted waters. God has a lot of explaining to do.

Carnivores are some of the most ingenious hunters on the planet. Perhaps the most amazing carnivores are the plants that catch and digest insects, like the Venus Flytrap. Unsuspecting prey are invited to enjoy its nectar until a spring mechanism traps the insect for leisurely digestion. Red ants have been studied in Siberia constructing mounds up to three feet deep into which they cram bodies of all sorts of victims killed for storage to last throughout the long cold arctic winters that can send temperatures low as minus 90 degrees F. In contrast, the American black bear can hibernate through winter up to six months without food or water and still survives. Science is trying to discover how they do that so it can be applied to astronauts on long space trips, like exploring Mars. There is a small horny toad in the outback of Australia that lives apparently only to eat ants. And the anteater has no teeth so it just sucks them up and swallows them whole. Ant colonies, by the way, seem to function as one integrated mind in going about their lives, sustaining and protecting the colony. Ants are estimated to be one of the oldest forms of life, dating back 50 million years or more. There is a small poisonous spider that preys upon ants successfully because it is made to look like one and therefore can sneak up on the victim unawares. The small archerfish in rivers of southeast Asia and India is known for preying upon land based insects, including grasshoppers, butterflies and spiders by literally shooting them down from plant leaves with jets of water drops from their specialized mouths. They have excellent eye sight that enables them to compensate for the light refraction through water when aiming at the prey. Their accurate range can be up to 2-5 meters long, which would be equivalent of a human spitting up to 40 feet with lethal force.

A small tropical fish living in rivers near the equator jumps out of the water to lay its eggs on overhanging plant leaves. The male then splashes the eggs with water to keep them moist until they hatch in a few days to drop into the river where they suckle on secretions from the scales of their parents. The praying mantis, more likely called the preying mantis, is a ferocious insect predator 50 million years old that comes in some 2200 different species all over the Earth. It has been photographed catching and eating small snakes, humming birds, butterflies, and field mice head first while they are still alive, not to mention females of the species beheading males during copulation. Lions hunt on the plains of Africa in packs which hunt together to take down larger animals, even up to giraffes, zebras, and elephants, when smaller animals are not available. Eagles and other flying predators can see prey hidden among grasses from a thousand or more feet above.

There is a small bird living in Yellowstone Park called the "nutcracker" that gathers pine nuts and buries them to eat during the long cold winters. The bird remembers all the locations and finds them even though buried under deep snow. The same is true of squirrels living in the Park. The sperm whale which grows to 70 feet long and 20-30 tons, migrates more than 2,000 miles annually from mild tropical waters to the arctic to feed its appetite for schools of squid. This predatory violence takes many forms on land and in the oceans, but the bottom line for life on this planet is kill or starve because it is a closed system. Animal life forms absorb oxygen and exude carbon dioxide while the plants do exactly the opposite. Some coincidence, huh. So, how much forest will have to be cut down by insatiable humans before the oxygen runs out?

Modern Homo sapiens have secluded the killing of food animals away in secured meat processing plants, but it still happens. If each person had to kill its own prey, perhaps there would be more vegetarians. The food chain seems to be in precarious balance on land and in the seas and everything is recycled, except for the species that man has driven into extinction by over-harvesting. Only by recycling the energy in matter can life survive. Is there anything more amazing than the electric eel that produces a jolt of 600 volts to paralyze its prey? Or the largest fresh water catfish that lives in the Amazon River and can breathe in air with its primitive lungs thought to be 100 million years in evolution? A mysterious sea creature in the south Pacific is the cuttle fish that comes in 100 species from two inches to 30 inches long and can instantly change its shape and color to confuse both predators and prey. And consider the life cycles of the migratory birds, mammals, and insects that are programmed to navigate the Earth, running a gauntlet of predators, in order to return to their origins to spawn and to die at the end of their lives.

Birth and death, predator and prey, are necessary complements to preserve life on Earth, and each must reproduce to feed the other in a delicately balanced, fragile food chain. Looking under bushes might disclose hordes of locusts consuming the flesh of plants in wide ranging attacks in arid regions that threaten the food source of many other life forms unless they can be restrained by effective interventions. Insects of all species could be the most survivable life forms on Earth since they appear to be the oldest, some dating back 360 million years in their present form. Someone calculated the weight of all cock roaches to be ten times that of Homo sapiens. Think of the food supply there if we could overcome the taboo of eating roaches. Actually, some sheeple do eat insects of all kinds...good protein. Modern hotels and homes also seem to be infested with an outbreak of bedbugs, (cimicidae) a pest very difficult to detect and to destroy. Like mosquitoes, they feed on the blood of animals and sheeple, so you better check for bite marks each morning. All in God's will of course...AIGWOC.

While most species are defined by their need to survive and reproduce, species Homo sapiens seems to be more creative and even intentionally cultivates other species for food. A most bizarre example could be the fishermen in Yangshuo, China who have trained a flightless bird, the Cormerant, to fish for them at night. They tie a string around the birds' necks so they cannot swallow the prey which they catch and then haul them back into the boats to retrieve the fish from their throats. In Mongolia, humans train golden eagles to catch foxes, deer, and wolves, before they are returned to the wild to nest and repopulate the species. In contrast, the flying pigeon was used by soldiers in both world wars to carry secret messages hundreds of miles back to their roosts. They appear to use the magnetic field of Earth for navigation. More than 40,000 human pigeon fanciers still race the birds competitively in England. In a typical year, U.S. human beekeepers produce about 250 million pounds of honey from billions of bees. Their hives are precisely formed and maintained with 30 perfect hexagonal cells per square inch oriented to true magnetic north. Unfortunately, honey bees seem to be disappearing for some unknown reason, threatening the supply of all crops that require their pollination services. Some investigators think over use of toxic insecticides to increase food production could be the cause.

Explorers visiting planet Earth might be shocked to see how the species Homo sapiens seems to kill each other simply for power and control, sometimes one at a time and sometimes in mass slaughter. Empires come and go fighting for centuries to establish rights in religions, politics, or natural resources. But, always the rise of one empire is eventually transformed into its fall and the rise of another in its place. This behavior seems to be an extension of the animal world in which males must endure mortal combat in order to mate and assure procreation of the species. Tribes of Homo sapiens may be defined many ways, by their geographic boundaries, by ethnic culture, by religions, by patriotic ideas, by goals and desires, by racial blood lines, etc. Many sheeple decorate their bodies with cosmetics, tattoos, and bloody scarring to enhance their perception of beauty and to display their warrior natures. Whereas in the past the struggle was among nations in Europe and then between them and the north American natives, this trait is most prominent in the Middle East and Africa presently where sheeple still live in male dominated families among tribes and nations that continually attack each other as they have been doing for millennia. These primitive roots are seen in the body tattooing and piercing that is becoming an acceptable art form in modern cultures. The process of evolution seems to go backwards sometimes.

A wonder of this planet likely to be missed by explorers from space is the way that Homo sapiens have learned to discover, refine, and use its natural resources. Many sheeple live in undeveloped areas where they share resources with the other mammals and predators in a fine balance of mutual respect. From the burning of wood for warmth and cooking to using it in construction to the discovery and use of coal, oil, gas, and all the minerals and metals on planet Earth, one must be amazed at the way it all has unfolded in time. Now, most of the easily found and refined materials are used up so it is becoming more and more difficult to keep up with the increasing demand. Gold, for example, that was found in surface deposits and river streams now must be harvested from microscopic deposits in subsurface rocks that only geologists with exotic instruments can discover. The most productive gold mine is more than two miles deep in South Africa. Production of oil products, which has enabled society as we know it to move and fuel industry may have peaked, leaving the rest to be ever more expensive to find and refine. The future will require every new and unimagined way of replacing these natural resources with whatever comes next. So, if visitors from outer space have any new ideas they surely would be appreciated.

Along the river shores in Ethiopia there grows one of many species of sycamore fig tree that provides a glimpse into the mind of God. But you have to look very closely to see all the details. It may be one of nature's oddest couples; a tiny wasp that can barely be seen, and a giant fig tree, which shelters a remarkable menagerie of wildlife among its limbs. The wasp and the fig depend on each other for survival. Without the wasp, the tree could not pollinate its flowers and produce seeds. Without the fig, the wasp would have nowhere to lay its eggs. Filmmakers spent two years camped out documenting the tree's pivotal role as a source of food and shelter for everything from gray hornbills, Africa's largest bird, to swarms of invading insects searching for food. The resulting documentary, "The Queen of Trees," produced in high definition video could help Homo sapiens see their role in the overall plan of life more clearly if they only took time to see the way this tree participates in the wide variety of life dependent upon its existence. From the parasitic insects that live within the fruit to the animals that consume the rotted droppings, each participant in the stream of life plays its defined role. Elephants and giraffes devour the fruit and seeds are spread and new trees spring up to keep the cycle going. Every leaf on the fig tree has its purpose and does it in a unique fashion. And so it is with each of us. Every sentient being has its place in the grand scheme of the universe in space/time and no one can say which one is more important than another.

What may appear to be an insignificant individual fig tree in the vast stream of life forms occupying Earth is actually a single, but indispensable, unit in a fantastically complex interlocking system of elements that make up the whole. Only the species Homo sapiens seems to have the power and the inclination to intentionally destroy its own habitat as well as each other. Never do they cease to conquer space and time and to seek and fill each nook and cranny of the planet with evidence of their existence while they quarrel over ideas with no consequence. They are both compassionate and cruel, intelligent and stupid. Perhaps explorers at some future time will find their remnants and wonder why they came to exist here at all. With all the craziness going on, one might reasonably ask if the planet would not be better off without the species Homo sapiens. After all, it existed long before they ever came.

One thing about planet Earth that space explorers could miss is that it seems to be getting warmer repeating a cycle between ice ages. More precisely, it appears that the ice fields at the north and south poles are melting, something not seen for 50 million years. From ice cores drilled in Greenland, it appears that Earth has endured several long term cycles of ice ages followed by warming trends during its four billion years of existence. The Earth also sweeps through an orbit around the Sun that expands and contracts in radius during a repeatable cycle, swinging from a circle to an ellipse. Normally it wobbles very precisely on its axis tilted at 23 degrees during its orbit around the Sun to create the predictable moderate changes in the seasonal climates. In addition, the impact of the Sun on surface temperature of the Earth is a lot more complex than first imagined. The magnetic storms on its surface of the Sun may have a modulating influence upon cosmic radiation that affects the Earth in very complex unknown ways. Historical temperature cycles seem to track the density of carbon dioxide in the atmosphere, and the present debate is over whether consumption of fossil fuels that produces carbon dioxide is threatening future climate stability.

Researchers are searching valiantly to better understand these phenomena. No doubt, the rampant burning of fossil fuels by Homo sapiens must be included in the research. Some scientists fear that by 2050 the ominous trend towards present overheating may not be treatable so they want a panic stop to burning fossil fuels. The Union of Concerned Scientists that watches such things has warned all world governments of the measured melting of the ice caps at both north and south poles. Icebergs of long standing are melting into the oceans and the polar ice caps are receding, which means less Sun energy is getting reflected and that accelerates the warming in a vicious cycle. Melting ice is causing the oceans to rise by a foot every century, but a hundred years is too long for most planning by Homo sapiens. In addition, skeptics are convinced the scientists are fudging the data to support political goals that are inconsistent with impartial investigations. Nevertheless, to hedge their findings, many nations and charitable foundations have constructed the Svalbard Global Seed Vault, a gigantic seed storage facility deep under the arctic tundra of Norway, to safeguard crop seeds at zero degrees F in case the world's agriculture may need to be restarted from scratch one day to preserve human life.

Previous life-destroying cycles of planet cooling and warming occurring every hundred thousand years have been detected in deep glacier cores and accounted for by theories of volcanic eruptions, release of methane gas from ocean deposits, strikes by comets, cycling solar magnetic flares from the Sun, and even changes in the orbit of Earth around the Sun. The Earth is still a molten caldron of iron and nickel at its core that erupts from time to time through vents that produce life-destroying volcanoes. Some of them are more active while others lay sleeping waiting for the next cataclysmic eruption. [Yellowstone National Park is the largest known charted volcano with an active caldera more than 60 miles across. It has more geothermal rifts than the rest of the world combined. Volcanologists estimate it is 50,000 years overdue for its next gigantic eruption which could destroy much of North America.] Consequences of the apparent accelerated change in the warming of Earth are being debated by opposing sides; those who want to believe it is caused by the burning of fossil fuels to feed the lifestyles of Homo sapiens and others who want to believe it is part of the historical cycles of cooling and warming that have been seen in the distant past.

Nobel winner, ex-Senator and Vice President, Al Gore estimates that consumption of fossil fuels is spewing about 70 million tons of carbon dioxide into the air every day, far too much for the atmosphere to absorb. Combined with the clearing of old growth forests, this is an ominous trend, according to him. If it continues, oceans could rise up to 40 feet this century, displacing a billion or more sheeple and disrupting life as we know it. One thing that seems certain is that unless the planet warming is slowed and reversed the rising ocean levels will impact countless millions of sheeple living near the shorelines of all the continents, and some animal species may be threatened with extinction. More than that, climate change could affect fundamentals of food production and basic needs of life in ways that are scary and unpredictable. When Homo sapiens are confronted with insurmountable challenges, they often respond with flight or fight reactions, but not until it hurts too much not to, and this one is no different.

All life forms on Earth seem to live according to their divine design, so why should Homo sapiens think they are different from other forms of creation? To be sure, the works of Homo sapiens on Earth have left their marks even on the moon where there is an American flag and the NASA platforms posted to mark their visitation. From the Great Pyramids of Egypt to the Greek Parthenon [where stone masons fitted hundred-ton marble blocks to accuracies of one twentieth of a millimeter in the fifth century B.C.] to cathedrals to the gods to the Great Wall of China [which was under construction for two thousand years] to Hoover Dam to the Empire State Building, the Brooklyn Bridge and the Golden Gate, The Panama Canal, Disney World, the Eiffel Tower, the great cities and the slums, and the cemeteries and unmarked graves that contain warriors and victims of them lost in ubiquitous battles, the 800-mile long Alaskan oil pipeline and the thousands of oil drilling rigs planted in the oceans offshore; the works of men have bent the Earth to their will. The latest building monuments to mankind are being constructed in Dubai, all with oil money, to show how high they can reach, one of them nearly a half-mile tall. They also have created the means for destroying all of it and choking it with their pollution. When the late Saddam Hussein was driven out of Kuwait in 1991, he left more than 600 burning oil fields that cost $3 billion dollars to extinguish and consumed a billion barrels of oil per day for nine months.

Ocean feeding birds like Albatross are dying from eating plastic debris floating in their feeding zones in the North Atlantic Ocean. Americans discard 1500 pounds of plastic containers per person per year... and much of it ends up in the oceans. They discard enough plastic water bottles to circle the Earth 190 times every year. Pollution flowing into the oceans is making them more acidic and threatening existence of life forms at the lower level of the food chain that have survived millions of years. Destruction by natural forces also disrupt life on the planet including recent earthquakes, tsunamis, and hurricanes. Danger comes from the stars also. Going back much further, explorers might discover that the age of dinosaurs came to an abrupt end about 65 million years ago when a gigantic asteroid six miles wide hit the planet at the Yucatan Peninsula and left only the underground animals to survive and slowly evolve into modern species, eventually producing Homo sapiens. They now seem to be threatening their own future existence with sexually transmitted diseases, exploitation of natural resources, climatic pollution, and weapons of mass destruction. One may legitimately ask if the planet would not be better off without them on it. After all, it apparently existed just fine for billions of years before they came along, so it certainly does not need them. And impressive as some creations of mankind are, they are nothing but temporary zits on the scale of history timeline of the planet.

Mother Nature not only provides the rainbows and the roses, she also provides the predators and prey. The top of the food chain thinks it is the crown of creation, but that attitude could be just the crown of hubris. The species Homo sapiens has adapted to its many different habitats on Earth, but it still acts in many ways as the animal from which it evolved. Its primary role is to reproduce the species and its secondary role is to conquer its neighbors. It also seems to be destined to convert the mineral resources of Earth into waste products that are unusable. Through mining and drilling, refining and processing, humans rapidly are using up reserves that took eons for Earth to produce. Metals and minerals are fast disappearing from the easily removed supplies. While it reshapes the planet and exploits its resources for "improved" standards of living, it seems to be hell bent upon destroying its own habitat and exhausting the resources it was given for survival. Oil is the most visible of these resources since it drives all forms of transportation, but the many others that are taken for granted also are nearing their maximum production. From extremes of rich and poor, Homo sapiens seem unable to learn how to distribute health, wealth, and happiness fairly or to live at peace. They devote one hour per week to spiritual life, but spend the rest of their time in competitive power struggles. The Bible says in Genesis 9:7 that God told them to multiple and subdue the Earth, but then what? Can there be too much of a good thing?

One of the more interesting things about life on this planet is that much of it is in the past. Archeologists often find and dig up remnants of species and cultures that are no more. The origin of life forms, i.e., that which moves, processes food, and reproduces, has been traced through fossil evidence back two billion years, half the life of the planet. From the extinction of the dinosaurs some 65 million years ago to the mythical lost continent of Atlantis, there could be as much of us buried as there is on the surface. Scientists estimate that fully 99 percent of all once living species now are extinct. That trend line does not bode well for the rest of us. Humans of primitive form may be as long as two million years old. But, the species Homo sapiens seems to be so very young in time, they are a mere blip on the history of the planet, emerging some 200,000 years ago. So, whether we are just on the beginning of a new trend in some experiment of creation yet to be tested remains to be seen. It certainly is not a homogenous bunch when you compare the technology and lifestyles of the most advanced with the least developed among us. They say the stone age did not end for a lack of stones, but some sheeple just have not got the message yet. Why there must be such widely varying lifestyles among us, and what role each individual in the species has been given only God the Almighty One knows.

Watching the "Life" series on Discovery Channel, one might conclude that Homo sapiens are nothing special. They do some very insane and bizarre things to carry out their various lifestyles. They appear to be little more than hairless gorillas with hubris...researchers are looking inside their brains to try and find out how they work. But a very close look might disclose there is more than flesh and blood here. The invisible but indispensable exchange of oxygen and carbon dioxide between plants and animals would be a good example. The operation of laws of physics and the use of mathematics to explain them would be other examples. There also is a spirit, soul, and universal energy that soars above the visible to fuel the invisible. It drives continuous change and mutation of species to evolve and to adapt between themselves and each other. And where they begin and end nobody knows. The late astronomer, Carl Sagan (1934-1996) saw the Earth as a small blue dot in the universe and described it as follows; "That's home. That's us. On it everyone you love, everyone you know, everyone you ever heard of, every human being who ever was, lived out their lives. The aggregate of our joy and suffering, thousands of conflicting religions, ideologies and economic doctrines, every hunter and forager, every hero and coward, every creator and destroyer of civilization, every king and peasant, every young couple in love, every mother and father, hopeful child, inventor and explorer, every teacher of morals, every corrupt politician, every superstar, every supreme leader, every saint and sinner in the history of our species lived there - on a mote of dust (12,000 miles in diameter) suspended in a sunbeam."

For centuries, sheeple have dreamed of leaving the Earth to explore outer space. But, first, it will be necessary to colonize the Moon because it would be necessary to launch explorations to other planets. The first thing that you have to understand is that Earth and the Moon actually orbit a common center of gravity. This place is about 4,700 km from the center of the Earth. In other words, the Earth wobbles back and forth because of the orbit of the Moon. Some scientists have even proposed that the Earth and the Moon actually are a double planet because of their relationship, but this would only be the case if the common center of gravity was outside the surface of the Earth. The orbit of the Moon is about 385,000 km from the Earth on average. Like the planets in the Solar System, the orbit of the Moon isn't circular; it actually follows an elliptical path around the Earth. At its closest point, called perihelion, the Moon is 364, 397 km from the Earth. And then its most distant point, called aphelion, is 406, 731 km.

You might have heard that the Moon is slowly drifting away from the Earth. Although the Moon is tidally locked to the Earth, always presenting the same face to our planet, in about 50 billion years from now the Moon will complete an orbit once every 47 days, and it will remain in exactly the same place in the sky. One half of the Earth will be able to see the Moon, and it will be hidden from the other half. Of course, the Sun is expected to become a red giant in about 5 billion years and potentially destroy the Earth and Moon during its terminal implosion, so this time may never come. But, scientists are not sure what will happen to Earth as the orbit of the Moon changes. It could experience a shift in axis causing horrific climate change and rotation that could relocate the oceans and destroy all life on the Planet...or not. Scientists also think it is overdue for a major reversal in its magnetic field. This magnetosphere aids all the migratory species find their way so just what it will do to life in all forms is not certain, although it appears to have happened many times before. The Mayan calendar ends on December 21, 2012, and many scientists are wondering what the meaning of that might be. Some say it marks the approach of a super asteroid that will disrupt life on Earth with many geological wonders, while others say it predicts a shift in magnetic radiation from the Sun that could disable all communications on Earth. Those living then will certainly find out who is right.

Now if you look at some of the pictures of Earth taken from the international space station in orbit 250 miles above, none of this activity is visible. It may even seem to the astronauts that none of it exists at all. The Earth just appears like a blue and green globe with white smudges floating around on it. In addition to wondering where it is all going, the basic unknowable question is why does it exist at all? Moreover, what is going on with all those other dots of light in the universe that may include planets not yet imagined by mankind? Noted humanist, naturalist, adventurer, and essayist, Barry Lopez defines wisdom as understanding "that the world will always be there, no matter how sophisticated our technologies for probing reality become. The great mystery will be there forever. And it's the sense that it's not yours to solve. And the search for a solution to a mystery is perhaps not a sign of wisdom. I am perfectly comfortable being in a state of ignorance before something incomprehensible. And it's in that moment that you're driven to your knees and you believe - I wouldn't call it religious. It's just what happens when you open up again to the extraordinary circumstances of being alive"...on planet Earth. Planet Earth certainly is a miracle of creation that we know very little about. Nevertheless, at the finish of its creation, the Bible says God saw everything that he had made and said it was good...several times. But, the Bible also said it turned sour and eventually will be demolished and replaced with a new heaven and new earth...believe it, or not. All beginnings come with endings.

This is now, but what about the future? Could anyone have predicted a hundred years ago what life would be like today? Could they have foreseen cell phones, space craft or the Internet? Some sheeple who are sensitive to such things feel an energetic shift is happening as a result of transitioning into the second millennium A.D. Astrologers may say we are entering the "Age of Aquarius." From a spiritual, intuitive reference they believe we are entering into a new era which is driven by female energy. In contrast to the male energy which is directed and aggressive, the female energy is collective and nurturing. For the last century and more many "new age" gurus have talked about the need to balance the male and female energies. Most everyone who is spiritually grounded sees this time as a transition phase, shifting energy from the philosophy of the West to that of the East. But what about all the other species living on this planet? What is their role? The Psalmist observed, "What is man that thou are mindful of him…?" It is obvious that mankind needs the planet to survive, but Earth does not need mankind for its survival. So, why are we here? Where are we going? When Job got his long awaited interview with God, he was soundly admonished for daring to compare his insignificant self-righteous attitude with the greatness of the creation. And he replied, "How can I reply to you? I put my hand over my mouth." (Job 40:4) Feel good inside no matter what happens outside. If you can. Now that you know how you fit into planet Earth, we can go on with the rest of the story.

2. Every Bell Curve Has a Bottom Side.

Ever since mankind learned to write there have been some who got rich telling others how to gain health, wealth, and happiness. They claim that if you can just believe it you can have it. After all, Jesus said so. "..if you believe, you will receive whatever you ask for in prayer." (Matthew 21:21) But, as Jesus also predicted, we still have the poor and destitute among us. (John 12:8) Trappist monk, Thomas Merton [a.k.a. Fr. M. Louis] (1915-1968) explained careers in No Man Is An Island (1955), "Some people find in the end that they have made many wrong guesses and that their paradoxical vocation is to go through life guessing wrong. It takes them a long time to find out that they are happier that way." What is wrong with this picture? In the most brutal of wartimes, there are sheeple who survive easily and prosper while many others perish and suffer miserably. In the calmest of peaceful historic periods, there are many who suffer great pain and failure. That is the way it is, and if it were not so it would be different.

In the theater of life we are cast into many reciprocal roles. Some of them include that of student-teacher, child-parent, employee-employer, member-leader, sick-healer, etc. In each role we are given to imagine an ideal performer and to compare it to the real performer that we are. The gap between the ideal self and the real self is a measure of success, but it also creates stress, discontent, and unhappiness. Some stress is good in that it stimulates striving to become better, but too much stress can become frustrating and create guilt, remorse, and even self-loathing in the extreme. The task of life is to do the best we can under the circumstances, and to accept the real person that we are no matter where our natural level of performance occurs. Feeling unsuccessful, by whatever measure, is a dis-ease of society that must be accommodated. Comparing yourself to others is a sure way of feeling unhappy and making you unhealthy. Living in the gap of chronic failure to match the real self to the ideal self can lead to mental depression and even suicide if it is not recognized and treated.

Unfortunately, some sheeple seem to turn everything they touch into gold while other sheeple must exist all their lives on minimum wage drudgery. Oil mogul, J. Paul Getty (1892-1976) said if you took all the wealth of a country and distributed it equally among everyone it would very soon be reallocated like it was at the beginning. He said it seems to be a natural law for some to be rich and others to be poor. Someone must clean up the tables and wash the dishes after the rich finish eating their banquets in fancy restaurants. And someone must slaughter the cattle and pick the fruits that they enjoy during the meal. Someone must mow the grass and dress the greens on the golf courses, and someone must clean the bathrooms and remove the trash in the hospitals while doctors enjoy their exalted social status.

One of the most difficult tasks of Homo sapiens is to accept their station in life when it becomes obvious that further development is not likely to happen. In every contest only one comes in first and last; the rest are distributed above and below the middle in the form of a bell curve under normal conditions. After mid-life most every one will have to accommodate to their social and financial status on a scale much like the bell curve used for grading students in school. Passed the age of 50 or so the die is cast for old age and nothing much will change the trends in life that are established by then...unless you happen to win the lottery of course. And, every bell curve has a bottom half. For example, the average retired person in America lives on only $16,000 per year; $12,000 from Social Security and $4,000 from personal savings, investments, and pensions. That's the fact, Jack. Many baby boomers are not going to be prepared for that shock when they retire.

Nowhere is this principle more evident than in attempts by social educators to make all students equally proficient in all their subjects, as in the "No Child Left Behind" policy of Pres. George W. Bush.

Nationally, about one third of students do not graduate from high school, and among many inner cities it is more than half, including Washington, D.C., because success is defined by the wrong standards. One size does not fit all. C.G. Jung noted that "the shoe that fits one comfortably pinches another." Prince Charles of England got some public criticism for complaining that educators who imply all students are equally capable of superior performance were doing them a gross disservice. He wrote in a private note that got leaked to the press and was printed in a newspaper, "What is the matter with everyone these days? Why do they all seem to think they are qualified to do things far beyond their natural capabilities? This has to do with the learning culture in schools as a consequence of a child-centered system which admits no failure. This is the result of social utopianism which believes humanity can be genetically and socially engineered to contradict the lessons of history."

Prince Charles may not have realized that he was echoing an idea proposed by Adolf Hitler (1889-1945) in Mein Kampf, (1926) "The best constitution and the best form of government is that which makes it quite natural for the best brains to reach a position of dominant importance and influence in the community...The first consequence of this fact is comparatively simple. It demands that those elements within the folk-community which show the best racial qualities ought to be encouraged more than the others and especially they should be encouraged to increase and multiply." Actually, some sheeple have attempted to promote just that through a movement known as "eugenics" that was proposed by a cousin of Charles Darwin, Sir Francis Galton (1822-1911) It is defined as "the organic betterment of the human race through wise application of the laws of heredity." Its goal is nothing less than raising the average intelligence level of society by restricted breeding of the lower class. After all, if animal, fruit, and vegetable stock can be improved by genetic manipulation, why not humans too? Must the species be weighted down by the lowest performing cohort of each generation? Of course, the opposite view claims that all students can do equally well, given the best of teachers and classroom resources. But, no matter what scale is used, there always will be a bottom side to the bell curve.

The pioneer of birth control in America, nurse Margaret Sanger (1879-1966) advocated eugenics by empowering women to intentionally regulate pregnancy and birth in opposition to law and the Church. She lived to see the Supreme Court strike down Connecticut state law in 1965 that prohibited contraception by upholding the rights to privacy. A socialist and atheist, Sanger advocated in 1932, "A stern and rigid policy of sterilization and segregation to that grade of population whose progeny is already tainted or whose inheritance is such that objectionable traits may be transmitted to offspring." Today eugenics is widely regarded as a brutal movement which inflicted massive human rights violations on millions of Jews during the Holocaust. Adolf Hitler was defamed and criticized for his stand against interracial mating, "The result of all racial crossing is therefore in brief always the lowering of the level of the higher race; physical and intellectual regression; and hence the beginning of a slowly but surely progressing sickness. To bring about such a development is, then, nothing else but to sin against the will of the eternal creator. And as a sin this act is rewarded." However, developments in genetic, genomic, and reproductive technologies have raised many new questions and concerns about what exactly constitutes the meaning of eugenics and what its ethical and moral status is in the modern era. The U.S. Declaration of Independence, as well as Marxism, declared that "all men are created equal," but this obviously is not true by any metric whatsoever. Some educators are critical of the present national policies that they claim are "dumbing down" all Americans in order to uplift the lower class. All in God's will of course...AIGWOC.

When you consider the average American voter barely graduated high school, let us hope that God makes all the selections for political office. With all the misinformation and the downright lies and emotional appeals in political campaigns, no one really knows the candidates they vote for. No two voters enter the booth with the same perception about the candidates, so how could they be making rational choices? Elections often produce a slim majority for the winner as a consequence and the voters remain divided. Less than half of registered voters vote and elections usually are won by very small majorities. Moreover, most voters actually expect their leaders to make the tough decisions for them, and that is why the founders created a representative republic rather than a democracy that would be controlled by the dumbest majority. Contrary to modern Christian common sense, our lives are not our own to live as we choose but rather to live as God chooses for us. So if you think that voters actually choose their leaders, think again. From the predestined stories of Isaac and Ishmael and the brothers Jacob and Esau in the Old Testament, including the role of Pharaoh in Egypt to enslave the Jews, God obviously has favored some sheeple over others to show the power of his will, according to the teachings of the prophets, Jesus, and the writing of Apostle Paul. (John 9:1-3, Romans 9:6-18)

The Koran says much the same thing to Muslims. That is the conclusion drawn in his popular book, The Purpose Driven Life, (2006) by mega-church pastor Rick Warren. It begins, "It is not about you." For it is God who has the power to make from the same lump of clay "some pottery for noble use and some for common use." And we are in no position to argue with him. (Jeremiah 18: 2-6, Romans 9: 20-22) In fact, the Bible contains many scriptures that govern the relations between slaves and their masters, so it is apparent that God included human slavery in his creation. "Your male and female slaves are to come from the nations around you. From them you may buy slaves...you can will them to your children as inherited property and make them slaves for life...Slaves, obey your earthly masters with respect and fear and sincerity of heart, just as you would obey Christ." (Deuteronomy 25:44-46, Ephesians 6:5) If God is sovereign it is impossible to defeat his will and, therefore, man is not responsible for his condition, neither collectively or individually. So who are we to judge those assigned to the bottom of the bell curve or to exalt those at the top in this life? This inescapable logical conclusion flies in the face of the argument for free will and the eternal and universal damnation of mankind for Adam's original sin, does it not? But, of course, God must have created that delusional idea also or else it could not exist.

The Prince of Wales could have invoked the model of the bell curve to explain why some students excel and some fail. For everyone who comes in first someone must come in last in any normal classroom distribution. Perhaps a good example is the way sheeple run a marathon race from the winner to the stragglers. If a certain number of sheeple are dumb, wealthy, sick, or evil an equivalent number must be the opposite; smart, poor, healthy, or good. Developed by renowned German mathematician, Carl Friedrich Gauss, (1777-1855) the standard normal distribution of any set of data distributes around a center with the shape of a bell. This seems to be true no matter what scale is used or what criteria are used for analysis. It is based on the math of probability and statistical theory. The center of that curve defines the location of the "standard deviation" developed by Sir Francis Galton (1822-1911) who imparted laws of statistics to human populations. He also started the debate between nature and nurture to explain human behavior. Experiments in childhood development have shown that appropriate sensory and intellectual stimulation are needed before the age of two if the human brain is to achieve its potential. If it is deprived of what it needs to grow properly, the infant must run on its basic input-output program, not unlike a personal computer. The track of brain development may be set by the age of three, as any pre-school teacher can attest. But, this is not the whole story.

Holocaust survivor, Victor Frankl (1905-1997) argued that "we live in three dimensions, soma, psyche and noos (body, mind, spirit). Our genetic material, by definition, is a purely physical expression (the manufacture of amino acids), but with profound effects on and interaction with psyche and noos. Because most of our physical needs are met in the environment, much of the variability measured in nurture studies are in the psyche (mind and intellect). We cannot account for the noetic (spirit) part of our existence in nature-nurture studies, and this variability is folded into arguments for hereditability or environmentality. Thus we never see it." If nature and nurture do not add up to one, the remainder may be attributed either to free will or the will of God the Almighty One, take your pick. So, Bill Cosby may grow up among poor black families raised by a single mother in Philadelphia and become a rich and famous comedy-actor who earned a Ph.D. degree in education, while his peers remained attached to their roots. In marked contrast, Jeffrey Dahmer grew up in a white middle-income professional family, but he became a drunk and serial killer, convicted of murdering 15 sheeple in gruesome crimes and was killed by a fellow inmate in prison. All in God's will of course...AIGWOC.

There are opposites to everything, and the bell curve is no exception. Jesus seemed to turn the bell curve upside down when he proclaimed in a parable about the kingdom of God, "...the first shall be last and the last shall be first." (Matthew 19:30, Matthew 20:16, Mark 9:35,

Mark 10:31, Luke 13:30) The ability of God to do as he wishes with mankind is shown by the many ways that he elevates some who seem to possess little merit. The U.S. Congress is full of them. To cite one such example, the success of A Course in Miracles (1975), claiming to be a new revelation from Jesus by Helen Schucman, defies reason. But, so does the Catholic Mass, which proclaims the body of Christ literally is present in the sacrament of the Eucharist and the raging public success of Glenn Beck and Joel Osteen. Neither of these public figures completed college and Beck is a self-admitted recovered alcoholic and converted Mormon. The main skill they have in common is the power of personal oratory, not unlike that of Adolf Hitler, which resonates with their followers and commercial supporters.

All three are examples of emotional passionate zealots who seem to be empowered beyond reason for the work they do and the followers they attract who in turn make them into cult leaders. By the age that older sheeple realize their plight is not changing, the message of relief and hope from such orators seems like the only remaining places to turn for any comfort and security, so they return again and again to their words in search of some hope for health, wealth, and happiness. This is the human ego seeking control when none is possible. The "Course" teaches from Hinduism that inner peace is found by choosing spirit-mind and rejecting ego-mind. But, who or what it is that does the choosing is never explained. The ego-thought system, which is the default thought system of humanity, is prone to conflict, haunted by guilt in the forms of an inner sense of threat and unworthiness, is constantly fearful and deeply suspicious. As the "Course" points out, when threatened, our ego will very likely go from suspicious to vicious.

Given this understanding, it is no surprise that A Course in Miracles (1975) is highly threatening to human egos and has been associated with controversies of various sorts since its thought system of Oneness teaches that individuality, the separation of bodies, and sensory world are illusions, much like looking at the image of a hologram. [A hologram is a three-dimensional projection of an object into space using a system of laser beams.] It proclaims, "My salvation comes only from me...it cannot come from anywhere else." But the "Course" seems to contradict itself by claiming, "God's will is all there is...Disobeying the will of God is meaningful only to the insane. In truth it is impossible...God's will be done. It cannot be otherwise...there is no will but God's, and...there is no substitute for the will of God...Free will is part of the ego's delusional thought system and part of its cherished array of gifts. There is no free will in Heaven, and Heaven is here and now, for free will implies choice, and choice implies alternatives that can be differentiated among, an impossibility within the Oneness of spirit that Jesus reminds us is our reality...what is opposed to God does not exist...the mind which believes it has a separate will that can oppose the will of God also believes that it can succeed. That this can hardly be a fact is obvious. Yet, that it can be believed as a fact also is obvious. Therein lies the birthplace of insanity." If all this be true, then the illusion of separation of ego from spirit that it condemns also must be the will of God, so further discussion is moot. Nevertheless, more than two million sheeple think this "Course" is some new form of gospel that merits their study and support, although it merely restates ancient principles of Vedanta Hinduism.

[It should be noted that Christians believe God has begotten only one Son. But that idea conflicts with the inclusion principle of Hinduism, that all of the souls that God created are his Sons, and if you also believe that the Sonship is One, then every soul must be a Son of God, or an integrated inseparable part of the Sonship that Jesus prayed for. (John 17: 20-23) If you do not find the concept that the whole is greater than the sum of its parts difficult to understand, you should therefore not have too great difficulty with this. The Sonship in its Oneness does transcend the sum of its parts. However, it loses this special state as long as any of its parts are missing. This is why the unity cannot ultimately be resolved until all of the individual parts of the Sonship have returned. Only then, in the true sense, can the meaning of wholeness be understood and manifested. The correction of this error is the At-One-Ment. Islam attempts to correct this error by proclaiming there is no God but Allah. Of course there must always be an opposite thought, and it was provided by Prof. Stephen Prothero, chair of the religion department at Boston University, in his book God is Not One. (2010) By describing beliefs and practices of eight world religions he hopes to gain more tolerance for the vast diversity among religions. But some critics argue that he failed to prove his objective.]

Rarely, an evolved soul is born with this insight. One such was juvenile philosopher and poet, Mattie Stepanek (1991-2004). At age six, he wrote this poem:

"We are many colors of skin and languages
We are many sizes and many countries
But we are one Earth and we have one heart and one life
We are growing up together
So we must live as one family."

Religion is psychotherapy in that when folks pray they accept a higher power to be in charge of their lives and to reduce their swollen egotism and feel humble. It is in humility and calm submission that mental health lies. St. Theresa of Lisieux (1873-1897) declared, "Jesus does not demand great actions from us but simply surrender and gratitude." Ultimately fear emanates from belief that one has a self, big-ego Self. To heal fear one must reduce ego to merely calm submission like that expressed by Job after God removed all his children, servants, herds, and then struck his aging body with boils all over. "Though he slay me yet will I trust in him," (Job 2:8-10) If one does not want to feel any kind of fear at all one must give up the entire ego, i.e., the wish that things should be different...if they could be they would be. In most cases, the human ego, which serves usefully in society to modulate the urges to both good and evil on opposite sides of the bell curve, will not commit suicide so it must be crucified in order to be resurrected in a different form. Such crucifixion may occur from two sources; either a personal trauma or crisis and from a religious conversion. Either experience removes control from the ego and puts the subject into awareness of existential anxiety. Crucifying the ego can take many crises in life, but the bottom line is loss of control at the hand of God. Of the rebirth necessary to enter heaven Jesus explained, "With man this is impossible but with God all things are possible." (Matthew 19:26, Mark 10:27)

This is the lesson of Job in the Old Testament, plus Jesus on the cross in the New Testament. Both of them were caused to suffer by God, physically, intellectually, emotionally, and spiritually, in order to remove their own self righteous ego and fall into submission to the creator. "Then Job answered the Lord: I am unworthy - how can I reply to you? I put my hand over my mouth. I spoke once, but I have no answer - twice, but I will say no more." (Job 40:3-5) Jesus died as a suffering ego that cried out from the cross, "My God, why have you forsaken me?" (Matthew 27:46, Mark 15:34) This was painful and gruesome to both mortals, but all very necessary to the plan of God for without the crucifixion there could be no resurrection to life everlasting. Peter declared to the Jews, "Jesus of Nazareth was a man accredited by God to you by miracles, wonders and signs, which God did among you through him, as you yourselves know. This man was handed over to you by God's set purpose and foreknowledge...Now, brothers, I know that you acted in ignorance, as did your leaders. But this is how God fulfilled what he had foretold through all the prophets, saying that this Christ would suffer." (Acts 2:22-23, 3:17-18)

Many saints have had to suffer feeling separated from God, strung out at the bottom of the bell curve in human society at the end of life. According to her biographer, Mother Teresa, the saint of Calcutta, came to stop praying and withdrew from Jesus during her terminal aging which lasted ten years while declaring, "My soul is no longer one with you." This was after she concluded that, "God does whatever he wants with whoever he wants whenever he wants." Those who are born with disabling illnesses suffer the most, while their families either grow stronger...or not. Others have reported some crisis, such as losing a spouse or close loved one, financial or natural disaster, disabling accident, etc. that disordered their concepts about basic beliefs and required a restructuring of the psyche to re-stabilize and go on. Some fall into irreversible addictions or even criminal behavior and never return to normal. For others, the anticipated resurrection experience raises their consciousness of spirit to levels not previously known.

Perhaps, some of that suffering can be avoided if we can just accept everything as God's will. The process requires letting go of the ego-control that cannot be sustained and replacing it with some understanding and acceptance of a higher power, whatever that may turn out to be. Jesus proclaimed it the "Holy Spirit" and he reassured his disciples; "... the Counselor, the Holy Spirit, whom the Father will send in my name, will teach you all things and will remind you of everything I have said to you. Peace I leave with you; my peace I give you. I do not give to you as the world gives. Do not let your hearts be troubled and do not be afraid."(John 14: 26-27) But, this claim seems to violate human nature which is naturally afraid to face the end of life at the bottom of the bell curve. Sometimes it means losing all you have in order to adopt a different lifestyle that avoids the ego drive for more, more, more. For example, one can think of the highly successful football pro, Michael Vick, who nearly destroyed his life by supporting illegal organized dog fighting. His rehabilitation after serving in prison is on a different plane of life than before. Of course, some spend the rest of their lives in prison or even lose their lives in the process of restitution to society. All in God's will of course...AIGWOC.

Perhaps C.G. Jung would say that terminal suffering at the bottom of the bell curve is necessary to purify the soul and crucify the ego, turning dross into gold as it were. One might even assume that subconscious forces may work to remove the barriers to this experience, such as might be that called the "kundalini" crisis described in Asian mysticism. This is not so much different than the plea of St. Tereas of Avila (1515-1582) to God, "Either let me suffer or let me die." The problem is that many healthy, wealthy, happy Homo sapiens are given to think they are some kind of exception, and it will never happen to them. Among humans there is a form of socially derived natural selection, as among animals, that assures each one a unique place on the bell curve. Sheeple, like the animals they are, can be ranked on a two-dimensional scale of dominant to submissive and independent to dependent. The dominant-independent ones make things happen, legal or illegal, while the submissive-dependent ones watch what happens and obey the others. Some sheeple naturally are more dominant and independent while others naturally are more submissive and dependent. Problems occur when either behavior is carried to extremes. This is not right or wrong, it just is. All in God's will of course. AIGWOC. Think you can handle that?

National public radio celebrity, Garrison Keeler describes fictional "Lake Wobegon" as a place that defies statistics where "all the men are good looking, all the women are strong, and all the children are above average." This only happens in fantasyland, because in real life every bell curve has a bottom side. The U.S. Census Bureau announced that 15 percent of Americans are living in poverty in 2010, the highest level since 1994. The government defines poverty as a family of four living on less than $22,000 a year. No matter how you scale it, there will always be 15 percent of sheeple at the bottom 15 percent of incomes. The top 20% now get half the income while the bottom 20% gets less than 5%...Get it? Jesus seemed to recognize this principle when he observed that there would always be poor sheeple ...no matter what scale is used. (Matthew 26:11) Politicians seem intent on ignoring this principle, and they try changing the bell shape of income distribution, health, education, and other public issues. One such public policy is the guaranteed minimum wage. When the government-set minimum wage fails to fit the bell curve, other market forces seem to work against it. Employers just hire poor immigrants instead at illegally low wages. That could be a major reason for the failure to enforce immigration laws. Some economists suggest that having more workers willing to work for lower wages actually improves U.S. ability to compete on world markets.

As Americans rise up the bell curve, more poor immigrants are admitted to fill up the bottom half. Employers pay poor immigrant workers without documentation less than the stipulated government wage while law enforcers look the other way. World-wide, the United Nations estimates that 1.5 billion sheeple must live on less than two dollars per day. Some of the poorest sheeple in the U.S. live homeless and scrounge garbage to eat; they are called "dumpster divers." Many of them are drunks and drug addicts, prostitutes, and mentally deranged but some are just down on their luck, some even with college degrees. Many cities have made it illegal to sleep in cars or in public spaces, hoping that will make them go away. Out of sight, out of mind. How bad can it get? Some sheeple in Africa starve and the poorest in Haiti eat mud pies because it must import most of its food. In spite of spending more than six trillion dollars on the "war on poverty" since President Johnson initiated the "Great Society" in the 1960s, about the same percentage of sheeple occupy the poverty ranks as before. Only the scale of the bell curve has been changed; its curve remains the same.

The bell curve is not always fair as some reap more than they deserve beyond what they earned during their working years. F. Scott Fitzgerald observed, "The rich are different from us." And Ernest Hemingway explained, "Yes, they have more money." The IRS reported that the nation's 400 highest-earning households reported an average income of

$345 million in 2007 — up 31% from 2006 — and that their average tax bill fell to a 15-year low. Their incomes soared again in 2009 to more than $500,000. Most of their income came from dividends and capital gains on investments. On the lower scale, government estimates place 19 percent of Americans over age 65, 14 percent of those between 18 and 64, and 18 percent of children as living below the poverty level. Although slavery no longer is legal, the richest among us still benefit from the labor of others while the poorest scrape the bottom. Jesus taught his disciples, "Thus the saying one sows and another reaps is true. I sent you to reap what you have not worked for. Others have done the hard work, and you have reaped the benefits of their labor." (John 4:37-38)

Some inherit wealth and win the lottery through no effort of their own. Others seem to do no wrong as everything they touch turns to gold. Wealthy and internationally famous, comedian Bob Hope (1903 - 2003) observed, "I have always been in the right place at the right time." The successful career of actress Carol Burnette was launched when some anonymous benefactor loaned her the money for relocation from Hollywood to New York. If Dino Martini had not met Jerry Lewis, (by accident?) neither of their careers may have amounted to much. Many skyrocketing careers depend on such synchronicity. A few seem to find no resistance in mounting the mountain of success. But the bell curve among incomes in the U.S. is badly skewed among the general population with a few at the top and many at the bottom. For every rich executive there must be many more poor working employees. That seems to be a law of economics.

Over the past 20–30 years Americans have experienced the greatest increase in income inequality among rich nations. The more detailed the data we can use to observe this change, the more skewed the change appears to be... the majority of large gains are indeed at the top of the distribution. Of those individuals who were older than 25 years of age, over 42% had incomes below $25,000 while the top 10% had incomes exceeding $75,000 a year in 2005. In 2007, the top 10 percent of American earners pulled in 49.7 percent of total wages - a level higher than any other year since 1917 and even surpasses 1928. The average weekly wages of American workers, the ones who were working, in 2009 was about $610. Do the math and you easily see they don't live on easy street. At the bottom are homeless beggars who live on discarded garbage and the retirees in public housing living on social security payments, then comes sheeple receiving only government disability benefits and those working poor who earn the minimum wage. How bad this must get before the poorest rise up in revolution is indefinitely uncertain.

At the other end of the bell curve are the 400 richest folks who all are billionaires according to the latest Forbes list. To get that wealthy, one must either excel as a sports or acting hero, or be a successful employer, landlord, or investor of other sheeples' money. Steve Schwarzman, CEO of the Blackstone investment fund took home $702 million in 2008. Possibly the ultimate in wealthy decadence may be *The World by ResidenSea*, a floating 40,000 ton 650 foot long twelve story condominium ship that plies the oceans visiting the most exotic ports just for the opulent lifestyles of its 165 owner-occupants, including a smoking lounge offering $38 cigars and a driving range with biodegradable golf balls. It even has its own radio and television station, plus a theater and on-board casino. How this wealth is distributed must be the will of God the Almighty One or it would be different.

Of course, there are social advocates who claim that distribution of sheeple on any scale is subject to human free will, because every thought must mirror its opposite. The reality seems to be that sheeple cluster in groups that are very congenial and occupy about the same place on the bell curve. Sheeple who try to move up the curve often find their old social club indifferent and even antagonistic to their rising status. When sheeple leap into wealth by winning the lottery they often run into social and personal difficulties. There seems to be some form of natural selection governing populations in all forms of social hierarchies, much of it based upon racial and ethnic clustering. But, there is no such thing as a one-sided thought. So, one day perhaps eugenics or cloning will be an accepted form of income control through selected breeding of humans as well as animals. It was attempted by the German Nazis in WWII, and we see evidence of it in controlling professional and Olympic sports where only the best performers are permitted to participate. But, no matter how the bar is set, there always will be a bottom half and there always will be a lower class. However, Jesus seemed to teach that those who honestly tried to improve would be rewarded while those who hoarded their meager talents would lose it all. "I tell you that to everyone who has, more will be given, but as for the one who has nothing, even what he has will be taken away." (Luke 19:26) So no matter how little one has it seems that it is intended to be used and not hoarded.

The bottom side of the bell curve comes with significant burdens to society. A report titled, "Mental Health, Resilience and Inequalities," prepared for the World Health Organization in London, links mental health to "levels of social and economic injustice." "Individual and collective mental health and well-being," says the report, "depends on reducing the gap between rich and poor." The report also notes that "The adverse impact of stress is greater in societies where greater inequalities exist, and where some sheeple feel worse off than others. This stress impacts everyone, not just the poor. Deep-seated inequality heightens status competition and status insecurity across all income groups and among both adults and children." Researchers concluded that the absence of positive mental health will put you at greater risk for cardiovascular disease than smoking. Chronic stress beats down our body's immune defenses, upsets our physiological balances, and leaves us open to disease. Living in poverty, coping with deprivation and disadvantage, day in and day out, wears us out. But stress doesn't just come from deprivation, trying to make do without the material basics of life. Stress comes, perhaps even more powerfully, from the constant pressures that come with life in deeply divided societies, the report says. "The adverse impact of stress is greater in societies where greater inequalities exist, and where some people feel worse off than others." It adds, "This stress impacts everyone, not just the poor. Deep-seated inequality heightens status competition and status insecurity across all income groups and among both adults and children."

The human ego needs to experience reliable self as well as environmental control; do this - get that. It can tolerate some limited amount of disappointment if there is hope for better days ahead. If going to school gets one a good job and diet and exercise promotes health, save money to enjoy retirement, logic dictates more of the same. But, when ego perceives no connection between efforts and results, when savings disappear overnight, when college graduates are unemployed, the mind becomes troubled and sick with anxiety and depression. Even slot machines must pay off occasionally or sheeple quit playing, and the lottery winners assure plenty of hopeful gamblers. It is as though the ego says, if at first you don't succeed try and try again, and then quit because there is no sense in continuing to fail. So, mental health requires the satisfaction of trying and succeeding at least some of the time at some level of performance. Coming in last all the time really sucks. Would that we could all adopt the attitude of Thomas Edison (1847-1931) who said after failing to find a reliable material for the filament of his light bulb, "Now I know a thousand things that won't work." He also lost the battle with George Westinghouse over adoption of alternating current for power transmission. But, it was actually Nicola Tesla (1856-1943) who invented the transformer that made it all possible. He was hardly recognized for his efforts and died with none of the fame and fortune attributed to Thomas Edison.

[Many Tesla fans accuse Edison of stealing much from Tesla who worked for Edison during his early years when he first emigrated from today's Croatia via Paris in 1884. They claim Edison was a thief and that he died a rich and powerful man surrounded by friends because he robbed Tesla and others like him. Meanwhile, Tesla died broke and miserable and lonely with his closest friends being wild pigeons he had enticed into his room at the Hotel New Yorker. For example, Edison did not invent the first light bulb. Joseph Swan was installing them in homes and landmarks in England a full year before Edison got his light bulb patented and working. Edison was buying out other sheeple's patents and when Swan eventually sued Edison and won, Edison had to take him in as a partner in Edison's British company. As a poor but ingenious immigrant, Tesla claimed Edison offered $50,000 ($1.1 million in 2007, adjusted for inflation) if he redesigned Edison's inefficient motors and generators, making an improvement in both service and economy. In 1885 when Tesla inquired about the payment for his work, Edison replied, "Tesla, you don't understand our American humor," thus breaking his word. Earning only $18 per week, Tesla would have had to work 53 years to earn the amount he was promised. Tesla immediately resigned when he was refused a raise to $25 per week. Edison and Tesla came to open conflict in the late 1800s when Tesla's AC (alternating current) power systems that are used all over the world today came into competition with Edison's DC (direct current) power systems. Tesla also developed theories for the wireless transmission of radio energy put to use by Marconi plus fluorescent lamps and AC electric motors. Tesla's technologies were bought by railway air brake inventor George Westinghouse who developed them into what became the multinational Westinghouse Company. A friend of Tesla claimed he was "a scientist or engineer who was also a poet, a philosopher, an appreciator of fine music, a linguist, and a connoisseur of food and drink." Edison is the godfather of General Electric, presently the world's 12th largest company. But the reasons why Edison died rich and famous while Tesla died broke and lonely are known only to God the Almighty One.]

Many sheeple in the United States may be dangerously close to forgetting that its founders traditionally promised only the equal right to try and fail in the pursuit of happiness. The Federal Reserve Board, mandated by law in 1913 to assure price stability and full employment without achieving either, has documented gains by America's wealthiest one percent of more than $2 trillion during the latest Bush administration... more than everyone in America's bottom 90 percent combined. We are now the most unequal wealthy nation on Earth and have reversed the relationship we had to Europe when the founders of this country rejected aristocracy. Today Europeans come to the United States to marvel at the excesses of wealth beside shameful poverty. Many of us would like to lift up those at the bottom, but few of us want to bring down those at the top, especially if you are one of them. Since the "New Deal" of President Roosevelt, politicians have attempted increasingly to solve all personal problems of everyone, something that they cannot do and will bankrupt the government trying.

Dr. Laurence Peter proposed in his book, The Peter Principle, (1968) the reason for so much insanity in organizations is due to the fact that sheeple always get promoted up to their first level of incompetence. Thus, all organizations are run by the most incompetent. One may only wonder how many such sheeple have occupied the White House and the U.S. Congress as well as the corporate headquarters of Wall Street banks. The widest gap between the richest and poorest income earners lies in New York State; think about it. The optimum society would be one in which each person reaches his highest level of competence, but no higher. You may become the captain of a grade school soccer team, but it still is a grade school team. When government policies manipulate the natural distribution of the bell curve, there must always be a natural correction, even if it takes a war or recession to do it. This is what happened in the banking melt-down of 2008-09 after corporations lost sight of the need to create services and products to create income and substituted manipulation of financial instruments to make money out of nothing. The resulting distortion of the bell curve, shifting income from producers to manipulators, could not be sustained after the top ten percent were earning more than all the rest combined. Such things cause social and military revolutions. All in the will of God the Almighty One, of course.

When you apply the bell curve to human spiritual development, you get tribal warfare and belief in shamans at the bottom and total emancipation from superstition at the top. Among Homo sapiens, the range of evolution that exists throughout the world still includes those primitive tribes that have not developed much at all in the course of history. The middle contains a vast range of religious and social variations between the extremes. At the top are a very few saints who really get it and at the bottom are poor souls only to be pitied and succored. However, as with all rules, the bell curve comes with indefinite exceptions. Adding the income of college dropout, Bill Gates, founder of Microsoft, to that of average workers skews the results unrealistically. Some sheeple do rise from the lower ranks to the top, but they are few and often they benefit from events beyond their control, although they may not admit it. Although anyone can win the lottery only one person does. And no one can predict when some unpredictable event, like Hurricane Katrina or a cure for cancer, will occur. Great moments in history often occur when some "black swan" comes along to muck up conventional statistics. So we must live with the anxiety of indefinite uncertainty.

So, wherever you end up on the bell curve, it must be God's will or it would be different. Think you can handle that? Giving up the desire for things to be different is one of the most difficult challenges we face as terminal aging gathers steam. Difficult, but not impossible.

3. CONSIDER THIS HUMAN BODY.

So long as it works as needed we take our human bodies for granted. Unless something malfunctions or we have an accident that damages part of it the old "bod" just goes on doing its things pretty much unnoticed. But, if we stop to take note of it, the miracles of its functioning seem beyond science and medicine to explain. As invention of the telescope made it possible to view the cosmos, so has invention of the microscope made it possible to look inside cells of human organs. But, just when they think they have it figured out some new discovery is made that confounds medical scientists and demands ever new and emerging tests and theories to investigate it further. For example, the human body is thought to be composed of some ten billion individual cells. But it is host to possibly ten times that many in various forms of parasites, bacteria and viral life forms. They go about coexisting so long as the immune system keeps it all in balance. [One such parasite is a flatworm called the "Lung Fluke," (paragonimus westermani) that passes from crustaceans like crayfish through human stomach walls into the lungs where it reproduces and lays its eggs. When it is coughed up and reswallowed, it is passed out and finds its way back through crayfish to infect others. This is just one of hundreds of parasites that can infest the human body, often unknowingly until they cause acute discomfort.] And just how the cells in various organs including the heart, lungs, stomach, kidneys, liver, pancreas etc. and especially the human brain, know how to do what they do all in cooperation with the others still is a mystery beyond medical knowledge.

The amount of ignorance and superstition that sheeple have applied to the body are staggering to the intellect. Consider that the standard of medical practice for many illnesses was to withdraw blood from the patient as recently as one century ago. And, until 1952, female sexual desire actually was treated as a disease called hysteria. Plus, there are modern church leaders who believe in the exorcism of demons to quell emotional paroxysms which were called conversion reactions. Indeed, the mechanisms by which sheeple take in information and make use of it is a mystery. Memory and imagination are total enigmas to neuroscience. So is the property of sleep that is common to all forms of mammals. No one knows why we sleep or what happens during that period of unconscious existence, especially the time spent dreaming. Research into not-so-rare conditions of fatal apnea or insomnia shows that sleep is controlled by a sometimes faulty inherited gene that goes bad, causing a loss of consciousness and death in a few months. And whatever is meant by consciousness has yet to be understood.

Much of what goes on in the body is unconscious and involuntary, grouped into several different but interacting systems. [How these systems are coordinated and respond to mortal attacks by disease and to medical interventions still is a mystery to science. The practice of medicine has been fractured into untold specialties, with each specialist largely ignorant of the whole. Is the Type I diabetic sick because his pancreas produces insufficient insulin or does he produce insufficient insulin because he is diabetic? Such confusion between correlations and causation are rampant among medical theories as they are in social theories and natural science. For example, some studies show that drinking diet sodas correlates with obesity...maybe because the subjects think they can eat more junk food than ever...or perhaps diet sodas actually cause obesity?] There is the endocrine system, the skeletal system consisting of 206 bones, the digestive system, the reproductive system, and so on. They are all fueled by the circulatory system which transports nutrients and the pulmonary system that filters oxygen from the air we breathe. Human blood carries ancient mythical and spiritual roles in addition to its biological function. The need for a blood sacrifice to appease the gods is basic to many religions, including traditional Christianity, beginning with the story of Cain and Abel in the account of Genesis. Blood is a highly specialized circulating tissue consisting of several types of cells suspended in a fluid called, plasma. Its cellular constituents are: red blood cells (erythrocytes), which carry respiratory gases and give it its red color because they contain hemoglobin, (iron-containing protein that binds oxygen in the lungs and transports it to tissues in the body), white blood cells, (leukocytes), which fight disease, and platelets (thrombocytes), cell fragments which play an important part in the clotting of the blood. Anatomically, blood is considered a connective tissue from both its origin in the marrow of bones and its function. As the ancients suspected, the life indeed is in the blood because of the many crucial functions it performs. Among them are transporting oxygen to the tissues, carrying nutrients, removing waste including carbon dioxide and urea, detecting foreign materials, transporting messenger hormones, and regulating body temperature among others. One of the unconscious miracles is how the pituitary gland in the brain secretes a hormone called ACTH that flows through the blood to regulate the adrenal glands which sit atop the kidneys and produce another substance called cortisol that regulates precise production of glucose from food digestion to fuel each individual cell of the body.

Possibly the most complex and least understood of many systems in the human body is the endocrine system. It is made up of glands that produce and secrete hormones; some even seem to come from the bones. Hormones are chemical messengers created by the body in several different glands. These hormones regulate the body's growth, metabolism (the physical and chemical processes of the body), and sexual development and function. The hormones are released into the bloodstream and may affect one or several organs throughout the body. They transfer information from one set of cells to another to coordinate the functions of different parts of the body. The major glands of the endocrine system are the hypothalamus, pituitary thyroid, parathyroids, adrenals, pineal body, and the reproductive organs (ovaries and testes). The pancreas also is a part of this system; it has a role in hormone production as well as in digestion. The endocrine glands appear unique in that the hormones they produce do not pass through tubes or ducts. The hormones are secreted directly into the internal environment, where they are transmitted via the bloodstream or by diffusion and act at distant points in the body. In contrast, other glands including sweat glands, salivary glands, and glands of the gastrointestinal system secrete the substances they produce through ducts, and those substances are used in the vicinity of the gland. The regulation of body functions by the endocrine system depends on the existence of specific receptor cells in target organs that respond in specialized ways to the minute quantities of the hormonal messengers.

The endocrine system is regulated by feedback in much the same way that a thermostat regulates the temperature in a room. For the hormones that are regulated by the pituitary gland, a signal is sent from the hypothalamus to the pituitary gland in the form of a releasing hormone, which stimulates the pituitary to secrete a stimulating hormone into the circulation. The stimulating hormone then signals the target gland to secrete its hormone. As the level of this hormone rises in the circulation, the hypothalamus and the pituitary gland shut down secretion of the releasing hormone and the stimulating hormone, which in turn slows the secretion by the target gland. This system results in stable blood concentrations of the hormones that are regulated by the pituitary gland. When this system works properly the human body is healthy and strong, able to fight off invading parasites, virus and bacterial agents. But as it gets older this system can malfunction in many complex ways that are extremely difficult to diagnose and treat with modern medical understanding. Artificial hormones are not yet very effective at replacing the originals so one must live with the inevitable results. We also could discuss the complex systems of the senses whereby sight, touch, taste, and hearing are converted into consciousness, but that is far too complex for this venue. It all is just another of the many ways in which God the Almighty One shows us who really is in control. Believe it, or not.

Consider the human digestive system. The digestive system is made up of the digestive tract - a series of hollow organs joined in a long, twisting tube from the mouth to the anus - and other organs that help the body break down and absorb energy from food. The digestive tract also contains a layer of smooth muscle that helps break down food and move it along the tract. The digestive glands that act first are in the mouth - the salivary glands. Saliva produced by these glands contains an enzyme that begins to digest the starch from food into smaller molecules. An enzyme is a substance that speeds up chemical reactions in the body. The esophagus is the hollow tube that leads from the throat (pharynx) to the stomach. Upon swallowing, muscles must close off the windpipe so food cannot enter and cause choking, then a wave of contractions moves food down through the esophagus into the stomach, which has a valve at the top that closes to prevent regurgitation of acids during digestion. The walls of the esophagus propel food to the stomach not by gravity, but by rhythmic waves of muscular contractions called peristalsis, all automatically without conscious control of any kind. And that is just the beginning. Digestion is the process by which food and drink are broken down into their smallest parts so the body can use them to build and nourish cells and to provide energy. Food and drink must be changed into smaller molecules of nutrients before they can be absorbed into the blood and carried to cells throughout the body. A thick mucus layer helps keep the acidic digestive juice from dissolving the tissue of the stomach itself. The digestive process requires production of bile from the liver that is stored in the pancreas and released or recycled as needed. Cancer of the pancreas is most to be feared as it takes lives rapidly and relentlessly.

After the stomach empties the food and juice mixture into the small intestine, the juices of two other digestive organs mix with the food. Other enzymes that are active in the process come from glands in the wall of the intestine. Most digested molecules of food, as well as water and minerals, are absorbed through the small intestine. The lining or mucosa of the small intestine contains many folds that are covered with tiny fingerlike projections called villi. In turn, the villi are covered with microscopic projections called microvilli. These structures create a vast surface area through which nutrients can be absorbed. Specialized cells allow absorbed materials to cross the mucosa into the blood, where they are carried off in the bloodstream to other parts of the body for storage or further chemical change to fuel regeneration of billions of individual cells throughout the body. A common and serious malfunction of this system is the faulty absorption of nutrients by the individual cells. This process is regulated by the production of a hormone called insulin made in the pancreas attached to the stomach. Insufficient insulin production is Type I Diabetes, and insensitivity to insulin is Type II Diabetes. The primary symptom in both types is elevated glucose in the blood, which signals starvation of the cells through failure of insulin to activate the cell receptors and that leads to serious complications that often become life threatening. Amazing, isn't it. And not very appetizing either. What was that about free will again?

Consider the miracle of the human-animal eye, how it converts light into sight. The iris regulates the amount of light it admits through the surface cornea, the lens focuses the light photons onto the thin gossamer retina that then transitions light into nerve impulses onto the macula that travel the optic nerve into the brain where they are converted into sensible observations. Although its functions may be modified by external interventions its basic operations are beyond the control of science. One of its little understood miracles is how the lens of the eye changes shape in only 350 milliseconds to accommodate the precise focus of objects from long distance to close up. Theories about how the brain senses the need for change in the iris to admit the right amount of light and then makes it happen still are being developed. More amazing is the way objects from near and far are automatically focused upon the retina by miniscule muscles that control the shape of the lens. The other senses of hearing, touch, smell and taste are no less miraculous although they are taken for granted until some malfunction or accident causes permanent disability. What is that about free will again? All the major organs including the heart which circulates the blood, lungs, kidneys, and liver are assumed to be understood so well they can be transplanted from one body to another and still function while the immune system tries to reject the foreign object.

The captain of the ship, the human brain, is still an enigma, i.e., a perplexing and baffling thing. The brain accounts for only two percent of body weight but consumes 20 percent of its energy. Movie maker, Woody Allen once quipped that his brain was his second most favorite organ. It is thought to contain tens of billions of specialized cells called neurons that communicate like a giant parallel information processor through electro-chemical spurts between gaps called synapses. Since living neurons cannot be studied directly, their functions are inferred only from external observations by instruments such as magnetic resonance imaging (MRI) and positron emission tomography (PET) scanners. Suffice to say the brain seems to be composed of three main bodies, the primitive limbic system that may be the seat of automatic functions at the base of spinal column which controls instinctive reactions to perceived danger, the amygdala which is a middle level system that seems to house the functions of emotions for connections with others, and all the rest used for conscious reasoning culminating with the frontal lobe that seems to define the whatever that makes one a unique human being. The materialist may say that is all there is to being human, but there obviously is more.

These three brain subsystems may somehow be evidence for the three elements of behavior identified by Sigmund Freud that he called the id, superego, and ego; the id saying "just do it," the superego saying, "just say no," and the ego being the moderator between them that interprets ethical reasoning for response to situational impulses, i.e., the thinking part. The process of evolution has laid one subsystem upon another for reasons of survival and human development. How the brain takes in information from the senses and converts it into knowledge and behavior still is a dark mystery. And the link between neurons and consciousness is even darker. Behaviorists stumble over such as gratitude and vengefulness, love and fear, as two necessary sides of the human coin. Without the sensory transducers, humans would be little more than the animals they were near the dawn of their evolution from lower forms of life, reacting from instincts driven by the limbic and amydgala more than reason in the frontal lobe. Unless, of course, you believe that God made man full and complete in his own image and likeness about 6,000 years ago which the Bible seems to declare.

That begs the question of how and why sheeple believe as they do about many things, which causes no end to conflicts and disputes, while also enabling them to cooperate at various levels of society for individual and group survival. Words like understanding, memory, learning, feeling, reasoning, etc. are used to describe functions of the brain that are symbols which are poorly described by evolutionary language which, of itself, is a miracle of creation that seems to define humans above their nearest animal relations. However, our nearest relative the chimpanzee has demonstrated better short term memory than humans. The brain needs to rest, what is called sleep, but that is a different state than unconsciousness displayed in various levels of coma. The deepest form of coma is called a persistent vegetative state in which only the most automatic of body functions are sustained. Without continuous artificial support life cannot be sustained at this level.

The brain is split between left and right hemispheres connected by a bridge of immense nerve cells called the corpus callosum that enables the left brain to communicate with the right side and vice versa of the body. Women have more of such ability than men. The brain seems to have self-healing properties that enable it to recover from attacks like strokes and accidental impacts up to a point of no return. A very intriguing discovery has been that of "mirror neurons" in the parietal-frontal area of the brain. These are energized when someone observes joy, suffering, or pain in others, providing the experience called empathy, i.e., grasping another's situation from a first person perspective from the inside. They come with both benefits and burdens. They tend to repel sheeple from situations that are threatening. But, if they are disabled or malfunction, the person can be induced to offensive or brutal criminal behavior that is harmful to others. This finding helps to explain the mob psychology that works in sports teams and street gangs and military battles. And, if they are less sensitive, they may enable caregivers to perform services for the sick and needy that otherwise could be repulsive or repugnant. Perhaps Mother Teresa, who devoted her life to serving the outcasts in slums of Calcutta, illustrates the benefits of detached mirror neurons. But, intentionally harming someone is a different matter. In military combat, empathy for the "enemy" must be turned off in order to kill fellow human beings under orders, while defense of the unit must be exhalted to the ultimate sacrifice. Such controlled behavior naturally sets up conflicts among normal brains that often cannot be easily reconciled after returning from the battlefield. Are the choices we make really free? Many scientists now believe that there can be no such thing as free will - they conclude our genes, our inheritance, and our biology are in control. But, who controls that? Could it be God?

Experiments seem to confirm that biochemical events occur in the brain some 300 milliseconds before conscious awareness happens as a "thought." The job of the brain is to take the available information about what is going on now, and then to decide the best way to act in the next moment, up to 300 milliseconds later. By the time you think a thought it has already occurred. Think about that. The average person cannot process signals more frequent than one every 300 milliseconds, or about three signals per second. Therefore, for reliable regulation of events that are faster than three signals per second, a human could not act as the controller and, in fact, computers have been given control functions in factory automation of rapid processing for everything from beer to candy bars for this reason. Neuroscientists are almost convinced that free will is an illusion because we do not control our own thoughts, which create our actions. A baseball batter must begin his swing before the pitcher releases the ball, and a football quarterback throws the ball into an open place on the field where he predicts the receiver will be when the ball gets there. Both are acting through unconscious impulses. Experimenters show that our brains allow us to think we are controlling our bodies, but our movements begin before we make a conscious decision to move in some preconscious domain not yet accessible to present research.

Researchers at the Bernstein Institute in Germany report experiments that show the brain actually engages decisions several seconds before they become conscious. But, they don't know where thoughts come from, unless of course the source may be God. Some researchers have already been asked to testify in court that the defendant is not to blame for anything they did because of this discovery. A scary future awaits for common sense in jurisprudence. Leading brain scientist, professor, and best-selling British author, Susan Blackmore says that free will doesn't matter - we can live a moral and meaningful life without it. In fact, Blackmore claims that consciousness itself is an illusion, i.e. it may exist but it is not what it seems to be. If it does not exist, it surely can be observed; at least the absence of it can as when we are asleep. She apparently does not see the dichotomy in her own reasoning...we cannot have free will but we can use it anyway. Such is the ability of the human brain to confuse itself with inevitable dualities. Illusions must exist to balance realities. The larger question of who is this "I" that either has or has not free will is...well, is impossible to contemplate. The further we explore into the unknown of how the chemical processes in the brain are converted into individual experience, the deeper and blacker gets the pit of apparent uncertainty. Some things really may be unknowable. All in the will of God the Almighty One of course.

Take mirror neurons, for example. Only a little thought can help illustrate the cognitive dissonance that mirror neurons may cause in the brain of an obedient, but sensitive, soldier who is commanded to kill his fellow men after being taught that murder is a sin. Little wonder that so many of them return from combat confused and unable to reconcile the dichotomy, too often leading to their suicide or criminal behavior. Such was the case with Maj. Nidal Hasan, an army psychiatrist and Muslim, who shot and killed 13 soldiers at the deployment center in Fort Hood, TX because his loyalty to Islam trumped his commitment to defend the U.S. Constitution. Possibly the best example of the total lack of empathy is Gary Ridgway, who (although married with a son) pleaded guilty in 2003 to murdering 48 prostitutes in the Green River area of Seattle, WA over a period of 19 years, and having sex with their dead bodies before cutting them up. Although similar but a lesser offense, Bernard Madoff pleaded guilty in 2009 to running a "Ponzi" financial scam that defrauded thousands of investors out of billions of dollars, without any empathy for his victims. Neither of these criminals seemed to have functioning mirror neurons.

When something goes wrong inside the brain, you can imagine how difficult it is to diagnose and treat. Only in the past 50 years have drugs been developed that seem to affect mental disorders, but no one knows precisely how they work. At the center of the brain there is located the walnut-sized pituitary gland topped with the little pea-sized hypothalamus. From there come many chemicals called neuropeptides that flow through the blood stream and attach to the cells that work as a liver or a kidney or a stomach. These chemicals seem to hold the secret to all hormones that drive the human body. But where do they get their instructions from? Little wonder that the human brain is labeled the most complex creation in the universe, except possibly for our genes. But, since our thoughts drive our behaviors, they must also drive our genes, or is that vice-versa? Hence, the notion of unconscious contagious thoughts, called "memes," that seem to have the singular purpose of replicating themselves no matter the consequences, just like bacteria and viruses. How else to explain the rapid popularity of best selling books, movies, and the explosion of personal social networking on the Internet, not to mention international social and political movements? The recent organizing of protests of government actions in Arab lands as well as this country seemingly overnight on Google are cases in point. It also seems from research that the brain automatically and unconsciously sets up immune reactions for defense whenever one sees sickness in others. Perhaps this is how medical care givers can work among the sick without succumbing to the illnesses that they treat. With its unfathomable complexity, it stands to reason that only a small quirk or malfunction in the brain can cause havoc and chaos among the functions of the human body, as well as the social institutions among Homo sapiens. If that body occupies the White House or Congress, social chaos can result. Whatever the definition of personhood may be its malfunction or absence certainly is discernable, as in psychopathology and Alzheimers discasc.

To top off this miracle of creation called a human being, there is thought to be jam-packed into the nucleus of every one of the many trillion cells in the body a molecule called deoxyribonucleic acid, or DNA. It contains the genetic instructions used in the development and functioning of all living organisms. Each cell contains abut three billion elements of DNA that now are understood to act like many micro-machines to carry out their work. All components must be present and working perfectly in order for the cell to thrive. The main role of DNA is the long-term storage of information, and it is often compared to a set of blueprints since DNA contains the instructions needed to construct other components of cells. Segments of the DNA molecule that carry this instructional information are called genes, and they are composed of four basic protein elements coded into a helical strand thought to be the most densely packaged set of information in the universe. If unraveled, it might reach all the way to the moon. The information carried in the genes is what makes us the unique individuals that we are, not just physically but behaviorally too.

Science thinks that cells continually die and are being replaced, replicating the entire body about every seven to nine years. But the genetic DNA is not altered in the process. The question for all time is where do the genes come from and what drives them? Gene researcher, Matt Ridley, called their source the Genome Organizing Device (G.O.D.) But, if genes are driven by contagious thoughts called memes, perhaps there is a meme organizing device, (M.O.D.) Now isn't that interesting? But, just how cells are formed into organs that seem to operate with innate intelligence is unknown, as in what makes a liver to be a liver or a kidney to be a kidney. Fueled by electro-magnetic energy and organized according to a unique DNA blueprint, the various organs, glands and systems of the human body function independently, yet as a whole. The heart, lungs, kidneys, pancreas and nervous system all have specialized jobs requiring specialized resources. However, to maintain health, all systems and organs must be in constant communication and interacting correctly. If communication breaks down, or if excessive or prolonged stress is placed on one system or organ, an imbalance can develop, first presenting warning symptoms and then more severe challenges. It is thought that thousands of specialized chemicals, called neurotransmitters, circulate through the blood and enter cells through a lock and key type of mechanism that is very fragile to control organic functions. When this endocrine system breaks down chronic diseases like diabetes often result.

British biologist, Rupert Sheldrake has proposed that some form of "morphic energy" is behind that process, but his theory is not yet proven. The latest development is merging physics and biology to come up with a system that integrates these divergent fields into a new approach to health and medical treatment not dependent upon pharmaceutical drugs which all come with undesirable side effects. In this new model, health can be compromised by intruders including physical and emotional trauma, toxins, microbes, parasites, bacteria and fungi, radiation, poor nutrition, etc. Likewise, health can be restored by reforming the life energy with a spiritual epiphany, physical cleansing and detox, improved nutrition, massage and acupuncture, homeopathy, herbal supplements, and reinforcing the body's energy fields. But, don't expect the existing medical system to embrace it. You can research it under "info-energetic systems" or "biophysics." Founders of this new science who probe into the subatomic realm of the body find that brain, blood, and bone give way to invisible forces, waves, fields, and particles whose interactions underlie all of matter. Molecules give way to atoms that dissolve into subatomic particles governed by the laws of physics as well as chemistry. In this system of human quantum mechanics, symptoms of illness in the body, whether physical or emotional, arise first not in the biology of cells but as distortions or blocks in the underlying energy and information pathways in the body-field. Treatment is focused on unblocking these pathways and replenishing the information fields so it threatens the business plan of the pharmaceutical drug companies. As with many inventions, new developments often arise from the failure of traditional methods. Necessity IS the mother of invention.

At the level of the quantum universe it appears that information fields order the physical world. It is not a giant leap for some to assume our bodies have inherent links to these underlying energy fields which can neither be seen now or fully investigated, only experienced. This seems to be one of those "when you believe it you will see it" developments. The mere act of raising your arm engages countless interactions among numberless cells that must all be coordinated by some force. Probing into these levels exposes questions that take on metaphysical overtones. Where is the boundary between the deterministic understanding of chemistry and biology of human cells that runs into the probabilistic questions of energy fields in quantum mechanics? At what level in the body does matter and energy take on the mystery of life? What makes the difference in function of a liver, heart, lung, or kidney? What is the difference between a person and a corpse? We call it life, but what is that?

The connection between body and soul, if there is one, still is a mystery. Maybe Jesus gave us a clue when he quoted Deuteronomy 8:3 by saying sheeple do not live by bread/food alone, but by every word that comes from the mouth of God. (Matthew 4:4.) He seems to be reinforcing the teaching of Moses that whatever life is experienced by sheeple, it comes from God. Perhaps the miracle healings by Jesus indicated that he understood and had mastered these matters. He told his disciples, "I have food to eat that you know nothing about." Then his disciples said to each other, "Could someone have brought him food?" "My food," said Jesus, "is to do the will of him who sent me and to finish his work." (John 4: 31-34) Perhaps this is so for everyone. The new model of human body-fields integrates physics and biology to reveal a stunning new horizon of research into how the body works at the sub-atomic level. It also integrates a new science of mind that extends its boundaries infinitely beyond the brain and the body and transcends the limits of time and space. But, don't expect your doctor to tell you about it, because scientists who have a career invested in some legacy paradigm limited by surgery, radiation, and drugs understandably are reluctant to let go of it. So, future developments often come from investigators outside the box. Michael Farraday (1791-1867) who developed the first modern theory of electricity, including invention of the electric motor and the battery, was trained originally as a bookbinder. His interest in science prevailed and through a “fluke” dismissal of a chemical assistant at the Royal Institution of London he was able to get the position and to pursue his second career which brought us to nuclear power plants and personal cell phones.

Physicists used to know of only two basic particles of matter, electrons and protons. Now there are sixteen or maybe four hundred. The most basic of all particles, the Higgs Boson, is yet to be detected. In 1964, Peter Higgs, a shy scientist in Edinburgh, came up with an ingenious theory that gave scientists the mathematical tools to explain how two classes of particles, which now appear to be different, were once one and the same. His theory proposes the existence of a single particle responsible for imparting mass to all things - a speck so precious it has come to be known as the "God particle." If it is detected in particle accelerators being constructed now, they say the origin of the Universe could be explained. The new science of biophysics applied to the human body in labs and universities throughout the world may bring a revolution in medicine and health management far surpassing what can be imagined at present. More and more evidence emerges in favor of the theory that life, at a level more fundamental than explained through chemistry, is dependent upon fields or waves of information. A cell knows how and when to divide, a protein knows how and when to change its structure, a muscle knows how and when to react to the conscious or unconscious intention of someone to move an arm or leg. A healthy kidney or lung or liver or heart knows how and when it is supposed to function. Cells throughout the body obviously have some kind of intelligence and actively cooperate in some complex communication network between the body and its environment that is not explained by Western science.

Many researchers are teasing out the information processes in the body and they are finding the networks are directed by quantum theory and not biology. It appears that we exist in two worlds simultaneously. The first is that of classical physics, the five senses, the laboratory and time/space-related events. The second world is that of quantum wave interactions that are taking place all over the universe as a spontaneous activity of matter all here now. Maybe that is the residence of God where the spirits dwell. This unseen, but real, quantum world directs what happens in the macroscopic physical world. During the three-day journey back to Earth from the moon aboard Apollo 14, Astronaut, Edgar Mitchell had an epiphany while looking down on the Earth from space. "The presence of divinity became almost palpable, and I knew that life in the universe was not just an accident based on random processes."

Following his spaceflight, Mitchell and others founded the Institute of Noetic Sciences structured to uncover the secrets to human consciousness and the relationship between the seen and the unseen. Over its thirty-five years as an Institute there has been an explosion of popular interest in the interface of mind and matter, mind and body, psycho-spiritual experiences and the creative and causal powers of consciousness. Scientific understanding is shifting rapidly, and new findings could make present conventional medicine obsolete. But, much of it is not new as the traditional medicine of Asia has relied upon intuitive techniques for millennia that are resisted and ignored by Western science. Maybe the insurance companies and drug producers should change their business plans to permit more proven Asian practices to go mainstream.

A strong trend towards merging world-wide mind-body practices with the conventional radiation-drug-surgical model is changing American medical services, but it must overcome the powerful drug and insurance lobby to gain momentum. A leader in this effort is Dr. Andrew Weil, best selling author on the subject, who has influenced several universities to broaden the training and experience of students in medical schools, including the famous Mayo Clinic. Patients are taking matters into their own hands and creating a growing demand for complementary and alternative therapies throughout the country, creating work for naturopaths, acupuncturists, nutritionists, energy healers, osteopaths, and hypnotists, among others. The human body just is too complex to be treated by only those methods that are approved by the Food and Drug Administration.

Thousands upon thousands of activities and millions upon millions of chemical reactions are occurring in your body continually that control your health unconsciously. Hundreds, if not thousands of bacteria, viruses, and parasites invade the body continually. The immune system keeps the body in perfect balance until something goes wrong, and there are thousands of things that can go wrong. Some of them are disgustingly grotesque. Consider the man in Indonesia who is cursed with incurable runaway warts on his useless hands and feet so badly that sheeple call him the "tree man" because they are thick as bark. Or, how about the twin girls born with two heads upon one body. The right head controls the left side and the left head controls the right side. Imagine them getting a drivers license. They actually can play soccer. But they are better off than the twin girls born with one body and two heads pointed in opposite directions. But, hey, they may be better off than the young man, age 24, born with cerebral palsy who has no control of his body. He must be diapered and fed through a feeding tube injected directly into his upper intestine. The lives of his mother, father, and normal brother are consumed with his care 24/7. Can we say that such a body has no value and might just as well be exterminated? There is something about his existence that will not be terminated before its time, while others are terminated violently and by disease and disasters all too often.

We [whatever that is] have no conscious control over the beginning or ending of this body, and what happens after it dies is unknowable. So what makes us think we [whatever that is] have any conscious control over what happens in between? But there is more than we can see, test, or treat to the human being. A western monk approached a Bhuddist monk and said, "My master can do miracles, what can you do? He replied, when I am hungry I eat, when I am thirsty, I drink, and when I am lonely I cry." We may know a lot about the human body but we know scarcely anything about the human being. Especially when no one knows just what consciousness really is…yet. Perhaps you have been taking your body for granted. Perhaps you have been taking your self for granted. Perhaps it is time for you to stop. [Whoever "you" are.] Feel good inside no matter what happens outside. That's an order.

4. THE GATHERING CROWD.

There is a critical storm brewing in the U.S. economy...revising the system of medical care. Costs are rising too fast to be sustainable and there seems to be no consensus on either the cause or solution to the problem. Underlying it is an elephant in the living room - aging of the baby boomer population, those 76 million born from 1946 to 1965, and the demands they will make on taxpayers to keep them alive as long as possible. It is an epidemic spreading across the land that will bankrupt the nation if not debated and treated. As aging adults move beyond the empty nest, they are confronted head on by their senior years, and most of them are not prepared emotionally or financially. Neither are their families. Having enjoyed the years of parental freedom in the empty nest, they now must deal with the issues of aging that will lead ultimately to helplessness, uselessness, and loneliness. The transitional senior years can bring many other life changes and take their toll on adult children and close relations who have no preparation for this type of crisis in their lives.

Studies indicate the baby boomers are less healthy than their parents at the same age because their financial success led to a sedentary and lethargic dietary lifestyle full of junk food and couch potato gluttony. You can see it in public venues all over the country as the baby boomers move into their senior years. The toll on their offspring is just beginning to be felt. Some of them are living a sandwiched existence between caring for boomerang children returning to live at home for lack of jobs and elders from the Great Depression unable to care for themselves any longer. About 65 million families now include care giving for an elder with average age of 77 years. With retirement and aging of the baby boomers this number will likely double the next decade and continue growing throughout the century. The findings hold significant and sobering implications for health care because they suggest that sheeple now entering their 60s could have even more disabilities, putting an added burden on an already fragile medical system and boosting health costs for society as a whole. Instead of thinking about how much life remains after retirement, life for the old-old is regarded by how little time may be left and what challenges it will bring.

The main growth industries this century will be hospital emergency rooms and funeral providers. Each year of aging starts to make the circle of friends and family peers dwindle as death comes to claim them one by one. Contact with children and grandchildren separated by occupations and dysfunctions can become less frequent causing loneliness to become a regular visitor in their lives. The loss of a spouse creates a huge cavern unexplored in their experience. If it hasn't already happened, depression reaches out and grasps them. Lack of company, lack of ability to keep up, and failing health all create a fertile growing medium for the seeds of darkness that bring depression. The fear of ending life broke and abandoned in a nursing home on Medicaid becomes a specter too real to ignore. As seniors become a larger and larger portion of the population, this storm is going to become more prevalent in society. Anti-anxiety drugs, psychotropic drugs, and sleeping pills, along with the latest generation of narcotics find their way into their treatments. While many of these drugs are effective in improving the mood of those suffering from depression, more innovative ways than drug therapies need to be explored to address aging transitions. Families need to draw together to provide for the needs of the aging members in order to diminish the feeling that the senior is no longer valued by those around them, but in a way that avoids catastrophic emotional and financial crises. This reality cannot be entirely overcome by drugs. It requires caring sheeple to help accommodate the loss of usefulness to seniors in ways they can participate in decisions about their care. But, don't hold your breath or expect any miracles. Things are going to get a lot worse before they can improve because sheeple will not change until it hurts too much not to. AIGWOC...all in God's will of course. Think you can handle that?

As the generation of baby boomers retires at the rate of more than three million annually, 7,000-10,000 per day, beginning in 2011, more and more of them will encounter physical and chronic medical disabilities like no previous generation ever imposed upon society or their families. More than half of them could live to 80 years and beyond, marking the threshold of old-old, with some of them still working if they have a job because they cannot afford retirement. Half of all medical expenses per capita are spent during the last six months of life. Half of the baby boomers cannot afford adequate medical care. When all those old-old sheeple are put on life support, who will pay all their bills? State demands for Medicaid for the indigent will likely double in a few years, so care will be rationed and funds shifted from other uses. Moreover, who will feed them, bathe them, and change their diapers?

No one wants to "pull the plug on grandma," but they don't want to pay for keeping her alive either. One estimate says the unfunded liability for Medicare insurance for those over age 65 is $35 trillion dollars and the fund will go bankrupt by 2018 unless revisions are enacted. This much debt amounts to $300,000 for each American family. If you live long enough, one day you will realize you are part of the problem and not the solution. Then what? Something has to give. That something is less government support of the aging. The medical reform act signed by Pres. Obama on March 23, 2010 removes half a trillion dollars from the budget for Medicare to help pay for adding more than 30 million uninsured younger sheeple to medical insurance. Reductions in payments to doctors by Medicare are forcing almost half of all general practitioners to avoid new senior patients. When this shock sets in, recoil from the families of baby boomers could turn violent.

Even so, Government-promised entitlements for social security and medical services for all the aging baby boomers will break the backs of taxpayers among their children and grandchildren. Keeping them alive during their last two years could bankrupt the nation unless taxes are increased dramatically and medical services are cut, so both are likely to happen. Many of the baby boomers will find they are unprepared for the financial and emotional impact on their families and traditional social order they will bring with them. Half of all personal bankruptcies are caused by catastrophic medical bills. More and more aging sheeple will become paupers from acute terminal illness that does not kill them soon enough. Many of them could become dependent upon their own adult children for housing and nursing care. Three-generation households will become more common as they are in less wealthy nations. Someone concluded that married couples should arrange to have three daughters, as they are the most likely team of elder care givers. In fact, surveys indicate 44 million adults now are caring for their aged parents. Many will have to live in three-generation homes like sheeple did during the great depression of the 1930s. But, children of most baby boomers are too few and too poor to provide the care and pay all the bills. Are you ready for the grizzly impact of 76 million aging baby boomers?

Consider this real life story in the news: A 90-year-old woman was found living in a house with the bodies of her three dead siblings, one of whom may have been dead since the early 1980s, police in suburban Chicago said in November, 2008. The skeletal bodies were found by police who were called by a seniors advocate, said Evanston police Cmdr. Tom Guenther. The 90-year-old woman was taken to a hospital for observation. The Cook County medical examiner's office said that the siblings had died of natural causes, but it would not say how long they had been dead. Neighbors described the woman as alert and aware, and they said she was well-liked on their close-knit block of large historic homes. She enjoyed gardening and shared her plants with others, they said. One longtime resident said the woman explained away the absence of her siblings by telling neighbors her brother had gone to live with other relatives and that one of her sisters was agoraphobic - afraid to leave the home. The resident said neighbors, who often took the woman food and groceries, were never inside the house. There was no mention of any care giving relatives.

What little help is given by society to destitute aging sheeple comes grudgingly because it is a drain on limited financial resources that must be rationed between the haves and have nots and between the young and the old. No one ever promised everyone a Rolls Royce automobile so where did they ever get the idea that everyone gets the maximum gold standard of medical care, whether they can afford it or not? Decisions between patient and doctor always are mediated by the payer, insurance company, or government. Rationing of treatments is emotionally and morally repulsive but logically necessary. Some drugs that merely extend suffering a few months cost more than $10,000 per month. A single treatment to dissolve blood clots in heart attack patients in emergency rooms may cost $20,000. All drugs used in western medicine upset normal balance in the human body and thus cause side effects too, some of them life threatening. No one knows how a drug that may help one harms another. Nevertheless, drug companies spend more than $15 billion annually on advertising to convince consumers they have viable solutions to all illness, which is just not true. All their treatments are experiments with outcomes that are indefinitely uncertain. One thing they all have in common is the 17-year patents that control distribution and the outrageous prices charged to recoup investment in their research at exhorbitant profits. Even worse, they can discontinue making a drug if it does not make enough money, leaving patients high and dry. And there is nothing the Food and Drug Administration (FDA) can do about it. All in God's will of course...AIGWOC.

There are many natural herbal treatments sold for many diseases but they cannot be patented so drug companies ignore them and therefore most doctors are not informed about them. Medical historian, Harris Coulter, (1932-2009) went so far as to claim that financial profit drives the pharmaceutical industry that will not permit alternatives to compete fairly with their patented drugs based upon results. He, probably more than any other writer, exposed the adverse reactions and harm done by the prescription drugs so highly prized by medical doctors. Coulter claimed the medical profession is well aware that drugs used to treat one disease can cause many others, each requiring more drugs for treatment. Coulter says the AMA has successfully stifled any publicity on alternative therapies that would threaten their business. In some cases, a placebo (sugar pill) works as well as the drugs, and nobody knows why. He quotes C. Everett Koop when he was surgeon general (1992) "One of the major confessions that medicine has to make today is that we have been working for years without knowing what works and what does not work in the practice of medicine...for not only is there complete uncertainty of the efficacy of cancer treatments today but there is the possibility that treatment may make the survival time of cancer cases less."...Soooo, who you gonna believe?...especially when there is no way of telling what alternative therapies may have worked after the fact. All in God's will of course...AIGWOC

Courts are full of litigation by drug companies protecting their precious rights to patented drugs. Alternative nutritional and diet treatments are not often understood or discussed by doctors who rely upon pharmaceutical companies for their options. One source for these alternatives is the Health Sciences Institute, publisher of information about natural source remedies. (Visit: www.hsionline.com) Many of them are standard products in Asian apothecaries, but you won't find them in American standard drug stores or covered by medical insurance. Another alternative form of treatment is homeopathy based upon the discovery of Dr. Samuel Hahnemann (1755-1843) that "like cures like." He proposed that a healthy "vital force" would repel any potential invaders, so his method of treating the sick was to reenergize it instead of fighting the invader. Thus, a highly diluted form of a substance that causes disease symptoms in healthy patients can trigger body healing responses in sick sheeple much as vaccinations wherein dead viruses prevent flu and polio.

After the invention of the microscope and subsequent discovery of bacteria, western medical researchers abandoned homeopathy and pursued biological treatments with synthetic drugs (allopathy). But, their failures to cure and toxic side effects have stimulated a resurgence of interest in alternative treatments by suffering patients. Allopathic doctors brag about how much drugs they can give without poisoning the patient, while homeopaths boast as to how little they can give and effect a cure. (Visit: www.homeopathyworks.com) Other alternative treatments including chiropractic, osteopathy, and acupuncture are rebuffed by the American Medical Association even though patients seek out these options. Some claims are supported with scientific double-blind studies compared with placebos but many are not.

To hear their purveyors tell it, there is no reason to tolerate symptoms of aging because there is a natural treatment with no side effects that can beat even the most effective drug products. They even push the envelope and imply that aging and death may not be inevitable if you just consume their recommended supplements...maybe instead of eating toxic food products sold in America. One resource offers a database of 72,000 alternative natural supplements, so choosing the one best treatment for any ailment is impossible. All medical treatments come with indefinite uncertainty because all benefits come with burdens/side effects that affect each patient differently.

On the other hand the FDA seems to be controlled by drug companies and often approves drugs with insufficient testing, so "caveat emptor," buyer beware. [Modern western drug therapy evolved from chemical theorists in Germany and France during the late 19th century. Critics claim the clinical trials used to obtain FDA approvals for drugs all are flawed by lack of homogeneity among the patients and lack of absolute standards in isolating and diagnosing diseases.] Since American medicine is driven by drug companies, the various options of available drugs approved by the FDA, and many uses that are not, will almost all be tried by doctors before any other treatments possible are considered. Drugs often are sold for more than one application to increase profits. A typical example is Finasteride sold separately as Proscar for possible slow acting prostate reduction in men and as Propecia to help grow hair restoration. This is just one way drug companies extend the patents they need to control drug prices. In the past 20 years only about 15 percent of new drug patents issued actually were for new drugs. Imagine that.

Never doubt the marketing power of the drug companies and medical services providers which begins to influence students in medical schools with gifts, promotions and other perks. They are in business to make money off of sick sheeple because that is the way of American capitalism. The only matter of debate is who makes the decisions, the doctor or patient. Patients who are uninformed may rely upon doctors who usually do not explain all the burdens that come with the uncertain benefits of treatments, ranging from toxic drugs to radiation to surgery. They assume that complications from side effects will impact only a small fraction of patients, and they will cross that bridge if and when they come to it. But, the bottom line is that no matter what medical interventions are applied, the human body has the last word on what it will do with them. At their best, interventions whether drugs, radiation, or surgery may buy the aging a little more time, but no one can tell how much. There may be no mistakes, only choices and consequences. All in God's will of course...AIGWOC.

[Information about all available FDA approved drugs is posted online at www.rxlist.com and www.drugs.com. It pays to look up the drugs prescribed by your doctor to avoid being surprised by side effects and to learn about long term results, if nothing else. Another powerful online resource is a rating of drugs and descriptions of side effects by actual using patients found at www.askapatient.com. These web sites should be bookmarked on computers of all family caregivers and all patients prescribed medications by doctors. Just remember that all drugs are dangerous chemicals and when taken orally they will impact every cell in the body, not just the ones targeted for intervention.]

Medicare and Medicaid reimbursements for geriatric care were set in Federal budgets of the 1980s and scarcely have been updated since then, so many doctors refuse to take aging patients on Medicare, or charge excessive premiums. Now, the system is facing financial and moral bankruptcy from demand for all the best medical teams can provide to keep sheeple alive as long as possible. Add to that the motive for insurance companies, nursing homes, and hospitals to maximize profits, and you get a stinking immoral unethical elder care system in this country. Medicine has potentially extended life times by countering, with unimaginable technology including organ transplants and artificial joints, chronic diseases that would have killed previous generations much sooner, but at rising costs that no longer are sustainable for everyone. Most physicians and nurses are poorly trained for alternative palliative approaches to end-of-life care because they see it as a failure of their profession. Hospice is a logical alternative but it rarely is employed until the final two weeks of life, and then requires that family care givers be available and willing to provide needed procedures at home. Caring for bodies that are contaminated with disease and pending death can feel disgusting and repulsive even to professionals unless they are somehow prepared for it by disconnecting their egos, which demand control over death, from the loss of control that comes with terminal medical reality. The emotional trauma from providing the terminal care for a loved one who is dying can be more than some can handle.

Those who are unprepared to face dying may practice avoidance and denial as defense mechanisms to protect the ego from the shock of facing reality. Consequently, more older sheeple will live longer under conditions of multiple chronic ailments and disabilities, often in assisted living centers and nursing homes under abusive humiliating and embarrassing, but expensive, painful professional care which will stretch human emotions and financial resources to the breaking point. More than two thirds of the expenses of the Federal Medicare and Medicaid programs and twenty percent of national income are spent keeping sheeple alive during final years of their suffering chronic disabilities. One third of Medicare expenses are incurred during the last year of life as cost of treatments escalates. The problem is that dead sheeple have no monetary value to the drug companies and the medical services providers so they need sheeple to suffer as long as possible, otherwise they have no business and no profit. Your doctor is not your friend. Remember that. Little wonder that both Medicare and Medicaid are forecasted to go bankrupt in a few years, and the government is seeking some kind of alternatives.

The overwhelming percentage of sheeple surveyed about their own deaths say that they want to die at home, either alone or with family around and without pain. About 1200 sheeple a day make it out the door this way. The other 5300 on an average day die in a hospital, surrounded by machines and strangers, often in pain and panic of facing hell, and probably bankrupt. Officials claim we have the best system of medicine on the planet. But that is an illusion. In communist Cuba, there are 117 sheeple for every doctor and they get paid $15 per month, and the annual cost for medical care is about $375 per person. In the U.S. there are 470 sheeple per doctor and they get paid $20,000 per month and more, while the annual cost for medical care is more than $7200 per person. In both countries, the median age at death is 78, so obviously spending a lot of money does not extend human life, but only increases human suffering. What is wrong with this picture?

Turning to religion for comfort in old age may be a frustrating venture. In all five major world religions, Christianity, Islam, Judaism, Hinduism, and Buddhism, suffering is a necessary component of being human. But, they also condemn uncleanness and separate the animal nature of man from the lofty angelic spirit of saints. Some even claim that in the secret universe of saints there are neither suffering nor death. However we live in this physical realm where sickness, suffering and death are ubiquitous. This condition does not testify well for the god of love that they worship who seems more intent upon punishing his creation than nurturing it in the end. Speaking to Air Force cadets, Senator Margaret Chase Smith (1897-1995), who was widowed at the age of 43, instructed, "...just as fire tempers iron into fine steel so does adversity temper one's character into firmness, tolerance and determination." It can also crucify the ego and convert determination into calm submission. When actor Charlton Heston confronted terminal Alzheimers disease he concluded that he "must reconcile equal measures of surrender with courage." The idea that suffering buys some form of grace in a future life is little comfort during the labors of approaching death. After serving the suffering souls in slums of Calcutta all her life, Mother Teresa (1910-1997) concluded, "We must give what he/God takes and take what he gives with a smile." She herself suffered variously for ten years during her final travail before she died.

British theologian, C.S. Lewis (1898-1963) found that when you go to the door of grace for comfort while suffering it seems to be locked and bolted on the other side, the lights are out and no one seems to be home. He concluded in A Grief Observed, (1960) "The conclusion I dread is not, so there is no God after all, but, so this is what God is really like. Deceive yourself no longer." So towards the end of life, any hope for a miracle cure or even respite from suffering by this god of creation must be released and replaced with some other belief that will bring a measure of inner peace. The whole U.S. medical industry is based upon delivering technical interventions, not aiding the final transition or nurturing the departing spirit. Churches also ignore this need because to openly admit their impotence would drive away members who are needed to support their treasuries. When terminal illness destroys human dignity and reduces one to helpless dependency, when is enough too much? Each situation may be unique, but perhaps it is time to work on a new general transition model that Western society can live and die with that does not impose more horrifying suffering upon sheeple than we spare our family pets.

This crisis in aging of baby boomers comes with a lack of traditions and even vocabulary to deal with it. The founding fathers included among our inalienable rights life, liberty, and the pursuit of happiness. They did not include death with dignity and comfort. Nevertheless, their fantasy of everyone being created equal loses its basis soon after birth as wealth, health, and happiness become more and more unequally distributed. According to Buddhist teaching, the drive for such is the cause of much suffering arising from discontent and the desire for things to be different. If they could be they would be. All in God's will of course...AIGWOC. This is opposite to America where unfulfilled desire is the driver of change and progress. German existentialist philosopher, Friedrich Nietzsche (1844-1900) observed, "Hope is the worst of all evils for it prolongs the torments of man...if there is a why to live one can bear almost any how...one should die proudly when it is no longer possible to live proudly." Invoking hope in the face of inevitable death may be the cruelest form of suffering, but this is standard practice in American medicine which never will take hope away from a terminal patient or the family. No matter how bad things get they can always do more, and will if someone pays for it. One doctor proclaimed, "I can keep a stone alive."

Psychiatrist, Victor Frankl, who survived three years in the German Nazi Holocaust, observed that worse than loss of physical control was the suffering caused by the loss of meaning or purpose in life. Although the purpose of each person may be unique, when it is threatened and one becomes a burden upon care givers and lacks a future without any direction or worth, life energy ebbs to say the least. Frankl said that humankind cannot live a full life without the experience of grief and suffering. But, how much is enough? Even during terminal suffering, happiness can be untangled from distress by detaching from desire that things should be different for those who are given so to do. The rest suffer. Why this should be no one knows, except for God who causes it all.

Buddhism thrives on pacifism and accepts that suffering exists only in the illusion of this world which is really one of only apparent awareness and discernment. Ultimately, samsara (the cycle of birth, life, death, and rebirth) and Nirvana (liberation from the realm of samsara the extinguishing of desire and hence the elimination of suffering) are one and the same. The world may be all an illusion for spiritual gurus, but the rest of us must live in its physical reality. Calm submission seems to be best solution when all else is moot. Thus, Tibet would not seek revenge when China invaded in 1951 to set up a communist government, killed monks and demolished Buddhist temples and drove the Dalai Lama to exile in India after a bloody secular uprising in 1959. Things change and repeat. Tibet again got world attention as China hosted the 2008 summer Olympic games. They are not happy campers but attempts to shake off the Chinese yoke were met in the streets by militia inflicting even more punishment. In addition, the Muslim government of Sudan has destroyed the homes and habitat of its Christian residents in the Darfur region without intervention from the United Nations because it produces oil that drives the highlife of the Chinese economic capitalists.

It goes on and on. But Jesus claimed, "The spirit gives life, the flesh counts for nothing." (John 6:63) Pope Benedict XVI, a.k.a.: Joseph Cardinal Ratzinger, said in his Eschatology, Death and Eternal Life, (1988) that human suffering "provides the ground upon which the love of God can be expressed as it was on the Cross." This may seem to be a very remote concept to the homeless wretches in Darfur and Tibet and Haiti, but it also is rare in the nursing homes of America. Too many Christian churches in America provide little to nothing in comfort and services to help the aging terminal members to "walk through the valley of the shadow of death" so it is little wonder that older members often are left to drift away to make the journey alone with no one to help support their transition. They often are valued like customers in movie theaters, rated only by how much they contribute to sales. There is little difference between many churches and medical providers selling health, wealth, and happiness. Both are in business to make money, only the churches are tax exempt. All in the will of God the Almighty One of course.

The social psychology of America is to attack and conquer any adverse force that prevents the goals of plenty and more to be pursued, i.e., we think there is no circumstance beyond our control if we throw enough money at it, especially death. One publisher offers a book titled, "Seventeen Ways to Defeat Aging," as though that actually were possible. While selling his national medical reformation, Pres. Obama declared, "I do not support death." Whatever happened to the freedom to die in peace and comfort? There was so much emotional recoil against his proposal to finance end-of-life counseling for terminally ill patients by doctors that it was withdrawn. Consequently doctors often avoid talking about dying or discussing hospice care when they know death is inevitable. In generations past, sheeple just got sick and died. The new generation of baby boomers is more likely to die by inches as first one and then another of their life skills is eroded. Senility creeps up on them slowly but surely over several years until some crisis explodes their reality into view when they look into the mirror one day or the doctor declares, "I am sorry but there is no intervention I can offer you."

The changes can sneak up gradually, and there may be no one instant when the final line into terminal dependency is crossed, but it is there. Often, adult children must parent their parents much as children and even infants who need their care, and they are poorly prepared because they never thought it would come to that. As the old become more dependent someone in the family needs to step up and deliver their needed care if they cannot hire professionals to do the unseemly tasks. Sibling rivalries and unfinished business in dysfunctional families can leave scars that never heal. By the time their elders die, families often are so broken there is nothing left to repair. Ernest Hemingway (1899-1961) observed that "life breaks everybody, and some grow stronger at the broken places"...but he committed suicide at age 62. Nowadays, medical systems can keep dying sheeple alive interminably through shock of emotional trauma to themselves and family who must witness it while they bankrupt the patients and taxpayers who must pay for it all.

Many sheeple believe that everyone has a common right to the best medical care available, regardless of their ability to pay and the prolonged suffering it causes. To one family that would not consent to withdrawal of a feeding tube because... "we don't want Mom to starve to death"... hospice doctor, Ira Byock countered, "What would it be acceptable for her to die of?...we all are mortal and we all die...get over it...dying is not optional but the amount of suffering is." Viktor Frankl, author of <u>Man's Search for Meaning,</u> (1946) said that despair was suffering without any meaning such as he saw in Nazi concentration camps. Therefore, he concluded the search for meaning was the main goal in human life. Elisabeth Kubler-Ross, author of <u>On Death and Dying</u>, (1969) called death a natural transition. This may be a surprise, maybe even a shock, to the medical profession. From the way that doctors and churches both avoid the dying it seems more of a challenge than humankind can bear. T. S. Eliot (1888-1965) observed, "Mankind cannot stand much reality." Perhaps we are not meant to get used to it.

[Physician, Dr. Lloyd I. Sederer itemized issues surrounding death of his mother who spent her last year in the stupor of dementia... "Decisions abound during the process of finally declining then dying. Not to mention the often tortuous decisions about money, there are decisions about treatments: how should someone be treated for their illness as well as the cascade of complications that frequently befall someone as their immunity diminishes and their infirmity increases. There are decisions about care taking: home or institution, supplementing or not the staff of a facility or the family at home. There is the decision about whether to hospitalize during a crisis and then what is done at the hospital; the most well known decision is whether to DNR (Do Not Resuscitate), but the questions are far more nuanced, as a rule. (His mother was 90 years old and yet some surgeon wanted to give her a hip replacement.) Here is where a living will or health care proxy is a blessing; no need to guess about someone's wishes, because you know mostly about whether to use aggressive measures like a breathing tube and ventilator, or about using antibiotics, or food given through a tube or into the veins when someone cannot nourish themselves. When aversion to death results in no prior talks or clear wishes, we have added perplexity and potential family conflict to the already heartbreaking process underway...that often leaves so much trauma the grief never heals...I ask and find no good answers; how could the end of life be handled better?"] And that came from a doctor. When medicine cures all disease, then what will sheeple die from? A rhetorical question for sure.

There are but two choices in the extreme opposites; ending suffering or prolonging it. Medicine for profit will continue treating patients so long as there are options and someone to pay for them. It cannot feel your pain but it wants your money. That seems to be the crux of it. For all our churches and religions and promises of heaven, many sheeple don't want aging relatives to die for some reason. If we are going to heaven, what's to worry about? Apostle Paul declared, "So when this corruptible shall have put on incorruption, and this mortal shall have put on immortality, then shall be brought to pass the saying that is written, Death is swallowed up in victory. O death, where is thy sting? O grave, where is thy victory?" (1 Corinthians 15:54-55): It's all in the will of God the Almighty One. And if not, who can change it?

Never before have so many sheeple lived so far away from the relatives they may love, and never before have old sheeple lived so long. It is as though keeping the aged around longer makes up for all the absenteeism and neglect they lived with throughout their pitiful years. Many of them live in a world created by their grandchildren they no longer fit nor can afford. So families delay and delay making final plans until a week or so before death comes, and then they encounter such trauma as to leave permanent psychological wounds and unfinished business among the survivors. While hospice palliative care is recompensed for up to six months, fully one third of hospice admissions are delayed until the final week of life after all the money runs out. They are like the Jack Nicholson character in the movie, "A Few Good Men," who screamed, "You can't handle the truth." The question for modern medicine and surviving families is what would be an acceptable cause for sheeple to die of? Suffering in this context is a signal to get busy and change things, just the opposite of Buddhist philosophy of accepting things as they are and letting death come as it comes.

In fact, feeling alone, abandoned, depressed, and inadequate in the face of approaching death is perfectly normal among Homo sapiens, even though our medical system is designed to diagnose, treat, and cure acute illness, disease, and accidents quickly and efficiently. The medical system becomes befuddled and flummoxed when it encounters sheeple with long term chronic illnesses, like Alzheimer's or Parkinsons or MS or diabetes or cancer, or the many others to choose from that slowly but persistently remove the humanity from elder humans we may love. Students in med schools must experience a live birth, but few if any actually manage a dying patient so they enter practice with literally no preparation for treating terminal illness.

Despite a few rich family exceptions who can afford long term professional care of their elders out of sight and out of mind, or the destitute who qualify for government funded Medicaid, American society just is not equipped or staffed to maintain so many aging sheeple through years, and even decades, of debilitation and creeping senility in assisted living centers and nursing facilities if they cannot be cared for at home by family members. If admitted to hospital they will get all the treatments available until the money runs out. The medical reform act passed by Congress in 2010 scarcely touched this issue because opponents successfully raised the debate to rationing of medical care for the aged. The problem was so hot they could not even debate it. Elder care is one of the most distressing and depressing occupations if you resist normal symptoms of aging, but it can be a compassionate service if you accept them as a normal part of life. Under the best of conditions, elder fragility and infirmity is difficult to support, even by professionals because everyone knows they will get there soon enough.

The mirror neurons in our brains make us acutely aware of the suffering of others as though it were our own, as it will be. Avoidance and denial are excellent defense mechanisms to protect the ego from facing up to this reality. If we don't look maybe it will go away. Families in undeveloped cultures are not so shocked to see their elders age and die normally in the same household. But our very economic success has removed that process from common view so that when aging transitions of the baby boomers visit a family they often bring emotional, psychological, and financial shocks with little, if any, preparation. Dying too often means facing pain, emotional suffering, humiliation, embarrassment, and medical defeat in most Western cultures. The anxiety of death is a taboo subject in most households, and funerals of dead relatives often are quickly dismissed as though nothing happened so life may go on in denial and avoidance until a new crisis brings on the reality. But, undercoating this denial and avoidance is a fundamental spiritual aspect of humanity which can and must be enabled if the critical storm is to be absorbed. Death happens, and grief follows. All in God's will of course...AIGWOC. Think you can handle that?

God does not seem to make a big deal out of suffering and dying because he has made both a ubiquitous part of life for humans and animals alike. About 6500 sheeple die every day in America; that's 2.4 million deaths per year. Recall how often throughout history millions of sheeple have died in wars and plagues, more than 56 million in Europe during WWII alone. Jesus hardly spoke of loss and grief, briefly instructing, "Blessed are those who mourn..." (Matthew 5:4) He also did nothing to protect the Jews from their Roman slayers. "...do not be afraid of those who kill the body but can do nothing more..." but rather he told them to fear him who could cast them into hell. (Luke 12: 4-5) Jesus healed only to impress the Jews with his spiritual power and said to the mourner, "Let the dead bury their own dead." (Matthew 8:22, Luke 9:60) So, why do Homo sapiens make such a big deal out of it, even making a business out of anti-aging and keeping suffering sheeple alive far beyond any rational benefits? Many sheeple act like keeping their loved ones alive as long as possible, regardless of the suffering and expense, is the only way they can show that they care, and the more money they spend on heroic measures to extend life, regardless of the quality, the better. Little wonder that most medical expenses are spent trying to keep dying sheeple alive during the last two years or so of their lives. That attitude must change to allow sheeple to die naturally when they no longer can process food or drink on their own and death is imminent if social trauma is to be avoided. Dehydration and starvation must become preferred alternatives to the strokes, feeding tubes, amputations, seizures, blood clots, infections and other horrors that sheeple must suffer who are kept alive past their time. Human cells eventually stop replicating themselves and deplete their energy to fight off invaders and so they die. In the end, dying is traumatic to watch but it comes anyway. So why prolong it?

The only treatment proven to extend healthy life [tested among short-lived mice] is reducing calories by one third because digesting food actually causes oxidation of cells that reduces their ability to convert oxygen into energy. Cutting calories any more may actually reduce life expectancy because metabolism slows down with age. Although its quality may be improved, life may not be extended beyond its time. Cells without enough oxygen or nutrients atrophy and die. It appears that starving them triggers some genetic reaction that reduces metabolism and extends self preservation. But no matter how many anti-oxidant foods or vitamin supplements you ingest, metabolism slows with age and in the end you die, and the only sheeple who will remember you are a few close friends, family, and associates and that not for long. For most of us it is like pulling your hand out of a pail of water. Soon the ripples are still and there is no evidence of our presence at all. But each one occupies a necessary indispensable place in creation, or it would be different. The only problem with dying is that something must kill you, often very slowly. If one thing doesn't get you another one will, and unless it is a fatal heart attack or an accident the process often is very slow and painful and the treatment humiliating and embarrassing.

Remember this: no matter how bad things get, they can always get worse, and probably will before you die. It seems like God may have to remove all the reliance upon family, friends, government, and medicine, in order to get our reliance upon Him alone after faith in all else fails. When there is nothing left to turn to on Earth, then we turn to God. Security is not the absence of danger, but the presence of God no matter the danger. As the battery of life runs down it reaches a threshold beyond which it can no longer resist predatory invaders or recover from traumas, such as surgery and critical illness. By then you may have survived for years in chronic discomfort alone in some institution with bed sores, untreated constipation or diarrhea or urine incontinence and complete self-annihilation before the body finally dies. It is amazing how much suffering the ego can tolerate before it finally gives up desire for control. Some of them never do and must be crucified. Typical of this scenario was the final two years in the life of actress and model, Farrah Fawcett. (1947-2009) She finally died of complications of anal cancer after making a documentary television movie of her suffering attempts to remain alive as long as possible. Her life partner, Ryan O'Neal now has those traumatic memories to live with the rest of his life. She was wealthy enough to foot the bills, including charter flights to a clinic in Germany, but most sheeple will need taxpayers for support to stay alive and suffering. How much is too much?

There is a better way. It is called "Hospice." It provides palliative care for patients who have a prognosis of no more than six months - and it ranges from in-home care if family members are able to stand-alone centers to special wings in hospitals. It does nothing to artificially lengthen or shorten life, focusing mostly on a patient's comfort and social, emotional and spiritual support for the family. [Palliative care can be provided at any time in the U.S. It is focused upon comfort and has no time limit, whereas hospice is reserved for the last six months of life.] Hospice care has grown from about 25,000 patients in 1982, when Congress approved coverage under Medicare, to 1.45 million patients in 2008. Sheeple on Medicare account for the vast majority of U.S. deaths, and care in the last year of life accounts for roughly a quarter of Medicare's budget. So, increased use of hospice could mean sizable savings for the government, particularly if patients entered it sooner. Still, only about 39 percent of Americans who died in 2008 were in hospice. The average patient spent a little more than two months under that care; about a third moved to hospice only in the last week of life. The prevailing American medical perspective is "Do something! Do something! Do something!" Death is an intolerable failure for the medical ego, so many terminal patients are hospitalized repeatedly, often getting unnecessary tests and useless treatments before finally succumbing. Obviously, for-profit medical service providers are reluctant to recommend hospice for families with terminal patients because they lose money even though at least one study showed life extension of more than two months for lung cancer patients in hospice compared with traditional oncology treatment. Thus, each family must overcome the taboo and make their own decision, often in spite of medical recommendations to continue useless treatments that may supply hope but little else.

Developed in Great Britain in the 1960s, hospice cares for dying patients at home or in hospital and specialized facilities while making comfort the top priority. Palliative care for the dying is provided by the hospice movement that is covered by federal Medicare and Medicaid insurance during the last six months of life, but many sheeple avoid it because it means accepting the end is near. Hospice is not about cure, it is about healing relationships so the dying may find peace in their passing and survivors may let go with comfort and serenity without remorse. The clinical plan therefore addresses non-medical, social and spiritual needs as well as pain management. Families both receive care and are part of the care-giving team, which often stresses their emotional stability. If they can work through the emotional times and provide the necessary nursing care, close relatives may discover that caring for a totally dependent loved one during the transition can move from necessity, to satisfaction, to joy, to a privilege and even to a sacred honor. The key difference with hospice care, other than where care is provided, is that palliative care may occur while patients still seek a cure, whereas hospice is designed for sheeple who are never going to get better and know it. Otherwise, similar principles remain: comfort is a top priority, while emotional, familial and spiritual needs are paramount.

Hospice leader and crusader at Dartmouth, Dr. Ira Byock has concluded, "I believe that the root cause underlying the mistreatment and needless misery of the dying is that America as a culture has no position on the compass pointing the way. The health care professions and society's approach to care for the dying has been confused, inconsistent, and frequently ill considered. Often, efforts to extend lives have only made matters worse. If we are to achieve a solution to the crisis it must evolve one family at a time. Such a transformation of society cannot be legislated or implemented through public policy alone. Ultimately, a durable resolution of the crisis will require a transformation at the deepest level of the American culture." We must learn to give the dying permission to die and to let them go when their time comes. One might add that too many churches and their religious leaders also have looked the other way hoping that dementia and aging social concerns will not impact their cozy secure careers. Dig deeply into their catechism and one searches in vain among many churches for a direct response to issues in aging and the lifelong trauma that it often brings for survivors.

Why don't more sheeple receive hospice and palliative care for more than the final few weeks of life? Many families find it too emotional even for rational discussion before the need becomes a crisis because they have been conditioned to fear death. Churches are afraid to broach the subject for fear of scaring away their members, and there is some truth to that because human egos cannot stand much reality. Medical education ignores end-of-life family issues in training its professionals. Hospitals depend on high intensive care revenues, so only one-fifth of them offer palliative care. Federal policy precludes sheeple entering hospice care when they still might attain a cure, and the service is reserved for the final six months of life. Perhaps that should be extended to a year or longer. Doctors under-treat pain of the terminally ill for fear of prosecution for drug crimes or fostering addictions, and hospitals over-treat crisis patients for fear of lawsuits.

When it comes to the delicate and time consuming task of helping sheeple prepare for terminal medical decisions, doctors are woefully uneducated and poorly supported. More than anything else, though, the medical system has not shifted because consumers have not demanded it. Unlike the outcry over dialysis access for kidney failure in the 1970s, or the backlash against HMOs in the 1990s, the American public has not yet pressed health insurers, hospitals, doctors and the government to make the end-of-life as calm and pain free as it can be. But, Dr. Byock declared that no one should have to die in pain. Yet attaining that goal, compared with challenges like mapping the human genome or heart transplants, is far less costly and complex. What America needs is a mobilization across society to make certain that sheeple entering the most vulnerable days in their lives receive the greatest support and comfort at the end of their time rather than extending their suffering as long as possible, which can be very long indeed.

Arnold Relman, Professor Emeritus of Social Medicine at Harvard Medical School wrote this commentary about the present raging emotional debate about medical care in the U.S. "There are much greater financial incentives in the U.S. to use expensive technology, since health insurers pay doctors and clinical facilities most of what they charge for such services. In most advanced countries with universal medical coverage, the government determines how medical expenses are reimbursed, (call it rationing) and the income of health care providers from technical services is therefore more modest. Also, relatively more practicing physicians in those countries are paid salaries, and relatively more hospitals (where most advanced technology is concentrated) are controlled by government budgets. This limits the availability and use of expensive technology. Another very important but often overlooked reason for greater health expenditures in the U.S. is that, more than in any other advanced country, large parts of the system are owned by capitalist investors. As a result, the entire system behaves like a profit-driven industry (which it is.)

The commercialization of our health system dates back only a few decades, but its consequences are profound. Investors now own about 20 percent of nonpublic general hospitals, almost all specialty hospitals, and most freestanding facilities for ambulatory patients, such as walk-in clinics, imaging centers, and ambulatory surgical centers. These medical care businesses need increasing profits to satisfy their investors, and for this purpose they use marketing and advertising, directed at physicians and the general public." As bad as they already are, things will have to get still worse before major reform becomes politically possible because sheeple won't change until it hurts too much not to. The legislation likely to emerge from Congress will not control - and will probably even exacerbate - the inflation of health costs. The problem is that medical science has created "Rolls Royce" care, while the free market economy has failed to make it affordable to everyone. Somehow, priorities of care will be made. Sometime in the not-too-distant future, Federal health expenditures will become intolerable and fundamental reform will at last be accepted as the only way to avoid financial disaster. But, until there is a consensus about the problem of letting aging sheeple die, the solution will be evaded.

Navigating the transition from giving personal care to receiving personal care may be the last great indignity that human beings must suffer at the end of life. The late Dr. Elisabeth Kubler-Ross, (1926 – 2004) a psychiatrist specializing in terminal care observed that dying sheeple traverse the stages of denial, anger, bargaining, and depression before reaching acceptance of their condition. Her classic book, On Death and Dying, (1969) was met with skeptical reviews by medical professionals because she embraced dying as a natural process in life. She lived alone suffering from several strokes before she finally died. Dr. Ira Byock has laid out a system of tasks and landmarks that must be completed if the final transition is to be anywhere close to being tolerable. It can be found at www.dyingwell.org. Perhaps it is time for some institutional approach to education for dying that he offers. If not done by churches, then by whom? When living demands the last small measure of courage and surrender, it need not and should not be prolonged to appease dysfunctional family members or medical providers who view sheeple in terminal need as marketing statistics or consumers of Federally funded medical services.

In addition to the physical, intellectual, and emotional aspects of living too long, there is an underlying recognition of something more. Whether it is called spirit or soul, there seems to be universal acceptance that life energy can neither be created nor destroyed. Death and its aftermath likely always will be a painful journey for the human ego. Longevity has its place, but release and detachment from the body can and will be necessary to accommodate the financial and emotional cost of warehousing millions of old sheeple in conditions of suffering we do not even impose upon common house pets. Maybe it is time to begin a discussion of the unthinkable and the unmentionable...when and how to let the dying be dead. Soon it will be necessary to choose between treating the terminally ill and applying those resources to the younger healthier generation of taxpayers. When will it become necessary to reject treatment when it only means tolerating more suffering? Who should determine the acceptable limits to quality of life besides the person living it?

When the thought of aging comes to mind we think of gray hair or no hair, wrinkles, disabilities, and losing one's personality. We're afraid of looking old and we do things to our body to make us look younger.

Among some other cultures, aging is associated with spirituality and wisdom and leads to admiration and honor. For the aging Hindu, the negative characteristics of getting old are actually considered social status symbols, and they are given deference by the young. The signs of old age aren't looked upon as a decline in physical or mental states, but as a sign of entering a new life stage, a higher spiritual stage. Why not? Can we ever celebrate getting old, and praise those who have reached the latter stages in life? Perhaps instead of attempting to keep sheeple living as long as possible there should be a countering debate about letting them go, when and how, on their own terms. Such discussion will require a different basis for reference than most churches and medical authorities now provide. Make no mistake; the façade of civilization is very thin, and because most sheeple perceive that change is threatening they will oppose it. Social change, therefore, must always be imposed by God. But, since sheeple will not change until it hurts too much not to, the pain necessary to reach this threshold can be very stressful.

Psychologists know that sheeple encountering a threat they have never seen before are like deer caught in the headlights; they can be paralyzed with fear and try to assume all is normal up until it is too late to take protective action. Personal security is assumed until it is gone among sheeple with this "normalcy syndrome." It takes a rare person to acknowledge his own terminal mortality and make preparations for it. Thus, we see that Hugh Hefner, founder of Playboy, married a young woman age 24 at his age 84. Of course, she will no doubt inherit a large share of his fortune while his daughter, age 58, who ran the business for 20 years is left out but hey, such is life among Homo sapiens. All in the will of God the Almighty One, of course.

5. FOUR QUADRANTS OF PERSONAL DEVELOPMENT.

Four is some kind of special number. Where there is assumed to be pairs of forces among couples, Swiss psychiatrist C.G. Jung detected four. There is a "him" inside of each "her" and a "her" inside of each "him." Jung called these the animus and anima respectively. Imagine the complications this causes in communications as the unconscious elements in each person produce coded messages with the other. There are four assumed forces at work in the universe. They are the weak and the strong nuclear forces, the force of gravity, and that of electromagnetic radiation. If you look closely, you will see the Chartres Labyrinth is composed of four quadrants. The number "four" seems to have special significance in the Bible. The number four is used 336 times, 276 of them in the Old Testament.

Possibly the most significant Bible usage occurs in the prophecy of end times. The return of Israel to its promised land was promised by God to the prophet Ezekiel after he had a vision of four heavenly cherubim. (Ezekiel 1:4-22, 11:17-20) The Four Horsemen of the Apocalypse are described in the last book of the New Testament of the Bible, called the Book of Revelation of Saint John the Evangelist, at 6:1-8. The chapter tells of a scroll in God's right hand that is sealed with seven seals. Jesus Christ opens the first four of the seven seals, which summons forth the four beasts that ride on white, red, black, and pale-green horses symbolizing conquest, war, famine, and death respectively according to one interpretation. Over the centuries many different interpretations have been offered by scholars to explain what these symbols may actually mean. Each new century, Christian interpreters see ways in which the four horsemen, and Revelation in general, speak to contemporary events.

Scholars note that with the Bible there may be multiple depths of meanings and that the events of the past may foreshadow things to come. This means that interpretations that the four horsemen have already come and gone and interpretations that the horsemen are yet to come are not necessarily mutually exclusive. Old Testament prophet, Zechariah also sees four horses (Zechariah 1:8-17, 6:1-8). During this account, first comes the Red, then Black, then White, and finally the "Grisled and Bay." They are referred to as "the four spirits of the heavens, which go forth from standing before the Lord of all the earth." Zechariah's horses differ from Revelation's in that their colors do not seem to indicate or symbolize anything about their characters; also, the horses in Zechariah act as sentries, not as agents of destruction or judgment. Zechariah's imagery probably influenced John, the author of Revelation, in the way he depicted the four horsemen. Also, flying or heavenly horsemen were featured in other mythology, both Jewish and Gentile, of the first century.

Whatever the ancient meaning may be, there is a modern usage of the number four that sheeple might be aware of for unusual benefits. It helps to explain the wide diversity and the unique personalities of individuals and, if made conscious, may enable them to develop more fully into the wholeness of being human. C.G. Jung described human personality in two methods of perception, i.e., sensing and intuition, and two methods of judging, i.e., thinking and feeling. Jung thought that sheeple were born with a preference for stacking these four functions in a definite series so that one function was dominant and the others provided subordinate backup and support. Thus he clustered sheeple into those who prefer sensing- thinking, sensing-feeling, intuition-thinking, and intuition-feeling...and vice versa for eight possible combinations. His theory of personality was adapted for use in the Myers-Briggs Type Indicator, (MBTI) possibly the most popular of such tools developed so far to help sheeple understand themselves and others. [MBTI is a trademark of CPP, Inc.]

Jung declared, "If one does not understand another person, one tends to regard him as a fool...Every man is so imprisoned in his own type that he is simply incapable of fully understanding another standpoint." The body we were born with is replaced every few years as cells mature, die and replicate, but the natural personality remains much the same throughout life. Further, Jung proposed that sheeple develop these attributes in a serial sequence as they age from birth from sensing, to thinking, to feeling, to intuition. Further, these traits can be either introverted, i.e., held inside, or extraverted, i.e., displayed openly. Each individual develops a unique combination of these traits, giving rise to a four letter depiction of personality that results in a total of 16 different possible combinations. [Actually there are 64 different possible combinations when all the variables are included.] A vast amount of research and investment in applying this model to human conditions have been developed by professional members of the Association for Psychological Type (APT) and its research arm, the Center for Applications of Psychological Type (CAPT). [You can read more detailed descriptions at www.personalitytype.com.]

Now, it is possible to extend this model of human development into a new more practical phase of usage by using different words to describe the four functions, i.e., physical for sensing, intellectual for thinking, emotions for feeling, and spiritual for intuition. These four elements of being human may relate to development of the four main divisions of the brain, i.e., the amygdala, the cerebral cortex, the neocortex, and the frontal lobe, or maybe some other combination. These divisions of the physical brain are rather arbitrary and are used for convenience of researchers as there are no known locations as yet for residence of sensing, thinking, feeling, and intuition. However, using some empirical observations about human behavior seems to make the distinctions of physical, intellectual, emotional, and spiritual more useful. Four observations are possible: 1) human development in these four quadrants is universal and unique to each individual, 2) their evolution with age is not linear or serial, 3) they can be developed with conscious effort, and 4) most sheeple never pay them much attention while they develop unconsciously.

Researchers into evolution speak of becoming "fully human" without ever defining what that actually means. Many different therapies are used to help those who feel less than human to develop more fully but there are no standard definitions of a model to follow. Mental illness is defined by a subjective and highly unscientific consensus of a group of practitioners who compose the Diagnostic and Statistical Manual, currently DSM-IV, (1994) which describes some 300 different aberrations in behavior that define treatable mental disorders. Insurance companies usually support treatments only for those for which there are interventions approved by the Food and Drug Administration. The others must be self-funded. Sheeple usually do not seek professional help until it hurts too much not to, and that often happens only after life has become unbearable. Life insurance often is denied anyone with a history of mental treatment because suicide is a possibility in such cases. If a model for being "fully human" could exist what might it contain? What is most important, sheeple seem to experience the world differently from these four different perspectives. That would include their perceptions of God, also. [Even the atheist must have a God not to believe in.] Here are some observations about humankind using the four element definitions. Read them carefully and you may find yourself among these descriptions.

Physical – Humans come in a wide variety of physical forms from the very small and weak to the very large and strong, from the ugly and undesirable to the beautiful and lustful. Whether defined by their attraction to the opposite sex for mating purposes or by their agility and performance, the species Homo sapiens seems to have no limits of physical development. Just when it seems impossible to develop further physically a new record is set in some sporting event that stretches the known into the unknown. Sheeple also come in a wide range of interest in their physical development. Some of them are content to "let nature take its course" and accept their bodies as is, while others never cease to attempt to break more physical records, whether in performance or longevity. The international Olympics has been organized to display the best of physical performance in organized athletic competitions, but many other sheeple regularly stretch the limits of their bodies in dangerous and challenging activities.

While sheeple go about their business the body does its thing mostly unconsciously until something malfunctions that demands attention, usually by some expression of pain. The maximum life expectancy now is estimated about 120 years, but half of all sheeple die by age 80 and most of the rest by age 90 in developed counties with adequate diet, rest, and exercise. Without such, the body ages more rapidly and dies at a younger age. Bodies that are born deformed or disabled and those that become so by accident or wars or diseases create disdain and even abhorrence among untrained observers. An ancient Chinese proverb says, "All (untrained) men have a mind which cannot bear to see the suffering of others." [Recent discoveries of "mirror neurons" in the brain may explain why suffering of others is experienced as personal pain when it is observed by others.] They will either present with concerned attention or aversive avoidance, and which is unpredictable. Perhaps the art of medicine evolved from the former. It can be shocking to see how much disability a human body can endure without dying. We may not be able to define the limits of human physical development, but we certainly are affected by obvious abnormalities in the handicapped.

Possibly the main defining physical attribute of Homo sapiens are what we call senses. These include taste, smell, hearing, sight, and touch. Senses are the body's response to physical stimulants. As such they are reactions and not actions. For example the smell and color of a rose are not properties of the rose but rather sensory responses to properties of the rose. If we had no sense of smell or color or touch the rose would not make any impression at all. Senses are the windows to the mind, that element of humans which has never been fully defined or understood, because without mind senses would convey no meaning at all. A deficiency of the senses limits what the physical body can do, and fear of their loss prompts the victims to react with horror and depression. The range of performance among the senses in sheeple also is very wide and enables or disables them in many directions. When it all works it is truly amazing, and most sheeple just take it for granted until something stops working properly. Sheeple with a preference for the physical quadrant likely pursue experiences and activities that stimulate the senses, whichever ones are dominant. This would include their ways of seeking and experiencing God, whether in church or among the sensory experiences of nature. For them, God is in the volcano as well as the flower.

The science of neurology is teasing out slowly the mysteries of how our senses and brains interact. Anyone with low resistance to chocolate, tobacco, ice cream, beer, the smell of a rose or the sight of a lover, not to mention the ultimate pleasure of orgasm, will understand that much of our reactions to sensory data are beyond conscious control. Addictions abound among Homo sapiens so anyone who has not been undone by some sensory thrill cannot understand how powerful sensory stimulants can be. It seems that chemicals in the brain called neurotransmitters produced in response to sensory inputs can overrule logic at any time, and often do. It may even be that the illusion of free will can some day give way to the dominance of unconscious neurons in the brain. One need only watch the cases on court tv to see how sheeple can get into trouble when their reason is overcome by unreasonable behaviors. It would appear from these court cases, as well as the scandalous escapades of rich and famous celebrities, that an epidemic of stupidity rages among the human population that is driven by their senses without any modulating influence from the use of reason.

<u>Intellectual</u> – By this is meant the ability to learn, to store what is learned in memory, and to apply it to the process of living using processes of logical reasoning. The game of chess, for example, is said to be a challenge to the intellectual capacity of its players and so may be the talent for playing card games like poker and bridge. The discovery and evolution of mathematics would be another example. This process evolves with age and reaches its peak sometime in the middle third decade of life, possibly with development of the frontal lobe of the human brain. This development occurs across a wide range of cultures among Homo sapiens and in a wide range of geological climates from north to south and from east to west. The resulting diversity among societies of sheeple is one of their distinguishing traits. However, sheeple who never travel widely or who do not learn much about the world beyond their own immediate surroundings can be totally unaware of their place in the wider scheme of things. Further, it seems that the tolerance for diversity and the ability to acquire knowledge and use it within reason varies widely from person to person. That some are more intelligent than others is taken for granted. Efforts to measure and rank human intellects have included use of tests for intelligence quotients (IQ) and other such instruments.

[Mensa is the largest and oldest high-IQ society in the world. It is a non-profit organization organized in 1946 in Oxford, UK and open to sheeple who score at the 98th percentile or higher on a standardized, supervised IQ or other approved intelligence test. Mensa's constitution lists three purposes: to identify and to foster human intelligence for the benefit of humanity; to encourage research into the nature, characteristics, and uses of intelligence; and to provide a stimulating intellectual and social environment for its members. Mensa is formally composed of national groups under the umbrella organization Mensa International. Mensa International consists of more than 110,000 members in 50 national groups. Individuals who live in a country with a national group join the national group, while those living in countries without a recognized chapter may join Mensa International directly. The two largest national groups are American Mensa, with more than 56,000 members, and British Mensa, with about 23,500 members.]

The limits that bound normal from abnormal intelligence are quite broad and allow for variations about the norm that provide many benefits as well as burdens for society. For example, consider that one who graduates at the bottom of his class in medical school still is called a doctor. The range from the highest to the lowest scores among those graduating from colleges and universities and the military academies does not define how they will perform throughout their careers. How much of intelligence is inborn and how much can be developed is uncertain, except we usually can tell intellectual deficiencies when we see them. Children born with Downs Syndrome, for example, never can be expected to function fully as human beings because of their mental handicap although they may function adequately at their level. Sheeple who are severely handicapped intellectually may be wards of the state and housed in special institutions unless family resources can care for them. Out of sight out of mind.

Unfortunately, intellectual handicaps are not readily apparent as are physical disabilities, and therefore they can cause severe societal problems before they are detected. Many habitual criminals probably are intellectually challenged. Moreover, the modern trend in legal policies elevates personal freedom above public safety so that too often crimes must be committed before sheeple with mental deficiencies are identified and isolated. In this country, we don't imprison sheeple for what they think, but only for what they do. Unfortunately, not thinking before acting is not a crime. Perhaps it should be. Sheeple with a preference for the intellectual quadrant likely engage in activities that stimulate the mind and challenge the logical reasoning processes. They may prefer to seek God among the sciences or the study of formal logic and philosophy, putting two and two together as it were. And sheeple without such preference won't, no matter how much pressure is applied by teachers, relatives, or friends.

<u>Emotional</u> – Perhaps left over from more primitive ancestors and housed in the early formation of the human brain, the reactions to perceived danger including fight or flight or freeze are the most obvious of emotions. However, among the higher developed primates more complex emotions are observed. These take names such as love, compassion, stress, fear, anger, rage, depression, grief, elation, joy, empathy, etc. Such reactions to situations in relations to others are observed in children by the age of two or so. Although they must serve a useful purpose for survival, when they are dysfunctional, they pose serious issues for society and for the individual in all sorts of relationships with others. At one extreme they may evoke clinging dependency and at the other they may cause danger and attacks to others. Although C.G. Jung, being a thinker and not a feeler, devoted little effort to defining what he meant by feelings, he did say that emotions are reactions to situations that can be measured by blood pressure, heart rate, sweating, and other physical manifestations. Again, the range among Homo sapiens of the experience of emotions varies quite widely within the boundaries of normal. When they go out of socially set boundaries there usually is some form of policing reaction that attempts to return them to the set points.

Beyond normal, the manifestation of emotions can be seen when they are inappropriate for the circumstances. Thus, the diagnosis of bipolar disorder derives from the wide limits of mania and depression and wild swings from one to the other without sufficient provocation. Such disorders can be seen among the very young, but they often go undiagnosed until they cause relationship issues among adults severe enough to be socially disruptive. Preferred thinkers may be uncomfortable with their feelings and often hide them in the subconscious in order to avoid them. Not until a situation becomes a crises may they emerge, and then they can rule the behavior with serious negative affects. C. G. Jung used the term "shadow" to describe powers in the subconscious that may dominate behavior. It is said by experts that to be fully human is to experience emotions as appropriate without being overwhelmed or disabled by them.

One sign of maturity may be the ability to hold opposites and yet function appropriately, i.e., both/and rather than either/or. Denying or avoiding them may be dysfunctional defense mechanisms that cause undue harm and may even hasten other symptoms that mimic physical illnesses. The mental health professionals call this event a "conversion reaction" and treat it with education and developing awareness and tolerance for the appropriate role of emotions in healthy living. Sheeple with dominant emotional preference may engage in a lifestyle that is full of drama and involves others with the same goal. One may find these types in churches and other social gatherings that emphasize the presence of God among them. They may feel extreme ecstasy that must be expressed in song and dance when God is experienced in their way. Sheeple without such dominance may seem aloof, withdrawn, and even antisocial. Jung used the terms extravert and introvert for such descriptions. It is said that if you don't know what an extravert is thinking you have not listened, and if you don't know what an introvert is thinking you have not asked.

<u>Spiritual</u> – It may be agreed that the previous three quadrants are functional elements of the physical/chemical interactions among biological cells/neurons in the human brain. After all, using modern MRI scans visual observations of brains at work can be linked to actions, thoughts, and feelings. Some may say that these three quadrants represent the evolution of brain physiology throughout development of Homo sapiens on planet Earth, rising from the primitive brain stem to the central amygdala and culminating in the advanced functions of the frontal lobe. Many would like to stop there and avoid contending with the fourth quadrant because it is not so easily explained since it cannot be housed in the brain or seen on MRI scans. It also turns modern theories about humanity onto religion and that ends it for many sheeple...but not for everyone. Jesus said, "The spirit gives life... the flesh counts for nothing." (John 6:63) Another word for spirit could be intuition, according to C.G. Jung. Sheeple who are driven consciously by senses, intellects, and emotions can be studied with empirical methods...but what the heck does one do with intuition? Sheeple aware of their intuition/spirit are a very small portion of the

population of Homo sapiens. Most of the scientists are not interested in the whole topic of non-sensing perception, and that includes the ones who go to some church and call themselves religious.

Spirit often is expressed in some form of religious practice that invokes God or levels of consciousness that are experiential but non-material. In fact, religious practice in most Christian churches is a highly sensuous affair, with all the visual symbols, visual aids, the music, and verbal assaults on the hearing. There is very little room for spirit in the average church service on Sunday morning. Sheeple who go to church cannot check their reason at the door in order to assume their roles as committed worshippers with no minds of their own. A more intuitive approach to spirituality may be exhibited by those who practice silent meditation in isolated retreats and those who enjoy the yoga rituals from the eastern religions, Buddhism and Hinduism. In the concept of spirit, words even lose their ability to convey the experience of its awareness. When he was asked if he believed in God, C.G. Jung replied, "I don't have to believe...I know."

Among this spiritual quadrant one finds the imaginative creators, the artisans and the poets, the inventors and the architects of ideas, of whom the writer is one. They prefer observing the world more than participating in it. They are few and far between among Homo sapiens, amounting possibly to less than two percent of the whole population. Of such, Albert Eintsein (1879-1955) said, "Imagination is more important than knowledge." As such, it may be the greatest miracle among Homo sapiens. For intuitives, God is beyond words, senses, and relationships and symbols. As with Einstein, their religion is a cosmic force that unites all the elements of the universe into one grand jigsaw puzzle. Each piece is seemingly insignificant and yet indispensable to the sum of the whole.

Persian mystic philosopher, Omar Khayyam (1048-1131) expressed it this way, "Truly, during the days of your existence, inspirations come from God. Do you not want to follow them? Tell unto reasoners/thinkers that, for the lovers of God intuition is guide, not discursive thought." His was a form of Gnostic self discovery expressed in first century religion of the Middle East. However, western practices of religion now are so dominated by the senses that few aspects of the first century Gnostic intuitive form of worship still remain. Perhaps that is why churches have become so ineffective in developing the whole human being and are so impotent and irrelevant at the end of life. Now, intellectual/sensory religion and intuitive spirituality may be two mutually exclusive things.

Those who exhibit symptoms of spirituality in public may even be suspected of some mental disorder since the profession of psychiatry is populated by many who admit they are agnostic and atheist, with little to no interest in metaphysical things. Consequently, the line between spiritual epiphany and mental illness often is difficult to establish. Take the increasing practice of speaking in tongues (glossolalia) that has emerged in mainline churches the past century for one example. In a few churches in remote areas sheeple handle snakes as part of the ritual to prove their faith in spiritual protection from harm as instructed in the New Testament. (Mark 16: 15-18) Another may be the rapid increase in diagnosis of bipolar disorder and the application of spiritual practice to addictions including alcoholism. [This work may be seen by some as the output of a troubled mind searching for relief from the indefinite uncertainty of existential anxiety, or it might be seen as a new revelation from God exposing the face of reality. How does one explain the formation of a new theory of Theism in Theofatalism™ without invoking the inspiration of spirit?]

Intuition or faith is a more appropriate construct to discuss in terms of spirit. Faith was defined by Apostle Paul; "Faith is being sure of what we hope for and certain of what we do not see." (Hebrews 11:1) C.G. Jung was not very religious, but he was very spiritual. He said that intuition was the "ability to see around corners." This is similar to the creative imagination described by Albert Einstein as being more important than knowledge. Nothing happens, not even sin, that has not first been imagined, which is spiritual and not physical. The existence of spirit or soul may not be proven yet by physical means, but its development among sheeple is plainly seen in their behavior and accomplishments.

[In his book, <u>Blink</u>, (2005) Malcolm Gladwell showed that some sheeple have more ability than others to "think without thinking." They seem to solve problems by directly uncovering the mysteries unconsciously without lengthy deliberations or rational analysis. Some are able to jump directly to the right conclusion while others must slog through experiences without much results, i.e., some are luckier than others. They know how to "thin slice" the overwhelming flood of data and use only the most relevant to make the best decisions. In some experiments, human brains reach conclusions before their owners are conscious of it. They see opportunity in change while others see only danger. This finding seems to oppose common sense that claims good decisions demand rational analysis. J. Paul Getty, (1892- 1976) founder of Getty Oil and pioneer multi-national corporation mogul, was one such person who remarked, "Some people find oil and some people don't."]

However, as with the other quadrants of human wholeness, this gift varies widely among humankind and seemingly has a mind of its own in each individual. Abd-ru-shin [a.k.a. Oskar Bernhardt (1875-1941)] attributed this diversity to God; "All teachings were at one time willed by God, precisely adapted to the individual sheeples and countries, and formed in complete accord with their actual spiritual maturity and receptivity." Spirituality does seem to develop with aging and may evolve more as sages find limitations among the other quadrants that leave much to be desired. When all three of them fade, what is left may be only spirit. Sheeple with preference for spirit may likely appear to be highly introspective and more attached to another world than this one. What they see can either be fearful or comforting. All in the will of God the Almighty One, of course.

Sheeple develop these four quadrants of human development in a unique order of preference as they mature normally. One quadrant seems to be dominant with the others supporting it. The dominant preference usually does not preclude some use of the others in relationships and decision making, and sheeple may employ them in very helpful ways as backups in times of crises. However, in some extreme personalities, one or other of them maybe so concentrated as to exclude the others. In such sheeple, hyper-dominance in one of the quadrants may restrict their behavior in ways that are self-destructive or even harmful to others.

Unfortunately, such concentration of power sometimes has vaulted individuals into national leadership which caused much suffering and even wars. The dominance of sensing (S) and thinking (T) in America is so obviously seen in its devotion to the visual entertainment media and professional sports that there is little tolerance for the intuitive/spiritual or the feeling nature of emotionally driven sheeple. The growth of S-T society is like a dragon that must be fed its victims in ever increasing portions in order to sustain its insatiable appetite. We see that goal manifested in reducing information to ever smaller bites punctuated with seemingly unlimited sensational elements. For example, try to count how many individual scenes are displayed in a typical television commercial. Meanwhile, the quieter and subliminal energy in the spirit and emotional life has been muted so much that it scarcely has a voice in the western cultures anymore. The difference is as plain as that between carnivores and herbivores for those with eyes to see.

Normally, the highly developed dominant preference can tolerate some of the others, but only rarely is one so balanced as to find little variance among the four quadrants. Indeed, one who has not developed a definite preference by end of the second decade in life may find difficulty in communications and in decision making to the point of dependency upon others for normal functioning in life. Also, one or more of the least developed quadrants may be hidden in the subconscious mind, laying in wait to jump into dominance under stress or conditions perceived as a threat. Then, control may be taken by the lesser developed, dark side hidden in the shadows of the personality causing much woe and destruction. These patterns are described and used for analysis in the Myers-Briggs Type Indicator (MBTI), a diagnostic questionnaire, which was based upon his theory of personality by psychiatrist, C.G. Jung.

Counselors adept at administering the MBTI may help anyone to determine their own unique personality preferences and use them in conscious ways for the best possible outcomes in human relations. Assuming that others use the same combination in the same variance as oneself is a sure way to prevent useful communications. C. G. Jung said, "If one does not understand another person, one tends to regard him as a fool...Every man is so imprisoned in his own type that he is simply incapable of fully understanding another standpoint." His corollary to that was, "The most terrifying thing is to accept oneself completely." Of course, this implies knowing oneself first. Since we cannot see oneself, the best we can do is obtain a vision of it reflected from others. It is a wise and rare person who can see things from many viewpoints. Without such understanding of themselves and others, sheeple easily can apply faulty reasoning to various judgments that create crises which can escalate into violence and even wars. Such may help to explain why so many marriages end in divorce. Sheeple who do not understand themselves scarcely can make mature relationships with anyone else.

The conclusion of the matter is this: all sheeple are different and develop in differing ways. But the pathway taken by each one may the only one for them, like walking the Chartres Labyrinth...there is only one way in and one way out. Whether they are criminals or not...geniuses or not...charitable or not...wealthy or not...healthy or not...happy or not... all in God's will of course...AIGWOC. Think you can handle that? The differences can be explained by many useful models but one that may have more benefits than so far have been implemented is the notion that humanity has four quadrants or aspects to consider, physical, intellectual, emotional, and spiritual. These could be functions of the human brain not yet well understood. Concentration on one of them may be the normal inheritance we are born with. But, the others can be developed if they are recognized and moved from the subconscious to the conscious. We may be born with unconscious incompetence, but the first stage of human evolution is conscious incompetence. This model of humanity may help reduce conflicts among sheeple and may even prevent some wars. All it takes is assuming the benefits of continuous human development outweigh the burdens. Beyond that lies the will of God the Almighty One. Everyone is right where they need to be in this process or it would be different. Feel good inside no matter what happens outside...or not.3

6. AGING TRANSITIONS.

Some modern success gurus would have us believe that healthy aging boils down to eating right, balancing rest and exercise, maintaining friendships and family relations, continuous learning, keeping up a positive attitude, avoiding tobacco, alcohol, and illegal drugs, having a supporting faith, and performing some service useful to others. It also helps to inherit good genes, and it does not hurt to be rich. Fair enough. But, there is far more to the story. Israel Prime Minister, Golda Meir (1898-1978) said, "Old age is like flying in a plane through a storm. Once you are onboard there is nothing you can do about it." Unfortunately, many sheeple just don't want to believe that is true so they attempt to avoid the unavoidable. They want to not only live to be 100 but to do it in a 25 year old body. Is that insane, or what?

Since it has had the longest time to develop, perhaps the model of patriarchal life cycle in Hinduism offers some useful aging concepts to begin with. It recognizes four main stages of life. The first stage is that of the student, during which a boy traditionally is expected to go to live and study with a teacher for several years. After student-hood, the next stage of life is that of householder, usually entered into through an elaborate arranged marriage ceremony. It is during this stage that a man has children, forms a family, establishes himself in a career or job, and strives to be an active member of his community. With his wife, the householder is now responsible for ensuring that the rituals of domestic life are carried out at their proper times and in the proper manner. This stage is important because it carries the responsibilities of looking after and supporting sheeple at all other stages, both male and female. The third stage of life is that of retirement. When a man reaches old age and his son has a family and is ready to take over the leadership of the household, he and his wife will retire. On the one hand, their household responsibilities - both religious and secular - diminish significantly. On the other hand, they become free to contemplate the meaning of their coming death and rebirth. They may choose to withdraw into a secluded area or they may involve themselves in more active worship of Hinduism's plethora of gods and goddesses.

The fourth stage of life breaks the progression of the other three; it is that of the ascetic, who in Hinduism is called the sadhu or the "sannyasin." This stage is a rejection of life and all that it means in exchange for a search to attain moksha, that is, release from the cycle of "samsara" or reincarnations. The rejection of life requires rejection of the household duties and responsibilities of all stages of life. It also requires the rejection of the religious beliefs that no longer provide any comfort. Indeed, the ceremony making one a sannyasin includes the burning of copies of the sacred Vedas, a symbolic rejection even of one's role in maintaining the cosmos. It is such a powerful rejection of life that a person even loses their caste affiliation in India. [Imagine Christians burning their Bibles at this stage of life or Muslims burning the Koran. Not likely.] Some widowed sannyasins become wandering hermits, living life without any shelter or possessions. They eat when they can acquire food, but never enter into any work to acquire it; it must be given or found. They become holy men, seeking spiritual enlightenment and power, striving to achieve the true wisdom of the cosmos. Does this sound like anyone you know in your family?

Nowadays, we can see the process of human aging through time lapse DVDs and old movies on television that show the careers of actors through the decades. It can be shocking to see them age from youth to senility right before our eyes in decades of cinematography. But, our own aging usually goes unnoticed until something changes to make us realize we are not young anymore. For many living in technology driven cultures, aging is a race between retirement and obsolescence and the latter wins. Although marketers of products and services for senior citizens may focus on the benefits of freedom from work and joys of living if you are wealthy and healthy enough, the time comes when things change, and for many it comes as a shock. You can see them everywhere in airports, shopping malls, theaters, and just walking around the streets of America. There are many government agencies on aging transitions, and many service-for-profit providers, but few institutions actually meet this need of aging sheeple, so maybe one should be organized. Churches could be the place to start since the medics only want to sell more treatments. When the treatments don't work any more, then what? Where can one go to face the aging transitions?

The Bible is no help at all. Curiously, one of the last things spoken by Jesus as recorded in the Gospel of John to Simon Peter was, "I tell you the truth, when you were younger you dressed yourself and went where you wanted; but when you are old you will stretch out your hands, and someone else will dress you and lead you where you do not want to go." (John 21:18) And, although he promised those who mourn would be comforted, (Matthew 5:4) he also instructed, "Let the dead bury their dead..." (Matthew 8:22, Luke 9:60) Reading further, it seems that Jesus claimed to have control over the death or life of his disciples. "If I want him to remain alive until I return, what is that to you?" (John 21:22) No ifs ands or buts. Not much comfort there. He could just have said, what's it to you what I want to do with his life?...or yours?... or anybody for that matter? Just wait, your turn will come. After all, I am the potter and you are the clay. Mother Teresa learned, "We must take what he gives and give what he takes." Get it? It is as though each individual in creation has a unique life to live and no one else can do it for them. So whether others are rich or poor, strong or weak, what is that to you? Each of us has his own life to live and his own way to die. Studies indicate that physical dependency is the greatest fear among aging sheeple. Try sitting around in a wheel chair wearing ear plugs and a blindfold for several days to see how you like it. Aging requires that one adapt to physical deterioration and awareness of pending death while relinquishing whatever life we have to others destined to live on after we are gone. But, more than that are the changes in intellectual, relational, and spiritual transitions that also must be accommodated with age.

Rabbi Zalman Schachter-Shalomi issued a futile call to recognize the benefits of aging and the possible contributions to society that come with wisdom in <u>From Aging to Saging</u> (1997). While it is true that modern lifestyles enable some elders to enjoy social benefits far longer than their ancestors, the fact is that after a certain age, one just becomes irrelevant in the transition from productive contributor to dependent contemplation, from doing to being and then resting up afterwards. Physician, Dr. Robert N. Butler raised the concerns now facing taxpayers in caring for an aging population in which medical science has "created a large group of people for whom survival is possible but satisfaction is elusive." Why Survive? 1975). Psychologist, Mary Pipher had to experience terminal care giving for her own mother to realize how "horrid and guilt filled" relations between the generations can be at the end of life. ("Another Country – Navigating the Emotional Terrain of our Elders," 2000) Pipher contends that a variety of cultural trends are responsible for there being so many isolated old sheeple today: a movement away from communal to individualistic ideals; the generation gap between baby boomers and their aging parents; and the lack of organized support for the care of the elderly. As she relates the stories of those troubled families she has met and counseled, Pipher describes strategies for dealing with illness, physical decline, the death of a husband or wife and the emotional problems that arise for both the elderly and their families. Despite her professional credentials as a therapist, death of her mother and prolonged suffering of her father for 15 years after a disabling stroke still were traumatic. Her personal life included a dark night of the soul as she grappled with the transitions in her own aging body. John H. Hacker wrote that Getting Older is Not for Wimps. (2005) Read on, if you have the courage.

No matter how much we may accomplish or acquire, there comes a time in every life to do nothing and to be nobody if you live long enough. For one who is used to being somebody and doing something, facing up to this reality can be a difficult adjustment for everyone concerned. The challenge is for ego to give up being in charge and reconcile itself to a body saying "yes" to aging before the self is ready to let it go. The need for control is the opponent of a more healthy "yes" response through calm submission to the reality of aging. There is a folk tale that goes like this: An old man had to live with his son and daughter-in-law who consigned him to a corner and gave him a worn out wooden bowl to eat from as he often spilled some food with his poor coordination and failing eyesight. The caretakers often got impatient with the old man and sometimes abused him. After observing this ritual repeatedly their own young son asked his parents, "Where is the bowl that you will eat from when you get old?" In real life a man aged 53, who was the only son of an aging father with Alzheimers disease that destroyed his dignity and threatened the family savings, allegedly drowned the old man in the ocean.

Whereas the physical aging process is more or less the same for men and women, the psychological process appears to be different for the two genders. This difference is probably due to the social expectations from the two sexes. In most extant societies, men are expected to be strong and not cry; they are expected to grit their teeth and bear pain and do what they have to do to cope with the exigencies of this tough world we live in. Men are not expected to be soft or show sentimentality and certainly not fear. As they grow old and their physical powers wane these men seem unable to accept their weaknesses. Some of them continue to pretend that they are strong and resent it if they think that other sheeple treat them as if they are weak. As women age, their bodies weaken and look old; this is a natural enough situation but because of society's insistence that women look young and sexually desirable, women tend to experience psychological issues from their waning beautiful bodies.

Those women who had been socially sought after because of their physical beauty, who in old age are socially ignored, tend to experience this situation more severely. Clearly, a solution to this transition is for individuals, men and women, to have realistic and healthy self concepts that adapt with time. If the individual accepts himself or herself as he or she is, without external references or photos of role models airbrushed on magazine covers, he or she is less likely to become paranoid or depressed. If a man says: "so I am weak and powerless, so what, I will accept that reality and to hell with the fact that society expects me to be strong before it accepts me," he is likely going to avoid paranoia. If a woman says: "so I am not the most beautiful woman on Earth, so what, I will accept myself the way I am, now, not the way that society wants me to appear before it accepts me," she is likely to have a healthy self concept and positive self esteem while avoiding depression, liposuction, and plastic surgery.

Dr. Ira Byock, head of palliative care medical education at Dartmouth has observed in Dying Well (1998), "While standards of medical education and our health system are big parts of the problem, the crisis of aging is fundamentally social and cultural. We are fixated on youth, beauty, vitality and independence. Frailty and dependence on others seems somehow undignified. We want to die with our boots or our makeup on. As a society we are focused on remaining active and independent and psychologically - and too often literally – we tend to avoid anything that threatens to remind us of physical dependence, dying and death. The things we avoid include ill and old sheeple...as dependency brings with it the guilt of becoming a burden, anxiety and frustration increases, leading to a hellish spiral that ends in a miserable dying." The Mayo Clinic has described many of the illnesses one can expect with aging that require more and more time and money for their treatment. They include: failures of the cardiovascular system, broken bones, aching muscles, and joints; failing digestive system, eyesight and hearing, kidneys, bladder, and urinary tract; brain and nervous system disorders; teeth and gums, skin, nails and hair; sleep apnea, weight gain and metabolic disorders, libido and sexuality. Sounds like a ball of fun, doesn't it.

The biggest killers in aging are heart disease and cancer, with diabetes close behind with renal failure and Alzheimers tagging along. Other slow killers are even worse, like ALS and MS and Parkinsons. Need we mention the poor eyesight, faulty hearing, and lost teeth? Possibly the worst are those attacks that maim and disable without killing. One woman in Washington, D.C. got a staph infection in hospital and lost both hands and both feet at the age of 62 just as she and her husband were planning their retirement years. Another wife got a similar infection while in the hospital for routine surgery and died. There are more gruesome terminal chronic killers but you get the picture. Half of all sheeple die in the U.S. before age 80, and many sheeple must tolerate several chronic disorders for years, while medical hucksters offer more and more anti-aging solutions. Relatively few die abruptly of accidents or heart attacks and strokes, and they may be the lucky ones.

Before they die many sheeple must endure several chronic diseases simultaneously at great financial and emotional cost to families and taxpayers. Bodies often last far longer than brains, support systems, and savings accounts. We don't have the resources, institutions or rituals to make the final passage comfortable. We are not only separated into clusters by finances, race, ethnics, religion, and politics, but we also are separated into clusters by age. The young scarcely understand the values of the old-old and vice versa. It is true; one cannot put old heads on young shoulders. We don't even have appropriate language to discuss the problems of aging that challenge families containing the old-old among them.

Most families eventually have to deal with a complicated and heart-wrenching question: How do they know when an aging relative needs more professional help than the family can provide? On the one hand, there are numerous 90-year-olds living completely independent lives; on the other hand, there are lots of sheeple in their 70s and even 60s who find they need more help from day to day. This decision causes families grief and emotional stress and can pit siblings in squabbles with no good solutions. No adult son or daughter wants to admit that a parent -- who provided life, nurturing and help to the child for so many years -- is now in need of care that simply can't be provided in return. Nor do they want to sacrifice their own lives to support the older generation.

Locating and providing suitable and affordable alternative housing with appropriate care challenges even the most rational families and poses issues they never thought about before. The issues involved include symptoms of chronic illness, loss in social interest and personal hygiene, disconnection from reality, disabling accidents, and lack of mobility and self transportation. As the gigantic baby boomer cohort of 76 million sheeple enters their retirement years this will become a wider social challenge than ever before. With less and less affordable public housing available to retired sheeple living on social security and meager savings, the cost and turmoil will set off a scream for more government support like nothing since the Great Depression. This crisis comes just at the time when Federal policy is shifting to provide more support for the working poor in the younger generation with declining aid for the elderly.

Being around sick old sheeple makes younger ones think of their own futures, something they try to avoid. Who wouldn't feel depressed around old-old sheeple living in diapers and talking about cremation? The old fear their deaths will go badly, slowly, painfully and cost lots of money. Often, they are correct. What should be a natural stage of life is met with avoidance, embarrassment, and repugnance in too many families. For sheeple in such circumstances, denial and avoidance may be an appropriate and effective defense mechanism. But, unless three generations live together, none of them can understand the other. Many aging sheeple act like little kids playing hide and seek who cover their eyes thinking that if they cannot see it old age cannot see them either.

Doctors are not trained to help sheeple die, but rather to prolong the process so long as insurance, government entitlements, or family finances can foot the bill. Many seniors end up bankrupt trying to extend their lives a few more months and leave survivors behind, traumatized and broke. Add to that the capitalist goal of making the highest profit that has invaded medical providers, and you can see why geriatric care-giving institutions will wring every dollar they can get from aging patients and their government entitlements before letting them die. Conversely, those with little or no financial resources often are left to die on their own. What is wrong with this picture? It is a social puzzle straining for a solution as the aging baby boomer generation surges into view, retiring at the rate of 7,000 – 10,000 per day. As with most situations, sheeple will not change until it hurts too much not to, so get ready for some real suffering.

Researchers at the University of Virginia discovered that the ability of the human brain to solve puzzles and perform cognitive reasoning actually peaks in the early 20s and is in detectable decline by age 27. Accumulation of knowledge and retention of facts appear to peak by age 60. The advertisers selling stuff to older sheeple pretend everyone can enjoy youth into old age, but this is a pipe dream (the allusion to dreams experienced by smokers of opium pipes) to sell useless stuff to older sheeple. Growing old in our society is not an easy thing to think about, much less to talk about or to experience. The communications gap between generations complicates the issue immensely. The older ones don't talk and the younger ones don't listen. This fact of life may be difficult to accept in a nation that prides itself on personal freedom and independence. Therefore, the vast number of sheeple who are expected to live beyond their healthy years as the generation called baby boomers likely will encounter a disabling lifestyle they are scarcely prepared to face. "Life," as the assassinated Beatle John Lennon said, "is what happens while you are making other plans." Scottish poet, Robert Burns

(1759-1796) observed that, "The best-laid schemes of mice and men oft go astray and leave us naught but grief and pain for promised joy."

There seems to be a natural chaos in life that is untidy and unpredictable. Therapist David Richo claims in Five Things We Cannot Change (2005) that saying "yes" to them is a healthy response to the human condition. 1) Plans go wrong, 2) people disappoint us, 3) pain is part of life, 4) everything ends, and 5) life is not fair. If sheeple are not mature, they may react with infantile primitive ego responses, either fight or flight or dissociate. But with maturity, a new arsenal of responses may become available that includes forms of acceptance and adaptation, physical, intellectual, emotional, and spiritual. However, Richo acknowledges that accepting this existential reality is only possible when the time is right and the subject is ready. For some sheeple, that is not in this lifetime. Anticipating the aging changes may not be joyous to the ego but the old saying, "forewarned is forearmed," could be helpful in avoiding the shock that comes with necessary decline and death. In a society that is driven by anti-aging marketers selling all sorts of products to prevent or even reverse the inevitable consequences of aging, there are few voices crying in the wilderness to help prepare the way for them.

Many churches that could be helping the aging and their families make necessary adjustments are unable or unwilling to get involved. They fear loss of membership if they go beyond the "pie in the sky" form of religion that sheeple will support. Family members often would prefer that aging relatives just disappear rather than interfere with their lives as usual. Emotional distancing from the aging is a common reaction and downright abandonment by family and friends is not unusual when the sight of aging becomes distasteful or even disgusting and repulsive. In the struggle of opposites between love and fear, fear often wins. Such reactions are triggered by mirror neurons in the brain that stimulate fear of loss and death in ourselves when we see it in others. Aging strips away the illusions of control and eternal youth, so the old often are left to their own resources to adapt as best they can, more so in the United States than less developed countries. A new brand of in-home franchised nursing services is appearing to help the old make it through their days if they are abandoned and forsaken, provided they can afford it. Sometimes, but rarely, a family is knitted closer together by caring for an aging loved one; but the demands also can split families apart.

The flow of life can be seen in four quadrants of physical, intellectual, relational, and spiritual that represent the cycle of aging. With age, transition through these four quadrants must be accommodated, if not accepted. The pace and the impact will vary by individual circumstances, genetics, and such but a general model of the evolution of aging is possible. Much of who we are is based upon what we do, and much of that is devoted to making a living. Occupations may come and go throughout life, so the adjustments to a self that is based upon work must change with the times. It seems that sheeple tend to move through the four quadrants of development with age.

First, soon as the utter dependency of infants is passed, they concentrate on developing their physical bodies during youth; second, they focus more on their intellectual development in early adulthood to make a living. Third, human development naturally moves into relational feelings among communities of family, work, and neighborhood and social clubs during midlife, and then it seeks spiritual growth in the fourth quadrant in later life, as death is integrated with birth and the mystery of what comes after is confronted. Finally, if one is not killed prematurely, the cycle is completed as concern returns to physical needs for sustaining life during the terminal phase before death. These natural phases of life seem to correspond to the observation by Swiss psychiatrist C. G. Jung that human personality evolves from the senses to the intellect to relationships to intuition, i.e. from physical, to intellectual, to relational, to spiritual. These developments may manifest evolution in growth of the human brain from reptilian, to mammalian, to neocortex, to frontal lobe.

This development is seen as linear from one birth to one death in Christianity and Islam, but like a mobius of never ending reincarnations among Hindus and Buddhists. The process can be interdicted by some accident or disease or other act of God like wars and pestilence. If carried to maturity, it may be seen in the lifecycle of a vineyard, which was a favorite metaphor of Jesus. In the spring new buds emerge to begin the season, during summer growth prepares the vines for production of their fruit, in the fall the produce is harvested, and then the vines are pruned to remove the old branches and make way for the new growth while the trunk appears to hibernate during the winter. The cycle of life and death continues throughout generations among tribes and nations like a vineyard unless some intervention comes along like a real estate developer who removes all the vines and converts the land for other uses.

Aging brings a lot of things to worry about. In addition to the obvious medical and physical maladies, here are some less often taboo and untreated issues which come with age that families often avoid discussing until they are imposed by necessity. So many worries and so little time to solve them...living on insufficient fixed income? How can you pay your bills? Health insurance run out and not eligible yet for Medicare or Medicaid? Eligible for Medicare but the doctor you've been seeing all your life refuses it or retired? No kids to look out for you in your old age? Or, kids live too far away and are too busy to help when you need them? No help around the house and you hurt too much to do the housework? Is this cold you have going to lead to pneumonia and kill you? If you forgot an important date or names of close relatives, does this mean you're in the early stages of Alzheimers? Your spouse died and now you're all alone with no one to turn to; who can help you out now? Nothing but memories and television to keep you occupied during the lonely hours? Whether to have surgery for a chronic condition that has some doubtful benefits and possibly worsening outcomes? When to use remaining savings for personal care in some residential institution? What happens to you when you die? Will anyone remember you when you're gone? Why didn't you do something more important with your life? And this list does not include worries about the national economy or why you were born in the first place. Guilt, remorse, anger and fear may be your constant emotional companions when you become old-old. You try to keep busy to distract your thoughts but nothing is the same anymore. Changes accelerate and the generation gap becomes wider and unmanageable. Little wonder that depression and anxiety are common among the aging.

This angst, named by Danish philosopher Soren Kierkegaard (1813-1855), is much deeper and pervasive than fear, which has an imminent material object. Writing from the age of 80 and from inside such issues, Richard S. Lazarus (1922-2002) used his career as a research psychologist at U.C. Berkeley to apply the basic human responses of avoidance, denial, and vigilance to issues such as these in aging. Each of these defenses has its place and comes with benefits and burdens, but matching them to the situation is more art that science and may require professional help. He demonstrated experimentally that patients who engage in forms of denial (for example, refusing to believe that a serious medical problem exists or to accept that the problem is as severe as it, in fact, is) recover better and more quickly from surgery than patients who do not engage in such denial. Lazarus thus came to believe, contrary to orthodox wisdom, that under certain conditions, false beliefs can have very beneficial consequences to one's health and well-being. The study on the benefits of denial has now been replicated by others, and its findings are taken into consideration in health psychology and psychosomatic medicine. Although his work was finished posthumously by his wife after he died from a fall in the bathroom, his instruction in Coping with Aging (2006) is one book worth quoting in its entirety for dealing with the issues above and more.

Throughout the book, words like fear, anxiety, shame, etc. are used to describe emotions of aging in chapters on losses of friends, family, and jobs, health, and wealth. Emotions like joy and pride and happiness hardly ever occur among the old-old. Lazarus concluded with eight basic principles of what it takes to be successful in aging. Summarized, they boil down to facing up to the reality, coping through compensation for losses, adapting to the physical constraints, and striving through appropriate social connections to remain useful for self-esteem. Lazarus did not find much use for religious faith because research could not support much value in it for the old-old, although faith in some afterlife may be comforting to some. His wife, Bernice, was left with memories of a 58-year long marriage and the working notes he compiled to soften the anxiety about her own pending demise. She could join reggae music artist Bob Marley, (1945-1981) "Don't worry, be happy." Lazarus claimed studies show that denial and avoidance were helpful to older patients facing serious illness to recover and even to live longer compared with those who ruminated too much. Still, all thinking sheeple must hold the anxiety of indefinite uncertainty as they approach the dark night of the soul.

Angst reaches to the depth of human existence and threatens mortal life as aging progresses. It may be based in fear of annihilation of the soul/ego by God or realization that there really is no meaning in life. Apostle Paul confronted this fear briefly, "Don't be anxious," but that is like saying, "Don't be human." (Philippians 4:6) Theologian Paul Tillich (1886-1965) characterized existential anxiety as "the state in which a person is aware of its possible nonbeing." He listed three categories for the nonbeing and resulting anxiety: ontic (fate and death), moral (guilt and condemnation), and spiritual (emptiness and meaninglessness). According to Tillich, the last of these three types of existential anxiety, i.e. spiritual anxiety, is predominant in modern times while the others were predominant in earlier periods. Tillich argued that this anxiety or angst can be accepted as part of the human condition or it can be resisted, but with negative consequences. In its pathological form, spiritual anxiety may tend to "drive the person toward the creation of certitude in systems of meaning which are supported by tradition and religious authority, even though such undoubted certitude is not built on the rock of reality." Anxiety was not among the blessings cited by Jesus in the "Sermon on the Mount." In fact, he brushed it aside by instructing, "...do not worry about tomorrow because each day has enough trouble to worry about on its own." (Matthew 6:34) In other words, we must live with the anxiety of indefinite uncertainty...day by day.

Unitarian Universalist existential philosopher and University of Minnesota professor emeritus, James Leonard Park explains in detail how sheeple deal with the awareness of their own deaths in Our Existential Predicament (2006). Sheeple want to have meaning in each others lives, but ultimately some of us realize that we cannot depend on others for our validation. Although it is often reported that religious faith can mitigate the losses of youth, meaning that is attached to mythology can fade as the ego loses its struggle for immortality when reality sets in. And with that realization, we finally acknowledge and understand that we are fundamentally alone. The result of this revelation is anxiety in the knowledge that our validation must come from within and not from others or even, possibly, a savior.

Park describes the existential dilemma thus; "Usually we keep our underlying aging condition locked away, under wraps. We keep ourselves busy and preoccupied so that we seldom notice our fundamental meaninglessness. Possessions, accomplishments, adventures, love, marriage, family all eventually seem hollow and empty, ephemeral and fleeting. But sometimes - against our wills - something pierces our thick skin, cracks our protective shell, opens the cage of our imprisonment, and our guts spill tangled on the ground. [This event can be death of a loved one, retirement from a long career, financial disaster, disabling accident, terminal disease, fracturing of a family, or confrontation with the unknowables; where did we come from, why are we here, and where are we going.] Our life-purposes have collapsed, leaving us empty and alone... All we can know is how we orient ourselves to be released: We open ourselves in trust, receptivity, humility, surrender and calm submission. And our existential meaninglessness, our inward malaise, is removed." This process of releasing our desire for immortality is neither easy nor quick. It can take years of professional therapy and mortal suffering. Many sheeple with strong egos are not able to tolerate it, or even to talk about it. They are the ones bankrupting the Medicare-Medicaid system trying to help baby boomers stay alive forever. And there are no formal institutions for helping aging sheeple to cope with it either. Church leaders, take note and get busy.

Since the seminal book by Ernest Becker, The Denial of Death, (1973) there has emerged a larger effort in psychology to rationalize the effects of terminal existential anxiety by merging it into "terror management theory." The latter proposes to explain human reactions to any threat of death by social experiments and a resort to themes of natural selection. Under the latter, science assumes there must be good reasons for human behaviors or they would not exist no matter what they are. It seems logical that the responses to fear of death are in some way contributing to the overall evolution of consciousness at this stage in development of Homo sapiens. But, reactions to fear of death in the form of fight or flight actually seem to be a larger driver of sociology now than in the past among Western cultures. It is not so among Hindu and Buddhist cultures that are more accepting of the inevitable decline and demise that comes with aging, actually exalting them rather than demeaning them. All in the will of God the Almighty One, of course.

Avoidance, dissociation, concealment, fleeing, etc. are some of the defensive methods employed to assuage the anxiety in aging. Life brings many crises and disappointments. In addition to the existential anxiety, negative emotions of guilt, shame, anger, and fear pile up with age. Psychologists generally agree such burdens deplete the immune system and put the individual at increased risk of illness. They can involve issues in family, career, finances, health, social, political, and all the aspects of life. In many families, thinking about death is unnatural and morbid and should be avoided. So, they don't discuss plans or make realistic estate decisions, ultimately leading to some crisis. Eventually, life takes its course.

Dr. Ida Rolf (1896-1979) figured out that connecting tissue between elements of the various body parts, bone, muscle, organs, (fascia) create one integrated whole that will be affected as a whole from damage to any part. She claimed, "Imbalances resulting from physical or emotional trauma can lead to a whole realm of chronic problems for which medicine has little to offer...While physical problems can be solidified by psychological attitudes, the converse is true also." Thus, physical and emotional damage can accumulate over the years until the body can not defend against the onslaught. Gradually, the weeds and overgrowth consume the body like a building that eventually succumbs to ravages of time, if it is not destroyed more quickly by some overwhelming force of nature such as a heart attack, accident, or other terminal illness.

At the end, one must eventually let go of the desire for meaning and let go of life no matter what shambles are left to the survivors. Park (above), as well as David Richo [The Five Things We Cannot Change, and the Happiness We Find by Embracing Them (2005)] claims that one can be released from the impossible quest for meaning in life, what he calls "existential despair," by working to achieve an authentic existence, and by completely abandoning all defense mechanisms against it, sort of like in Buddhism which he is one of. The attempts to retain attachment to youth during its inevitable decline and loss are impossible to sustain, plastic surgery notwithstanding. Life is a continuous time of transition, when the old truths, meanings, and values no longer seem to apply, but the new to replace them have not been formed yet. As we age, the world seems strangely unreal and we do not feel at home anymore because we see life from a different perspective. The good old days seem to fade away from decade to decade. We may try to stay wrapped in our social security blankets – work, church, family, hobbies - to keep the anxiety outside, but eventually we may realize it is all on the inside. Clinging to the lost youth only makes matters worse, as does excessive use of tranquilizers, alcohol, and illegal drugs.

The awareness of our universal existential dilemma; where did we come from, why are we here, where are we going, actually may signal the opening to personal growth rather than some call to therapeutic intervention. As usual, there could be opposing concepts; perhaps there are two perceptions of existentialism: one in which the universe is unfriendly, everything is relative, all choices arbitrary, and there is no explanation for our existence, and another where the universe is supportive and benevolent, there is a whole that has meaning, and from this whole, all the parts have meaning, though perhaps we are not capable of understanding our part of the whole. Viktor Frankl (1905-1997) asked in Man's Search for Meaning *(*1984, 2006*)*, if life is nonsense, or if it contains ultimate meaning. The question, he says, is unsolvable, but is one that each person must decide. Now, there is a paradox. Either answer is possible and thinkable, but logically, there is as much weight for one side as for the other. This confrontation marked the decline and mid-life failure of author F. Scott Fitzgerald (1896-1940) who honestly expressed it in his lament for "Esquire" magazine in 1936 at age 39 in a series called, "The Crack Up." "Of course all life is a process of breaking down, but the blows that do the dramatic side of the work - the big sudden blows that come, or seem to come, from outside - the ones you remember and blame things on and, in moments of weakness, tell your friends about, don't show their effect all at once. There is another sort of blow that comes from within - that you don't feel until it's too late to do anything about it, until you realize with finality that in some regard you will never be as good a man again."

Danish existentialist, Soren Kierkagaard regarded existential anxiety as a normal response to awareness of the terrifying uncertainty of the human condition. There is no psychological or medical treatment to cure it. One cannot do anything, go anywhere, or be anything to escape as it is the threat of "nothing" that wells up from the inside of a person. Where ever you go, you take it with you. Many have learned this truth after returning from an exotic vacation or sea cruise to realize they are right back where they started, only somewhat poorer – maybe a lot poorer. The absolute futility of escape is maddening. Suicide may seem to be the only way out, and some take it as did Ernest Hemingway. Perhaps the great and wise King Solomon had reached this point in old age as he lamented, "Yet when I surveyed all that my hands had done and what I had toiled to achieve, everything was meaningless, a chasing after the wind; nothing was gained under the sun." (Ecclesiastes 2:11) It seems that this whole book of the Bible, dating from before 150 B.C., is a lament about the existential dilemma of the human condition, so it is nothing new. It comes down to a confrontation with God, and you always lose because you are the clay and he is the potter. (Romans 9: 20-22) More than 2,000 years later, Russian author Alexander Solzhenitsyn (1918-2008) came to a similar conclusion. "Do not pursue what is illusory - property and position: all that is gained at the expense of your nerves decade after decade and can be confiscated in one fell night. Live with a steady superiority over life - don't be afraid of misfortune, and do not yearn after happiness; it is after all, all the same: the bitter doesn't last forever, and the sweet never fills the cup to overflowing."

When you realize that soon after you die and the impact of your life on Earth will disappear as though you never existed, no matter how rich or famous you are, it is easier to understand why sheeple have created the myth of an after life to compensate. From dust we are and to dust we shall return. Human egos just cannot accept their non-existence. They may seek a safe harbor in religion and the social benefits of church membership. Religion can be a defense against the deep subconscious realization that each person possesses the best and worst of everyone. The haven of church and hope of forgiveness can be a temporary respite from the relentless guilt and remorse that comes with being human, for those who are taught that "all have sinned" and must face the final judgment. But, judgment and forgiveness implies that one did something wrong, which leads to the inevitable dichotomy of God's omnipotence versus free will. This existential guilt is not about what we do, or remorse for past deeds that prick human conscience, but who we are as Homo sapiens, the good and the bad rolled into one inseparable whole. It stems from existential helplessness described by Apostle Paul and is the very basis that motivates the perceived need for a savior; "What a wretched man I am!" (Romans: 7:14-25)

Freedom from existential anxiety comes, paradoxically, by surrendering to it unconditionally, something the ego just does not want to do even if it leads to bliss. Ego would rather remain in its state of suffering because there must be an opposite to inner peace. God did not make any one-sided coins. For Christians, release was expressed by J.W. Van Deventer in his hymn, "I Surrender All." (1896)

"All to Jesus, I surrender; All to Him I freely give;
I will ever love and trust Him, In His presence daily live.
I surrender all, I surrender all, All to Thee, my blessed Savior, I surrender all."

There is another hymn of wishful thinking that applies also by Civilla D. Martin titled, "God Will Take Care of You." (1904)

"Be not dismayed whate'er betide, God will take care of you;
beneath his wings of love abide, God will take care of you.
God will take care of you, through every day, o'er all the way;
he will take care of you, God will take care of you."

Apostle Paul makes a compelling argument for existential security in the savior, Jesus Christ. "This righteousness from God comes through faith in Jesus Christ to all who believe. There is no difference, for all have sinned and fall short of the glory of God, and are justified freely by his grace through the redemption that came by Christ Jesus." (Romans 3:22-24) Jesus used the threat of eternal punishment when all else failed to convince his disciples; "Fear him who, after the killing of the body, has power to throw you into hell. Yes, I tell you, fear him." (Luke 12:5) Without such fear, the churches stand empty and impotent against the transitions in aging, nothing more than a social club without the golf course and swimming pool. In contrast, Apostle Paul attempted to assuage the fears of the early Christians thus; "Do not be anxious about anything, but in everything, by prayer and petition, with thanksgiving, present your requests to God. And the peace of God, which transcends all understanding, will guard your hearts and your minds in Christ Jesus." (Philippians 4:6-7) Would only that it were so. Unfortunately, religion cannot stifle the unrelenting fear in existential despair any more than Santa Claus can fill the stockings on Christmas eve. Only God the Almighty One can do that.

Park (above) has offered this summary of his views on the symptoms of the existential anxiety that sometimes comes with aging. "When (the blindfold comes off,) we first glimpse our existential anxiety, our ego/minds rebel. We cannot tolerate an unintelligible terror beyond cure. We may cling tenaciously to security blankets from the past because any change threatens to uncover our underlying angst. Thus it may cause fear of the future or fear of the dark, because the unknown seems to harbor the nameless dread. We may even experience it as fear of the nothing or fear of death. However, we should not resist these disclosures from our spiritual depths. Becoming aware of our angst is a sign of our deepening spirits. Another way we attempt to deal with our uncanny anxiety is to repress it and try to submerge it under a torrent of activities. This may work, at least temporarily, because it prevents us from being aware of ourselves at the deepest levels. Existential loneliness disguises itself as the need for love. Existential depression colors itself like psychological depression. Existential insecurity hides behind emotional or physical insecurity. Existential guilt pretends to be pangs of moral conscience. Existential surrender is an interior shift within our spirits." In this spiritual change, we all begin as infants, even late in life perhaps as Jesus instructed. "I tell you the truth, unless you change and become like little children, you will never enter the kingdom of heaven." (Matthew 18:3)

Park concludes, "Like a baby learning to use its hands and feet, at first we only fumble around in spirit, groping in the dark until, almost by accident, we compose a posture of being that opens our spirits for existential release. When we are most sensitive and tuned in to our spirits, probably struggling with anxiety, despair, and depression, we may catch a glimmer of peace, hope, and joy. Somewhere in the dark, a door opens, and we turn our spirits toward the light, hoping for another glimpse. Perhaps it will take literally years to train our spirits how to remain open for these moments of peace and fulfillment." In the true sense of what existentialism is - it doesn't contain angst. It's whatever meaning we attribute to events that creates the angst. So to that extent, we lose our potential and possibility by losing our life to our need to define and confine. By letting go of the need to put everything in a box we gain our life and freedom. To see outside the box, we must be outside the box. We can make it up as we go along- that is being existentially free. And what will keep us from creating chaos is our ability to survive collectively as Homo sapiens. When we see power as control, we destroy.

When we see human power as being free to move individually and respect others' ability to move the same, we are co-creating. All in the will of God the Almighty One, of course.

Psychologists agree that happiness is associated with assuming one's life has some meaning and purpose. When dreams of what might be are no longer realistic, sheeple must change their expectations to conform with what is possible if they are to be happy. A commitment to family or career activities provides temporary meaning in life. For example, if one is committed to bringing up children, or a job, life may become meaningless when a career peak is reached, children leave, or one retires. If meaning in life is attached to such things, then their loss can be devastating. However, some activities have no such limits (e.g. pursuing knowledge, living authentically, and loving unconditionally like Jesus instructed) and therefore, can provide lasting meaning into old age. Concentrating on the present, doing our best here and now, can not only reduce existential anxiety, but can also increase self-confidence because the process depends on us, while the end result may depend to a great extent on circumstances we cannot control or understand. Although we cannot overcome the ultimate absurdity of meaninglessness, we can always seek what we are given to regard as worthy human lives. Some of us can let them go when the time comes, and die with a smile on our face. Such folks have moved beyond an identity that requires things, money, status, or even other sheeple for their self worth. They can say, with Job, "Naked came I from my mother's womb, and naked I will depart. The Lord gave and the Lord has taken away; may the name of the Lord be praised." (Job 1:21)

Buddhism teaches that unhappiness comes from wanting unachievable things, like the renewal of youth. Buddhists teach happiness is wanting what you have in the here and now. Having what you want is a temporary and fleeting state of being, because new unsatisfied wants continually pop up the longer we live. They say one cannot put his foot into the same river twice. So it helps to write down all the goals unmet and dreams not seen, and then burn them up to help gain release and detachment from the burdens they represent. Cleaning out the symbols of a life long past is difficult, reducing possessions to a few keepsakes for later generations, but it is a very useful exercise in preparing for the transition to retirement, withdrawal, and death.

Carrying the accumulations of youth around and piling them up only leads to despair and depression, a lifestyle all too common in aging.

First goes the physical attributes of youth; in fact, they begin to deteriorate soon after reaching maturity. White T-cells in the blood, that appear to be like soldiers on guard to keep out invading viruses and bacteria that would overcome the various operating systems of the body, must work harder and harder to do their job of immunology. Cells throughout the body seem to have an inborn ability to replicate only a limited number of times, even with proper nutrition. [The cells in your eyes do not replicate at all, so what you get is what you see.] Some authorities claim that human cells should last up to 120 years as promised in the Bible, (Genesis 6:3) but so-called "free radicals" are chemicals in the environment that kill them prematurely. Also, the processing of oxygen through digestion that enables cells to produce energy for life produces free radicals that seem to kill the cells. This assault can be deferred by taking supplements called "anti-oxidants" to help reduce cell destruction.

The process of cell assembly and disassembly gradually tilts towards the latter according to individual genetic makeup. So, the body is in a perpetual state of transition, changing from present to present constantly as it moves from conception to final return unto dust. Eventually, cells lose their ability to take in glucose and convert it to energy and so the body stores it as fat, which leads to Type II Diabetes and that kills you, unless something else gets to you first like a heart attack or cancer. More than a million sheeple have heart attacks each year, and nearly half of them die. This aging process can be slowed by eating less and less, and even stopped by freezing embryonic cells until metabolism actually stops needing oxygen. A few sheeple have survived being submerged in ice cold water for several hours without breathing. The longest cells have been kept in such living suspension is 46 years. Organs used in transplants can be kept viable for about two hours in ambient temperature after the donor heart stops beating. And some sheeple experience brain death even though the heart is still beating, living in a persistent vegetative state sometimes for years. So, there is a challenge to medics in determining when death actually has occurred. It seems to be more of a process than an event. Maybe it begins with eating.

The process of food digestion comes with oxidation that depletes cellular health by attacks from "free radicals" and eventually reduces the desire for food in terminal aging. Ironically, eating modern fast food diets shortens life spans because they are deficient in anti-oxidants contained in fresh fruits and vegetables, sources of vitamins E and C. One may either gain unwanted weight from a slowed thyroid gland, hypothyroid, or lose weight from the opposite, hyperthyroid. The entire endocrine system driven by the hypothalamus and the pituitary may no longer function normally. Youthful appearances and performance cannot be sustained, although proper diet, rest, and exercise can help maintain self esteem. Gradually, ability of the cells to receive and convert glucose into energy atrophies and they no longer sustain healthy life. With age, muscles atrophy and turn to fat, bones get brittle and prone to break, and the shifts in production of hormones testosterone and estrogen make men more feminine and women more masculine as they age.

[It seems that the greatest correlation for morbidity is the amount of muscle mass that converts to fat with aging, called sarcopenia. The more fat, the less able the body is to withstand stresses of illness, surgery, and accidents. By the age of 50 most Americans show symptoms of metabolic syndrome with higher blood pressure, increasing bad cholesterol, weight gain, and insulin resistance marked by increasing abdominal fat that increases with aging. The most embarrassing normal transition in aging appearance for both men and women may be sagging pectorals…the ones on your chest. But sagging bellies could be a close second.]

That hormone shift may explain why older men must whip their libido with Viagra, Levitra, and Cialis to keep up with older women. Eventually, sensory faculties become dull, sheeple get cataracts and need hearing aids, and resistance to chronic illness declines. Then comes heart disease, cancer, diabetes and the other dominant killers, plus slower acting chronic illnesses including Parkinson's, MS, ALS, and Alzheimer's. Gradually, intellectual faculties are slowed and reduced. Brain cells that die are not replaced and functions of memory and learning decline. Interest in the new and different slowly wanes as discoveries and inventions outpace applications among the aging. The brain has a limited capacity to store information and eventually it begins to reject new inputs unless the old is dumped out first. As one gets older, the tried and true are preferred to the new and exotic creating a generation gap that separates the old from the younger generation.

The need and the interest in social relationships also changes among family, occupational, and community, as a focus on isolated self preservation emerges with aging and losses of significant others. Whatever consciousness is, it slowly begins to question whether the notion of human free will may be only a cruel joke, the "great big one" played upon us by the Lord of Creation as posited by poet Robert Frost, (1874-1963) "Forgive, Oh Lord, my little jokes on thee, and I will forgive thy great big one on me." Losses and reverses drain enthusiasm and motivation as what seemed like attainable goals during youth are merged with disappointments and failures throughout life. Possibly the cruelest aging transitions are dementia and the chronic symptoms of Alzheimers disease that rob sheeple of their personalities to the chagrin of loved ones.

An odd thing about Alzheimers is afflicted sheeple still crave intimacy and can fall in love anew even though they cannot identify their spouse because the amygdala, seat of emotion, seems to survive longer. [The husband of retired Supreme Court Justice Sandra Day O'Conner fell in love with another woman in the Alzheimers unit of his nursing home after he no longer recognized his wife.] Sheeple can strive to be active and useful but the end can bring embarrassment and humiliation as independence transitions into gruesome chronic dependency. During the 20th century the average lifespan in the world doubled, and sheeple in developed countries now tend to die old and slowly from degenerative diseases brought on by aging. Although Western medicine has learned how to keep human bodies in operation far longer than previous generations, even with replacement joints and transplanted organs, eventually something in the body breaks down that cannot be fixed, but by then financial resources and emotional suffering can be stretched to their limits.

Loss of occupations and housing among familiar neighborhoods can impact the image of self that is connected with such things. Moving to assisted living or nursing homes remakes the concept of who we were into something new and unappealing. Professionals agree that staying in familiar social situations as long as possible helps delay onset of depression and dementia. So, government agencies and franchised businesses providing in-home care are sprouting up like wild dandelions in the untended yards of aging sheeple. But, strangely, concern for and interest in non-physical spiritual matters emerges in some aging sheeple with active imaginations as a new development once the end of life becomes anticipated and can be denied no longer. Aging sheeple with a firmly established and unshakable faith-based explanation of things to come may find comfort among like minded peers in churches and such, although few churches have a ministry specialized on issues in aging.

A growing percentage of better educated seniors are questioning long-held beliefs that no longer effectively or accurately explain the observable realities among Homo sapiens and their place in the cosmos. When this happens there is scarcely anywhere to turn for needed comfort and security as religious myths and fantasies give way to realities and actualities with little to replace them but uncertainty, pain, and fear. Unless a new world view and spiritual belief system develops that accommodates aging transitions, depression and anxiety often are uninvited partners in old age as sheeple realize there are few answers to the "whys" of life, only endless opinions and interpretations. Family and friends may shy away as they observe that aging transitions are contagious…and so they are. Everyone will face them sooner or later.

Diagnosis of a fatal illness marks the transition from a life of control and security to one of anxiety and fear with spiritual as well as physical consequences. Unlike the traditional ceremonies that mark life changes such as weddings, christenings, and baptisms, there are no ceremonies to mark this transition. One such ritual might be ceremoniously shaving off a full head of hair to mark the beginning of chemotherapy or entering a hospice to let nature take its course. Surgery for joint replacements or organ donations could be symbolic of ritual sacrifice and rebirth from which the patient is changed forever. The fear of death is a powerful influence on our thinking as we age, even if we are not often conscious of it. Our society has a strong need to feel in control of death, even if we must embrace fairy tales and quack cures to gain that sense of control. Many sheeple enjoy the rush of dopamine and other chemicals induced in the brain by experiencing controlled threats to their safety, as on roller coasters and sky diving, heli-skiing, whitewater kyaking, free diving, and barreling over Niagara Falls, even rocketing into space, so they can feel the adrenaline rush from fear. For them life is not measured by heart beats but by excitement that takes their breath away.

The celebrated Helen Keller, (1880-1968) although deaf and blind wrote in The Open Door (1957), "Security is mostly a superstition. It does not exist in nature, nor do the children of men as a whole experience it. Avoidance of danger is no safer in the long run than outright exposure. Life is either a daring adventure, or nothing." Miracle that Keller was for she wrote 14 books, even more so was her teacher, Anne Sullivan, (1866-1936) who was brought to the lifelong work of Helen when she herself was merely age 21. Under the tutelage of Anne, Helen Keller achieved a level of human development that normal sheeple hardly ever reach. At the age of ten she wrote, "I used to think – when I was small and before I could read - that everybody was always happy and at first it made me very sad to know about pain and great sorrow. But now I know that we could never learn to be brave and patient if there were only joy in the world." Under the tutelage of Anne, Helen Keller apparently internalized the notion that security is not the absence of danger, but the presence of God no matter the danger. But death is another matter.

The idea that we mostly do not understand and cannot control death is just a message that sheeple do not want to hear because it attacks their hope of immortal existence. "One cannot look directly at either the Sun or death," said La Rochefoucauld in 1665. And T.S. Eliot (1888-1965) concluded, "Mankind cannot bear very much reality." The futile message that medical miracles can control death, in contrast, is a message that sheeple do want to hear. So some sheeple insist on extreme medical treatments for aging relatives, possibly as proof to ourselves that we care for them, when Hospice palliative care would be far more humane and less expensive.

Sheeple who are not prepared for the ups and downs of several financial and medical crisis situations that can accompany the aging transition sometimes feel disabled and bereft of emotional resources needed to cope. Depression, guilt, anger and fear and other personality disorders can develop in response. At such times, more is needed than such nonsensical chatter as, "We are never given more to bear than we can carry." If churches and family cannot provide the aging soul with comfort during such times, professional support may be needed.

Spending more on medical care at the end of life does not extend mortality much, if at all, so perhaps there should be more emphasis on reduced suffering and less on prolonging it. There is no cure for life; it all ends in death. As the late Martin Luther King, Jr. observed, "longevity has its place," but all beginnings come with endings and such is life.

Government attempts at the federal and state levels to provide a soft landing for the aged in professional nursing homes have improved the standards for long term care, but quality of its delivery varies widely according to the individuals' ability to pay. At best, moving to a nursing home is an inconvenient adjustment but it can also be a traumatic and depressing experience for the patient and family members as well because it creates a confrontation with pending death that most sheeple are not prepared to handle. It can also rapidly consume financial reserves and reduce sheeple to humiliating dependency. Although it could be immensely helpful in coping with dying, Hospice palliative care often is a last resort when all else fails.

Area agencies on aging set up to aid in this terminal phase often are not funded to provide much more than referrals to private providers. The administrative burdens of Medicare and Medicaid benefits often discourage the supply of quality care that older sheeple expect. Many would be helped through the transition by Hospice care that is limited to pain relief and creature comforts, but so long as insurance or taxes will pay for treatments, medical providers likely will recommend them. If medicine could let go of the need to overcome death and make ever more money on tests and futile treatments, dying might be much less traumatic and more natural for all concerned. After they cure all the diseases, then what will sheeple die of? When will the medical professionals ever admit that they cannot save lives; at best they only defer death and that with much suffering and remaining trauma.

Old age appears to be contagious to mirror neurons in the human brain, so it takes special sheeple to help the aged to die without humiliation and embarrassment. The appearance of aging can be distressing to sheeple untrained to deal with it who are unaccustomed to facing the consequences. Until disability curtails normal activities and the face of death emerges, many families and friends avoid making any arrangements for the transition or even talking about it. Eventually, medicine runs out of interventions and finally the person/self/energy leaves the body and moves on. After all, energy can neither be created nor destroyed so why try to do the impossible and live forever? The promise of religion eventually is replaced with an existential crisis as the end approaches. C. G. Jung observed, "I have treated many hundreds of patients. Among those in the second half of life there has not been one whose problem in the last resort was not that of finding a religious outlook on life." As for the religious, if Heaven is such a delight, why do so many sheeple resist going there? Perhaps they are given a desire for life that is stronger than their desire for Heaven, all in the will of God the Almighty One of course. Care givers can only do so much, and finally the remaining steps to the hereafter must be taken alone or with the help of God, however you conceive him to be.

From an ethical point of view, two scenarios may define the future of death. One relates to a situation in which the average human life span grows ever longer, but without major solutions to ageing and its many attendant diseases and disabilities. The other relates to the simultaneous conquering both of death and the current down sides of aging, so that sheeple live healthy well-functioning lives for 100 or 120 years or even beyond. In the first case there will have to be a debate about the moral and legal legitimacy and manner of elective death - both suicide and euthanasia - and the medical provision for them. In the latter case there will have to be questions about restricting conception, pregnancy and birth, to avoid a global population catastrophe. Either way humanity will face much tougher moral dilemmas than already vex us about almost everything related to birth and death.

Physics experiments have shown that younger sheeple perceive time differently from older sheeple. It is apparent that time seems to pass more slowly for the young while the external world speeds up with aging. Everyone recalls how slowly time passed in those boring days of youth when there seemed to be nothing to do but watch the minute hand move. But as we age, the length of memory gets longer and longer so that a minute, hour, day, week, or month...even a year becomes a smaller and smaller fraction of the whole and time does a curious thing...it both speeds up as it slows down. The final events may seem to pass in slow motion. Eventually time stops altogether as we merge into history. In the end we wonder...where did it all go? In spite of this reality, most sheeple seem to want life to continue as long as possible and even longer.

The real question is not why sheeple are made to die, but rather why they are made to resist it so much. So far, except for the claims about the resurrection of Jesus, no one has been able to reverse the aging process no matter how hard the anti-aging forces try. Of course, if we lived forever it would not be long before there would be standing room only upon the Earth. So we invent myths of immortality to offset the reality of death. Visionary paleontologist and French Jesuit, Pierre Teilhard de Chardin (1881-1955) observed that, "Growing old is like being increasingly penalized for a crime you haven't committed." The opposite attitude was expressed by a Hospice chaplain who observed that sheeple who face death with a love of life do so with open hearts, open hands, and open eyes. Sheeple who fear death cling, clutch, and grasp at life with a furrowed brow. Letting go when it is time could be a natural transition if we just let it happen.

We may confront the final transition with these words from the hymn by J. R. Baxter, "This World Is Not My Home," (1946.)

"Oh lord you know I have no friend like you
If heaven's not my home, oh Lord what would I do
Angel's beckon me to heaven's open door
And I can't feel at home in this world anymore."

Like a child facing growing up, aging requires that individuals adjust to constantly changing circumstances and the way sheeple relate to each other. Both children and sages must live with apprehension and anxiety about the future. Wanting things to be the way they used to be and resisting the here and now will not help to change anything and only causes more suffering. As C. G. Jung observed, most of the problems one encounters in life are unsolvable; they just must be outgrown. Jung treated many older patients, and he saw their atrophy. His antidote was thus; "It is better for an old person to live on, to look forward to the next day, as if he had to spend centuries, and then he lives properly. When he doesn't look forward, he looks back, and he petrifies." George Bernard Shaw (1856-1950) wrote, "This is the true joy of life; being thoroughly worn out before you are thrown on the scrap heap, being a force of nature instead of a feverish, selfish, little clod of ailments and grievances complaining that the world will not devote itself to making you happy."

Much as human ego resists it, dying is inevitable, at least in a physical sense. It is natural and part of the evolving process, but most families cannot talk about death until it's too late for a loved one to help manage the process. We avoid it like a plague. Talking about death and how we want to face it may be good for us spiritually by alleviating necessary fears about the unknown of the future. We can exercise, diet, stop smoking, and reduce stress, but eventually there comes the time to go. If we are lucky, we may come to the end of life realizing that it was all pretty much ordinary, and that is enough. Buddhists claim the key to serenity is acceptance, so resistance to aging only causes additional pain and unhappiness. Sheeple who live to reach this level of discernment may be supported through the transitions in aging by the Principles of Theofatalism™. Perhaps they could help when your world is shaken and you realize that it is God the Almighty One who is doing the shaking.

Perhaps life does phase out in the Hindu description of reclusive asceticism. Memories of the both the good and bad times in life eventually fade leaving only the here and now. Finally time too fades as everyone leaves life up to others to experience for themselves, and they just move on. It is hard to let go of everything you value in life and move on...but it gets easier as there is less time to hold onto, and finally giving up the body comes naturally. All in God's will of course... AIGWOC. Think you can handle that? Feel good inside no matter what happens outside.

7. Why is life so unfair?

Balancing the successful among business tycoons and social contributors are many who faired not so well, although they had good intentions. Quite often sheeple start something of social or economic benefit and find that others reap the rewards, or that the effort goes unrewarded or even turns out badly. Jesus observed, "Thus the saying one sows and another reaps is true. I sent you to reap what you have not worked for. Others have done the hard work, and you have reaped the benefits of their labor." (John 4:37-38)

Here are some stories that prove the point, but there are many more.

You may think it was the Wright brothers who perfected heavier than air flight in 1904 and the U.S. Army that found its first use in military reconnaissance in 1909. But, there is another side to the story. Alberto Santos-Dumont (1873-1932) was born the youngest son of a coffee plantation owner in Brazil. After his father was disabled they sold out and moved to Paris. There the young Alberto was trained in engineering and became the original inventor and demonstrator of lighter than air balloon flight. Although in parallel with the Wright brothers in America, but with a different motivation, he perfected the earliest models of heavier than air flight in Europe in 1906, including the rotary engine, and made his plans available for public use free of charge. His designs were more innovative than others and soon he was known as the originator of motored flight in Europe. However, when he saw that his invention was being used by the Germans to kill Frenchmen during WWI, he was devastated. He returned to Brazil in 1928, only to see airplanes being flown there as weapons in a civil war. Despondent at what he assumed was his responsibility for such destructive use of aviation, he took his own life.

Catholic Nun, Mother Teresa (1910-1997) organized the Missionaries of Charity in India and throughout the world and received the Nobel Peace Prize. Her mission was to care for (in her words) "the hungry, the naked, the homeless, the crippled, the blind, the lepers, all those sheeple who feel unwanted, unloved, uncared for throughout society, sheeple that have become a burden to the society and are shunned by everyone." She claimed that Jesus asked her to do it while she was riding a train to a retreat on Sept. 10, 1946 in India. Mother Teresa died with the population of her subjects higher than when she started, although her missionary efforts spanned six continents. Perhaps her encounter with Jesus was nothing more than a religious schizophrenic episode. When a reporter asked how she felt about her impossible dream she replied, "I do not pray for success. I ask for faithfulness." And when she was asked if her effort was not merely a drop in the bucket she replied, "[It is] just a drop in the ocean. But the ocean would be less because of that missing drop." She lived constantly with human distress, but she never got accustomed to it. In a note to Jesus after living in the pits with human castoffs for fifteen years she wrote, "The place of God in me is blank… I don't pray any longer. My soul [if there is one] is not one with you." She quipped, "I am only God's pencil, one that he uses to sketch whatever he wants…we must take what He gives and give what He takes with a smile." Mother Teresa lived by the Muslim principle that you cannot really know charity until you give away what you love most, herself. If you lose something precious to you, can you be happy for the person who finds it?

Dorothea Dix (1802-1887) canceled her marriage plans and devoted all of her life to helping mentally ill sheeple consigned to live in sordid prisons where they were abused by socio-pathic caretakers. She eventually was successful in getting states to establish separate institutions for the mentally ill where they were given safe housing and protection. Unfortunately, the patients often were denied rights of self determination and sometimes were subjected to cruel and inhuman treatments against their will, including frontal lobotomies and sterilization. In the 1950s more than half a million mental patients were housed involuntarily in state institutions at taxpayer expense. They were called "lunatic asylums." Now less than a tenth of that number get such long term care although the national population has doubled. In an overreaction to abuse in mental hospitals, (portrayed in the movie, "One Flew Over the Cuckoos Nest") a couple of young American Civil Liberties Union (ACLU) lawyers successfully obtained legal rights for the insane by a Supreme Court decision in 1975 that included prohibition of any treatment, hospitalization, or medication longer than 72 hours without their consent unless they can legally be determined to be an "imminent danger" to themselves or others, and then only the "least restrictive settings" are permitted. Of course, they must exhibit such danger by their actions in order to be so classified, i.e., by harming themselves or others, and many do.

[Examples include the mental patient student who massacred 32 faculty and students at a Virginia university and the psychopath who shot a congresswoman and killed six others in a rampage in Tucson, AZ.] Then the subsequent Health Insurance Portability and Accountability Act of 1996 assured that records of the mentally ill are not available to law enforcement agencies. Personal civil rights have trumped the public safety, thanks to the ACLU. Recall the massacre of 32 students and faculty on the VPI campus by a psychotic suicidal killer and the murder of her four children by an insane mother in the nation's capital and the insane mother in Texas who cut up her newborn son and ate its brains after being released from a psychiatric hospital and refusing medications. States immediately used this Supreme Court ruling as an excuse to shut down their mental institutions to save money, so they were remanded to family members or left alone on the streets.

Persons with mental illness and those recovering often are among the poor and oppressed, the outcasts of society, not much different than they were in the Middle Ages. The lucky ones end up in prison for life. It is estimated that up to 80 percent of homeless sheeple have some mental illness. Sheeple walk on by to avoid being contaminated. Although a lofty ideal, deinstitutionalization of the mentally ill failed, due to a lack of sufficient community education and social support networks and a lack of sufficient financial and medical personnel infusion into community mental health systems for preemptive treatment. How crazy is that? Consequently, many of the mentally ill are abandoned again and left to rot in homeless shelters and worse on public streets if their families cannot care for them, or in overcrowded prisons if they commit crimes. Civil liberties have trumped public safety. Although new medications may help support a nominal lifestyle for chronic mental patients, too many are uninsured and cannot afford them. And, too many sheeple with a sick mind cannot recognize they are ill so they refuse treatment which, of course, increases their risk of incarceration or homelessness. There are too few good Samaritans concerned about them and the name of Dorothea Dix is rarely known among them.

Brownie Wise (1913-1992) was hired by Earl Tupper, inventor of the ingenious "burping seal" that made his Tupperware refrigerator storage containers a household word. She conceived, organized and ran the highly successful original marketing method of hosting home parties to showcase the products and book orders. Brownie and Earl got into a power struggle and he fired her at the peak of their success, then he removed all evidence of her contribution to the company, even burying her books on company property. He sold the company and retired to an island, while Brownie lived in obscurity and relative poverty because she had no stock options or golden parachute and worked only for a salary. She attempted to start a cosmetics business based on home party marketing but it failed. Many women have made some handy money selling Tupperware at home parties around the world at the rate of one every two minutes, but not Brownie Wise who started it all.

Greg Mortenson, and journalist David Oliver Relin, recount the journey that led Mortenson from a failed 1993 attempt to climb Pakistan's K2, the world's second highest mountain, to successfully establish schools in some of the most remote regions of Afghanistan and Pakistan. By replacing guns with pencils, rhetoric with reading, Mortenson combines his unique background with his intimate knowledge of the third-world to promote peace with books, not bombs, and successfully brings education and hope to remote communities in Taliban country. Their book, Three Cups of Tea, (2007) is at once an unforgettable adventure and the inspiring true story of how one man really is changing the world - one school at a time. In 1993 Mortenson was descending from his failed attempt to reach the peak of K2, the highest mountain in central Asia. Exhausted and disoriented, he wandered away from his group into the most desolate reaches of northern Pakistan. Alone, without food, water, or shelter he stumbled into an impoverished Pakistani village where he was nursed back to health. While recovering he observed the village's 84 children sitting outdoors, scratching their lessons in the dirt with sticks. The village was so poor that it could not afford the $1-a-day salary to hire a teacher. When he left the village, he promised that he would return to build them a school. From that rash, heartfelt promise grew one of the most incredible humanitarian campaigns of the century. In an early effort to raise money he wrote letters to 580 celebrities, businessmen, and other prominent Americans. His only reply was a $100 check from NBC's Tom Brokaw. Selling everything he owned, he still only raised $2,400. His efforts changed only after a group of elementary school children in River Falls, Wisconsin, donated $623.40 in pennies, which inspired adults to begin to take action. Since then, he's established 78 schools throughout remote villages of Afghanistan and Pakistan.

In pursuit of his goal, Mortenson has survived an armed kidnapping, fatwas issued by enraged mullahs, repeated death threats, and wrenching separations from his wife and children. Yet his success speaks for itself. The work Mortenson is doing, providing the poorest students with a balanced education, is making them much more difficult for the extremist Taliban madrassas to recruit and convert into suicide bombers. But, when you contrast his struggle with the rich and seemingly effortless success of Dr. Robert Lawrence Kuhn, neurologist, financier, expert on China, author, and philosopher who apparently needs little sleep, one must wonder at the will of God the Almighty One.

The American Revolution had its share of abandoned heroes. Thomas Jefferson, writer of the Declaration of Independence and third President, founder of the University of Virginia, died bankrupt and bereft from loss of all his family except one daughter and her bankrupt husband. He concluded, "whoever controls your money has more power than a standing army." After his death on July 4, 1826, all his personal property at the 5,000 acre Monticello, which he had inherited, was sold at auction to pay off his debts. He lamented, "Grief, what is the purpose of it?"

Thomas Paine was a free lance writer who left his wife in England under patronage of Benjamin Franklin to help promote patriotism during the American Revolution. He wrote a series of pamphlets called

The Crisis from 1776 to 1783 that helped General Washington to raise and motivate the fledging army needed to rout the British so well that he was commissioned as an aide de camp. He then went to France to engage public opinion in its revolution and was imprisoned in Paris for his efforts. During his French imprisonment he wrote a scathing rebuke of the Bible called "The Age of Reason" in 1795. For that effort he was abandoned by his American supporters, including Washington. Returning to America, he was all but forgotten by the new government and was pensioned by the state of Pennsylvania and was granted a small farm that was foreclosed by New York. He died a pauper in a rooming house in New York City. They say only six sheeple attended his funeral, and two of them were freed blacks. His body was exhumed by a reporter and returned to England where it somehow got dismembered and scattered about Europe. Many sheeple recognize his name but don't realize how many basic American political values come from the genius of his writings.

Alexander Hamilton, born illegitimate about1755 in the West Indies and raised as an orphan, became an architect of the U.S. Constitution in which he argued for a strong Federal government and central bank. He mastered clerking for international shipping and was sponsored to attend Kings College in New York in 1773. He grew into an opinionated collegiate and delegate to the Constitutional Convention with a chip on his shoulder, then gained some fame as a field commander in the revolution. He wrote key elements of the Federalist Papers to convince the states to ratify the U.S. Constitution sans the Bill of Rights. He earned the full confidence of George Washington as his chief of staff, who then appointed him as the first Secretary of the Treasury.

Hamilton organized the central banking system and the stock market in order to pursue his vision of a powerful industrial nation with a strong central government, over objections of Thomas Jefferson who wanted an agrarian economy with independent states rights. After Washington retired he returned to a law practice in New York and invested his hopes for political influence in his eldest son, Philip. Unfortunately, Philip inherited his father's tart tongue and died on the field of honor in a senseless duel at age 26. Hamilton became entangled in a blackmailing adulterous affair which he made public to redeem his integrity. Hamilton's caustic but well deserved commentaries about his character insulted Aaron Burr during the campaign for president in 1804. Another duel ensued early on the morning of July 11 in New Jersey and, without firing his weapon, Hamilton suffered a mortal wound and died after 31 hours of agony at the age of 49. Although he was given a state funeral by citizens of New York, his body lies buried in a tomb hidden behind Trinity Church, and his widow and surviving seven children disappeared into the shadows of history. He left a letter to his wife exalting her as the loveliest of women and the best of mothers.

The history of Christianity is full of unfair life stories. The earliest copies of the New Testament are in Greek by unknown writers and date to about 200 CE. The Roman Catholic Church held tight control of its fourth century Vulgate version of the Bible in Latin so that common sheeple could not read it for themselves. Long before Martin Luther, there was John Wycliff who opposed the Pope's intrusion into secular politics. A resident professor at Oxford, he studied history, law, philosophy, and religion receiving the Doctor of Divinity. He accomplished the first translation of the Bible into English around 1384, but that was before printing so the few issues made had to be copied by hand. The Church reacted by getting the Constitution of Oxford passed in 1408 which prohibited translations of the Bible into English. Then came William Tyndale who was a scholar educated at Cambridge and Oxford. Tyndale worked secretly with aid of some wealthy families and his Bible was first printed and distributed in Cologne, Germany by 1536. Unfortunately for him, Henry VIII had him arrested and executed for sedition when he returned to England. After he was buried, the Church dug up his body and burned it to assure he would not be resurrected at the Second Coming. Only two original copies of the Tyndale Bible remain in museums, although you can buy facsimiles. However, things changed.

During the next generation, King James I authorized an English translation of the Bible that was issued in 1611 with approval of the Church of England. That had been formed by King Henry VIII over rejection by the Roman Catholic Church of his desire to divorce Catherine of Aragon to marry Anne Boleyn in 1533. She became a rousing opponent of the Church and was an active player in the Reformation movement. However, the King had her beheaded under trumped up charges of adultery, incest, and treason. One of her religious advisors, Matthew Parker, would become an architect of the Church of England under her daughter Queen Elizabeth I. During this time there arose in Portugal, France, and Spain, the infamous Inquisition, persecution, torture, and execution by strangulation and burning, of religious dissidents that would not end until the mid 1800s. With this background one may understand why the First Amendment to the U.S. Constitution proclaims that "Congress shall make no law respecting an establishment of religion..." Nevertheless, in 1870 it proclaimed Christmas as a Federal employee holiday in Title 5 of the United States Code 5 U.S.C. (6103) [1]. Go figure.

Here are some more short stories to demonstrate the will of God the Almighty One in action. It must begin with the tale of Joan of Arc (1412-1431) who led the French army in routing the English occupation forces before her age of nineteen under the inspiration of three saints, only to be taken prisoner by the British and charged with religious heresy for dressing in male garb, among other charges, and immediately burned at the stake. She was posthumously exonerated and beatified by the Church. The poetry of John Keats must be read by every student of English as a supreme example of the language. But, Keats lived only to age 25 and died horribly in 1821 from tuberculosis after losing his mother and a brother to the dreaded disease. He died without knowing of his success because during his lifetime critics panned his work and only after 30 years was it finally exalted in the circles of English literature posthumously. The second architect of the U.S. Capitol, hired by Thomas Jefferson to correct the poor design of Dr. William Thornton which was selected by George Washington, Benjamin Latrobe, was forced into bankruptcy twice and died penniless in 1820 of yellow fever in New Orleans after he was unable to sustain any political connections in Washington. Today, Latrobe is called the founder of architecture in America.

Thomas A. Edison is credited for inventing the incandescent light bulb, but it was Nicola Tesla, (1856-1943) an immigrant engineer born in Croatia who made possible with his 200 patents the system of alternating current electric power that we enjoy today. His partnership with George Westinghouse fell upon hard times and Tesla died alone in a New York hotel room mostly unknown to the users of wireless cell phones who use his technology worldwide. Col. Harlan Sanders (1890-1980) sold Kentucky Fried Chicken to a lawyer and one investor from Texas for $2 million. They took it public and resold it to Hublein, Inc. for $285 million...how could this be unless God the Almighty One willed it so? Everyone knows about the insane success of Steve Jobs and Steve Wosniak, cofounders of Apple Computer, but few know about the missing third founder, Ronald G. Wayne. He sold his interest in Apple for $2300 and lives on social security benefits near Las Vegas. He holds a number of patents but has never had enough money to develop any of them. Could there be another like Frederick Douglas (1818-1895)? Born as a slave, he somehow learned to read and write when slaves were prohibited an education, he became a freedman thanks to sponsors in England who bought his release from his owner, and he became a vocal abolitionist and peer of Abraham Lincoln. He published a newspaper and was far ahead of his time in seeking equality for blacks and women. All in God's will of course. AIGWOC.

Possibly the greatest American author, humorist and philosopher Mark Twain [a.k.a. Samuel Clemens] (1835-1910) made and lost a fortune and then made another, but he lived to bury all his children and his wife, leaving no heirs to inherit his estate. Maybe the greatest American actor, Marlon Brando (1924-2004) lived to age 80. But his son served time in prison for killing his sister's lover and died broke at age 49 while the sister committed suicide at age 25. His best friend and neighbor, actor Jack Nicholson, bought his rundown mansion for $6 million and had it demolished to protect Brando's legacy. President Teddy Roosevelt (1858-1919) is remembered for his zeal in creating the system of American national parks and Federal monuments. But each of the parks carry the memory of unnamed and all but forgotten pioneers and naturalists who devoted life and incomes to their recognition and protection from unregulated settlers for decades before Congress finally understood their pleas. One of them was John Muir who devoted his life to preserving Yosemity national park, but he failed in preventing San Francisco from damming the Hetch-Hetchy valley as its watershed.

Frank Lloyd Wright (1867-1959) was a famous architect. He also was an infamous cad. He left his wife and six children for a lover and thereby ruined his reputation and his career. If it had not been for a wealthy benefactor and client named Darwin Martin who described himself as "either sucker or angel," Wright might have found himself destitute and his Guggenheim museum in New York would look much different designed by someone else. One might also mention the nameless general who devoted his life to building the last 1,000 miles of the Great Wall of China and commanded an army to defend it against the invading Mongols during the 16th century and then died in obscurity. How about General Douglas MacArthur, who engineered defeat of Japan and General Eisenhower, who defeated Germany in WWII. "Ike" became President but MacArthur was removed from command in Korea by Pres. Truman and just "faded away." The geologist who published the idea of plate tectonics in 1915 to explain the shift of the continents that causes earthquakes died rejected and lost while exploring Iceland without ever proving his theory was correct. His name was Alfred Wegener (1880-1930). It took fifty years for his theory to be accepted and for proof to be found by others in Iceland. Now, geologists have discovered similar ecosystems in Appalachia and southern China that can only be explained by a connection of the continents in some distant past before they gradually separated.

French impressionist painter Claude Monet (1840-1926) was so despondent about his financial poverty early in his career he attempted suicide by jumping into the River Seine in Paris. Recently one of his paintings brought $80 million at a London auction. J.K. Rowling, billionaire author of the famous "Harry Potter" series of childrens' books began by writing stories for her children because she could not afford to buy them any books. Henry Miller, organizer and first president of the International Brotherhood of Electrical workers organized the union at age 33 in 1891, but he died at work falling from a power pole in the dark of night at age 38. Moonshiner, David Marshall Williams (1900-1975) was sentenced to 30 years in prison for killing a Federal deputy during a raid on his still in North Carolina on July 21, 1921. He was released after serving only eight years and went on to receive 41 different patents for gun technology. One of his inventions was the gas recoil mechanism that became the standard for military repeating carbines during WWII. Paul Smith (1921-2007) was a self-made man. Born with cerebral palsy and unable to hold a paintbrush, he taught himself how to make glorious pictures by locking a manual typewriter in the upper-case mode and using the symbols above the numbers at the top of the keyboard one character at a time to transfer his mental images onto paper. His wit and sensitivity made his talent a unique contribution to art that will last far beyond his lifetime.

In Philadelphia, the "City of Brotherly Love," Joaquin Rivera, a respected school counselor and musician died in the emergency room after waiting 80 minutes to be treated for a heart attack, and some homeless drug addicts stole his watch right under the video security camera. Poet laureate, Robert Frost (1874-1963) lost his wife and four of five children by his age 62 and then lived to age 84 to think about it. J. Paul Getty (1892-1976) devoted his life to building a vast global empire on oil drilling, refining, distributing, and selling gasoline. He had five wives and five sons. None of them were able to take over the business and in the end he was alone among strangers. After he died, Texaco and Pennzoil conducted a hostile bidding war for Getty Oil which caused Texaco to declare bankruptcy. Today, the Getty brand is owned by Petrowes, the oil division of Netherland's Westerhoudt Group and is only a blip in the history of American capitalism, but his grandchildren live on the trust funds he set up for them. Lastly, born to conquer, Alexander the Great conquered much of the known world in only one decade and died at the age of 33 in 323 B.C., not to see all his conquests reversed in short order. He is so diametrically opposite to Jesus of Nazareth, who conquered no one during his 33 years, but yet still influences the lives of Homo sapiens world-wide. AIGWOC.

Must we assume that some sheeple are called to their vocations by God while the rest of us must figure them out for ourselves? St. Theresa of Lisieux (1873-1897) [she was the youngest of five surviving daughters of nine children, who died of tuberculosis at age 24.] asked this question and was given this answer: "I often asked myself why God had preferences, why all souls did not receive an equal measure of grace. I was filled with wonder when I saw extraordinary favors showered on great sinners like St. Paul, St. Augustine, St. Mary Magdalen, and many others, whom He forced, so to speak, to receive His grace. In reading the lives of the Saints I was surprised to see that there were certain privileged souls, whom Our Lord favored from the cradle to the grave, allowing no obstacle in their path which might keep them from mounting towards Him, permitting no sin to soil the spotless brightness of their baptismal robe. And again it puzzled me why so many poor savages should die without having even heard the name of God. Our Lord has deigned to explain this mystery to me. He showed me the book of nature, and I understood that every flower created by Him is beautiful, that the brilliance of the rose and the whiteness of the lily do not lessen the perfume of the violet or the sweet simplicity of the daisy. I understood that if all the lowly flowers wished to be roses, nature would lose its springtide beauty, and the fields would no longer be enameled with many lovely hues. And so it is in the world of souls, Our Lord's living garden. He has been pleased to create great Saints who may be compared to the lily and the rose, but He has also created lesser ones, who must be content to be daisies or simple violets flowering at His Feet, and whose mission it is to gladden His Divine Eyes when He deigns to look down on them. And the more gladly they do His Will the greater is their perfection."

But, what about the thorn bushes, criminals, and warmongers? Every year, more than 16,000 sheeple are murdered in the U.S. by criminals and deranged psychotics because our laws do not ban criminal thoughts, only its behavior. Adolf Hitler was responsible for the death of more than 55 million sheeple during WWII. How does God look down on him?

Apostle Paul reminds us that God said, "...I will have mercy on whom I have mercy, and I will have compassion on whom I have compassion. It does not, therefore, depend on man's desire or effort, but on God's mercy. For the Scripture says of Pharaoh: "I raised you up for this very purpose, that I might display my power in you and that my name might be proclaimed in all the Earth. Therefore God has mercy on whom he wants to have mercy, and he hardens whom he wants to harden...One of you will say to me: Then why does God still blame us? For who resists his will? But who are you, O man, to talk back to God? Shall what is formed say to him who formed it, Why did you make me like this? Does not the potter have the right to make out of the same lump of clay some pottery for noble purposes and some for common use?" (Jeremiah 18: 2-6, Romans 9: 14-21) [This God takes special eyes to see, otherwise the shock would be too great.]

Was the power of Jesus to change Israel intentionally restricted by God in order for the Jewish nation to be annihilated in 74 A.D. by the Romans? Did Napoleon Bonaparte act under the power of God when he all but destroyed the French society after he plundered Europe? Was Adolf Hitler being obedient to God as he plundered Europe and exterminated millions of Jews until he was stopped and the German Nazi nation was all but destroyed? What prompted beautiful young Eva Braun to give up her life and be his mistress from age 20 to 33, hidden from pubic view until their mutual suicide after the reign of terror in WWII? Was her life totally wasted, or was it precisely the will of God? Beloved opera diva Beverly Sills mothered a daughter who was born totally blind and had multiple sclerosis and a son born with some disabling mental disorder. She commented, "There are no short cuts to anything worthwhile." She died of lung cancer although she never smoked.

Perhaps we all merely are doing the work that God sets before us because it seems that everyone plays an indispensable role in the evolution of Homo sapiens. Apostle Paul instructed, "Each one should retain the place in life that the Lord assigned to him and to which God has called him. This is the rule I lay down in all the churches." (1 Corinthians 7:17) No better example may be the life of Mary Ann Wade (1777-1859). At age eleven, child of an outcast single mother, she was shipped from London to Australia as punishment for stealing a dress, after her death sentence was commuted by King George III. During a life of struggle she managed to birth 21 children in three marriages and lived to see 300 of her heirs survive in five living generations. She literally may be the mother of Australia, with tens of thousands of eventual heirs. All in God's will of course...AIGWOC. Get it?

In stark contrast, another woman who was left undiscovered until long after her death was Emily Dickinson (1830-1886). Now upheld as the leading American poet of her century, had her devoted sister, Lavinia and sister-in-law, Susan, not worked to publish her 1800 poems after she died, they may have disappeared into the dark crevass of reclusive existence that was her life. Confined to the family house in Amherst, MA as chief gardener and baker with her sister for many years nursing their invalid mother, the virgin Emily poured out her lamentations in secret rhyme that no education in the English language now is complete without. Here is her signature poem that illustrates her lifelong attempt to reconcile the omnipotent, omniscient and benevolent God with all the loss and suffering she encountered, including the bloody U.S. Civil

War. As any thinking person would, she wrestled with the existential; why a benevolent God first laid out rules and then enabled/induced man to break the rules and then responded with the evolution of mortal pain, suffering, and grief.

"Apparently with no surprise
To any happy Flower
The Frost beheads it at its play
In accidental power
The blonde assassin passes on
The Sun proceeds unmoved
To measure off another day
For an approving God."

We can sympathize with the blooming flower slain by the seasonal frost because we know that in our time we also will be cut down by impersonal forces created by "an approving God." But, unlike the "happy flower" that seems oblivious to its pending doom, Homo sapiens have the unhappy facility of anticipating and imagining their demise. We all perish, often prematurely and violently, while observed by "an approving God." God, working through frost in the human garden, induces not love but fear and terrifying inferences of inscrutable destructive power rather than any comforting religious revelation. This poem became the centerpiece of his biography of Emily about her lifelong existential quest by Patrick J. Keane, <u>Emily Dickinson's Approving God</u>. (2008) He comments: "No sensitive reader can fail to respond emotionally to the flower's sudden, brutal decapitation and to the human and theological implications of that death by frost...different readers may judge the drama's tone as awed, or resigned, or dismayed, or angry, or even blasphemous." Emily came to understand that joyous life and grievous death are two inseparable sides of the same coin, but she never came to like it. One might observe there is nothing "accidental" about it.

Perhaps that is the only way to think about the killing spree of more than four dozen...yes, four dozen...young female runaways in the Seattle area for more than two decades that was finally admitted by Gary Ridgway...a married man with a steady job who seemed in all other respects normal until DNA evidence linked him to one of the crimes. The prosecution plea-bargained a life sentence in return for his confessions and the locations of as many bodies as he could recall. At the sentence hearing families of the victims were permitted to confront him and, while one father expressed forgiveness because "that is what Jesus taught," Ridgway sat through it all showing no emotion or remorse. All in God's will of course...AIGWOC. Can you believe that? There is the county fair and the state fair and the world's fair, but life often is unfair. Why is that?

Apostle Paul assumes that man does not even have the right to ask that question because God can do as he pleases with his creation as he molds the clay for its various uses, some to hold the choicest wines and some to receive the chamber waste. (Romans 9:20-22) Nick Vujicic was born sans arms and legs, (www.lifewithoutlimbs.org) but he learned to use his voice and stage presence to show sheeple that the will of God the Almighty One, like gravity, does not need your permission and does not care if you believe it or not, and maybe even create your belief or unbelief. (Romans 9:14-21) Question the will of God the Almighty One, and the only response from religion is, "that is none of your business." Jesus admonished one apostle who questioned his intentions about another; "If I want him to remain alive until I return, what is that to you? Come, follow me." Right to the cross. (John 21:22) It seems that Jesus was claiming sovereignty over his disciples independently and separately, and so it may be with each of us in relation to God the sovereign of all. [BTW...he has been gone now for nearly 2,000 years and the Jews never have accepted him as their Messiah.] Today, God might say, "If I want Nike to make all their shoes in Vietnam while the starving sheeple in Haiti must eat mud pies, what is that to you? And if I want some sheeple to die peacefully in their sleep while others suffer long through terminal illness or are killed in murders, accidents, and wars...and if I want predators to eat prey alive...and if I want hurricanes, tornadoes, earthquakes and volcanoes to destroy human habitat...and if I want to destroy all of my creation and start over anew...and if I want the writing of one author to be a best seller and that of another to languish in obscurity...if I want millions of sheeple to watch Oprah Winfrey become rich and famous while countless women are starving and homeless refugees...what is that to you?" Some teachers may claim that Jesus taught that anyone can have anything they want if they just believe they have it. He did say such things, but he also said that some would reap what they did not sow. (Mark 11:22-24, Luke 19:22-22) Where is the justice in that? Where is the justice in the cross of Jesus who came "to save his people from their sin," when they all forsook him and revolted against Rome only to be massacred and spread abroad for 2,000 years? Only by act of God could they survive all those years to be reconstituted in the land of Israel again in 1948...or was that just the work of Pres. Harry Truman?

Do you think Sarah Palin woke up one morning in Alaska and said to herself, "I am tired of being a nobody so I am going to be rich and famous instead." First she had to become mayor, then governor, then campaign for vice president...and then be enthroned as the queen of media...all in Gods will of course...AIGWOC. So, who are we to question the Source of all behavior in lives of sheeple we may know no matter how insane they may seem to be? As Job was reminded by God, the creation is in no position to challenge the motives of the creator. (Job: 38-40) Job must submit to the irresistible evidence of God the Almighty One, sovereign and unchallengeable...or not.

So, if God created everything, and that includes an unjust world, then God must not be just. And we are in no position to argue with him. God does whatever he wants with whomever he wants whenever he wants...including blindfolding them or revealing himself in reality or in disguise...one little glimpse at a time...Get it? For those who are given to believe in Karma, these examples may illustrate its power in all the sentient beings of creation, each one reaping the consequences of previous lives and sowing seeds to reap during the next ones in their progression towards Nirvana. Although we cannot see our place in the cosmos of time and space from where we stand, it does appear that everyone, including every atom and molecule, is an indispensable link in the evolving chain of life. As the English poet, John Donne (1572-1631) declared, "No man is an island..." All in God's will of course... AIGWOC.

8. WHO DO YOU THINK YOU ARE, REALLY?

This is not a moot question because someday when your body begins to die you will be required to give up your present identity for the one that really matters. What you think about that will determine how much suffering you will endure before the end. The condition of your mind will drive the way your body lets go of life when the time comes. [Notice that we refer to "my body," "my mind," "my hand," "my soul," etc. without ever stopping to wonder who or what that owner really is.] When diagnosed with Alzheimers the late actor, Charlton Heston opined, "I must reconcile courage and surrender in equal measure." Who is the "I" speaking? American writer and historian James T. Adams (1878-1949) instructed, "Seek out that particular mental attitude which makes you feel most deeply and vitally alive, along with which comes the inner voice which says, 'This is the real me,' and when you have found that attitude, follow it." Professional therapists all know they cannot help others until they have learned who they really are themselves. A helpful model for seeing clearly is a four-fold one based upon a paraphrase of Socrates by Shakespeare from Hamlet, Act I Scene III as follows: "This above all: to thine own self be true (Know thyself), And it must follow, as the night the day, thou canst not then be false to any man."

In other words take the beam out of your own eye before attempting to work on the other for indeed it is as Apostle Paul discerned that we all see through a dark glass of cloudy distortion from a lifetime of piled up "engrams" (distortions of reality) in the brain that obscure the clarity we were born with. L. Ron Hubbard, founder of the Church of Scientology, may have been right in the goal to see more clearly, although his methods and motives may be suspect. A four fold inventory is helpful in finding out who one really is: 1) examine the social-political-economic environment in which we grew up, 2) discover the natural personality that we have, using the Myers-Briggs Type Indicator based upon a model by C.G. Jung (chapter 5), 3) forgive and release the dysfunctional family that influenced our survival and 4) surpass the religious dogma that was heaped upon us, or lack thereof, to enter the world of Spirit that has no beginning or end and is not limited by space or time. Few sheeple ever attempt this personal inventory so they become inoperative, so to speak, in the world of other sheeple who do likewise thus causing much damage to each other and to the world.

The Gnostics of first century Israel believed in two parallel worlds, the physical and the spiritual. So apparently did Jesus who said, "The spirit gives life, the flesh counts for nothing." (John 6:63) Apostle Paul also separated the spiritual man from the carnal man, citing how the conflict kept him in a perpetual state of "wretched man." (Romans 7:21-25) The doctrine of Christian Science discovered by Mary Baker Eddy in 1879 distinguishes two realms, the real immortal Spirit and unreal Mortal material. In the Church of Scientology the spiritual entity is labeled "thetan." "Man is held to consist of three parts - thetan, mind and body. The thetan is the spiritual being. The thetan is the individual. One is a thetan who has a mind and who occupies a body. The thetan is that which animates the body and uses the mind, i.e., the self. One of the most basic tenets of Scientology is that man is an immortal spiritual being whose experience extends well beyond a single lifetime and whose possibilities are unlimited, even if not presently realized in this life. The term is taken from the Greek letter *theta* for thought or life or the spirit. It is used to avoid confusion with previous concepts of the soul."

The word "spirit" occurs 569 times in the Bible, 201 times in the Old Testament. In the Old Testament contact with spirits was prohibited under penalty of death. (Leviticus 9:31, 20:6, 20:27, Deuteronomy 8:11) This prohibition was carried on by the Catholic inquisition and still persists to this day, although it would seem to conflict with the authorized practice of praying to the saints. The "Holy Spirit" emerges without introduction or explanation in the New Testament and drives the life and teaching of Jesus. (Matthew 1:18) Unfortunately, there also is mentioned "evil spirits" that control mankind too, at least some of them coming from God. (Judges 9:23, 1 Samuel 19:9,) Why this should be is not explained, unless the one is needed to balance the other in order to affirm the principle of diametric opposites. When Jesus died, it is said that he gave up his spirit...implying that something owns it with power to give it up...who or what that is still is a mystery. (Luke 23:46, John 19:30) Apostle Paul also referred to himself as the owner of " my spirit" leaving us with the mystery of its ownership unsolved. (1 Corinthians 14:15) Perhaps it all will be made clear in due time. AIGWOC...all in God's will of course. Think you can handle that?

The physical image we see in a mirror has been given a name composed of letters in our alphabet which is made audible in speech. But, to the storage device that holds the checking account in your bank, that name is just a bunch of magnetic blips in binary code. Moreover, the you in the flesh is changing continually as cells die and replicate so the body you had yesterday is not the same body today. The temporary habitat of flesh and blood organism, which reads these lines is not you. Hard to accept, isn't it. This very moment, millions of photoreceptor cells in your eyes scan the pixels on this page. Other neural systems in your brain identify their signals as words, locate their meanings from a lifetime of memories and make sense of each sentence. Within the span of a heartbeat, numberless action sites in the brain called synapses fire electrically to enable billions of brain cells called neurons to comprehend the final meaning of what you read now. You (whoever "you" is) have almost no awareness of the complex processes which manage the timely comprehension of the world of "you." You inhabit a massively knowledgeable machine into which nature has accumulated, over millions of years, unbelievably large lodes of operating instructions all working unconsciously.

At the moment of conception, in a single fertilized human egg, the coded DNA instructions alone contain information equivalent to about six billion chemical letters, which could be recorded in a thousand 500 page books. [After that moment, the parents can do little to alter the future human life except provide for the physical needs of the infant. It seems from studies of twins separated at birth that DNA controls not only our appearance and longevity, but our behaviors as well. Such twins live very similar lives although they may live in vastly different families. When rejoined in later life, the twins usually are amazed at the way their choices have mirrored each other.] In a grown human body, with the DNA in each cell containing a sequence of over 3 billion chemical nucleotide bases, the total of those codes in the body would fill the Grand Canyon fifty times over! Actionable biochemical instructions in your genes, which can fill cubic miles of books, manage your every activity which composes "you." Even your thoughts demand vast galaxies of subterranean knowledge. It is not the intangible you, but the information system, which decides to move even your little finger.

Researchers at the Bernstein Institute for Mathematical Research in Germany report experiments that show the brain actually engages decisions several seconds before they become conscious to the mind. It is the same with your speech. You become aware of it only after your information system speaks. Within the blink of an eye, actually about 350 milliseconds, the brain gathers ideas, locates words, arranges them grammatically and moves your muscles and pushes air through your vocal cords to enable speech. You become aware of your choice of words only after they are uttered in the brain. Just as naturally as lilies bloom in the field, your words of love or anger originate from one of the many inbuilt intelligences within your brain. Without your awareness, those intelligences manage your circulatory and digestive and reproductive processes unconsciously. An invisible coded intelligence manages your immune system to protect your body from infection or dangerous invaders, all unconsciously. You exist as an intangible awareness of a very limited portion of the myriad processes which click and whir in the background. So, who do you think you are, really?

French mathematician and scholar Rene Descartes, (1596-1660) father of modern philosophy observed, "I think, therefore I am. I know that I exist; the question is, what is this 'I' that I know?" And who is it that knows? Socrates admonished, "Man, know thyself." Sheeple often refer to themselves as "I" and claim ownership of parts of their bodies as in "my arm," "my heart," "my mind," etc...but this language fails to account for whatever or whomever this ownership phenomenon describes. When we say, my self, who is the owner and how does that differ from universal self? What is a self, anyway? The Great Commandment says, "Love the Lord your God with all of your heart, all of your soul, and all of your mind." Who is the doer in that commandment that possess heart, soul, and mind? How does the soul differ from the mind? What does it mean to love God with your medial ventral prefrontal cortex? That is a burning question that can keep you awake all night. The ancient Hindus referred to something called the "self" that existed before birth and will continue after death and so was separate and distinct from the body.

This idea was exported through ancient Greece to Rome and became the basis for religious claims for a "soul" and that translated into constructing the separation duality of mind and body. Along the way was added the inclusion of "spirit" as opposed to physical existence. The first century Gnostics believed in a spirit world that was the kingdom of God coexisting with this sensible universe, but in a realm that was undetectable from this one. Modern physics proposes the existence of multiple, maybe infinite, universes around and amongst this one in which all possibilities exist at once. The part cannot see the whole because it would have to be removed first and that would diminish the whole. In many religions and parts of philosophy, the soul is the immaterial essence of a person. It is usually thought to include one's thoughts and personality, and can be synonymous with the spirit, mind or self. In theology, the soul is often believed to live on after the person's death, and some religions posit that God created all the souls and then rested. But, Jesus claimed that God is still working in the act of creation. "My Father is always at his work to this very day, and I, too, am working." (John 5:17) [Perhaps this gives God some allowance for experimenting a bit and backtracking or making corrections along the way say, with the human genome for example. One could assume he got the great white shark about right from the start but he is having more difficulty working out the details among Homo sapiens.]

In some cultures, non-human living things, and sometimes inanimate objects are said to have souls, a belief known as animism. The terms spirit and soul often are used interchangeably, although the former may be viewed as a more worldly and less transcendent aspect of a person than the latter. The words soul and psyche can also be treated synonymously, although psyche has relatively more psychological connotations, whereas soul is connected more closely to metaphysics and religion.

The Bible speaks of a soul 136 times with an owner of it...some examples follow: "He who gets wisdom loves his own soul; he who cherishes understanding prospers." (Proverbs 19:7-9) "Love the Lord your God with all your heart, and with all your soul, and with all your strength." (Deuteronomy 6:5) What good will it be for a man if he gains the whole world, yet forfeits his soul? Or what can a man give in exchange for his soul? (Matthew 16:25-27) Even God seems to have a soul; "The Lord examines the righteous – but the wicked and those who love violence his soul hates." (Psalm 11:5) In one case Jesus inferred some form of existence beyond the dead body, "I tell you, my friends, do not be afraid of those who kill the body and after that can do no more. But I will show you whom you should fear: Fear him who, after the killing of the body, has power to throw you into hell. Yes, I tell you, fear him." (Luke 12:4-5) Thus, the love of God described in John 3:16 seems to be conditioned upon acceptance of Jesus as Lord and thus, it is not unconditional at all. All this implies that after death of the body, there is still a "you" that can be cast into hell. Since Jesus claimed he would be the final judge, was he referring to himself? He expanded the lesson with the parable about a beggar who was ignored by a rich man. The beggar went to heaven and the rich man went to hell. He saw Lazarus in "the bosom of Abraham" and pleaded that his living brothers might be warned to repent by father Abraham. But Jesus replied, "If they do not listen to Moses and the Prophets, they will not be convinced even if someone rises from the dead." (Luke 16:31) Jesus warned, "What good will it be for a man if he gains the whole world, yet forfeits his soul? Or what can a man give in exchange for his soul? (Matthew 16:26) So, when sheeple say "my soul" or "my spirit," who is the owner speaking?... as when Jesus ended his ministry by saying, "Father, into thy hands I commit my spirit." (Luke 23:46) We refer to "my self" as though there were an independent owner of it. And when sheeple introduce themselves with "I am..." who is the I that is speaking?

This question leads to some very challenging research into what is called consciousness and "self psychology." Soon after birth, the infant becomes aware of separation from mother as it was totally integrated in the womb, even sharing the mother's blood. By the age of two when they normally are weaned from mother's milk, baby sheeple begin to set boundaries between self and other as their egos emerge to take control. This separation between self and other then defines life among Homo sapiens until death. The physical self identity that we live with temporarily may not be our original immortal self, however. Whether consciousness survives death in some form is unknown and maybe unknowable because memory does not seem to connect the spiritual and physical realms. So, if we existed before conception we do not remember it. But the existence of an unconscious realm now is taken for granted by some in psychology and psychiatry and is referred to as spiritual psychology or transpersonal psychology. What psychology calls the self is merely an idea that cannot be seen, except by inference from its effects, like the force of gravity. Trying to understand the unconscious self is like spinning around fast enough to see your own backside. Some things really are impossible. There is a whole field of professional self psychology that is wrestling with this dilemma.

So we have the true self, real self, false self, ideal self, authentic self, etc. etc. etc. Sigmund Freud kicked off the search for consciousness by declaring there was a lot of harmful stuff buried in the unconscious that makes sheeple sick, and so he began the search for methods of treatment of troubled minds that could enable sheeple to achieve mental health by cleaning out the garbage piled up in there. There still is no general definition for mental health, although it can be separated from mental illness or disorder using criteria in the psychiatric diagnostic manual which describes some three hundred mental maladies. In the meantime physics was developing the theory of matter and energy and the basic laws of thermodynamics. Like; energy can neither be created nor destroyed - and for every action there is an equal and opposite reaction - that one explains how jet engines and space rockets work. The concept of human energy fields was invented from ancient Asian theories that consider illness and disease to be a disruption of normal balance in this life force. Perhaps there will someday be a new theory on life and death based upon energy fields rather than the biology of cells. The beginning of such may be found in the ancient Hindu practice of Aryuvedic medicine that is described in his many books by Dr. Depak Chopra who teaches the integration of mind/body treatments for physical illness.

The ancient Egyptians thought the brain merely was the source of phlegm and that thought originated in the heart. Modern neurology researchers are trying to find the location of the "self" in the brain. That it can be influenced unconsciously from such as advertising, argument, education, hypnosis, music, art, and religion is acknowledged. No doubt its neuron cells can be rearranged by illness and recovery from illness. And no doubt this process is continuous so long as it lives. But researchers cannot define what consciousness or thinking is much less locate cognitive processes precisely in the brain beyond rough guesses. Researching the brain with an MRI scan presently is like exploring the moon with a telescope.

The fact is that while there might be some rather narrow results in neuroscience about which all researchers agree, they are only beginning to probe the brain as the seat of human consciousness and the source of mental illness. As soon as they start talking in generalities about mind, mood, self, and mental disorder, there's inevitably a variety of opinions about how to interpret the evidence among practicing neuroscientists. What they are discovering challenges traditional views of mental health and even the basis for assuming free will and that scares the hell out of all those religious unwilling to let go of responsibility for sociopathology. [Take, for example, the television reality family of Jim Bob Duggar in Arkansas that includes nineteen kids and still counting. Why they have so many children just because they can is beyond imagination.]

The traditional religious refuse findings of modern science and cling to ancient mythical ideas more than two thousand years old, while unaware of the mental disorder that represents. The fact also is that providers of medical health care are marketers first. They continually seek drugs or treatments that can be sold to suffering clients and paid for by insurance companies. Mental diseases often are defined by the methods that are available to treat them. Thus, frontal lobotomies were replaced by cognitive behavioral therapy which was replaced by various drugs that are applied on a trial basis to see what works or not. This is an ongoing process that is continually replacing one treatment with another to increase sales, which is the primary motivation for all research and development. In primitive societies where this motivation is lacking, Homo sapiens live now as did their ancestors centuries ago. All in the will of God the Almighty One, of course.

Even so, researchers are reporting the ability to use MRI scans to recognize patterns in the brain that correspond to words, feelings, and memories. This work is beginning to expose the essence of consciousness as blips in the neurons of the brain that occur up to six seconds before their conscious awareness. Companies are rushing to market commercial applications for this technology. But, how memory and imagination work still is a mystery. [Savants are mentally ill sheeple with a concentration of ability in one single area. Among the 50 known savants in the world, Kim Peek has become a celebrity because he can recall any and every fact he ever read, like the entire U.S. directory of zip codes or the cards dealt in a poker game. The subject of the movie, "Rain Man," Kim is now in his mid-fifties and is the subject of memory research at several universities. No matter what he is asked he knows the answer, but he cannot conceptualize a metaphor like "get a grip on yourself" or dress himself and brush his teeth. Some might call him a miracle so his father must take care of him.]

Many sheeple still seek answers to the unknown in some religious teaching or other. Census takers report that 25% of Americans believe in witches, 50% in ghosts, 50% in the devil, 50% believe that the Book of Genesis is literally true, 69% believe in angels, 87% believe Jesus was raised from the dead, and 96% believe in a god or a universal spirit. Some scientists actually are looking for segments of the brain that contain these beliefs. A few even think that the need for some form of religion is bred into human genes. The endless variations there do not help understanding but rather they provide a forum for broadcasting the many differences among human belief systems. And the worst cases are those who claim some direct channeling from God or deceased sheeple speaking through them. That gives them authority to lead a stumbling and ignorant flock into eternity...whatever that is. Where do they get such ideas and why do so many sheeple agree with them? The greatest miracle of religions is that so many sheeple believe in them to the point of slaughtering each other to justify their claims. For many sheeple religion and science are mutually exclusive. For others the only way to future peace among Homo sapiens is by some accommodation of measurable phenomena with imagination and myth.

Myth dies very slowly and imagination not at all. It took immense sacrifices by Copernicus and Galileo and more than a hundred years for the Catholic Church to acknowledge that the Earth was not the center of the universe. To do so would destroy the myth of its infallibility. The

Church also imprisoned Roger Bacon for his research into light and optics that seemed to take the magic of miracles out of the rainbow and replaced them with natural laws of physics. Now it is obvious from space travel that Heaven does not exist just above the atmosphere, labeled the firmament in the Bible, and volcanology shows that Hell is not magically at the center of the Earth. And the Church even says it is OK to believe there might be alien life on other planets in the universe because "the Bible is not a book of science." But most folks still insist on believing that something which survives death will reside in Heaven or Hell after some day of judgment, so they are a bit leery of tempting the ultimate barrister beyond the point of his tolerance. Sheeple who make lifelong careers in religion and philosophy and tax-exempt church business are evidence that something about Homo sapiens will not let go of the notion that "I" am not this body. We say so and so died, but who is it that dies…really? Language will not let them go as we say so and so "is" dead. A being verb.

Mary Baker Eddy (1821-1910) developed her theory of Christian Science (1879) around the notion that sensory existence is really an illusion that includes sin, sickness, and death, which do not really exist in the world of Spirit. She never mentions geological disasters like hurricanes, tornadoes, earthquakes and such that destroy the imaginary habitat of humankind. She also never mentions wars, so perhaps they are imaginary also. Helen Shuchman (1909-1981) did much the same with A Course in Miracles (1975). "Nothing real can be threatened, nothing unreal exists." This is not a new idea and dates back to Christ and before. "The Spirit gives life, the flesh counts for nothing." (John 6:63) There is a growing amount of pseudo-science that claims to prove the theory of reincarnation and the everlasting life of souls that comes from the Hindu faith of Asia.

Now, using hypnosis, therapists with Ph.D. degrees, led by Michael Newton, claim they have regressed clients back into previous lives and got them to re-experience relationships and lifestyles in widely ranging cultures that are remarkably consistent with investigative evidence. Is this evidence for some kind of contagious imagination or communications from an energetic level that is everlasting? What comes out of the mouths of their clients during hypnosis often is incredible, and even includes accounts of their existence between lives and influence upon living partners. Throughout their hypnotic recalls, the identity of the person remains constant no matter what form the various previous life experiences take. A few of the researchers have documented evidence for recurring lives that seems difficult to refute, but whether they are true or merely creations of active imagination cannot be known. So, it may be that the identity we carry in our wallets is only temporary for this particular lifetime, or not. However, when sheeple are blocked from any such realization of former lives, past-life therapists lay the fault to some form of amnesia that they say is given at birth to prevent such memories from being contacted. If God created everything and then rested, obviously the subsequent appearance of various life forms was predetermined. But, where it all leads to is still unknown.

[One of most interesting bits of such history involves the sisters, Margaret and Kate Fox of Hydesville, NY. They are credited with starting a meme-wave of belief and practices in séances for communications with the dead in 1848 at the ages of 11 and 14. Their experience quickly was duplicated by thousands and spread to Europe where even Queen Victoria tried to contact her deceased husband. The wife of Pres. Lincoln also held séances in the White House. After they reputed the claim of clairvoyance in 1888 and then recanted their confessions a year later, the sisters both died of acute alcoholism. The present practice of "channeling" voices from the other side is said to have begun with them in the U.S. but it existed before that throughout Europe. Even the Catholic Church has gotten into the act by declaring that it believes in the feasibility of communication with the dead. The Rev. Gino Concetti, chief theological commentator for the Vatican, said the Church remains opposed to the raising of spirits by mediums, but he declared, "Communication is possible between those who live on this Earth and those who live in a state of eternal repose, in heaven or Purgatory. It may even be that God lets our loved ones send us messages to guide us at certain moments in our life." Fr. Concetti said the key to the Church's attitude was the Roman Catholic belief in a "Communion of Saints," which includes Christians on Earth as well as those in the after-life. "Where there is communion, there is communication," he said.]

Beginning when parents select the names for their babies, the original "I" is subject to social forces so strong there is little chance of self development without outside influence. Research and experiments show that the child's brain develops very rapidly before age five and actually can be taught much more than usual before the age of three, if appropriate adult tutoring is available. Whatever this "self" is, quite likely it gets distorted very early as children are farmed out to day care centers and preschools just at the very time that it is being formed. In such a structured social environment there is very little opportunity to develop the spontaneous creative self that exists during infancy. As school years progress, the student is cast more and more into a rigid schedule and curriculum spelled out by school boards and learned "educators" to prepare them for the world of work and society in which they will live. Whatever creativity they had often is stifled and warped into conformity with the needs of that environment. Little wonder then that their adult relationships are so tenuous and full of conflict. By then, their creative neurons have been overgrown with "engrams," like wild creeping ivy that can stunt a tree and even bring its early death.

Few sheeple understand this process, much less ever get the treatment needed to remove the overgrowth and let the true self emerge. Its efforts to break out often are marked by successive marriages and divorces, jobs lost, and relocations while it attempts continually to find its own unique expression. Sometimes, it takes a serious illness or threat of death for the self to emerge from its darkness into a life of light. The few who refuse to conform with social paradigms often are considered weird, but the few who break out sometimes achieve very special accomplishments. Rarely, a trusted loving parent, teacher, friend, or counselor may facilitate the emergence of a butterfly from the cocoon like a sculptor exposes the figure hidden beneath the marble. But they must overcome the continual impact of a culture that would smother it over again.

The ancient Greeks provided two different words for time to distinguish activities that nourish the soul from those that just make money; "kairos and kronos" respectively. Most everyone recognizes only the latter. In contrast, "kairos" implies a special and unique relationship between time and place where souls meet throughout eternity. If you go to India and study the ancient Vedic Hindu culture under the teaching of a guru in an isolated encampment (ashram) when you "graduate" you are given a new name that symbolizes your emergence into spiritual consciousness. This state is a unification of the original Trinity; body, mind, and spirit with its creator. Thus, Harvard professor, Dr. Richard

Alpert became "Ram Dass" after his enlightenment in India and became a spiritual teacher to the West. [You may enjoy his teachings at www.ramdass.org.]

Ram Dass instructed everyone to be present in the here and now because the past and the future exist only as memories and imaginings, respectively. The here and now is the only reality that we have. Even then, reality is only what our senses and intellect tell us it is and what we believe about it; thus reality is a creation of the mind, and modern physics is telling us that may all be an illusion. Objective reality may not exist at all. Modern physics suggests that reality is more like a two-dimensional hologram than the three-dimensional world of our senses. As Apostle Paul proclaimed, we do indeed "see through a glass darkly." Like Pierre Teilhard de Chardin, he learned that, "We are not humans having a spiritual experience; we are spiritual beings having a human experience." The Bible proclaims as much: "The Lord will call his servants by another name." (Isaiah 65:15. "To him that overcomes I will give a white stone and on the stone a new name written that no man knows but the one who receives it." (Revelation 2:17) It seems necessary for Spirit to be manifested in matter and form in order to express Itself. Can you believe that?

You may think you have some solid and fixed physical identity. The problem is that this fixed sense of self is completely conditioned by past emotional pain and projected imagination about the future. It also changes continuously. Imagination may be the greatest miracle. Modern yoga mystic, German/Canadian Eckhart Tolle thinks reality is otherwise. "This false sense of a fixed self prevents you from living in the present, where you have direct access to your true essence which is no other than an expression of the universal life force. All things (from planets to pebbles to flowers to animals) are expressions of this universal life force. The false identification with the past and future has the world and the human race on the brink of extinction. You have all sorts of roles and personas in relation to others. However they are time bound and don't fully capture your essence. Your true essence could never be captured by an occupation, a gender, a religion or a personality type. Your true essence is beyond words and description. Fortunately, this crisis is sparking many sheeple to move from an unconscious state to consciousness. In order to become conscious of your spiritual self, you must recognize that you are more than your ever changing thoughts and self image. Humans have evolved to the point where (some of us) have the ability to be aware of our oneness with the universal life force. As you learn to operate from your true essence rather than your ego, you will experience incredible transformation, and the planet will become a new Earth."

This true essence or life force appears to be common to all sentient beings, but still uniquely displayed in each one. C. G. Jung observed, "The shoe that fits one pinches another. There is no recipe for living that suits all cases. Each of us carries his own life form, an interminable form which cannot be superseded by another." This life force is apparently manifested in human behavior, but its locale and configuration is still out of reach for scientific inquiry. It is now an open secret that the will of the mind has enabled sheeple to achieve extraordinary physical feats, which proves beyond doubt for some there is a mind and body connection. But, what about the possibility of a universal mind, body, spirit connection? Tolle, and other gurus like him, are attempting to get modern Westerners to think like ancient Easterners. It may happen, but it will no doubt take centuries for the wide gulf separating the two philosophies to be blended into a common belief.

Meantime, as Tolle says, if you look up at the stars at night and are not overwhelmed by their implications, you have not really looked. To place your miserable little self in the context of such true greatness would make your associations with daily living of no consequence. Living in the flesh produces no end of mutually exclusive difficulties. Religion really is no help and actually can be a distressing detour until either/or merges into both/and. Jesus, son of God, declared the immense claim upon his followers thus, "If anyone comes to me and does not hate his father and mother, his wife and children, his brothers and sisters - yes, even his own life - he cannot be my disciple." (Luke 14:26) Contrast that with the Old Testament rule, "Cursed is the man who dishonors his father or his mother." (Deuteronomy 27:16) Jesus also said the second great commandment was to love your neighbor as your self. (Leviticus 19:18, Matthew 22:39) The God created by mankind obviously needs a revision if such dichotomy is ever to be resolved.

Throughout history, sheeple have employed various ways of attempting to contact the "kingdom of god within." These include drugs, trances, rituals, sensory deprivation, etc. to achieve an altered state of consciousness. Researchers are trying to find the locale of such behavior in the human brain. Neurologists think they have isolated it to a section of the right temporal lobe. The inability of the adult brain to retrieve earlier images experienced by an infantile brain creates questions such as "who am I," "where did I come from," and "where does it all go," which lead to the creation of various religious explanations. Humans are compelled to act out myths by the biological operations of the brain on account of the inbuilt tendency of the brain to turn thoughts into actions. But, the source of thoughts seems to be beyond current research methods. Abd-ru-shin [a.k.a. Oskar Bernhardt (1875-1941)] thought they all came from God. "All teachings were at one time willed by God, precisely adapted to the individual peoples and countries, and formed in complete accord with their actual spiritual maturity and receptivity."

German ex-priest Eugen Drewermann, one of the most prominent and controversial theologians in Europe, developed in two monumental volumes ("Modern Neurology," 2006) and ("The Question of God," 2007), a radical critique of traditional conceptions of God and the soul and a sweeping reinterpretation of religion in light of neurology, called neurotheology. Neurotheology assumes that the basis of "spiritual experiences" arises in brain physiology, for example a detectable increase of N-Dimethyltryptamine levels in the pineal gland, and he attempts to explain the neurological basis for those experiences. But, researchers know that correlation does not prove causality, so finding that two phenomena are correlated does not necessarily justify a conclusion that one causes the other. However, a few human subjects have described some sort of experience of God after receiving magnetic stimulation of the brain. For all the tentative successes that scientists are scoring in their search for the biological bases of religious, spiritual, and mystical experience, one mystery will surely lie forever beyond their grasp. It is likely that they will never resolve the greatest question of all; namely, whether our brain wiring creates God, or whether God creates our brain wiring. Which you believe is, in the end, a matter of faith and where that comes from no one knows. God still is the ultimate mystery. [For more than forty years, the magazine "Zygon," has been publishing authors from both science and religion who continually struggle with this dilemma. Visit: www.zygonjournal.org]

One of the oldest and most enduring attempts to achieve some higher level of spiritual awareness of a self is the practice of yoga, which has been exported from India around the world. Jesus said, "The kingdom of God is within you." (Luke 17:21) Yoga seeks the union or merger of inner and outer, of self with other, of man with God. To get there, a devotee must pass through planes of the gross, the subtle, and the causal in order to achieve the plane of divine consciousness. Maybe this is what C. G. Jung meant, "Whoever looks outside dreams; whoever looks inside awakes." But, gurus acknowledge that not everyone can go beyond the plane of attachments to the physical matter in spite of their desire to do so. This could be explained by the personality model of C.G. Jung where-in some sheeple prefer their sensing perception more than their intuitive perception. In the Western world, many sheeple are driven by their extraverted senses, which must be stimulated every waking minute. They are not able to engage their introverted intuition in order to enter the inner space where lies the spirit. Even church services are sensory-loaded settings with little opportunity to access the spirit intuitively. The many Catholic cloisters were formed in order to provide more opportunity for such inner contemplation without so much sensory distortion.

In contrast, the practice of yoga seeks to disable the senses and thinking in order to contact the inner world of intuition or spirit during the void of silence and meditation. The yoga practices common in various schools of India seek a release from the sufferings of "samsara" or life in the flesh by opening one to the mind and linking mind with spirit until the I AM identity emerges. Yoga practice is very complex and literally is transmitted from one teacher to another, although it comes with a library of instructional books by various "gurus." The meditative practices developed hundreds of years B.C. through yoga help in achieving an emotional balance through detachment from desire and create conditions where you are not affected so much by the happenings around you. This in turn creates a remarkable calmness and a positive outlook, which also has tremendous benefits on the physical health of the body, so they say. This state of sensory and intellectual renunciation is described as one living far above the storms of weather in the atmosphere or far below the storms on the surface of the ocean. Its ultimate goal is becoming conscious of the "Self" that is immortal and totally inseparable from the ONE source of all, i.e., God within. This concept of Hindu oneness in all things is just the opposite of perceived dualities between flesh and spirit in a Western world of separation and conflict between self and other. But it still leaves the mystery of who is it that becomes conscious of the self. Perhaps the "I" and the "myself" are merged into the subject and object as one. All in the will of God the Almighty One, of course.

Unfortunately, the modern fragmented frenzy of living produces such noise that unless one isolates from the hubbub in some isolated retreat setting there is little chance that the subtle voice buried inside will ever be heard. Many Western sheeple also possess immature dependent minds that must take energy from other co-dependent minds even if that includes tolerating abuse, alcoholism, and drug addictions. They are ingrained with the pop psychology of the entertainment culture. Deceased crooner, Dean Martin sang "You're nobody 'til somebody loves you...you're nobody 'til somebody cares...so find yourself somebody to love." And singer-actress Barbra Striesand intoned, " People who need people are the luckiest people in the world." In addition, the human body now is bombarded continually with untold amounts of man-made electromagnetic radiation from rapidly growing sources, including those ubiquitous cell phones, that were unimaginable a century ago, and no one knows what the long term impact will be. Find some quiet space for meditation is increasingly impossible. Some guru said that thirty minutes should be reserved for meditation each day unless you are very busy; then it should be one full hour.

If practiced properly, it seems that silent meditation somehow activates the vagus nerve that regulates heartbeat and digestion to slow down the affects of stress and produces deep relaxation. A devoted full time yoga initiate in India may be expected to meditate four to six hours per day in the disciplines needed to forego physical and mental attachments. Of such it is written, "He has neither father nor mother, nor wife nor son, nothing that he calls his own nor others, neither sin nor merit, neither this world nor the other, neither birth nor death, nor religion nor scriptures, for he has transcended them all." Jesus instructed his disciples similarly, telling them they must forsake all in order to follow him. "...any of you who does not give up everything he has cannot be my disciple." (Luke 14:26-33) This goal may be what is meant by being in the world but not of the world. Since few can spare the time and expense to take refuge in some ashram with a guru for several years in India, one must take a do-it-yourself approach to such enlightenment in the few moments that are possible during a busy schedule. The ancient yoga gurus found that self realization required disabling the senses and thinking to permit intuition to reign. This practice requires a full measure of introverted intuition, so those more tuned to their senses may not wish to participate. Few sheeple have enough self control to be fully here and now all the time.

Although she spent a career studying chimpanzees in Tanzania, naturalist Dr. Jane Goodall had another intuitive side. "It seems to me that there are different ways of looking out and trying to understand the world around us. There's a very clear scientific window. And it does enable us to understand an awful lot about what's out there. There's another window, it's the window through which the wise men, the holy men, the masters, of the different and great religions look as they try to understand the meaning in the world. My own preference is the window of the mystic." This state of spiritual awareness is described by mystic Eckart Tolle, endorsed by Oprah, who explains, "I lived in a state of almost continuous anxiety interspersed by periods of suicidal depression" until he had his awakening to spiritual reality. We all are an expression creating our aspect of source as we gain higher, wider, more expanded consciousness. Tolle claims the purpose of the world is to create the suffering that seems to be needed for the awakening to happen. And then once the awakening happens, with it comes the realization that suffering is unnecessary. When you have reached the end of suffering because you have transcended the world, it is the place that is free of suffering, so he says. That sense of deep crisis - when the world as you have known it, and the sense of self that you have known that is identified with the world, becomes meaningless. Perhaps it is not everybody's path in this lifetime, but it seems to be a universal path like that depicted in the Chartres Labyinth used for the symbol of this book. All in God's will of course...AIGWOC.

This is the dilemma of the unenlightened consciousness: it is torn between seeking fulfillment in and through the sensible world and being threatened by it continuously. A person hopes that they will find themselves in it, and at the same time they fear that the world is going to kill them, as it will. That is the state of continuous conflict that the unenlightened consciousness is condemned to - being torn continuously between desire and fear. It's a dreadful state. It's only when there is complete surrender to the now, to what is, that liberation is possible, according to Eckhart Tolle. The willingness to let go is surrender or calm submission. That remains the key. Without that, no amount of practice or even spiritual experiences will do it. It simply means to say "yes" to this moment, as Jesus let go in Gethsemane, "...not my will but thine." That is the state of surrender - a total "yes" to what is. The usual state of consciousness is to resist, to run away from it, to deny it, to not look at it.

Buddhism teaches when there is nonresistance to what is, there comes a peace. In the present time, we can't escape from the world; we can't escape from the mind. We need to enter surrender while we are in the world, where you are, right here, right now. There's no need to seek out some other place or some other condition or situation and then do it there. Wherever you are is the place for surrender and calm submission. Any other activity is ego-induced, and even doing good, if it's ego-induced, will have karmic consequences. ["Ego-induced" means there is an ulterior motive, doing something for something. It enhances your self-image if you become a more spiritual person in your own eyes and that feels good; or another example would be looking to a future reward in another lifetime or in heaven. So if there are ulterior motives, it's not pure and you are not there yet.] The Apostle James warned, "When you ask you do not receive because you ask with wrong motives...that you may spend what you get on your own pleasures." (James 4:3) Pastor Rick Warren declared in his best seller, <u>The Purpose Driven Life</u>, (2006) "It is not about you."

Here is a brief Zen Buddhist recitation that may help one realize the I AM of their reality is not the image in the mirror or the name on an ID card. You might print it out and keep it in a separate reminder form. Sit comfortably; notice whatever is arising in the body, externally and internally, without judging it, condemning it, chasing it, avoiding it, or desiring it. Just witness it, notice it and then let it go. After several moments of non-judging awareness, repeat these mantras to yourself:

> I have a body, but I AM not my body. I can see and touch my body, and what can be seen and felt is not the true See-er. My body may be weak or strong, sick or healthy, but that has nothing to do with the I AM that is aware of my body. I have a body, but I AM is not my body.
>
> I have desires, but I AM not my desires. I can sense my desires, and what I sense is not the true Senser. Desires come and go, in and out of my awareness, but they do not affect the I AM that is aware of my desires. I have desires, but I AM is not those desires.
>
> I have emotions, but I AM not my emotions. I can feel and sense my emotions. Sometimes they are clear and sometimes they are confused. What can be felt and sensed is not the true Feeler. Emotions pass through me, but they do not affect the I AM that is aware of my emotions. I have emotions, but I AM is not my emotions.
>
> I have thoughts, but I AM not my thoughts. I can know and enjoy my thoughts, but what can be known is not the true Knower. Thoughts come to me and thoughts leave me, but they do not affect the I AM that is aware of my thoughts. I have thoughts, but I AM is not my thoughts.
>
> I AM remains when I remove all ideas, assumptions, thoughts, actions, feelings and desires. I AM is pure awareness of awareness, a witness of all that arises.

The SELF is above and outside of the transient senses, intellect, and physical consciousness. It is fueled by the everlasting power of the "ishta deva," God within. Perhaps it was such awareness that prompted Apostle Paul to exclaim, "I have been crucified with Christ and I no longer live, but Christ lives in me." (Galatians 2:20), and for C.G. Jung to declare, "I don't have to believe, I know." To paraphrase Pogo, "we have met the puppeteer and he is us." Separateness disappears and all becomes the One. Anyone who understands this cannot harm another sentient being, because it would be harming oneself to do so. If you reach this level of discernment, perhaps you can begin to refer to the earthly form of your Self in the second person, as in he or she rather than I. This achievement is very difficult for Western minds, maybe even impossible, absent the tutoring of a guru, and years of silent meditation. Sheeple work years for a college degree or a career, but they expect enlightenment in a flash. Some sheeple may claim to have an instantaneous conversion experience, but enlightenment does not seem to work that way.

Ever since Sir Francis Galton (1822-1911) developed his statistical approach to eugenics, sheeple have debated whether nature or nurture controls more of human behavior. Studies of twins separated at birth to live in different families and cultures show that they are more alike than different. Now, we must include the role of genes into the mix, and even then some behaviors are not explained. Could there be some element yet missing from the equation that describes Homo sapiens? Could that missing piece be what is called soul or self? Maybe it is pure energy. After Albert Einstein showed with his famous equation that matter and energy are interchangeable, the door was opened to developing a religion that accommodates both the known and the unknown. When "Superman," the late actor Christopher Reeve lost control of his body below the neck in a tragic accident, his personality remained intact. The "he" that he was lived on in a body without any voluntary control of its limbs. However, aging patients with Alzheimer's disease lose the person that they were even though their bodies may remain functional. What may be even worse is losing your mind while you know you are losing your mind. Which of these conditions more accurately manifests the authentic self? Clearly, the word "Mind" does not sufficiently explain the true essence of self, much as Mary Bake Eddy (1821-1910) tried to make it so in her "Christian Science." Much of our identity is based on what we do and who we do it with. One day, you may wake up realizing that you really are nobody doing nothing with no one. Then, who will you really be?

9. THE PLACEBO EFFECT.

Medical research professionals know that a force beyond scientific explanation can enable some patients to experience the same healing effects from a sugar pill as from their exotic chemical potions if they are fooled into thinking the former is the latter. This effect was reported by army surgeons during WWI when they found that telling wounded soldiers that injections of saline solution was morphine often reduced pain among the battlefield wounded when they ran short of medicine. Often the healing results obtained, called the "placebo effect" [from Latin meaning "to take care of"], are similar to the real thing. Among physicians reporting to a 2008 study by the National Institutes of Health, Harvard University, and the University of Chicago, 62% said they believed the practice to be ethically permissible. About half of the surveyed internists and rheumatologists reported prescribing placebo treatments on a regular basis. Few of the responding doctors admitted actually using saline or sugar pills as placebo treatments, while large numbers reported using over-the-counter analgesics and vitamins as placebo treatments within the past year. Researchers have found that a medical encounter - a patient's visit to a provider - may produce its own placebo effects that can bring about significant symptom improvement. The part of the encounter that plays the greatest role in the placebo effect appears to be the physician-patient relationship, i.e., the energy transfer between them.

Harvard Medical Professor and placebo researcher, Richard Kradin documented the history of placebo medicine in The Placebo Response (2008) and concluded that until the scientific method using controlled experiments was employed about 200 years ago, all medicines provided by tribal shaman and physicians were placeboes. No one knew how they worked, and that is still true of many prescription drugs today. The first two drugs actually tested using controlled studies for efficacy compared with placebos were quinine, an extract of the Cinchona tree bark and aspirin, derived from bark of the white willow tree in 1763. The first mention of placebo in a medical journal was in the "New Medical Dictionary" in 1785. Until around then, medicine was closely related to religion and belief in mystical talents of healers. Here is a very puzzling discovery. The highest selling drug for anxiety attacks, Valium, has no effect unless you know you are taking it. In study after study, taking Valium unknowingly did not help resolve anxiety. What is going on here? Could this all be related to the religious concept that mind rules matter?

Jesus said, "If you can believe, all things are possible to him who believes...whatever things you ask when you pray, believe that you receive them and you will have them..according to your faith it will be done unto you." (Matthew 9:29, 21: 21-23, Mark 9:23, 11:24) Such scripture seems to say that human belief controls the power of God, and it supports a thriving industry of "positive thinking" self-help writers and motivational speakers duped by their own hubris. The religions called Christian Science, Science of Mind, Unity, and related phrases derive from the "discovery" by Mary Baker Eddy in 1879 that mind controls matter, so the cure for what ails you is to change your mind about it. "Who" it is that changes mind is unknown. Hypnotism seems to show that mind does control matter at least sometimes. Still, everyone dies so whether life is mind over matter or not remains to be proven.

Barbara Ehrenreich shows in her book, Bright sided – How positive thinking is undermining America, (2010) that it has a massive impact on business, religion and the world's economy. She describes motivational speaker conferences where workers who have recently joined the unemployed culture are taught that a good team player is by definition "a positive person" who "smiles frequently, does not complain, is not overly critical and gratefully submits to whatever the boss demands." These are sheeple who actually have less and less power to chart their own futures, but who are given, thanks to positive thinking, "a world-view – a belief system, almost a religion – that claims they were, in fact, infinitely powerful, if only they could master their own minds." Who the "they" is that has this power is never defined. But, it seems that such belief may not be under your conscious control. The late and rich actor and comedian, Bob Hope explained his success; "I always seemed to be in the right place at the right time." The late J. Paul Getty, billionaire founder of Standard Oil concluded, "Some people find oil and some people don't."

Nevertheless, many writers and "channelers" make a tidy living promoting the idea everyone can have whatever you want if you think you can by invoking the "law of attraction," i.e., what you put out you get back. They rely upon the teaching of Jesus, "Give and it will be given to you. A good measure, pressed down and shaken together and running over will be poured into your lap. For with the measure you use, it will be measured to you." (Luke 6:38) They ignore the opposing instruction of Jesus to avoid laying up treasures on Earth, (Matthew 6:19) his challenge to thinkers of his day (Matthew 6:27) and his beatitudes that provide heavenly solace for the meek, the grieving, the persecuted, and the poor in spirit. (Matthew 5: 1-12) He warned, "You cannot serve both God and money." (Matthew 6:24) If you complain about your lot in life they will say your complaints merely are attracting more of the same through the Law of Attraction, so think positively even when your house is burning down. There must always be something to be thankful for and your God-given task is to find it. That was an order from St. Paul himself to all Christians. (1 Thessalonians 5:18)

The earliest description of placebo seems to be grounded in a conflicted use of a special formula of oil that was ordered up by God in the Old Testament for use only as a consecration of priests, as follows: "Anoint Aaron and his sons and consecrate them so they may serve me as priests. Say to the Israelites, This is to be my sacred anointing oil for the generations to come. Do not pour it on men's bodies and do not make any oil with the same formula. It is sacred, and you are to consider it sacred. Whoever makes perfume like it and whoever puts it on anyone other than a priest must be cut off from his people." (Exodus 30: 22-33) The use of oil for this special anointing for consecrating priests is mentioned 135 times until it is given a different and, apparently, revised usage for healing the sick in the New Testament. "Is any one of you sick? He should call the elders of the church to pray over him and anoint him with oil in the name of the Lord. And the prayer offered in faith will make the sick person well; the Lord will raise him up. If he has sinned, he will be forgiven." (James 5:14-15)

Key to this instruction is the power of faith, i.e. belief that it will work. This sacrament is overlooked by most mainline churches except for the Church of the Brethren, membership about 128,000, which uses it sparingly as a healing ritual. This promise also is the basis for rejecting prescribed treatment by medical practitioners among some faith-based religious sects derived from the teachings in the Church of Christ, Scientist founded by Mary Baker Eddy in 1879. Sometimes, parents end up in court if the patient is under legal age to make such a decision. Obviously, if faith is not sufficient the oil as placebo will not work. Some have claimed of faith, "When you believe it you will see it." Jesus instructed when you pray believe that you have received and whatever you ask will be yours. (Matthew 21:22) But, where does such belief come from? And how does it work?

The idea of the medical placebo in modern times originated with one Henry K. Beecher, a researcher at the Massachusetts General Hospital. He evaluated 15 clinical trials concerned with different diseases and found that 35% of 1,082 patients were satisfactorily relieved by a placebo alone. (The Powerful Placebo, 1955). Other studies reported by Michael Brooks in 13 Things That Don't Make Sense (2008) have since calculated the placebo effect as being even greater than Beecher claimed. For example, studies have shown that placebos are effective in 50 to 60 percent of subjects with certain conditions, e.g., pain, depression, some heart ailments, gastric ulcers and other stomach complaints. And, as effective as the new psychotropic drugs seem to be in the treatment of various brain disorders, some researchers maintain that there is no adequate evidence from studies to prove that the new drugs are more effective than placebos. Beecher started a wave of studies aimed at understanding how something (improvement in health) could be produced by nothing (the inactive placebo). Studies in homeopathy show that you can filter out the medicine completely and plain old water will have the same effect, so they say. Unfortunately, many of the studies have not been of particularly high quality. In fact, it has been argued by skeptics that, contrary to what Beecher claimed, a re-analysis of his data found no evidence of any placebo effect in any of the studies cited by him. The reported improvements in health were real but they could be due to other things that produced false impressions of placebo effects. So, who you gonna believe?

What the re-analysis shows is that there are a number of factors that can affect many treatments and the evaluation of those treatments, making it very difficult to be sure just what it is about a medical intervention that produces improvement or perceived improvement. The randomized clinical trail for new drugs first proposed by clinical pharmacist, Harry Gold has become the standard of practice in testing new drugs since it was required by Federal law in 1962, but it is not a perfect procedure. Neurologist, Richard Kradin concluded, "Rarely a week goes by without some new result reported in the medical literature that is subsequently widely popularized by the press, only to be refuted by another study at a later date. This cycle appears to have a life of its own, with few questioning why this might be the case...evidence-based medicine from clinical research may in reality be less than fully reliable." In spite of the skeptics, modern drug researchers now compare results with a placebo as a standard technique in random clinical trials to determine effectiveness of new medications and procedures. Consequently, all the medicines and procedures delivered by medicals come with unpredictable side effects and unpredictable results. The Food and Drug Administration (FDA) is criticized for being too lenient in approving drugs that are only marginally able to relieve suffering but cause harmful side effects. So, when it comes to managing your medical care, it is all absolutely indefinitely uncertain. Think you can handle that?

In spite of the skeptics, modern drug researchers now compare results with a placebo, often a sugar pill, as a standard technique in random clinical trials to determine effectiveness of new medications and procedures, including even sham surgery. Professor Robert A. Burton, M.D. reported in On Being Certain, (2008) "...surgeons in Houston found that patients receiving sham arthroscopic surgery, in which only a skin deep wound was made, reported as much relief and improved mobility as patients who actually had the full procedure." Some of them were even told they had sham surgery with only a skin incision that left the same kind of scar and they still felt better, unethical as that may be. This capacity for self healing apparently involves dedicated but hidden pathways linking the brain and the healing system, which certainly look is if they have been designed to play this very role. This could explain the results obtained with homeopathic treatments. In this mode, the medicinal chemicals are removed from a water base through repeated dilution until no traces of them are left, although their healing effects seem to remain. In practice the dilution continues until only pure water is left with only a minute trace of the medicinal ingredients or none at all. Homeopaths claim this diluted remedy stimulates the natural immune system, i.e., the "vital force" of the body to cure itself through some unknown energetic force. This is counter to allopathic medicine that attacks the invading illness with some powerful external intervention.

[Homeopathy is based on the "Law of similars." It follows observations in nature and is different from the notion of opposing or killing invading illness by intrusive interventions. This was the beginning of preventive vaccine medicine by injecting inactive doses of viral infections to prevent such as polio and common flues by stimulating the immune system. Curing by similars dates back to 5 BC to Hippocrates, the Father of Medicine. It was familiar to Paracelsus, the renowned 16th century Swiss physician, and was formalized by Samuel Hahnemann (1755-1843) in 1796. Dr. Hahnemann tested the law of similars and established it as the cornerstone of a system of medicine he named homeopathy. Dr. Hahnemann stated: "Any substance that produces symptoms in a healthy person when given in full-strength form, will cure a sick person with the same symptoms when given in a very diluted minute form." He was discredited by the drug industy, but subsequent studies have supported his claim that the explanation lies in properties of energy not related to the biochemistry model of drug treatments. Homeopathy now is accepted medical treatment in Germany, France, Britain, India, Pakistan, Sri Lanka and Mexico. In the U.S. about 6 million sheeple buy homeopathic treatments each year, although drug companies pay it no attention since they are interested only in drugs that can be patented for price controls.]

The placebo effect has been observed when some sheeple respond to "faith healers" and similar non-religious therapies based on belief in the healing power of the transaction. Perhaps the miracle healings reported of Jesus were the earliest examples of the power of human minds to materialize a deeply held desire to get well. When he was asked how he could do such things he replied, "I tell you the truth, anyone who has faith in me will do what I have been doing. He will do even greater things than these." (John 14:12) Apostle Paul wrote, "Now faith is being sure of what we hope for and certain of what we do not see." (Hebrews 11:1) But, no one knows where such faith comes from. One doctor noted, "God heals but I get the fee."

Nevertheless, researchers think that expectancy – one might call it hope - has a lot to do with response to medical treatments. This could help explain why thousands of sheeple have journeyed to a psychic healer called John of God in Abadiania, Brazil for more than 25 years, expecting a miracle. He claims to succeed in about 85 percent of cases, including painless surgical procedures without anesthesia, although he has no medical training. He claims to be possessed by spirits of many different historical medical practitioners, although he is not a religious guru. Kradin (above) does not rule out the possibility of unconscious telepathic "communications" between doctor and patient that may affect the outcome of such treatment. This is a two-way street with feedback from the patient affecting the doctor's response, as it does in a psychotherapy encounter. Studies report the best results obtain when the patient is honestly spontaneous and the doctor shows interest in the whole patient, knows the patient over time, is sensitive and empathic, reliable and trust worthy, willing to adapt treatment to patient needs, and encourages patients in the decision making. Modern specialty team-based impersonal medical delivery systems fail to reach this standard, and the trend is getting worse. In response, the massive marketing of alternative treatments, dietary supplements, and nutriceutricals shows how much some sheeple desperately want to be healed. This trend could be evidence for separation anxiety caused by deficient or absentee parent succor during childhood that was sought in alternative sources such as teachers, relatives or street gangs. That could explain why even scientists and physicians are not immune from wearing copper bracelets, magnetic shoe insoles, or absorbing medicinal light sources without realizing the contradictions.

The proponents of drugs and science-based treatments can no longer ignore the growing public market for alternative treatments, which may attest to their placebo effects. But, sometimes they work in reverse. For example, patients who are worried about unpleasant side effects to FDA approved drugs often experience them and stop taking the medication. The placebo process can be reversed as when a voodoo devotee dies from fear in reaction to being cursed. This is called the "nocebo effect." Richard Kradin says that such sheeple are so conditioned to suffering that they actually resist all forms of treatment to maintain their status-quo. Their expectation of suffering prevents their healing. To get well is to change who they are, which is impossible without some powerful intervention. [This may be the case in Haiti and Afghanistan where sheeple are so conditioned to poverty for centuries that it seems impossible to change their conditions for the better.]

So it is that Catholic priests are being taught to conduct exorcism of demons as an injunction of the Church under new rules issued by the Vatican in 1999. Some conservative Protestant ministers also practice the service of ritual exorcism. Whether these rituals by a loving "Father" actually purge the mind of objective evil or merely provide supportive self-healing release from acute distress is unknowable. What is there about the human mind that imparts so much power to the mere suggestion by a doctor, priest, or even a concerned layman that some pill or solution or holy water or belief will produce healing results? No one would intentionally and consciously grant the power of chemical medicines to a sugar pill or salt water or a magician, so there must be some form of unconscious power yet to be understood at work in the placebo effect.

As recently as 1993 medical historian, Edward Shorter reported that nearly half of patients present symptoms to physicians that are psychosomatic and seem to change with the times like contagious diseases. French physician, Jean-Martin Charcot (1825-1893) and Austrian neurologist, Sigmund Freud (1856-1939) attacked such symptoms with psychotherapy and once exposed, they often disappeared spontaneously. But, they still appear in tribal groups with undeveloped medical services. Often attributed to "the nerves," no common theory has yet explained this phenomenon, except maybe one. The power of subliminal suggestion by an authority figure was discovered by Franz Anton Mesmer (1734 –1815) in the form of what he called "animal magnetism" and others later called "mesmerism." The theory he developed asserted that "cosmic bodies," through the force of their nature, caused magnetic fields to influence sheeple and could be directed in a controlled way with the right knowledge. In 1766 he achieved a doctoral degree in Vienna through a dissertation on the subject. Mesmer eventually developed a practical treatment program based upon his theories. Conflicts with the medical establishment of Vienna made Mesmer move to Paris. While there he enjoyed great publicity, but the interest of the public declined after his activities were dismissed as fraud by a scientific commission. The evolution of Mesmer's ideas and practices led Scottish neurosurgeon, James Braid (1795-1860) to develop hypnosis in 1842, and the practice spread rapidly from his work in Manchester, England. He attributed hypnotism to unexplained changes in the brain and spinal nerves. Jean Charcot (1876-1936) brought hypnosis to modern investigative scientific study, and Yale professor, Clark Hull's work in the 1930s did much to attempt a scientific understanding of it.

In America, hypnosis was promoted as a healing art by clockmaker, Phineas P. Quimby (1802- 1866) in Portland, Maine, uneducated son of a farmer and blacksmith after he was exposed to it by a traveling French practitioner named Charles Poyen. He is credited with starting the "New Thought" religious movement, with such branches as Christian Science, Science of Mind, Unity, and Scientology, that includes "mind treatments" as healing rituals for sheeple beset by a condition of nervous disorder then called "neurasthenia" by some medical doctors. Sheeple then had a lot to worry about in addition to common diseases including smallpox, diptheria, scarlet fever, tuberculosis, pneumonia, and even childbirth. It was a time of laissez-faire free enterprise when restraints upon greed and economic oppression were few and capital and financial power were concentrated in a handful of ruthless industrial dictators and bankers with little if any empathy for the laborers who created their wealth.

[George Fitzhugh of Virginia (1806-1881) declared the new universal liberty following the Civil War brought "selfishness, discord, competition, rivalry, and war of the wits..." Until now, industry had been controlled and directed by a few minds. Men were suddenly called on to walk alone, to act and work for themselves without guide, advice or control from superior authority. In the past, nothing like it had occurred; hence no assistance could be derived from books. The prophets themselves had overlooked or omitted to tell of the advent of this golden era, and were no better guides than the historians and philosophers." The new liberal economy merely substituted industrialists for slave owners without any obligation to care for their "free" workers. This seems a lot like the present attitudes of conservative Republicans.]

Railroad magnate, George F. Baer declared in 1902, "The rights and interests of the laboring man will be cared for not by the labor agitators but by the Christian men to whom God in his infinite wisdom has given control of the property interests of the nation." John D. Rockefeller, Sr. (1839-1937) proclaimed, "God gave me my money." So, who could argue with that? There were no government safety nets and labor was not organized to protect the working class, which created an extremely stressful way of life. Little wonder there was an epidemic of nervous disorders. Thought to be a condition among the intellegentsia arising from the uncertainties and risks in competitive economics that depleted nervous energy, neurasthenia was a precursor to depression and anxiety mood disorders in modern psychiatry. These would emerge later in the 1930s, but only after millions suffered for lack of commercial power. Outside of the family enclave the world was a realm of "dangers, disorders, and demoralizing temptations." There was little difference between being free and enslaved by those with a divine right to power such as proclaimed by Apostle Paul. (Romans 13: 1-7)

[The New Thought mind-curers are not far from theology of Luther and Wesley. They come with similar words of emancipation for troubled souls. They speak to persons for whom the conception of spiritual salvation has lost its traditional theological meaning, but who labor nevertheless with the same eternal human difficulty about what to do with existential anxiety about unequal distribution of health, wealth, and happiness. Things feel wrong with them and they ask, "What shall I do to be clear, right, sound, whole, well?" And their answer is: "You are well, sound, and clear already, if you did but know it." The whole matter may be summed up; "God is well, and so are you. You must awaken to the knowledge of your real being." The Rev. Robert Schuller made a personal international empire out this type of preaching from his Crystal Cathedral in Orange, CA until it went bankrupt in 2010.]

Today, the study of hypnosis is closely tied into spirit-mind-body alternative medical science which is being investigated at the National Institute of Health. Hypnosis happens when a state of mind is achieved in which suggestions by an authority figure alter someone's awareness, imagination, memory, or thinking and muscle control in a way that the hypnotized person responds to the alteration as if it were reality. The popular form that is sometimes used as staged entertainment actually demonstrates its effectiveness and power. Hypnosis is not a form of sleep, but of concentration that bypasses the usual critical or evaluative activities of the mind to get control of the unconscious mind. A few examples have shown that even self-hypnosis can produce a form of anesthesia that permits minor surgery without pain. A patient under self-hypnosis was reported to tolerate minor surgery of the hand for arthritis without any sensation of pain. Some leading edge dentists also use hypnosis successfully instead of pain killers during their procedures. Cult leaders also seem to have a hypnotic effect among their followers who can adjust their perceptions of reality to align with the cult beliefs. Such were the Heaven's Gate and the Jonestown cults that committed mass suicide upon command of their leaders. Perhaps the growing interest in hypnotic therapy that uncovers past life regressions and recovers "hidden memories" are other examples, although experts claim that memories can be fabricated imaginings. As such, memories may be more like reconstructions than recollections

Most studies suggest that about 35% of sheeple can be hypnotized easily, even by themselves, while about 20% just won't allow it. The hypnotizable person is more often the one who gets totally caught up in a movie or TV show - they can block off what's happening around them, suspend their detachment, and enter into the scene as if it were real and happening in their presence. Those who practice Asian meditation techniques also find it easier to enter hypnosis - they're used to being in a concentrative state where universal energy can be tapped as in being one with God. Mass hypnotism also could be the source of power by television and movie icons who exhibit destructive lifestyles which influence youths, as well as mass media televangelist ministers who also mesmerize audiences with their "spiritual" powers at religious conferences.

Elders may recall the massive crusades staged by the Rev. Billy Graham in which he persuaded thousands to get up out of their seats to make a profession of faith in Jesus Christ. Modern healers, like Bennie Hinn, claim they have miraculous powers and many sheeple believe they do. The same unexplained forces may be at work at mass rock music concerts and among those who think that powdered rhinoceros horn can increase libido and bear bile can cure diseases, or in the counseling chambers of modern therapists and priests. Quimby came to believe that his clients for hypnosis were healed more by their belief in the cure than the ministry itself, just like Jesus said. [In several cases, Jesus declared that faith of one could invoke healing in another. (Matthew 9:22, 15:28, Mark 5:34, 10:52, Luke 8:48, 18:42) How such faith came to be he did not explain. Moreover, Jesus gave us conflicting opposite instructions. On one hand he declared that all prayers are conditioned a-prior upon belief, and that only. (Matthew 21:22, Mark 11:4) And he also said that unanswered prayers were due to faulty motives. (John 16:23-24, James 4:3)]

The healing itself was mental and, thus, a new religion of "mind cures" was born. One of Quimby's patients was the Rev. Warren Evans, an ex-Methodist who is credited with writings that connected the religion aspect to the teachings of Jesus Christ. Mary Baker Eddy picked up the call and organized her Church of Christ, Scientist in Boston to fulfill its promise in 1879. Other entrepreneurs recognized a growing market and several branches of New Thought were organized, all capitalizing on mind-over-matter marketing while calling themselves churches for obvious tax exemptions. Perhaps this trend reached its zenith with the preaching of Norman Vincent Peale (1898-1993) at the Marble Collegiate Church in New York and his best seller, The Power of Positive Thinking, (1952) plus a steady stream of mind cure propaganda from his publishing empire. "If only you really want him to, God will give you anything...Believe you have it and you will have it...God obeys man." Peale's popularity rose much like that of Adolf Hitler as both men did not lead so much as follow the trends of the times. All successful politicians know the trick of leadership is to find out where your sheeple are heading and get out in front of them. Both men told their fans basically what they wanted to hear at the time. As such, both were creations of their audiences. Followers make leaders. Every politician knows the way to get votes is telling sheeple what they want to hear. Perhaps C.G. Jung realized this aspect of Nazism as he commented about Hitler, "You know you could never talk to this man because there is nobody there...it is not an individual, it is an entire nation." All in God's will of course...AIGWOC.

A similar rationale exists for the popularity of social spokespersons on radio and television talk shows. They, like Oprah Winfrey and Rush Limbaugh, are not leaders so much as vocal examples of the sheeple/ fans who create their popularity and commercial value to advertisers. Consider the fame and following of civil rights leader, Martin Luther King, Jr. His was a cause whose time had come. One may assume had it not been him, another orator would have been chosen to proclaim the message. One might also include the likes of Sir Winston Churchill, Napoleon de Bonaparte and Jesus of Nazareth as voices whose time had come. This is no different than the doctor who tells his sick patients a sugar pill will make them feel better and so it does because they want it to. Anticipation trumps reality when desire is driven by a higher power. But, there always is an opposite thought. Peale wrote, "No man however resourceful is a match for so great an adversary as a hostile world. He is at best a puny and impotent creature at the mercy of the cosmic and social forces in which he dwells." Jesus might agree with him. The only response to such a world was the supernatural power of God, and so it was for Peale to become rich and famous saying so.

More importantly, God was within [in the subconscious or the unconscious] and could be tapped for his limitless abundance, maybe even trained like a pet dog to do tricks. All it takes is belief in faith, or faith in belief. Peale minced no words; "...almost like a powerful drug dissipating a center of pain, the religious prescription dissolves the patient's trouble," and thousands subscribed to his weekly "Guideposts" devotionals to get his mind cure instructions. Historian of this era, Donald B. Meyer tried to explain it in <u>The Positive Thinkers,</u> (1965) "Peale had discovered the power of suggestion over the human mind... Cultivated ignorance of the economy as a whole was not the most drastic characteristic if mind cure...The wish for plenty was not a wish to have one's wishes fulfilled; it was the wish not to have to wishes of one's own at all. When you know God does not have to learn, grow, expand or unfold you begin to awaken from the dream of limitation and become alive in God. You need only live and consume the supplies that are provided for the taking...The student of the laws of mind knows absolutely that regardless of economic situations or personal circumstances he will always be amply supplied." Key word here is "amply" because the range of supplies among Homo sapiens is indeed very wide. After all, Jesus taught that one need not worry about tomorrow because God will provide. (Matthew 6: 25-34) Still, he did not explain all the suffering and starvation in the world, except to say they are necessary. Only the principle of necessary opposites accounts for that. God leaves much to be desired.

The power of primitive shaman to influence physical behaviors of uneducated sheeple is well documented, even to inducing the mysterious practice of voodoo hexes and zombie trance states of the highly superstitious in Haiti and the outback of Australia, sometimes resulting in death. If one may believe himself into sickness and even death, why not believe himself into health and eternal life? (John 3:16) But, hey, whatever works. Could more investigation of drug addictions help in understanding the ways that human brains can be influenced by non-chemical interventions? Perhaps thinking [whatever that is] really does influence reality as the ancient sages assumed long before Christ declared as much. If so, who or what controls thinking?

As with everything, there are opposing viewpoints. Skeptics point out that research in placebo effects is full of uncertainties. Nevertheless, the fact that an increasing number of medications are unable to beat sugar pills has thrown the drug industry into crisis. Two comprehensive analyses of antidepressant trials have uncovered a dramatic increase in placebo response since the 1980s. One estimated that the so-called effect size (a measure of statistical significance) in placebo groups had nearly doubled over that time. It's not that the old meds are getting weaker, drug developers say. It's as if the placebo effect is somehow getting stronger. Some drugs that have been on the market for decades, like Prozac, are faltering when compared with placebos in more recent follow-up tests. In many cases, these are the compounds that, in the late '90s, made Big Pharma more profitable than Big Oil. But if these same drugs were vetted now against a placebo, the FDA might not approve some of them. The side effects listed for new drugs might be enough reason to choose a sugar pill instead. The stakes could hardly be higher. In today's economy, the fate of a long-established drug company can hang on the outcome of a handful of tests. What the re-analysis of placebo reports shows is that there are a number of factors that can affect many drug treatments and the evaluation of those treatments, making it very difficult to be sure just what it is about an intervention that produces improvement or perceived improvement. One analyst concluded, "We must also consider artifacts such as the natural history of a disease (that is, the tendency for sheeple to get better or worse during the course of an illness irrespective of any treatment at all), the fact that sheeple behave differently when they are participating in an experiment than when they are not, a desire to please the experimental staff by providing socially desirable answers and a host of other factors unrelated to the pill we are administering independently of any mechanism that we believe is producing any observed effects."

Ironically, Big Pharma's attempt to dominate the central nervous system with drugs has ended up revealing how powerful the brain really is. The placebo response apparently doesn't care if the catalyst for healing is a triumph of pharmacology, a compassionate therapist, or a syringe of salt water sprayed by a priest. All it seems to require is a reasonable expectation of getting better. That's potent medicine. Belief, motivation, and expectation are essential to the placebo effect. One might even call it faith, and the success of religious faith healers may be the same as placebo effect administered in a religious setting. Indeed, faith in the healer may be the paramount resource in placebo effects. Jesus affirmed several times the power of faith and also lamented its absence as when neighbors in his home town rejected his miracles because they thought he was just the carpenter's son. To a blind man that he healed, and several others, he said, "Your faith has healed you." (Luke 18:42, Matthew 13:54-58) Perhaps that was evidence of the placebo effect. As with faith healing today, there is no record of how long the man sustained his sight. It is difficult to refute obvious results that obtain from sugar water or salt solution or personal touch or hypnosis or exorcism when they are substituted for what the patient thinks is official pharmacology. Research has shown that sheeple can be manipulated by subliminal advertising that induces them to make purchases from unconscious choices, as in buying snacks in movie theaters. It worked so well in movie theaters the practice was outlawed. The area between real and imagined is very murky.

Apparently, anyone can be affected by the placebo effect from time to time. Predicting when or how is impossible. There are several theories about why placebos work, but no direct generally accepted proof for any of them. There seems to be some kind of mind-body interaction going on that involves the immune system, but just what and how are not yet uncovered. There obviously appear to be needs for more research into placebo effects, but the economic power of drug companies in our capitalist business system would not be served well, and so it is not being done. Mysteries such as the placebo effect will not be explained until science resolves the issue of mind-matter intersection. So long as research stops at the brain matter there will be no accommodation of effects that cannot be sensed and measured, including placebos and thoughts and prayers. So, until the incestuous connection between physicians and druggists is broken, little will happen. Too many leaders of these institutions respond with amusement or contempt to mind-body discussions. There also may be threats to established religious dogma in discoveries regarding faith-based healing. If it turns out that placebo effects explain faith-healers, they could be put out of business. The essence of medical capitalism, making money, could be demolished if the placebo effect challenges Western medicine. And, only God can do that.

The latest placebo developments don't need a sugar pill. Some patients in chronic pain are gaining relief by observing their own brain scans on computer screens and merely thinking themselves into more serenity and comfort with biofeedback. Relief from emotional disorders also occurs from tapping certain of the acupuncture meridians with two fingers while concentrating on positive affirmations. These experiments show that the brain is controlled by mind, whatever that is, which may control the body. Perhaps Jesus had some insight into powers of the mind that we have yet to discover. "Believe me when I say that I am in the Father and the Father is in me; or at least believe on the evidence of the miracles themselves. I tell you the truth, anyone who has faith in me will do what I have been doing. He will do even greater things than these, because I am going to the Father. And I will do whatever you ask in my name, so that the Son may bring glory to the Father." (John 14:11-13) Eventually, all forms of medical treatment and placebos fail to prevent death, and at that point the medical establishment as well as the pulpit goes silent. While attention then may shift to religious support, that also fails to prepare sheeple for their dying in many cases. Witness how few churches have any form of institutional family death watch or even grief support for survivors. Even Jesus casually instructed, "Let the dead bury their own dead." (Matthew 8:22, Luke 9:60)

So, the questions remain. When you make medical decisions or act out your lifestyle, buy a book or go to a movie, even deposit your money into the collection plate at church, are you acting consciously or are you merely reacting unconsciously to stimuli your brain does not distinguish from reality? What is reality, anyway? Who or what actually is in control of your thinking and actions? Who owns the brain that thinks? Where do thoughts come from? Is there really some form of undiscovered energy available between sheeple that creates forces of health, wealth, and happiness as well as suffering and discontent? Is there some file of residual universal knowledge buried in the subconscious mind waiting to be tapped? Did Jesus of Nazareth, the carpenter's son, employ such knowledge during his ministry? If so, where did he get it from? Is it available to others? But, what about the forces for destruction, disease, and criminality also buried in the subconscious? Does everyone live because some energetic force wills it so as Jesus declared, "The spirit gives life, the flesh counts for nothing." (John 6:63) The bottom line in this discussion may be that, barring obvious physical attacks or accidents, we may never know with certainty why anyone lives to do whatever they do and then dies. And, after all, what difference does it make after they are gone? Theofatalism™ says it is all God's will as there can be no other. Think you can handle that?

10. Practice dying.

The human body can be likened to a battery that is given so much charge, i.e., vital force, at conception and eventually runs down, with only unsuccessful attempts at recharging with medical treatments at the end of life. Astronaut, Neil Armstrong (first man to step onto the moon in 1969) said, "I don't believe in exercise because my heart was given so many beats and I don't intend to use them up any sooner than necessary." Death is a permanent solution to a temporary problem (life) that comes to everyone, that is obvious. But most sheeple avoid talking about it as long as possible. Movie maker Woody Allen said, "I am not afraid of dying, I just don't want to be there when it happens." Jesus promised blessings to those who mourn, the peacemakers, the poor, etc., but he had nothing to offer the dying. For those he waved his hand and declared, "let the dead bury their dead." He just was not about this life. Jesus declared, "The spirit gives life, the flesh counts for nothing." (John 6:63) This may be the most important statement in the Holy Bible, but how many sheeple actually believe that?

For something so useless, we all seem to be very attached to our human bodies. But they don't last forever. When the time comes they stop processing food, and no matter how much we try to avoid it or delay it, they all eventually die. We may link up our bodies with others throughout life for temporary social, family, commercial, and military purposes but in the end all relationships end and each of us must die alone because no one can do it for us. So, why do sheeple continue resisting the inevitable? Answer: Human ego is made to want immortality and will not voluntarily commit suicide...unless God wills it so.

[Since its launch by Hugh Hefner in 1953, "Playboy" magazine has featured monthly airbrushed centerfolds of beautiful young women who are very proud of their bodies. Since then, 42 of them have died. The youngest was 23 and the oldest was 76. They died of heart attacks, cancer, accidents, murder, and suicide. The latest nude model declared, "My photo shoots were probably some of the best experiences I've ever had - they were such a rush! Playboy made me feel like a princess." But, she will die too.]

Some commentators have argued that baby boomers are in denial of their own aging. Many spend billions and undergo painful treatments trying to sustain a youthful appearance. However, beginning with the new millennium, there has been a growing dialogue on how to manage aging and end-of-life issues as the baby boomer generation ages. In the U.S. half of all sheeple die by the age of 80 and most of the rest by the age of 90. For many of them, the final years are not much fun. If you live past age 80 the rest is all downhill with the only variable being the slope of decline and number of hurdles before the end.

[The top ten causes of death in America reported for 2007 were: Heart disease: 616,067, Cancer: 562,875, Stroke (cerebrovascular diseases): 135,952, Chronic respiratory diseases: 127,924, Accidents (unintentional injuries): 123,706, Alzheimer's disease: 74,632, Diabetes: 71,382, Influenza and Pneumonia: 52,717, Nephritis/ Kidney Failure: 46,448, Bacterial Infections/Scepticemia: 34,828. In addition, the FBI reported 14,180 people were murdered in America during 2008 and 34,598 sheeple committed suicide. During the 20th century, more Americans were murdered by fellow Americans than soldiers died on active duty during WWI, WWII, the Korean War and the Vietnam War combined.]

A few sheeple die quickly without warning, like entertainer and sausage maker Jimmy Dean at age 81 and New York Yankees owner George Steinbrenner at age 80. But, most of us get a longer time to contemplate our pending demise after diagnosis of a terminal condition, as did actor Patrick Swayze who died of pancreatic cancer at age 57 and actress Farrah Fawcett who died of anal cancer at age 62, leaving a documentary film to record her terminal suffering. The greatest tragedies are deaths among younger folks who leave dependent children behind with their grieving spouses. Such was Prof. Randy Pausch, author of The Last Lecture (2008) who died at age 47 leaving a beautiful wife and three young children and also actor Christopher Reeve, "Superman," at the age of 53 after an accident that left him a quadriplegic for ten years. His beautiful wife, Dana died shortly after leaving their ten year old son orphaned. It isn't just the dying, it is the amount of disability that must be accommodated and the impact that has upon loved ones before the end actually comes. The fact is that the old must die and the young may die, and that something must kill us unless we do it to ourselves or to each other. Too often, it takes longer than is tolerable or affordable.

Since everybody does it, why is there such a fuss about it? Must the ego be involuntarily crucified in order to let go and move on? Apparently so. We are alive, therefore we will die and there is no explanation for why many must suffer so much before the end finally comes. This is the simplest, most obvious truth of our existence, and yet very few of us have really come to terms with it. Life under any conditions of suffering and disability seems to be preferred to the alternative for many sheeple. Human ego just does not accept its own demise without putting up a fight to the finish. One failing gentleman said he wanted to live so long as he could watch football and eat ice cream. To paraphrase Prof. Pausch; "We cannot change the cards we are dealt nor how we play the hand." Each of us must act out the script we are given in the theater of mankind as Shakespeare declared, "All the world's a stage and men and women are the actors." All in God's will of course...AIGWOC. Believe it, or not.

Thanatophobia, the fear of dying, is more common than sheeple probably want to admit or to talk about so the whole topic is taboo in modern western culture, and that makes the shock even greater when the time comes. New York movie maker, Woody Allen spoke for most of us when he said, "Life is full of misery, loneliness, and suffering - and it's all over much too soon...still, I don't want to live forever in my work; I want to live forever in my apartment." Although death seems to be the universal ending of life, very few sheeple anticipate it with pleasure and yearning. Nevertheless, as therapist Mary Pipher said in her chronicles of the old-old generation in Another Country, (1999) "We shall all experience our ship going down." She concluded, "All lives ultimately are tragedies. Not only does nobody get out of this place alive, but nobody gets out without loss and despair...everyone carries heavy burdens...everyone." And the only thing one can do finally is accept it for themselves and witness it in loved ones with courage and surrender. That realization put Dr. Pipher into a meltdown crisis in 2002 after watching her physician-mother suffer for a year before dying that she documented in her memoir, Seeking Peace. (2009) and caused her to close her therapy practice. She lamented, "We are in a crisis. We lack housing arrangements, social structures, traditions, and wisdom to make the last years of life manageable...There is a lot wrong with this picture."

The burden of life challenges she witnessed among her clients and the final year of her mother became too much and she crashed in burnout by forgetting the basic rule of therapists; do not listen. Not only did she listen, but she documented what she heard and thereby took on the weight too heavy to carry. Mary Pipher learned the hard way in her own personal crisis the Buddhist principles that acceptance is the key to serenity and gratitude is the key to happiness. And some things really are just unknowable, like what happens after death. She described herself as "the worst Buddhist in the world" and one who was running around "like a head with the chicken cut off." And, like the confusion among victims on the "unsinkable" Titanic, it can come as a great shock if we refuse or cannot accept our mortality and let go of the worthless body when the time comes while letting go of all concern for our survivors. They will have to look out for themselves.

Science assumes that life forms die to make room for new generations, not counting the ones consumed in the food chain and by wars and natural disasters, else the planet would soon be overrun and life would be unsustainable. Dying is said to be a natural process in the cycle of life to sustain life, except for the ego, which cannot tolerate its own demise so something must kill it. Perhaps it is not death we fear so much, but rather the loss of control that the ego cannot relinquish. How can the individual prepare for that? The process of aging and dying defies science because there seems to be no explanation for it since with the right food and recycling conditions, cells could theoretically replicate themselves forever. But, dying seems to be built secretly into our DNA, and everyone is born with a clock that ticks at different rates and eventually stops working. The longest documented record for human longevity seems to be a woman in France who lived 122 years. In fact, the Bible specifies maximum human longevity at 120 years. (Genesis 6:3) The latest craze in death prevention is personal in-home DNA testing that may disclose inherited tendencies to illness that may not be discovered by routine physical exams in time for treatment. But we still die.

Basically, sheeple die naturally when biological cell death exceeds cell division. Cells must be replaced when they malfunction or become diseased, and excessive cell proliferation must be offset by cell death or cancer results. This control mechanism is part of the homeostasis required by living organisms to maintain their internal states within certain limits. [Some scientists have suggested "homeodynamics" as a more accurate term.] Homeostasis is achieved when the rate of mitosis (cell division resulting in cell multiplication) in the tissue is balanced by the rate of cell death. Cell death is a completely normal process in living organisms and was first discovered by scientists over 100 years ago. Programmed cell death or "apoptosis" involves a series of biochemical events leading to a characteristic cell morphology and death; i.e., a series of biochemical events that lead to a variety of morphological changes. The word "apoptosis" is used in Greek to describe the "dropping off" or "falling off" of petals from flowers or leaves from trees. In the average human adult, between 50 and 70 billion cells die each day due to apoptosis. In a year, this amounts to the destruction of a mass of cells equal to an individual's body weight.

Research on apoptosis has increased substantially since the early 1990s. It is seen regularly in species that live to propagate and then die. One such is the curious life cycle of the cicada. This is an insect that appears once every 17 years from out of the ground to mate and then lay its eggs in the soil to hibernate until they hatch and repeat the cycle. Then the adults die and clutter up the sidewalks and lawns. In addition to its importance as a biological phenomenon, defective apoptotic processes have been implicated in an extensive variety of diseases. Excessive apoptosis causes hypotrophy, such as in ischemic damage, whereas an insufficient amount results in uncontrolled cell proliferation, such as cancer. In the adult organism, the number of cells is kept relatively constant through cell death and division. If this equilibrium is disturbed, one of two potentially fatal disorders occurs: the cells divide faster than they die, resulting in the development of a cancerous tumor that eventually destroys organ functions; or the cells divide slower than they die, causing organ malfunction and death. This condition may be caused by external shock or injury, disease mechanisms, failure of the feedback conditions, or internal cell malfunctions.

Sheeple die naturally as cell death exceeds cell rejuvenation. This condition is seen in the refusal of cells to receive glucose and metabolize it into energy so it builds up rapidly and is detected in the blood. Excess glucose is toxic and eventually disables organ functions required to sustain life. The most likely manifestation is seen in Type 2 Diabetes. The process of normal aging has been laid to production of free radicals in normal foods and chemicals that cause excess oxidation of cells, but anti-oxidant supplements have not been proven to increase longevity. Longevity among mice has been increased somewhat by reducing calories about one third but starving beyond that and life actually is shortened. When dying comes, it is not instantaneous as sheeple have been revived several minutes after the heart stops beating. Only when the brain stops functioning completely for lack of oxygen is one really dead, and that can take as long as it takes. About the longest a brain has survived lack of oxygen and recovered is twenty minutes, and then only if it is frozen.

From the instant of conception, living and dying seem to be opposing forces, and dying always wins. That's the fact, Jack. The question most sheeple avoid is this: What would you be willing to die for or of? If the answer is nothing, you are in trouble. Death is perceived by many not only as the termination of life, but also the termination of all memories of life, and that may be the worst of all because without memories we as egos do not exist, and the ego wants immortality above all else. Without our memories, we have no ego/self, as Alzheimer's disease so graphically demonstrates and is so appropriately feared. It is ironic, but the best way to enjoy life is to contemplate death. If one can detach from the mortal body and watch it decline from a distance, the process may be quite interesting to watch unfold. If we observe it in others, our own demise may not be such a shock, but in modern cultures we prefer not to be involved.

Rabbi Joshua Liebman (1907-1948) quoted Estonian poet, V.A. Koskeniemi in Peace of Mind, (1946) "Man is not free in life unless he is free from fear of death too. We can certainly not be free of it by not thinking of death, but only by learning to be at home with it, even by becoming accustomed to it. In preparing ourselves for death, we enable ourselves for freedom because only one who has learned to die is free to live." [Rabbi Liebman died at age 41 under mysterious circumstances while his book was on the best seller list. His book was such a success it was reprinted forty times after his death. It's popularity was no doubt enhanced by a full page ad in "Life" magazine on Sept. 30, 1946 taken by the publisher, Simon and Schuster. His work promoted cooperation between Freudian psychology and religion that was popular among Jews. Is that curious, or what?] It appears that God wants us to learn humility and to practice calm submission in life, but only after he gives us an ego that wants power and control, even if it takes several lifetimes or only part of one. When he wants us to, then we die. The old must die and the young may die. However it happens, it happens. All in God's will of course ...AIGWOC. Think you can handle that?

Our attitudes on death stem in large part from the way we raise our children. Young sheeple in America generally are sheltered from death and all of its horrors, unless they are raised on streets of inner cities. Video games and violent movies don't count. When grandfather/mother dies, for example, he/she is typically in a hospital room, nursing home, or hospice, isolated from friends and family. After their death, grandchildren may be told that they moved on to a better place, perhaps to Heaven in a magical world of eternal happiness where there is no longer any pain or suffering. In addition to being sold this fictionalized version of death, children do not typically have the opportunity to see their parents grieve openly over the loss of loved ones.

Mourning is a private process, which is often suppressed out of shame to hide weakness. Modern American society dictates that we must be happy, youthful, and fresh-faced at all times; there is no tolerance for drooling on your bib and for mourning in public much less messing up your diaper. Furthermore, children receive mixed messages from their daily media intake and video games, in which major heroic characters may die but they rarely stay dead. They become desensitized to simulated death, but the real thing scares them to pieces. Because parents cannot understand their own feelings about a subject as complicated and emotionally complex as death, they often recoil from having to grapple with it with their children, assuming their offspring will also be unable to comprehend it and engendering their own discomfort with death in their children. They are wrong of course. Children are much more resilient that supposed.

We could take lessons in death and dying from other cultures that integrate it naturally into life, but that would be too painful for most fragile American egos to tolerate. Life is so good that most Americans refuse to talk about death or simply ignore it, pretending it does not exist. We hand bodies of our dead loved ones over to professionals, who go to great lengths to make a very-dead corpse look as alive as possible. These professionals dress up our deceased in normal clothing, expertly apply lifelike artificial makeup to their faces and hands, and lay them to "rest" in expensive caskets with soft mattresses to ensure that they will remain fresh-looking for their never-ending nap. [In one case in Puerto Rico, the body of a youthful motorcycle rider was displayed mounted upon his bike in full riding gear for the funeral.] Those in charge of the funeral preparations, comprising the "death industry," in the United States represent a booming business, generating approximately $20-billion a year. With the American baby boomer population aging more every day, there is no end in sight to this boom. Death is a growth industry.

The subject of dying is so emotionally charged that rational discussion about it is almost impossible among average sheeple, so the churches avoid discussing it and driving away members. In fact, modern efforts to prevent death have become irrational while practically no resources are invested in helping sheeple to prepare themselves to die. Consequently, very little planning for end of life decisions is completed before it is too late to avoid serious emotional trauma. Even the discussion of insurance compensation and medical provisions for end-of-life counseling is taboo among legislators facing the social cost of measures to avoid dying because of the media frenzy that froze all debate.

Medical science considers death to be a tragedy, another form of disease to be conquered. After all, they can't make any money from dead bodies. When all diseases are conquered, then what will sheeple die from? Some few are having their dead bodies stored in a cryogenic deep freeze in hopes that some future discovery will enable them to be resurrected. Some futurists even predict that healthy living sheeple could be frozen at will for future preservation when technology permits. The unnatural transplanting of organs, complete with personality shifts, now enables life extension that was impossible a century ago, so who knows what may be possible one day? Perhaps one may be able to store and preserve infant stem cells to rejuvenate failing bones and organs ad infinitum whenever needed to achieve life everlasting. Animals have been cloned in this fashion, so why not sheeple? But, others look at death as a normal part of life to be embraced, maybe as a transition to something much better than this life. Some sheeple believe that birth is not the beginning and death is not the ending of life.

If death is the natural transition of life why is it feared and resisted so much in Western cultures? Could it be the medical profession, insurance companies, and drug companies all want it that way to assure we will spend as much money as we can and more to avoid it? Their advertising claims about "saving lives" merely mask the economic goals of capitalism because everyone eventually dies. Death and its preludes are battles to be won and endings to be avoided at all costs in Western society and the public literature. Could the churches avoid it for the same reason because, after all, they are primarily business social clubs that don't pay any taxes? When it comes to the real crises in life, they are both irrelevant and impotent. In past generations, death was always stalking around family members. In many parts of the world, it still is. Sheeple get sick and die in plain view. In previous generations, families prepared the body for burial or cremation, and most still do in poor countries. But, in the United States, sheeple are in a state of death denial because we have been deluded into assuming there is nothing medical science cannot fix, and if we cannot pay, the government will. But that is a fiction of wishful thinking that is rapidly bankrupting tax payers as the 76 million baby boomers enter their final years.

We somehow consciously or unconsciously believe that if we go to the gym, eat organic foods, maintain an appropriate weight, think positively, get yearly physicals… and focus on these healthy ways of living, well, the prospect of death disappears. We acknowledge intellectually that other sheeple die (more than 2.4 million annually in the U.S. or 6500 daily) and so will we, but, our demise always is an abstract and infinite number of years away - not to concern us! Then, we get to be middle aged and a relative or friend or celebrity about our age dies. We begin to think of our death - but, ever so slightly. As we progress in years more peers die, but it's still others, but not us. But, the clock still ticks. We use denial of our mortality to cope, but there is no cure for mortality. We always lose. Moviemaker Woody Allen caught the essence of the Western attitude toward death when he reportedly quipped, "I am not afraid of dying... I just don't want to be there when it happens." In contrast, Plato summed up wisdom for his students who were standing his death watch… "practice dying." Eastern religions embrace death as an inevitable and natural stage in life, but many Western churches and medical institutions either pretend to dismiss it or evade it or delay it or even try to prevent it. Is that insanity, or what? Maybe it is just good capitalist marketing, squeezing the last dollar out of our terminal existence.

Pierre Teilhard de Chardin (1881-1955) observed, "We are not human beings having a spiritual experience, we are spirits having a human experience." Jesus proclaimed, "The spirit gives life, the flesh counts for nothing." (John 6:63) A Course in Miracles (1975), channeled by Helen Schucman, proclaims the human experience is an illusion created by ego to sustain separation from the real world of spirit. And, sometimes, it sucks. It proclaims we live as if in a dream unaware of the real home we left and at death the body sleeps but the soul awakes to the realization of heaven which is its natural home. This could be the rebirth or resurrection in spirit that Jesus said was necessary to enter the kingdom of God. (John 3:5) But, in this life we suffer. Pope Benedict XVI, [a.k.a.: Joseph Cardinal Ratzinger] expressed in his "Eschatology," (1988) "Each and every human being is a suffering being. The moment of death is not our first experience of finitude. Finitude presses daily on body and on our soul. We must prepare ourselves for that limit which, whether we are more aware of it or less, is the recurrence of suffering."

Everyone dies, but very few sheeple plan for it so it usually comes as a shock for which we are totally unprepared. We cover our eyes like a child playing hide and seek and hope that if we cannot see it, death will not find us. But it always does. More than 2.4 million sheeple die each year in the U.S. and there are more than 23,000 sanitized mortuaries to dispose of the bodies. In Old Testament law, anyone touching a corpse was deemed to be unclean for seven days. (Numbers 19:11) Jews bury their bodies the very next day for this reason. Ever since then, death has been attached to the stigma of sin that supposedly caused it. Consequently, immortality was not given to humanity, which would have had to eat of the "tree of life" in the Garden to achieve it. "And the Lord God said, The man has now become like one of us, knowing good and evil. He must not be allowed to reach out his hand and take also from the tree of life and eat and live forever." (Genesis 3:22) It isn't that dying is so bad, it is the loss of control and the suffering and humiliation leading up to it that is so repulsive to the Western human ego. Whether one can practice for that is uncertain.

C. G. Jung (1875-1961) observed the first half of life to be achieving growth and the second as preparation for death, which he considered as not an ending but rather as a goal. "Dying is not something that happens to us, but rather something that we do when the time is ripe." After a near death experience during his heart attack he claimed, "...what happens after death is so unspeakably glorious that our imagination and our feelings do not suffice to form even an approximate conception of it...To the psyche death is just as important as birth and, like it, is an integral part of life to be celebrated rather than mourned ...I make a great effort to fortify the belief in immortality, especially in my older patients, for whom the question is crucial...the younger growing man is being prepared for the complete unfolding of his individual nature, why should not the older man prepare himself twenty years and more for his death...Dying has its onset long before actual death. It seems that the unconscious is all the more interested in how one dies, whether the attitude of consciousness is adjusted to dying or not...to set to rights whatever is still wrong...I should like to add that no one knows what psyche is and one knows just as little how far into nature psyche extends." No one knows. Therefore, it is rather that we should mourn for the remaining survivors who must go on with life to finish the task that is before them without their loved one with indefinite uncertainty about their own futures.

When he lay dying the Buddha instructed, "Be a lamp unto yourself." The ancient Chinese manual "Tao te Ching" says, "Life is sweetest when you know you are dying." Roman Emperor and stoic philosopher Marcus Aurelius (121 – 180 A.D.) wrote in his memoirs, "Consider that before long you will be nobody and nowhere, nor will any of the things exist which you now see, nor any of those who 0are now living. When its hour comes, how lovely the soul that is prepared to slough off this flesh. For all things are formed by nature to change and be turned and to perish in order that other things in continuous succession may exist... Adapt yourself to the things among which your lot has been cast and love sincerely the fellow creatures with whom destiny has ordained that you shall live... Everything that happens happens as it should, and if you observe carefully, you will find this to be so. Whatever the universal nature assigns to any man at any time is for the good of that man at that time...Be content with what you are, and wish not for change; nor dread your last day, nor long for it...Despise not death, but welcome it, for nature wills it like all else. Therefore the termination of life for every man is no evil, neither is it shameful, since it is both independent of the will and not opposed to the general interest, but it is good, since it is seasonable and profitable to and congruent with the universal." But as he hung dying on the cross Jesus lamented, "My God, why have you forsaken me?" (Matthew 27:46) If the Son of God felt abandoned by God when suffering the pains of dying, what chance have we mortals to go softly into that dark night of the soul? Perhaps these events are connected in some way not yet recognized by Western churches. Most of them seem to overlook entirely the ubiquitous act of dying, except for the sanitized version of funerals they conduct occasionally. That death comes to everyone is self-evident, but until it is imminent most sheeple prefer to avoid thinking about it much less talk about it, so they often are not prepared to face it, even if that were possible.

Dying is just about the most un-American event in the world. Most sheeple in Western cultures are so petrified of death and grief that they avoid it as much as possible until it is forced upon them. Comedian George Burns, who lived to be 100 years old, quipped, "I don't believe in dying...it's been done." In selling his medical reforms, President Obama declared, "I do not support death." The ego that will not volunteer must be crucified. More than four sheeple die every minute in America, 6,500 each day, but you would never know it. And, no one cares until someone dies in your family. For many, dying is imagined as a dark foreboding place beyond which lies an unknown and terrifying terrain even though they want to believe in some afterlife. It can even seem like a betrayal by God, and if you can't trust him who can you trust. First he gives you life and then he takes it back whenever he wants to. If death is sudden or brutal or accidental or untimely, the shock can drive stress for survivors right off the scale.

Questions on the meaning of life never are more urgent or more agonizing than when we see the final breath leave a body which a moment before was a living loved one. If it is violent or untimely the horror is multiplied. How different than when we see a young person striving for goals and shaping the future and compare that with an incurable invalid sinking reluctantly and impotently into the grave. We are painfully mindful of the feelings and look away and turn the conversation to a different topic because we see there our own future. Modern Western cultures have removed death so far from daily activities that many sheeple scarcely know how to behave or react when the door opens to whatever follows life, and that includes many medical professionals and church leaders. Death is the last great social taboo among otherwise highly developed nations, as though avoiding discussion of it will make it go away. Even Jesus seemed to minimize the impact of death as he told a would-be disciple to "let the dead bury their dead." (Luke 9:60) In the American death-avoiding society, psychological impacts of denial and avoidance abound. The market for "anti-aging" products and services encourages the myth that one can live forever. So the inevitable ending usually is traumatic and often leaves permanent psychological damage and emotional scars among survivors that might be avoided with more attention to the end of life issues before they become reality.

We have no control over our birth, but we could have much more control over our dying if sheeple could accept it is inevitable and plan accordingly which, it seems, goes against human nature. The ego just will never give up so it must be crucified on the cross of terminal illness. There is no formal institution to support this phase of life, so it is mostly a do-it-yourself project in spite of growth in hospice care options for the dying during their last six months on Earth. Most physicians have little formal education in the philosophy of human suffering, and very little training in management of the terminal phase of illness, much less in ego psychology, although this is changing slowly within geriatric specialties. The medical orientation toward suffering often still is either avoidance or alleviation; acceptance is not part of their treatment.

Many physicians and nurses and religious ministers have unexplored attitudes about death and see it as failure of their profession…so when a patient can no longer respond to their treatment they shift efforts to other patients who can be helped live a while longer. When a terminal diagnosis is presented both patient and doctor may at first react with disbelief. Only after they work through stages of fight and flight can they eventually pass through anger, bargaining, and depression to assume calm submission. Terminal illness strips away years of façade, persona, entitlement, and privilege leaving one to ponder who they really are and what really matters, medical professionals included. How deep they must go depends upon how well they are prepared; how well the ego is able to relinquish its demand for control. The ego seems to be reluctant, or even incapable, of accepting its own demise voluntarily.

A diagnosis of death challenges all relationships. The strongest ones may be reinforced, but the weaker ones sometimes shatter. Families that are wrapped up in enjoying life may recoil from anticipating demands for physical care of a dying relative because it is never easy and can be emotionally taxing, maybe even nauseating. Needs for feeding, toileting, medicating, and bathing may go on 24/7 for months and even years. Relatives who cannot cope often leave the dying alone in hospitals and nursing homes which then secretly transport the body to a sanitized funeral "home" where visitors sign the guest book and return to life quickly, as though nothing happened. At best they linger at the casket, displaying the deceased dressed and made up as though alive to cover the cold gray of death, a few minutes in silence and then retreat to make small-talk safely removed from the fear of contamination. Like moviemaker Woody Allen said, most of us don't mind the thought of dying so long as we don't have to be there when it happens.

Many sheeple reach middle age without ever witnessing death of a loved one, so the experience can be very unsettling when it does happen, to say the least. When you receive a diagnosis of terminal illness you enter a new and unexplored landscape buried deeply in the unconscious. All the emotions that have been repressed for a lifetime of being nice can boil up and explode into the room. You haven't really lived if you have not watched a loved one die, and now you realize how fragile and vulnerable life really is. But try to imagine what it must be like for the patient. The dying one must mourn the loss of a future and let go of attachment to life, no matter how bleak it may be. Perhaps the ultimate feeling of anxiety occurs when humans realize that they are going to die alone, for it is the final task that no one can do for us. We are alive, therefore we will die. This is the simplest, most obvious truth of our existence, and yet very few of us have really come to terms with it.

As members of Western society have distanced themselves from their rural past, they also distanced themselves from the most basic of funeral customs. Before the turn of the 20th century, rural Americans may have been more in touch with death and as a result less fearful of the corpse. Farm accidents and childbirth complications caused many deaths in a more agrarian and pre-medically advanced society. Traditionally, Americans used to keep the deceased in their homes until everyone had a chance to view the body. It was a family member who would wash and dress the body, preparing it for display and visitation within the home. Americans were at one time better versed in dealing with issues surrounding death and the physical remains left behind. If a body in the front room isn't disturbing; if handling and dressing the corpse were not odd, then future generations would learn to feel the same way. However, in 1910, the "Ladies' Home Journal" decreed that the "parlor" should be renamed the "living room" to disassociate it from funeral parlors. Children were discouraged from going to funerals. It was no longer appropriate or safe for the body to remain in the home. The body must be taken away and professionally sanitized before the funeral.

For most, dealing with death and cadavers is not a part of everyday life now. A cadaver is an unwholesome, unhealthy thing, best left to be taken care of by trained professionals. Nevertheless, the body retains human identity, and the idea of mistreatment or decay can be painful to assume for survivors. Physically, it is just a dead body. But the identity, the life, and the memories are symbolically dead as well. The idea of that beloved friend or relative being slowly consumed by insects or vermin or fire is more than most can bear. However, decomposition of the flesh is natural, and inevitable. Anyone who tells you differently probably is selling funerary services. It can cost from $2,000 to $12,000 for a commercial funeral, including unnecessary embalming to delay decomposition for a few months. The Church used to claim it was necessary to inter the body so it could be recalled upon resurrection, but no more. Now, cremation is much cheaper, and likely more sanitary as even the most elaborate caskets eventually deteriorate and permit the gases and effluent to seep into the soil.

The dying seem to be harmfully contagious to those egos that see their own futures displayed, and they are right. "Mirror" neurons have been detected in the brain that make sheeple feel the suffering of others as though it were contagious, so they put up defenses to avoid it as a method of self defense or try to help make it go away. Experiments have shown that brain cells in one person affected by some stimulant, like a flash of light, are accompanied by the same brain cell responses in another person although completely isolated in a different location. Albert Einstein puzzled over such "spooky things at a distance," without finding an explanation. Experiments such as this mystify even leading edge scientists because they suggest that at some level not yet understood we all are connected; what is called "entanglement" in quantum mechanics and what the sages say is the oneness of all things. Therefore, the health of all persons may be affected by the health of one person. A threat to anyone is interpreted as a threat to "me." The more active mirror neurons are, the more a person feels empathy for another of his own group who is suffering. This phenomenon accounts for the "selective pattern recognition" that helps sheeple identify threats from visual observations such as the Nazi swastika or the logo and colors of a rival sports team. Emotional contagion then prepares the brain for a reaction; fight, flight, bargaining, or submission.

This finding merely confirms an ancient Chinese proverb; "All [untrained] men have a mind which cannot bear to see the suffering of others." They will either present with concerned attention or aversive avoidance, and which is unpredictable. Perhaps the art of medicine evolved from the former. It can be shocking to see how much disability a human body can endure without dying. So, many families focus medical intervention upon the obvious symptoms while the process of dying is denied and avoided, much to the loss of everyone. If the death is sudden, violent, or unexpected many can only ask why me, why now, why us? But the response of Buddhist teachers is, "Do not avoid contact with suffering or close your eyes...be present with suffering to understand the nature of existence, which includes suffering." It is not easy to gaze clear-eyed at the troubling manifestations of terminal human conditions, especially among children who suffer through no fault of their own. With all our social and economic gains, many have lost the essential privilege of saying farewell and staying close to the departing until the end. Death refuses to follow our scripts and does as it wills, each time in a unique way. Since no one can predict exactly how and when it will happen, decisions often must be made at the last minute that cannot be anticipated in detail. So letting go and letting God will reduce much suffering from wishing that things could be any different. Just remember that emotions are contagious. So care givers and visitors all prefer to see a smiling, happy countenance rather than a sad, depressed demeanor, even during your last days. Sorry, but that is the way it is among Homo sapiens in Western cultures.

Often the dying move from loneliness into peaceful solitude as the known world dissolves and begins to disappear, exposing the great darkness of the radically unknown. Swiss psychiatrist, Elisabeth Kubler-Ross, (1926-2004) described in On Death and Dying (1969) how dying sheeple must travel through denial, anger, bargaining and depression to attain peaceful acceptance of their pending demise. Not everyone completes this evolution without resistance, and some remain in one stage or other before they expire, perhaps all according to the will of God the Almighty One. So do their survivors. Family and friends may scarcely be able to understand the transition going on with their dying loved ones, so they become befuddled and evasive the closer death approaches. These tasks are not trifles and may require great energy and professional care to work through. Some get stuck in one phase or other and die without feeling good about it while leaving great remorse and grief behind for survivors. And the more they must leave behind the harder it is to go.

Jesus said it was harder for a camel to pass through the eye of a needle than for a rich person to get into heaven. (Matthew 19:24) Kubler-Ross lived alone and bereft of comfort her last several years through several strokes, wondering why it was taking so long. Actor, Christopher "Superman" Reeve (1952-2004) seemed never to accept the limitations of being a quadriplegic after a tragic accident and fought for ten years to make it different. Soon after he died his lovely healthy nonsmoking wife, Dana, was diagnosed with inoperable lung cancer and died within a year at age 44, leaving a ten year old son. She remarked angrily, "I'll tell you it's another journey, and I'm ready to be finished with the journeys." The near-death experience reported by some sheeple is described as very pleasant and nothing to fear. Toward the end, sheeple's egos naturally lose interest in controlling life, and eventually they begin releasing their failing bodies. Production of enzymes an amino acids needed to process food digestion declines as energy no longer is needed, and sheeple eventually stop eating and drinking if they are permitted to die normally. When death is imminent, stuffing patients with feeding tubes and respirators only prolongs the agony for everyone and deepens the grief of survivors. What they need is comfort, not resistance.

Some would say that remaining in denial is an appropriate defense for the fearsome mystery of death and permits one to live actively as long as possible. Research psychologist, Richard Lazarus documented situations where sheeple recovered better from surgery if they were not informed of its seriousness. He died unexpectedly from a fall in his bathroom at age 80. So we replace the thought of dying with "passing away." For those who can let go of their dying bodies, the transition actually may be a pleasant experience as it is a natural thing to do. But, if the ego will not let go voluntarily, it will be crucified. That may require working through the phases of denial, anger, bargaining, and depression to accept crossing the bar. Egos that cannot let go of the need for control when the time comes bring additional suffering onto themselves and dying loved ones.

Among extended families often scattered across the country there could be much unfinished business, remorse, and alienation that must be reconciled for the ultimate separation to be easily accepted. Modern social networks are complicated often by several divorces and remarriages that rearrange the family loyalties and leave the dying members potentially alone in their final days of need. The result is that old age and dying is a foreign country to the young and middle aged, and they have no awareness of its challenges until they get there. Failing some family reconciliation, the end for elders may bring with it much contentious bickering and arguing for control and demands for medical interventions that not only postpone the dying but add additional burdens of emotional and financial scarring of survivors that never heal. It is as though sheeple think they can find immortality buried someplace under all the trivia. C. G. Jung observed, "Death is psychologically as important as birth... Shrinking away from it is something unhealthy and abnormal which robs the second half of life of its purpose." So why not arrange to view a departed mortal in a funeral "home" from time to time just to get used to the ambience? That way you won't feel so shocked when it is the body of your own loved one in the casket. Or volunteer some time at nursing homes among the ones with little left to do but wait for God.

Much as we know about life, death is a mysterious process hidden behind curtains of avoidance. It used to be different in America and it still is among cultures with fewer social defense mechanisms, where the ego/self does not disable the spirit. Each family got to rehearse the process again and again as dying relatives faded away one after the other in plain view. Modern medicine can and often does keep a stone alive when families cannot let go, so we have lost the spiritual significance of death and replaced it with trauma and suffering. Conquering death is a battle to be won at all costs, but we always lose. For those who are able to let go when it is time, a comforting form of palliative care is provided by the hospice movement. Hospice care was started in England around 1967 by Dame Cicely Saunders and was added to Medicare coverage in the U.S. in the 1980s. Under care of a physician, a team of nursing and social workers, religious, and volunteers help assure a terminally ill patient is clean and comfortable during the final six months while the agent of death is permitted to take its course. Many sheeple still are not comfortable with this service option or the option of making formal plans with "do not resuscitate" (DNR) orders and powers of attorney on file with medicals before the need occurs. Those family members who resist this form of departure often cannot let go because of unfinished business and remorse and guilt for a life poorly lived with too little expression of love. They may put the dying through humiliation and embarrassment of feeding tubes, diapers, and catheters for their own needs. Consequently, many patients wait until the last week or so to enter hospice care; too short for families and patients to get used to the idea.

After surviving three years in Nazi concentration camps, psychiatrist Victor Frankl (1905-1997) concluded, "Sometimes a man may be required simply to accept his fate and bear his cross...to accept suffering as his task. He will have to acknowledge the fact that in his suffering he is alone and unique in the universe. No one can relieve him of his suffering or suffer in his place." Sometimes the only appropriate feeling is despair, and sometimes the only response is to witness it. However, anticipation of suffering can be worse than the experience. Jesus sweat drops of blood in anticipation of his expected suffering on the cross, so if he was not exempt from such anxiety, how can we expect anything less? (Luke 22:44) Those who believe in reincarnation and the law of Karma may assume if they do not complete the suffering they contracted for in this life, it will be added onto their account in the next one. If doctors and churches do not help sheeple prepare to die, where can they turn when the grim reaper calls? Hospice doctor, Ira Byock has laid out a plan for making the journey across the bar. When you need comprehensive education about end of life care of a loved one or yourself, please visit www.dying well.org and also http://endlink.lurie.northwestern.edu/index.cfm

Dr. Francis Collins, leader of the Human Genome Project, observed that sheeple will always experience "a death rate of one per person." Leonardo da Vinci (1452-1519) summarized his life this way, "While I thought I was learning how to live, I was really learning how to die." Be not deceived by ego's temporary diversions and the medical industry's profit incentive to "save lives," which it cannot do because death will not be denied. All it can do is deliver treatments that often prolong suffering. Some studies indicate that patients under hospice care actually may live longer than those accepting aggressive medical treatments. Beyond the peaks of life there is the valley of Gehenna waiting patiently with its smiling face and beckoning arms among the smoldering embers of life ebbing away, whether we are prepared or not to cross the bar. Medical science often just prolongs and intensifies the suffering that comes when egos challenge God as they march under the flag of poet, Dylan Thomas as he commanded his dying father; "Do not go gentle into that good night...rage, rage against the dying of the light." Hope for a long and healthy, wealthy, happy life is the last to go. In fact, doctors usually prolong hope past the point of no return when sheeple should be given clear instructions for getting their goodbye time in order. In contrast, there is a Buddhist saying; "There are other worlds in which to sing." Dying really begins when the person stops resisting the physical dependence and permits the care giving team to perform the unmentionables, dressing, feeding, toileting, bathing, and turning. When it comes, death always is incomprehensible without intellectual, emotional, and spiritual preparation.

Since God obviously does not hesitate to kill off its creation, often violently, why do Homo sapiens resist death so much? Fear of aging and death has roots in fear of losing possessions, friends, and control of life, including the body, all that which creates a self-image for the ego. It might be wise to practice giving things away and releasing attachments to them so their loss no longer has any impact on that self image which is so dependent upon transient things. Hanging on to such only makes the passage more difficult. Life may finally come down to a hospital room or a bed in some nursing home. As death approaches, control, authority, and eventually the ego-self as well must all be released as they are taken away along with the illusion of immortality. Denial, rationalizing, and intellectualizing all become challenged, leaving only the reality of raw emotions to expose the person to terminal care. When death is imminent we may learn what really matters and how insignificant and unimportant what we valued really is.

Dr. Ira Byock, who specializes in hospice terminal care, describes the five final milestones to complete with dying loved ones as, "Please forgive me. I forgive you. Thank you. I love you. Goodbye." These simple statements are a powerful tool for easing suffering of sheeple facing life's end - themselves or a loved one. Dr. Byock has created an exceptional planned set of tasks and landmarks for end of life preparation in his milestone book, <u>Dying Well</u>. (1996) At first, this title seems like a cruel oxymoron. But, his plan is like closing up a small retail store when it goes out of business. The owner sells off all the inventory, discharges all the employees, closes all the accounts, cancels the utilities, and one day just closes the door and walks away leaving the empty facility behind with no concern for its future use. Song writer, Stuart Hamblen (1908-1989) caught this mood as he composed the classic ballad, "This Ole House." "...ain't gonna need this house no longer, ain't gonna need this house no more."

Dr. Byock says that no one should have to die in pain or alone if they don't want to. But, many do because doctors and families cannot say when enough treatment is enough. While most sheeple claim they want to die at home, many die alone in the impersonal wards of hospitals and nursing homes that afford little to no final empathy. Failure to find hope in their religion may be the last challenge for such sheeple. The day before he was martyred by the assassin's bullet at age 39, the husband and father, Rev. Martin Luther King, Jr. announced prophetically, "Like anybody, I would like to live a long life. Longevity has its place. But I'm not concerned about that now. I just want to do the will of God" - the Almighty One.

Jesus warned not to lay up treasures upon Earth where moth and rust can corrupt and where thieves break in and steal, but rather to lay up treasures in Heaven where they are eternal. (Matthew 6:19-20) He told the rich young ruler to sell all that he had to gain the kingdom of heaven. And he warned that it was easier for a camel to get through the eye of a needle than for a rich man to enter the kingdom of God. (Matthew 19: 23-25) Whether the descent is swift or takes years of surrendering resistance one stage at a time, the closed fist that clings to possessions and independence cannot be open to receive whatever comes next. But terminal suffering is never easy to experience or to witness, and it is always an open question whether we can marshal the inner resources to let go of everything we have ever held on to. The suffering of letting go, including control of our bodies, is an important achievement in completing the cycle of life.

Resisting the dying process increases the very pain that we fear and leaves trauma that never heals in loved ones who must watch it. It is like a fish caught on a hook; the outcome is inevitable and resisting only increases the pain and suffering. Sheeple who contemplate death are known to consume more sweets or other indulgence to placate their anxiety and to escape their fear. Many families and patients avoid discussing or preparing for the end so it often is accompanied by high drama that leaves a lifetime of emotional scars. However, with appropriate preparation it might be a natural experience that sustains survivors to face their own demise as it is in many undeveloped economies. The sage embraces sheeple, events, life, gain and loss, and death unconditionally as one. Death is either a transition or an ending and we may not know which even as it happens. By suspending the ego, the Chinese Taoist wrote, "The sage has no ambitions, therefore he can never fail. He who never fails always succeeds. And he who always succeeds is all powerful." My mother always said, "expect nothing and you will never be disappointed."

The law of conservation of energy in thermodynamics states that energy can not be created or destroyed, it can only be changed from one form to another. That means that energy exists outside of time and space. So, perhaps there is some clue in that about death and immortality. However, no one actually knows what energy really is or if there is some afterlife. The Buddha learned that we must light our own way into the unknown because no one can do it for us. The apprehension is absorbed in preparation. In yoga there is the posture of savasana, lying still on your back and pretending to be dead by letting gravity absorb into your body (monkey-mind lying still.) Make yourself as comfortable as possible and remain in this position unless you begin to experience real discomfort. Constant adjusting or fidgeting will prevent you from experiencing the effects of deep relaxation. It is recommended for five minutes each day. The immediate result of savasana is a state of near-perfect harmony coupled with quiet energy. Let go and let God, because he will win anyway. When you practice dying a little bit every day, it will literally change your living. Try it sometime. You may be surprised at the comfort you feel. Living in denial of death may be a sure way to meet it with dread and fear plus additional suffering. But go easy on yourself. Perhaps the most we can hope for is facing death with the belief that we did the best we could under the circumstances. Each day is one more and one less, whether we realize it or not. Live each day like it is your last one because one day you will be right.

Get this: you are born to die. You are not made to like it, just to do it. This body was not made to last. "From dust you are and to dust you shall return." (Genesis 3:19) Sooner or later something is going to break down in your body that cannot be fixed. Everyone dies in their own time in their own way when their journey is completed. It could be easy and short or long and hard. Just as we have an immune system that fights off physical death, so we seem to have a psychological ego to avoid being prematurely disabled by thoughts of terminal doom. But, there is something about Homo sapiens that wants to believe this troubled world is not our real home. Many sheeple believe we came from some place of peace and joy and we will return to it after death. A Course in Miracles (1975) assures us that we never actually left our home in heaven. That being so, it is difficult to imagine why sheeple have conjured up the opposite; a place of eternal suffering where there is "weeping and gnashing of teeth," according to Jesus. (Matthew 13:41-43) Perhaps this merely is another example of the necessary opposites needed to create a peaceful diametric center where all opposing forces are neutralized and only both/and remains in some form of black hole where no ego may survive. [The Chartres Labyrinth symbolizes the journey to such a place.] This wisdom was known by Heraclitus in 500 B.C. who said, "All things come into being by conflict of opposites." And William Blake (1757-1827) concurred in 1790; "Without contraries there is no progression. Attraction and repulsion, reason and emotion, love and hate, birth and death, all are necessary to human existence."

Medical researcher, Dr. Bernie Siegel, divided terminal patients into three groups. One group was ready to die, even welcomed it and refused any exceptional treatment beyond hospice comfort care. He described one such patient thus; "Prognosis abysmal, outlook cheerful." They die with no regrets and no loose ends. Another group docilely followed all the doctor's recommendations, possibly because they did not want to disappoint their close relations who could not let them go. A third group went all out to find the latest treatments and spared no expense to prolong the process, including use of world-wide alternative modalities and experimental procedures. In the extreme fringe are those few who arranged for storage of their bodies in a cryogenic deep freeze in hopes that some future miracle with enable their resuscitation. The group you are in must be the will of God the Almighty One, as there can be no other.

Even at the end of life the range of human experience remains vast, extending from intense suffering at one extreme, to a sense of comfort and genuine peace to, at the other admittedly limited extreme, a sense of profound wellness in heart and mind if not in body. When the late movie star Charlton Heston (1923-2008) was informed of his terminal Alzheimer's condition he opined, "I must reconcile courage and surrender in equal measures." So do we all when the ending comes. In the end, there is only surrender as all claims to self control are abolished. After a serious illness, C. G. Jung observed, "When you can give up the crazy will to live and seemingly fall into the bottomless mist then the truly real life begins...it is something ineffably grand."

Perhaps congratulations rather than condolences should be offered to those who survive the ones who achieve this goal. Jessie Pounds (1862-1921) gave us a reminder that helps to heal the final wound of loss in her epic song poem:

"Somewhere the sun is shining,
Somewhere the songbirds dwell;
Hush, then, thy sad repining,
God lives, and all is well.
Somewhere, somewhere,
Beautiful Isle of Somewhere!
Land of the true, where we live anew,
Beautiful Isle of Somewhere!"

You might expect that Americans would professionalize care of the dying and mourners, and so they have with the Association for Death Education and Counseling. This august group of academics, counselors, nurses, and physicians has succeeded in developing a vast amount of dialogue and curriculums for thanatology, the science of dying and grieving. While they give each other various awards and forums for self education, they have not had much impact upon public policies or the preparation of individuals to make the final exit less painful and traumatic. Something more is needed. Perhaps this can be done only by one person at a time. Composer, Wolfgang Mozart (1756-1791) wrote to his terminally ill father, "As death, when we come to consider it closely, is the true goal of our existence, I have formed during the last few years such close relations with this best and truest friend of mankind, that his image is not only no longer terrifying to me, but is indeed very soothing and consoling! And I thank my God for graciously granting me the opportunity of learning that death is the key which unlocks the door to our true happiness."

Death is not the enemy. It is the goal. Practicing is not doing, and with this task, you only do it once per lifetime. If we do it right, perhaps we can enjoy life, let it go when it is time, and die with a smile on our face. Maybe we can die feeling content, if not totally satisfied. But hey, sheeple get what they get in life, not necessarily what they deserve. Nearly dying changes nothing; dying changes everything. Christians who have a personal relationship with Jesus sing, "Why do I sing about Jesus? Why is he precious to me? He is my Lord and my Savior. Dying, he set me free." Faith as that of a child in Santa Claus, that is all. All in the will of God the Almighty One, of course.

Although death-denying practices have been mounting in American society over the past century, it is possible to ease into a new era in which we take death by the hand and begin to accommodate its anxieties. If we can manage to bring death into the light through discussion in children and adults as well as education about the realities of death, and the natural desire of human egos to avoid it, our nation may be better able to cope with loss and its accompanying emotions. It is necessary for us to eliminate the idea that death is something shameful or dirty, as well as to encourage mourning more openly among survivors. Some strides have been made in America in terms of death awareness in recent decades. Aside from rising numbers of sheeple being cremated, there also are new green cemeteries and other more environmentally-friendly disposal methods to consider.

In addition, we are slowly progressing emotionally. Can you imagine taking school children on field trips to cemeteries and funeral homes? Some elementary schools provide "death-ed" programs for fourth graders which includes discussions, art projects, and essays. Such programs allow children to express their fears and anxieties in a healthy atmosphere and to realize that they are not alone in their concerns. Grieving is necessary and natural, and it's up to society and the media to change our way of thinking and allow for expressions of sorrow when the situation calls for them. None of these changes are easy, but if we as a nation recognize the cost in distancing ourselves from our death-affirming roots and the unhealthy practices that followed, we will be able to return to these roots over time and to establish a healthier relationship with death.

Perhaps it is best just to live so that when the time comes, we can say with Apostle Paul, "...the time has come for my departure. I have fought the good fight, I have finished the race, I have kept the faith." (2 Timothy 4:6-7) St. Teresa of Avila (1515-1582) expressed her completion in words of her autobiography, "I sometimes say to Him with my whole will: To die, Lord, or to suffer! I ask nothing else of Thee for myself but this. It comforts me to hear a clock strike, for when I find that another hour of life has passed away, I seem to be getting a little nearer to the vision of God." And, of course, from the cross Jesus declared, "It is finished." In the end all we have left are the memories of life, and for some of us with Alzheimers not even that, so it seems like a good idea to pile up as many good ones as possible among those we leave behind. Jesus cautioned not to lay up for ourselves corruptible treasures on Earth but rather incorruptible treasures in heaven.

Perhaps Alfred Lord Tennyson (1809-1892) gave us a model for dying in his classic poem, "Crossing the bar," which he wrote three years before his death. "Sunset and evening star, And one clear call for me. And may there be no moaning at the bar when I put out to sea." His rhyme calls up imagery of retired sheeple enjoying the balmy recreational life on a fertile isle, like Hawaii, where there is a party on the beach each evening but surrounded by the vast infinity and darkness of the ocean horizon. You have arrived from the mainland anticipating a wonderful time of life when you can do as you please and rest up afterward, not realizing that it was a one-way trip. Such is life. Imagine that at the peak of a glorious sunset each day a small canoe appears with the tide that has someone's name on it. You watch each time as the one selected climbs into the small craft and disappears over the breakers, never to be seen again, washed out into the great unknown of infinite seas as the sky turns darker and then goes completely black. It takes the dark night of the soul to look up and see the stars spread out among the universe that remind us how small we really are, and then comes the day again.

We cannot be sure what lies upon the other shore because no one has ever returned to tell us. The New Testament authors wrote that Jesus gave opposing images. On one hand he described a place of "wailing and gnashing of teeth," based upon fear of a God who can cast you into hell after he kills the body. (Luke 12:4-5, Luke 13: 28-30, Luke 16: 22-25) On the other hand, he comforted his disciples with the instruction, "don't be anxious about tomorrow..." because, "who by worrying can add a single hour to his life?" and he used the image of lilies in the field to assure them the heavenly Father knows what you need. (Matthew 6: 25-34) Although each person may seem insignificant on the scale of the universe, they also seem to be absolutely indispensable in the eye of God, just like a sparrow that falls to the ground. (Matthew 19:29-31, Luke 12:6-7)

English poet and priest, John Donne (1572-1631) wrote in his meditations later penned as a poem, "No man is an island, entire of itself; every man is a piece of the continent, a part of the main...Any man's death diminishes me, because I am involved in mankind; and therefore never send to know for whom the bell tolls; it tolls for thee." Donne, who was a priest of many sorrows, cited Psalm 68: 19-20 in his final sermon before he died, "Praise be to the Lord, to God our savior who daily bears our burdens. Our God is a God who saves; from the sovereign Lord comes escape from death." In the sermon he declared, "...unto God the Lord belong the issues of death, that is, the disposition and manner of our death: what kind of issue and transmigration we shall have out of this world, whether prepared or sudden, whether violent or natural, whether in our perfect senses or shaken and disordered by sickness, there is no condemnation to be argued out of that, no judgment to be made upon that, for howsoever they die, precious in his sight is the death of his saints, and with him are the issues of death, the ways of our departing out of this life are in his hands. And so in this sense of the words, this exitus mortis, the issue of death, is liberatio in morte, a deliverance in death; Not that God will deliver us from dying, but that he will have the care of us in the hour of death, of what kind soever our passage be."

At sunset one day the canoe drifts up on the sand with your name on it and just sits there waiting for you to get in. And you recall the saying of the Apostle Paul; "...give thanks in all circumstances for this is God's will for you..." (1 Thessalonians 5:18) St. Theresa of Lisieux (1873-1897) declared, "Jesus does not demand great actions from us but simply surrender and gratitude." Feel good inside no matter what happens outside. Think you can handle that?

11. Rights to Passage.

Life among Homo sapiens is similar to that of a small fish photographed for the documentary titled, "Life" produced by Discovery Channel. After it hatches at the base of a waterfall it must climb up the rocks against the downpour until it reaches the calm water at the top where they live for a short lifetime. Many don't make it, falling back to become prey fish for larger species. At the top the strongest survivors must fight against the current until they can mature enough to spawn and lay eggs that are swept over the falls to repeat the cycle of life again and again. Nature is full of such stories. Another is the fate of the Pacific Octopus. The female reproduces only once and when the time comes, she deposits more than 100,000 eggs in a secure location about the rocks hidden from predators and protects them for six months without eating anything herself. As the hatchlings break free of their egg shells and float off into open waters, their mother slowly dies. There is a small amphibian frog that carries her newly born infants to safe lodging in the wide ferns of large plants and feeds each of them one unfertilized egg each day until they are big enough to fend for themselves. Many human societies have developed rights to passage that test the courage and stamina of young men to obtain the full benefits of membership. One such in Africa requires sticking their arm up to the elbow in a bees nest and absorbing the stings without flinching. On the island of Pentecost in the south Pacific, young men are expected to prove their bravery by "land diving" off of a 100 foot tall tower strapped by their feet so their heads barely touch the ground. This practice was the genesis of bungee-jumping. There are similar traditions for young women, including female circumcision, among some primitive tribes.

While there are rights to passage for youth entering maturity, [the Catholics have their First Communion and Jews celebrate their Bar Mitzwah] departing life has no such formal rituals in America [except maybe for the last rites of the Catholic church]. Poet Robert Frost (1874-1963) concluded near the end of his life, "It is hard to get into this life and hard to get out. And what lies in between doesn't make much sense." Apostle Paul wrote, "No temptation has seized you except what is common to man. God is faithful; he will not let you be tempted beyond what you can bear. But when you are tempted, he will also provide a way out so that you can stand up under it." (1 Corinthians 10:12-14) He obviously lied, because life often deals some sheeple blows they cannot contain. Jesus warned his favorite apostle Simon Peter, "I tell you the truth, when you were younger you dressed yourself and went where you wanted; but when you are old you will stretch out your hands, and someone else will dress you and lead you where you do not want to go." (John 21:18) Thousands of sheeple commit murders and suicide by violent means each year because life becomes too much. One recent example was a New York financial advisor who lost billions of his clients' money by investing in the illegal Ponzi scheme of Bernard Madoff. He just slit his wrists and sat at his desk until he bled to death. A fisherman who thought his lifelong profession ended with the oil spill in the Gulf of Mexico ended his life, leaving his wife and teenaged children to live on without him. Celebrated author, Ernest Hemingway concluded that "life breaks everybody." He committed suicide at age 62.

We expend a great in learning how to live but we invest practically nothing in learning how to die. The results are all too apparent. Without a psychology of dying Homo sapiens suffer the most of any species on the planet. Some religious leaders are convinced that sheeple should tolerate as much suffering as they are given in order to affirm some meaning to life before they die or maybe even to earn more grace in heaven. Buddhists may think that suffering must be completed in this life or it will just be deferred until the next one and the next. Mother Teresa taught her nuns, "We must take what he gives and give what he takes with a big smile." She was ill for ten years before she died. In the end she said she no longer prayed and wrote to Jesus, "My soul is no longer one with you." The founder of Logotherapy and a survivor of the Holocaust, psychiatrist Victor Frankl, (1905-1997) claimed that grief and suffering are necessary to experience a whole life among humankind. This is a curious line of reasoning as millions of lives are sacrificed in wars that have no meaning in the long run, as he should know.

Now we have preemptive wars to avert human suffering by causing suffering, but we cannot legally conduct preemptive suicide to avert personal suffering. Go figure. All religions seem to be driven by a universal need among Homo sapiens to find some meaning to a temporary life that ends in death with no certainty about what comes after. In contrast, the founder of western psychotherapy, Sigmund Freud (1856-1939) was aided to die by his physician in London where he had moved to escape the Holocaust. A heavy cigar smoker, Freud endured more than 30 operations to deter mouth cancer possibly related to his continuous cigar smoking. Finally, he prevailed on his doctor and friend Max Schur to assist him in assisted suicide. After reading Balzac's novel "La Peau de chagrin" in a single sitting he wrote, "My dear Schur, you certainly remember our first talk. You promised me then not to forsake me when my time comes. Now life is nothing but torture and makes no sense any more." [The novel is about a man who discovers a powerful talisman in an old curiosity shop. The talisman is in the form of an animal skin. It grants any wish, but shrinks slightly with each use, and the user is doomed to die when it shrinks to zero.] Dr. Schur administered three excessive doses of morphine over several hours that resulted in Freud's death on September 23, 1939. Apparently, he found no conflict with the Hippocratic oath to "do no harm."

Among the "certain inalienable rights" identified by our founders in the U.S. Constitution, the right to die peacefully as we choose was not listed among them. This omission has left a trail of suffering and family trauma in its wake ever since. What possible form of logic or religion would entomb a person in a suffering, worthless body who no longer wants to occupy it? Are not the terms of your final exit the most precious of all personal freedoms? Absent the freedom to die, once you are admitted to a hospital there is no limit to how much will be done trying to keep you alive unless you have specifically filed a legal "living will" that spells out your wishes, and maybe not even then. The argument that since only God can make a life only he should end it falls through the cracks of human terminal suffering. Those who claim the final suffering was a good time of personal growth and renewal of relationships only testify to how broken our society really is. English poet John Keats (1795-1821) had this opinion: "Do you not see how necessary a world of pain and troubles is to school an intelligence and make it a soul?" Perhaps without suffering we are just a head without a heart. Or, perhaps God created so much suffering so that death would seem like a blessing in comparison. Like, we suffer because it feels so good when it ends. It must be necessary or it would be different. In any event, the prohibition on ending one's life to curtail suffering makes no sense at all. It is time to begin the debate.

Dr. Jack Kevorkian went to prison for helping to end human life at the patient's request. Of death he wrote as the caption to one of his paintings, "Despite the solace of hypocritical religiosity and its seductive promise of an after-life of heavenly bliss, most of us will do anything to thwart the inevitable victory of biological death. We contemplate and face it with great apprehension, profound fear, and terror. Sparing no financial or physical sacrifice, pleading wantonly and unashamedly, clutching any hope of salvation through medicine or prayer. How forbidding that dark abyss! How stupendous the yearning to dodge its gaping orifice. How inexorable the engulfment. Yet, the disintegrating hulks of those who have gone before; they have made the insensible transition and wonder what the fuss is all about. After all, how excruciating can nothingness be?" Kevorkian claims he was doing his sworn medical duty in helping sheeple die by relieving suffering, but his critics claim he was doing harm, even murder.

You be the judge. Is it euthanasia to help a person in the final stage of life to terminate his torture when it becomes intolerable? For those who have no family care givers able to provide the necessary and humiliating terminal services, there needs to be the option of ending misery when the benefits of living no longer exceed the burdens. Perhaps it is time for legislators to look realistically at the emotional and the financial cost of keeping terminally sick sheeple from release of their suffering, if nothing else. Family members may need to face up to this reality and let them go with dignity when that is their choice.

Perhaps the fact that religions cannot provide the needed support and comfort when facing death makes some sheeple just try to defer it as long as possible. If the Church has not been able to prepare sheeple to die in 2,000 years, there is little hope it can change in a single generation. So, a secular movement is underway to help sheeple take charge of their own dying. If sheeple have the freedom of legalized birth control by abortion, which no one can deny is terminating a human life although we can argue about whether a fetus has any legal rights, why not also the freedom of legalized death control? If government permits a woman control of her living unborn defenseless fetus, how can government criminalize the control over ones own body at the end of life? This debate was brought to light with formation of the Hemlock Society by Derek Humphrey in 1980 (now replaced by several other seeded organizations) and its popular manual, "Final Exit." The Final Exit Network of volunteers was set up in 2004 to help sheeple with assistance when they are ready and determined to stop their own suffering. It trains and helps sheeple who no longer wish to suffer through terminal illness to relieve themselves of the burdens by saying goodbye and moving on when suffering becomes intolerable. Its manifesto claims; "In a spirit of compassion for all, this manifesto proclaims that every competent adult has the incontestable right to humankind's ultimate civil and personal liberty – the right to die in a manner and time of their own choosing." [www.finalexitnetwork.org] Opponents rightly fear that some family members may encourage or even coerce the old-old members who are merely financial, emotional, and physical burdens to opt out of life in order to save what is left of their meager inheritance.

Final Exit volunteers have been arrested in sting operations in Georgia and harassed in other areas by police actions initiated by some who think life should be preserved and suffered at all costs to the victims and their families, but their voice is being heard in Canada where freedom of speech is not abridged by religious bigotry. There you can attend "safe suicide" workshops by Dr. Philip Nischke of Australia. [www.exitinternational.net] But his attempts to conduct workshops in the U.S. are met with delays and restrictions on his visa applications. When life presents nothing but future emotional suffering, physical pain, humiliation, embarrassment, and defeat, why should sheeple not be able to decide for themselves how much is enough and with the aid of their physician, end it with some degree of comfort? Does not the same logic apply here as it does with fetal abortions? Why should a pregnant woman have control of her body with the aid of a physician to expel an unwanted living helpless, defenseless fetus, while the old and suffering ones have not the same option to vacate a body that is "nothing but torture?"

Although many states have rejected attempts to enact enabling legislation the issue of physician assisted suicide (PAS) is not going away as evidenced by the growing number of Internet sites discussing the issues. How long will it take for this policy to reach critical mass as a contagious idea whose time has come? Those who oppose this final medical service so emotionally assume that since only God gives life he should be the only one to take it, i.e., man should not play God. But they do all the time by invoking interventions that delay death, thereby playing God. Since the United States will not prevent doctors from aborting viable pregnancies, why do they wish to prevent medical aid for the final exit? Could it be that medical providers want to extend treatment so long as there is anyone to pay for it, including the taxpayers? When terminal illness destroys the personhood of one who is dying and leaves lifelong incurable emotional and psychological scars of post traumatic stress upon all the survivors and care givers, why should it not be shortened so the memories of a loved one will not be poisoned with recollections of horrific inhumane debilitation, humiliation, and suffering? Of course, the opposite idea is that anyone who can afford it and wants it should be treated so long as possible. But, who pays for those who cannot afford it?

Maybe it is better to live in blissful ignorance of the worst case scenarios than to face terminal suffering for all the lifelong pain and grief it causes for survivors. Where is the line between causing suffering and alleviating it in the Hippocratic oath that says doctors should "do no harm.?" Is it euthanasia to help a person in the final stage of life to terminate his torture when it becomes intolerable for the patient and emotional trauma for survivors? Those opponents who argue against termination of suffering and claim the "right to die" may become the "duty to die" may think differently when it comes their turn for hopeless suffering and life is "nothing but torture." Perhaps even the duty to die may not be far from debate as the cost of keeping all the baby boomers alive becomes intolerable to taxpayers. Reform of medical services must inevitably confront the impossible financial burden of keeping terminally ill sheeple alive during their last few years.

At present physician-assisted suicide is legal in the U.S. only in Washington, Oregon, and Montana and in the Netherlands, Switzerland, Luxemborg, and Belgium. Australia passed such a law in 1996 but the Parliament reversed itself after nine months in a fit of collective conscience after successful lobbying by the churches. It is legal in Switzerland for foreigners to travel to the country to commit assisted suicide, and dozens do so each year. One such journey to Switzerland was documented by PBS in a program called, "The Suicide Tourist," that depicted the decision by one man to avoid the terminal suffering in ALS by his own hand. One just drinks an overdose of sodium pantathal and goes to sleep forever. Opponents usually express emotional repugnance based upon religious beliefs rather than rational logic. They claim it is playing God to choose one's own death and suffering must be tolerated, but they ignore all the medical attempts to prolong life outside the will of God and the lethal abortion of a helpless fetus by an accommodating doctor.

If there is a God, only an unjust, uncompassionate, unfeeling God would allow the suffering that goes on to extend life when a person is already dying a natural death. So a terminally ill patient suffering the torments of hell may be totally justified in requesting physician-assisted release. However, surveys indicate that one fifth of physicians may be unable to rationally manage end of life support for their patients because they have not accepted their own mortality; and they just do not learn how to do it med-schools. This issue is not at all about the sanctity of life. There is dignity and even comfort in natural death. That dignity is lost and can turn into cruelty with well-intended attempts at keeping terminal sheeple alive until their money or insurance runs out. Any religion that says it's divine law that dying has to be suffered as long as necessary is a religion not worth serving. There is nothing in the Holy Bible or the Holy Koran to support that notion.

Under current law, assisting a suicide is a crime punishable by up to 14 years in prison in England and Wales. But, in the U.K. doctors may concur legally in a patient's decision to refuse food and drink, which can bring death in from 5 to 25 days. As a result, many patients travel abroad to foreign clinics in Switzerland, where assisted suicide is permitted.

Although relatives who arrange such trips are subject to prosecution when they return, no one has been arrested. Mexico and Uruguay permitted terminally ill patients to refuse further treatment, over vicious objections by the Catholic Church. A high court in Australia permitted a quadriplegic man to refuse water and food without prejudice to the nursing home where he had lived since 1988, and so enabled him to die in his own time. About fifty sheeple take their physician-assisted option in Oregon annually, while about ten times that number die by unassisted suicide when life becomes unbearable. Why so many suicidal sheeple decline the legal service has not been studied because the subjects are no longer available for analysis. Perhaps the main reason is the law requires medical certification of only six months left to live, and for many who take their lives that is far too late.

Future costs of terminal care for the aging baby boomers may tax social resources so much that physician-assisted suicide may be legalized nationally throughout the U.S. out of fiscal necessity. Until then, perhaps the best one can hope for at the end of life is "twilight sleep" or terminal sedation - the furthest reach of hospice palliative care - drugging a suffering dying patient into unconsciousness with a barbiturate and keeping him that way until he expires, days or weeks later for lack of food and water or treatment of acute disease except for symptom relief. The key word here is "terminal" because many doctors refuse such treatment to younger patients and those who may have some remote chance of life extension. Death must be confidently within weeks for most doctors to prescribe such drugs because they are addictive and are causing more lawsuits all the time among survivors. For some patients, the treatment may be worse than the illness. Failing that, suffering terminal patients may survive months or years in a chronic state of stupor, humiliation, and biological decay before death mercifully ends it. Can you imagine what a human body looks like that is ravaged by gangrene before it finally dies? Meantime, the patient, family, and friends can only be helpless spectators as the drama unfolds, and then live with the traumatic memories and financial burden that follows.

Terminal sedation is not practiced openly and is not without some controversy, but it does not seem to carry a high incidence of complication. The lack of it can make the end stage of life worse than death for patients and scar their survivors for life. More than seventy percent of respondents to an online survey by AOL said they would consider helping a terminally suffering loved one commit suicide if it were legal. When life comes down to nothing but suffering and struggle, what logical reasoning would result in prolonging it? The power of capitalism to continue treatments and threats by the Church of burning forever in hell easily overcomes logical reasoning among care givers of the sheeple who no longer may be able to care for themselves. When it is time to change because it hurts too much not to, perhaps sheeple who no longer abhor death and wish to leave their suffering bodies will be given socially and legally sanctioned physician assistance to leave it, just as unwanted fetuses are aborted now with physician assistance. Most religions teach that death is but a door to another and better home for the worthy ones, so why all the reluctance to make the passage? Perhaps many assume they are unworthy because so many will fight to the end, whatever the cost and emotional toll, to avoid the trip. As in all decisions, there are no mistakes, just choices and consequences. In this life one does not always get what he pays for, but most everyone will pay for what he gets. But God the Almighty One always wins.

The release of Dr. Jack Kevorkian from prison for assisting hundreds of terminally ill sheeple to commit suicide and release of a movie, "You Don't Know Jack," about his crusade to legalize medical termination of inhuman suffering, could bring this issue back to the front pages. Euthanizing pets is a common practice to alleviate their suffering and reduce terminal expenses, but we tolerate human suffering to such a degree that the post traumatic stress on families and survivors takes a lifelong toll which cannot be justified by any reasonable argument. The only possible opposition is based on faith-based belief that assisted suicide is a form of murder, and therefore is prohibited by God and should be by common law. Committing suicide voluntarily could land a person in Hell for eternity according to this belief. Faith-based beliefs claim that God never gives anyone suffering beyond their tolerance, and suffering provides a form of grace achievable no other way. Since only God can create the most precious gift of human life, he also should be the final arbiter on death, so they say. Opponents also claim that frail and indigent patients may be induced to kill themselves by family members wishing to preserve their financial inheritance. These arguments are easily countered by thinking sheeple. If God gives humans free will, then why not the freedom to set limits upon their own suffering? God does not seem to make a big deal of death in the creation, as it is all over the place, so why should we?

If government can legalize abortion of the living unborn and permit the flower of society to volunteer for death in military service, why not also legalize the right to die on your own terms. Perhaps the financial interests of medical and medicine providers should be removed from the debate, because so long as money is available for treatment they will seek it. Who is to tell anyone what to do with their money, whether to donate it to charity or leave it to heirs instead of squandering it on impotent medical treatment that only prolongs suffering for a few months. The claims that we are a nation under the rule of law that values freedom above all other values sets up a conflict that will require the wisdom of Solomon to resolve. When taxpayers can no longer afford to keep all the terminally ill baby boomers alive, the taboo may be overcome by fiscal necessity. But, sheeple will not change until it hurts too much not to, so the time is not yet. However, the Supreme Court has refused to overturn the assisted suicide laws in Oregon and Washington and Montana saying it was not a matter for Federal intervention. So the future or assisted suicide is up to the states.

In the meantime, the financial and psychological cost of maintaining terminally ill sheeple in a state of suspension for weeks or months or years before death is an increasing social burden that will demand a resolution before long. More than 44 million adults in the U.S. struggle to provide care for a dependent family member or loved one. This number will increase dramatically over the next decade as the baby boomers enter their terminal years. The system is broken, given that more sheeple are living longer with multiple chronic conditions, and few alternatives are available to them except expensive existence in a nursing facility that costs $400 - $500 per day. Per Day. If you live beyond age 80 chances are fifty-fifty you will spend two years or more in such a facility. When 76 million aging baby boomers are put on life support, who will pay for all their bills? More than half the cost of Medicare is disbursed in the final two years of life and maintaining the indigent under Medicaid is stressing the state budgets. If they have to choose between terminal care of aging and schools for the young, which should prevail? Long term treatment of patients with the four chronic killers, heart disease, cancer, Alzheimers, and diabetes will become unaffordable as taxpayers no longer can pay for the long term care needed. Family care givers now often are left bankrupt and destitute and emotionally scarred when a loved one dies after a long illness in old age, so it is likely that a debate about generational competition is inevitable.

As the baby boomer generation approaches its demise, the cost of sustaining their bodies in acute care past all hope of survival during the last months may no longer be financially sustainable. So this is not just a moral issue but a social one as well. The debate about universal medical care stumbles over the necessity of rationing treatment for the aged so those younger ones most likely to benefit from it for the longest time can be helped. Keeping old sheeple alive under conditions of imminent death not only is fiscally irresponsible, it also is cruel and inhumane. Until the past century, sheeple just got sick and died. Now, it is possible for medical science to "keep a stone alive" according to one physician, for those patients and families who cannot accept pending death of a loved one.

Billions of dollars spent on research for treating the chronic killers has only served to keep sheeple alive and suffering for longer periods of time. Therapist Mary Pipher described in Another Country (1999) the trauma of watching her mother, a doctor, die slowly and hospitalized the last year of her life. "She had diabetes along with its cruel problems – peritonitis, heart and liver failure, vomiting, chills, and leg cramps. She was bed ridden, bloated and brain damaged. She had skin cancer and osteoporosis and she hallucinated. She had months of ups and downs and then just downs and downs. My mother's last year was a worst case scenario, and then she died alone." One senior complained, "My age is my cage, and only death can free me." In the end, we all die leaving post trauma shock behind for the survivors.

Pipher concluded, "Everybody carries heavy burdens...everybody." Her trauma was so great she closed her therapy practice to avoid hearing any more such family stories. Dysfunctional families and those with unresolved issues of remorse and guilt often are the most ardent in deferring death at all cost. In contrast, sheeple who have lived a good life and reach the end of it are more likely to detach from a useless suffering body and say goodbye without the wrenching efforts to sustain a beating heart long after its usefulness is passed. This writer made the decision to decline life support for his comatose wife a week before she died, and although it might have prolonged her agony the outcome would have been the same with a lot more post trauma shock for survivors. But, the law is the law, so they say. Since we are a nation of laws, let's consider the law. A reasonable examination of this issue may not be delayed much longer as the debate on reforming medical care enters a critical and acute stage. The nation just cannot afford to keep all the aging terminal patients alive for as long as it can. That's the fact, Jack.

The Oregon Death With Dignity Act (ODWDA) exempts from civil or criminal liability state-licensed physicians who, in compliance with specific safeguards, dispense or prescribe a lethal dose of drugs upon the request of a terminally ill patient with estimated less than six months to live. Voters in Washington state approved a similar law in 2008. In a decision issued on January 17, 2006 the U.S. Supreme Court affirmed this usage of toxic drugs was "for a legitimate medical purpose by an individual practitioner acting in the usual course of his professional practice." Judge Antonin Scalia wrote, "The court's decision today is perhaps driven by a feeling that the subject of assisted suicide is none of the federal government's business." However, there still are more then ten times the number of conventional suicides as there are controlled DWD deaths in Oregon, 562 against 49 during 2007. What accounts for this disparity is unknown because the dead cannot be interviewed. Perhaps the sheeple committing suicides have undiagnosed and untreated mental illness or their doctors would not cooperate, or they just don't want to suffer more until they qualify for DWD, which must be deferred until the last six months of life. Or, as C. G. Jung concluded, "Sometimes the divine asks too much of us." Google "murder-suicide" on the Internet and you will find increasing accounts of couples and parents exterminating whole families when the burdens of life become unbearable.

As for the concern of the Church that assisting suicide is a form of murder and, therefore, punishable in hell, well whatever happened to permitting a person to die when his time has come? Where ever religion and law diverge, which should be the ultimate arbiter? The answer has been given in the abortion debate wherein a pregnant woman can terminate a life of her own choosing. If we can legally terminate life of innocent, helpless human infants, why not let the mature suffering ones do likewise? Should there not be room for both views according to the desire of the patient? Those who claim that assisted suicide is intrinsically wrong force many sheeple to take the matter into their own hands. How can any doctor rationalize taking the life of an unborn infant and refuse to help a rational adult to shorten his suffering?

The fact is, and doctors know it, that death often is hastened by withholding treatment, food, and water, or administering higher dosages of pain killers, which could be called assisted suicide, maybe even euthanasia, as it is. After all, this is the mode of exit among Hospice patients. Some doctors may take aggressive action, such as administering excessive morphine, phenobarbital or sodium pentathal, to hasten death. Most states permit sheeple to create a living will and a "do not resuscitate" (DNR) order if it is their wish to avoid extended terminal suffering, although less than 20 percent do so. Assisting suicide is not specifically illegal in seven states, but unfortunately, the rate of lawsuits for malpractice often induces hospitals to prolong suffering if some family members resist or oppose the final wishes of the patient to refuse further treatment. In a few high profile cases, a court of law has had to intervene when family members disagreed about end of life treatment.

If you go to hospital without a living will it is most likely you will be kept alive as long as possible, no matter the cost or suffering. So, it is very important for everyone to have a living will and durable power of attorney on file with the hospital and the doctor to assure that their wishes will be honored. Even then, it is uncertain whether they will be or not. Can we, as a society, assume the faith of Alfred Lord Tennyson (1809-1892) as he mused about his demise; "Sunset and evening star, And one clear call for me! And may there be no moaning of the bar when I put out to sea..." Will we take up the call of Dr. Jack Kevorkian and Dr. Philip Nitschke and let doctors fulfill their oath by first, doing no harm, when prolonging suffering of those with no hope is the cruelest act of all? Will we grant sheeple their final act of freedom? In the absence of a rational debate, many sheeple take this matter into their own hands when the struggle and suffering of life become too much. As recently as 2003, almost twice as many sheeple committed suicide as died from murder, and the rate of suicide is increasing. There should be a better way out when life becomes "nothing but torture" and suffering becomes intolerable.

There were 32,637 suicides in the U.S. during 2005. Elderly sheeple accounted for about fifteen percent of these. Suicides actually declined somewhat from about 13 per 100,000 in 1950 to 10 per 100,000 in 2003. This does not include medically induced deaths as no figures are kept for obvious reasons. The increasing baby boomer population will no doubt bring this option up for discussion in many families, or not. Families and medical teams often must grapple with the anxiety of uncertainty about the future cost and suffering imposed by terminal aging. C. G. Jung seemed to be ambivalent about suicide as he wrote, "The idea of suicide, understandable as it is, does not seem commendable to me. To interrupt life before its time is to bring to a standstill an experiment which we have not set up. We have found ourselves in the midst of it and must carry it through to the end. But, I have seen cases where it would have been something short of criminal to hinder the patient because according to all rules it was in accordance with the tendency of their unconscious. So I think nothing is really gained by interfering with such an issue. It is presumably to be left to the free choice of the individual. Anything that seems to be wrong to us can be right under certain circumstances over which we have no control and the end of which we do not understand."

[A hospice nurse tells a story on the Internet of one family she helped with the transition of their grandmother. There was a five year old little grandson who liked to crawl up onto the bed and have his grandma tell him a story, which she was happy to do. After the family watched her passage, the little boy crawled onto the bed, raised one of her eyelids and staring into her unseeing eye he asked, "Grandma, are you in there?" After getting no response he slid down off the bed and someone said, "Grandma is gone and she cannot tell you anymore stories." The little boy thought for a moment and then said, "OK."]

Death comes eventually and the only remaining issue is how much post traumatic stress and financial burden will be left for survivors to live with. Those facing terminal illness in Oregon who have requested physician aid for suicide have described concerns about such issues as losing autonomy, 89 per cent; cessation of activities making life enjoyable, 87 per cent; loss of dignity, 82 per cent; losing control of bodily functions, 58 per cent; burden on family or friends, 39 per cent; inadequate pain control or concern about it, 27 per cent; and financial implications of treatment, 2.7 per cent. Sooner or later the emotional taboo over this matter must be lifted so the legal debate can begin. When the ego no longer commands control of life it may seek control of death. And those who cannot abide the suffering may discover that the carbon monoxide used by Dr. Kevorkian illegally is available from the exhaust pipes of their own cars or a smoldering pit of charcoal. A 1.2% concentration of carbon monoxide can cause unconsciousness after three inhales and death in less then three minutes. Helium also works efficiently, but it is not so easily available. If you can tolerate the side effects, just eliminating water will cause fatal dehydration in about a week. Often, desperate sheeple use more bloody and gruesome methods to leave planet Earth. Sneaking some brand of Nembutal used for euthanizing pets from veterinary suppliers in Mexico is one of them. A nation that authorizes physicians to terminate the lives of an unborn fetus while criminalizing a terminally ill patient's desire to end his suffering when survival becomes moot is insane. Keeping all the baby boomers alive as long as possible also will make it bankrupt. All in the will of God the Almighty One, of course.

12. WHERE DO WE GO WHEN WE DIE?

Short answer: nobody knows. Long answer: read on. The hope of immortality runs deep in the psyche of Homo sapiens and extends back as long as written history. It seems to be the one question that everyone wants answered and the one that is most elusive, what happens after death? After loss of a loved one, or several, it seems that human nature cannot abide the thought that they are gone forever. It seems that Homo sapiens all want some reassurance that life goes on after death. But the proof is elusive. Every week it seems that another book that attempts to prove life after death is published for those who need such assurance. A search of "life after death" on Amazon.com produces 48,320 different book titles. One critic and skeptic wrote that they seem to, "...bring together a mishmash of quantum theory, neuroscience, personal accounts of paranormal experiences, and bad logic. They use the usual crank theorist characteristics of jumping to unwarranted conclusions and being highly selective about their evidence."

Nevertheless, something, maybe it is ego, wants to hope that life goes on and on and on. We suffer, as the Buddha reminds us, because we want to live in separated ego states, and bodies enable us to seem separated from each other. If we did not want to live in separation we would not suffer the pains of living in a temporary body. But if there is a world of spirit and spirit is not subject to physical suffering, now we get interested. But, alas, it is mostly just a hope even though apparently a necessary one for most sheeple. Even the words get lost in translations.

For example the Greek word for soul and life are the same. So, how can life exist after life? It makes no sense. But then, who said that religion must be sensible? In fact, there is nothing so unreasonable as the power of faith. Sheeple are determined to believe all manner of things for which there is no evidence or scientific proof. That is one of the things that makes humankind human.

The human ego just cannot stand the thought if its own extinction. The awareness of our mortality causes acute existential anxiety, so sheeple have created many myths in order to avoid the inevitable confrontation with death, which brings the greatest fear of mankind, loss of self awareness. When it comes to where we go after we die, there are many variations of opinions based in religions of varying origins, but no one knows for sure. No one. Not even Pope Benedict XVI, [a.k.a. Joseph Cardinal Ratzinger], who tried to explain it all in his <u>Eschatology, Death and Eternal Life</u>. (1988) His scholarly treatment of immortality leads only to the conclusion of Apostle Paul who called it a "mystery." (1 Corinthians 15:51) Although Christianity is based upon the assumed resurrection of the dead, the only proof is faith in the Bible scriptures which are subject to widely varying interpretations and various translations. Referring to Luke 17:20-25, which says, "the Kingdom of God is within you," the Pope wrote, "This statement is so hard to translate that every translation must be an interpretation...the mystery of the Kingdom does not disclose itself in this kind of observation...No one can turn the Bible into descriptive history what is still to come and has not yet been experienced...In the case of immortality, what the New Testament offers to reflection is a beginning, not an end." Thus, every generation of theologians has added its range of interpretations to the confusion of voices that rages on, whether from God or Satan, no one knows. Thomas Jefferson edited and wrote his own personal Unitarian version of the Jesus teachings, and the Jesus Seminar organized a group of theologians to annotate the gospel scriptures with their probability of authenticity in <u>The Five Gospels</u> (1996) from probably yes to probably no. Visit www.biblegateway.com for many different translations of the Bible.

Similarly, the doctrine of Purgatory, a temporary place after death of interim punishment for purification from venial (not mortal) sins apart from God, has a long history in the Church but a very slim

Biblical basis, if any. It is rooted in writings of Pope Gregory (540-604 A.D. and some claim in 1 Corinthians 3:10-15. The Bible can be very confusing so there is good reason for Catholics to rely upon the Pope for holy interpretations.

[Consider these contradictions for example: "Moreover, the Father judges no one, but has entrusted all judgment to the Son."(John 5:22) "You judge by human standards, I pass judgment on no one."(John 8:15) "I am not seeking glory for myself; but there is one who seeks it, and he is the judge." (John 8:50) "For judgment I have come into this world so that the blind will see and those who see will become blind." (John 9:39) Since Jesus claimed he would be the final judge, was he referring to himself? (Matthew 16:27)]

Pope Benedict concluded, "Only as the actual course of history unfolds does reality fill the scripture with content and shed light on the meaning of its various aspects...For this reason, the interpretation of scripture must be incomplete...And so the reader himself is taken up into the adventure of the world and he can understand it only as a participant, not as a spectator." Of that adventure he declared, "The only truly Biblical doctrine is that which holds that when a man dies he perishes, body and soul. The proper Christian thing is to speak not of the soul's immortality, but of the resurrection of the complete human being and of that alone." He referenced no scriptures to support his claim. That opinion of the Pope would seem to negate the possibility of souls with unforgiven venial sins living temporarily in Purgatory that the Church teaches. It also conflicts with the Catholic Catechism, Section 958, "Communion with the Dead."

Considering the infallibility claimed for the Pope, this notion seems in conflict with a statement of Jesus; "I tell you, my friends, do not be afraid of those who kill the body and after that can do no more. But I will show you whom you should fear: Fear him who, after the killing of the body, has power to throw you into hell. Yes, I tell you, fear him." (Luke 12:4-5) This implies that after death of the body, there is still a "you." The King James Bible uses the word "hell" 54 times, 31 in the Old Testament. Each of those in the Old Testament was replaced with the word "grave" by the New International Version, but not in the New Testament. Only in Psalm 9:17 does scripture specifically say that bad sheeple go there. Nevertheless, under Pope Gregory the Great in the 6th century, and later Dante Alighieri (1265-1321) in his epic poem "The Divine Comedy," the Church identified seven deadly sins that are pathways to hell as follows: lust, gluttony, greed, sloth, wrath, envy, and pride. Each of the seven deadly sins has an opposite among the corresponding seven holy virtues (sometimes also referred to as the contrary virtues). In parallel order to the sins they oppose, the seven holy virtues are: chastity, temperance, charity, diligence, patience, kindness, and humility. However, Jesus instructs several times in Mark, Matthew, and Luke (but not in John) to cut off your foot, or hand, or pluck out your eye if it causes you to sin and be cast into hell. Apparently he thought these body parts have a will of their own. He never mentioned the sexual parts, the ones that have ruined many careers of public celebrities and countless ordinary sheeple.

The word "Hades" is used five times, once in Matthew and four times in Revelation as a destination of the wicked. The complete human being is described in the Bible as spirit/mind, body/flesh, and soul. (1Thessalonians 5:22-24) Since these elements are integrated parts of the whole, where it goes they must go. But where they go after death is left up to interpretations, and there are many. The Catholic "Letter on Certain Questions in Eschatology" issued in 1979 by the Congregation for the Doctrine of Faith made conflicting statements; "3. The Church affirms that a spiritual element survives and subsists after death, an element endowed with consciousness and will, so that the human self subsists. To designate this element, the Church uses the word soul, the accepted term in the usage of Scripture and Tradition." And then later it says, "Neither scripture nor theology provides sufficient light for a proper picture of life after death." The latter statement would seem to negate the former. Go figure.

Whether death is a "sleep" or some form of annihilation is not clear in the Bible, either. The first reference to death as sleep is a prophecy assumed to be written about 530 B.C. by Daniel; "Multitudes who sleep in the dust of the Earth will awake: some to everlasting life, others to shame and everlasting contempt. (Daniel 12:3) Jesus refers to the death of Lazarus prior to his resurrection as that of sleep. (John 11:11-14) He said the same about a little girl presumed dead. (Matthew 9:24, Mark 5:39) Apostle Paul refers to death as sleep only once. "Listen, I tell you a mystery: We will not all sleep, but we will all be changed in a flash, in the twinkling of an eye, at the last trumpet. For the trumpet will sound, the dead will be raised imperishable, and we will be changed." That will be quite a miracle for all those bodies that have completely decomposed over the centuries and returned to the dust of the Earth. (1 Corinthians 15:51-52) However, Jesus claimed, "I am the resurrection and the life. He who believes in me will live even though he dies. Whoever lives and believes in me will never die." (John 11:25) And also, "I go to prepare a place for you..." but that was spoken for his disciples and not for everyone ever after who believes in him. He also said, "The spirit gives life, the flesh counts for nothing." (John 6:63) Whether a soul exists and survives to be resurrected again in heaven or hell is among the matters of faith in Christianity. It claims that sheeple all are born sinners and need the saving power of belief in Jesus to assure they will reside with him in some form of afterlife in a new heaven and a new Earth. The famous scripture of John 3:16 is used to affirm this conclusion. However, the Bible also claims that no one must suffer for the sins of their parents but each one must account for his own life on Earth. (Ezekiel 18:19-20, John 9:3) What happens to all those who never hear of Jesus or don't accept John 3:16 is left unexplained. Obviously, this does not account for all the other religions among mankind either. It also claimed that children are role models for heaven, so they must not be born sinners. (Matthew 18:3) Much is left indefinitely uncertain.

Islam is no better. The Koran uses the word "hell" 97 times, several times as the abode of unbelievers. The word "heaven/s" appears 275 times in the Koran, but not once does it say anyone actually is going there unless God wills. "Hasten to forgiveness from your Lord and to a garden the extensiveness of which is as the extensiveness of the heaven and the Earth; it is prepared for those who believe in Allah and His apostles; that is the grace of Allah: He gives it to whom He pleases, and Allah is the Lord of mighty grace." (57.21) The Koran does promise a reward 187 times to those Muslims whom Allah approves, but it is not specified. "Every soul shall taste of death, and you shall only be paid fully your reward on the resurrection day." (3.185) Therefore, let those fight in the way of Allah, who sell this world's life for the hereafter, and whoever fights in the way of Allah, then be he slain or be he victorious, we shall grant him a mighty reward." (4.74) "And whoever brings evil, these shall be thrown down on their faces into the fire; shall you be rewarded for aught except for what you did." (27.90) So, who you gonna believe?

If the Church obviously is confused, where else can we turn? There are many options. C. G. Jung identified several different variations of beliefs among Homo sapiens; rebirth, reincarnation, resurrection, reconstruction, and transmigration. Even a brief investigation of these claims discloses they all have serious flaws and come with no proofs. Nevertheless, many sheeple are given to believe that death is not complete extinction but rather a transition from one form to another as in matter to energy. A growing number of sheeple are being induced by hypnotherapists to produce rich fantasies of "life between lives" while in deep hypnotic trances complete with elaborate visions of spirit guides and a council of Elders who direct their rebirths. They want to believe there is more to their existence than a mortal body and so they are likely to hope that any theory which promises another chance to get it right next time in a better form is true. Everybody seems to need some assurance of immortality. Practically every known culture has some mythical belief about life after death. It seems that the human ego just cannot accept its own extinction. Why this is so is not known unless, of course, God the Almighty One wants it that way. Think you can handle that?

Many sheeple are turning to A Course in Miracles (1975) for the answer. It is claimed to be channeled by scribe, psychologist Dr. Helen Schucman (1909-1981) from the voice of Jesus. It declares; "...because reality is not understandable to the deluded, only a very few can hear God's voice and even they cannot communicate his message through the Spirit. (Why are they deluded unless God made them so?) They need a medium through which communication becomes possible to those who do not realize they are spirit. A body they can see and a voice they can understand and listen to...the body's function is to let God's voice speak through it to human ears." The "Course" claims that any discussion of dying and life after death is moot because there is only Spirit where only love exists at one with God, and human ego made this world one of illusion to propagate a fundamental error in belief that harbors fear and guilt. Why that must be so and who created ego and gave it that task is not explained by the voice of Jesus. But it must be so or it would be otherwise.

The "Course" seems to be an elaborate product of psychological dissociation to enable hope among all the conflict and suffering by creating an imaginary place of peace and harmony in a different realm called heaven which we left at birth, for some unexplained reason. We suffer and cause each other pain so ego can prove it is separated from the Source in a life of illusion. Mankind needs its illusions, we are told, to soften the shock of reality. His reality is so terrible that without illusions he must go mad. So he assumes he does not exist and, thus, cannot die. The despairing psychotic is in some ways more honest than we self-deceived and "adjusted" ones. The most troubled souls may seek answers in counseling and therapy. The fundamental contradiction undermining the therapeutic goal of psychoanalysis lies in the fact that the exposure of defenses and illusions that is supposed to liberate us in reality exposes us to unbearable reality of indefinite uncertainty in the face of which defenses and illusions are indispensable for mental survival. Go figure.

Author and writing consultant Yvonne Perry wrote in More Than Meets the Eye (2005) as if it were true; "Our loved ones who have crossed over communicate with us in a variety of ways. They may bring a familiar smell, or leave coins, feathers or other objects in our path. They may appear as a bird, an animal or take human form. They may come to us in our dreams, or may be the voice we hear in our head. No matter how you sense their presence you can be assured that you're not crazy. They really are near and they want to communicate." Even the Catholic Church has gotten into the act by declaring that it believes in the feasibility of communication with the dead. The Rev. Gino Concetti, chief theological commentator for the Vatican, said the Church remains opposed to the raising of spirits by mediums, but he declared, "Communication is possible between those who live on this Earth and those who live in a state of eternal repose, in heaven or Purgatory. It may even be that God lets our loved ones send us messages to guide us at certain moments in our life." Fr. Concetti said the key to the Church's attitude was the Roman Catholic belief in a "Communion of Saints," which includes Christians on Earth as well as those in the after-life. "Where there is communion, there is communication," he said.

Apostle Paul pictured a cloud of witnesses encompassing Christians on Earth. (Hebrews 12:1) [Perhaps that accounts for those who claim to channel messages from the other side and the books they claim come from such spiritual sources.] Fr. Concetti suggested dead relatives could be responsible for prompting impulses and triggering inspiration - and even for "sensory manifestations," such as appearances in dreams or possibly even seeing ghosts. Of this relationship, Pope Benedict XVI, [a.k.a.: Joseph Cardinal Ratzinger] expanded in his "Eschatology," (1988) "Even when they have crossed over the threshold of the world beyond, human beings can still carry each other and bear each others' burdens. They can still give to each other, suffer for each other, and receive from each other...The possibility of helping and giving does not cease to exist on the death of the Christian. Rather does it stretch out to encompass the entire communion of saints of both sides of death's portals." Hence the Catholic doctrine of prayer for those in Purgatory and the practice of vicarious baptism for the dead conducted by the Church of Latter-Day Saints (Mormons). From such as this the Mormons declare the uniting of families for all eternity even though Jesus claimed in heaven there will be no marrying or giving in marriage because everyone will be as the angels. (Matthew 22:30) This all seems to conflict with the notion that nothing survives death as the Pope said above. But the truth is no one who has died ever came back to tell us what is "over there," and if both body and soul perish at death, as the Pope declared above, there could scarcely be any relationship with the living. So, go figure, again.

Sheeple want to overcome natural anxiety about the unknown so they try to create certainty out of uncertainty by inventing myths, and some would say wishful thinking based upon pseudo-science. So there are plenty of sheeple with opinions and even beliefs that defy reason, some with advanced educations. A belief is not a fact unless there is irrefutable evidence for its truth. Some believe they will go to Heaven immediately after they die if they pass judgment and into Hell if they fail. Others believe that body and soul must wait for some future coming of Christ to be resurrected. Buddhists believe in countless reincarnations until they reach a level of development that needs no further growth, which comes after suffering and detaching from material existence and following the eight-fold path, when the soul reaches a state of spiritual perfection called Nirvana. If everyone could reach that level of enlightenment, there would be eternal peace and prosperity with no suffering. And, of course, there are the images of the Greek god of the underworld Hades, skeletons, and devils that inhabit a place of darkness and everlasting despair for many sheeple. Many writers, poets, and theologians, going back to ancient Vedic culture 2500 years before Greek mythology, have attempted to develop understanding of what comes after death. No one among them knows for sure what the truth of the matter really is, accounts of near-death experiences and poltergeists notwithstanding.

Several books by hypno-therapist, Dr. Michael Newton and others attempt to show how souls serve earthlings while they are in between successive lives on their pathway to reincarnation. Others employ his form of hypnotism for life-between-life therapy, objectives of which are not clear. Newton claims that more than 7,000 clients provided very congruent descriptions of the spirit world while in deep trance. Excerpts of his hypnotic sessions with clients show sheeple realizing that they have had one partner throughout many lives, sometimes in sexual roles that are reversed; that after previous deaths, the couple was reunited; and that after this incarnation, they will be together again. Clients find that the special person or soul mate is a spouse, relative, friend, parent, or sibling, and even a coworker in this life. Newton also investigates the nonhuman manifestations of spirits on Earth, including elves, fairies and ghosts. Newton also takes on belief in malevolent spirits; arguing that demons and the devil do not exist. But I wonder about his assumption about having one partner through many lives... what about all the divorces? Is it possible to miss a connection and end up with the wrong partner in this life? Does one then have to wait for some future life to get back on track with the right one, and how is all this affected by mental illness?

[It is interesting that belief in continuous reincarnations seems to incubate on the west coast around Los Angeles, where influence from Asia prevails. The Theosophical Society located in Pasadena, CA moved from New York City and the Theosophy Foundation of Georgia (where it does not play well with Jews and Catholics) founded on works by Helena Blavatsky, Henry S. Olcott, and William Q. Judge attempted to blend Hinduism and Buddhism with Christianity, while avoiding its "errors of orthodoxy," during the late 19th century with only modest success. Theosophy is the name Mme. Blavatsky (1831-1891) gave to that portion of knowledge called the Akashic records that she brought out of Tibet from the masters to the world. It comes from the term "Theosophia" used by the Neoplatonists to mean literally "knowledge of the divine." Many contemporary "ministers" have made careers from her writing without giving her appropriate credit for the original imagination. Self proclaimed Samael Aun Weor (1917 – 1977), born Víctor Manuel Gómez Rodríguez, Colombian citizen and later Mexican, was a prolific author, lecturer and founder of the Universal Christian Gnostic Movement which seems in content to be an extension of esoteric theosophy as promoted by Blavatsky and her followers. Numerous writers in this genre have come and gone but some remnants linger among churches along the coast. They are nothing if not prolific publishers about the Akashic records. Their work seems to be more imagination than insight, but who can tell the difference? And they all die like the rest of us. They attract sheeple drawn by promise of psychic guidance by the "ascended masters," most from India, who have reached a level of spiritual maturity not found among human mortals.]

One of the most flamboyant Indian gurus seems to have been one who called himself "Osho." [a.k.a. Bhagwan Shree Rajneesh] His followers established an ashram near Portland, OR and reportedly bought him 93 Rolls Royce limousines during the early 1980s. He ran afoul of immigration laws and was forced to return to India where he died mysteriously at age 58 in 1990. His modern disciples have converted his original ashram in Pune, India into a 28 acre resort with tennis courts and a swimming pool. He taught the potential of becoming a "new man" who was not trapped in social institutions such as marriage, family, political parties, or religions and spiritual belief systems and even nations. All that should be replaced by the commune, much like the first century Christians described in the book of Acts 2:44-47. In his view, the ego is sort of a screen through which reality is distorted as a self reflected from others. By being authentic one could avoid the distortions of perception that prevail among Homo sapiens, so prosperity and peace would prevail without really working for it. His lectures are recorded in many books translated into 55 languages. You can find his lectures on YouTube. "Thank God that he does not exist." He might be labeled a hedonist cult leader. His teaching has survived him through some 60 Osho centers located now throughout India and Nepal. Some critics have called Osho the most dangerous man since Jesus Christ who himself was one of the ascended masters. It seems that if one can be outrageous enough, some sheeple will believe anything. All in God's will of course. AIGWOC.

There are many branches in ancient Vedic culture of India, each seeking Sanatana-dharma, the eternal nature of the soul. Eight different forms of yoga have been developed to help sheeple achieve consciousness of God through meditation and contemplation. They teach that "money is not required to buy one necessity for the soul," and that life is for learning and it goes on in many forms of animals through reincarnation until one reaches a level of development or enlightenment where one attains Nirvana and further lifetimes are unnecessary. They believe experience in this life is due to behavior in previous lives, a system of cause and effect called karma, and conditions of future lives will be determined by the karma compiled during this one. As such, sheeple create their own future lives by the way in which they live during this one. It is merely necessary to live a lifestyle prescribed by the Vedic practices to accelerate one's consciousness and advancement into spiritual consciousness. These include yoga, meditation, chanting a mantra, following a spiritual guru, and study of the Vedic texts. Whether they suffer or advance or not, it is because they earned it by their willful behavior in previous lives. In this view, the purpose of human life is to shed all attachments to matter and to attain liberation from material existence to achieve spiritual perfection. When we act against the law of karma we disrupt harmony and cooperation and create stress, confusion, discontent, and anxiety. Why this is necessary and why everyone has not learned this lesson after 5,000 years is not explained by Hindus, it just is.

The ultimate state of humanity in Buddhism is said to be Nirvana, perfection that needs no further reincarnations. It is attained by following the eight-fold path of right living through right view, intentions, speech, action, livelihood, effort, mindfulness, and concentration. The Buddha is assumed to have reached this state in a single lifetime by practicing the eightfold path, and that was 600 years before Christ. Buddhists believe the reason we are born is that we haven't yet learned the lessons and so as a student we must continue with the classes until graduation and final exams no matter how many lives it takes. Being liberated from the drudgery of this unending cycle can happen in this very birth if one makes an effort to grow spiritually and realize Nirvana in this life by following the noble eight-fold path and surrendering his will to the will of God the Almighty One. This is the supreme spiritual goal anyone can have and leads to the cessation of suffering. However, if a person exhibits beastly character in this life they may return as a lower form of one in the animal kingdom. Whatever condition one dies in will be reinstated at the next life. That is Karma. But, what then?

His Holiness the 14th Dalai Lama, [a.k.a.Tenzin Gyatso] has described life between lives in the everlasting process of reincarnation. He explains, "Immediately upon death, the intermediate state begins during which a being has the form of the person as whom he or she is to be reborn. The intermediate being has all five senses, but also clairvoyance, unobstructiveness and an ability to arrive immediately wherever he or she wants. He or she sees other intermediate beings of his or her own type -- hell-being, hungry ghost, animal, human, demigod or god -- and can be seen by clairvoyants. If a place of birth appropriate to one's predispositions is not found, a small death occurs after seven days, and one is reborn into another intermediate state. If taking rebirth as a human, one sees one's future mother and father as if lying together. If one is to be reborn as a male, this sight generates desire for the mother as well as hatred for the father -- and vice versa if one is to be reborn as a female. Being desirous, one rushes there to engage in copulation; but upon arrival, one sees only the sexual organ of the desired parent. This creates anger, which causes cessation of the intermediate state and makes the connection to the new life. One has entered the mother's womb and begun a human life." He claims this process can be recycled at most six times, with the result that the longest period spent in the intermediate state between lives is forty-nine days. This means that those beings who, even a year after dying, report that they have not found a birthplace are not in the intermediate state but have taken birth as a spirit. Wow.

Here is the flaw in Buddhism. If the Buddha reached the level of Nirvana, he would need no further reincarnations, so the office of Dalai Lama is an institution without foundation. And if he must be continuously reincarnated, the Buddha never reached the state of

Nirvana. [There currently is a youth meditating in the jungles of India declared to be Buddha reincarnated by many devotees.] If we accept the Buddhist notion that living is a constant process of becoming it must also follow that life also is a constant process of dying as well. The necessary thing is to experience both, life and death, as a unity of both/and. In fact, including death in the concept of life, far from provoking anxiety, can become a way of accepting, if not overcoming, it. Anxiety is caused by uncertainty, and the only certainty in life is that we will die. All the rest is anxiety produced by indefinite uncertainty. So it is not a paradox to claim that encompassing life and death as a unity can contribute to transcending anxiety and experiencing existential joy.

The synthesis of living and dying which involves accepting nothingness as a valuable and necessary part of reality and ourselves makes the anxiety related to it redundant and consequently produces a sense of joy. There are many branches in Buddhism, each developed by a different teacher, but in all of them death is the separation of mind from body. The body decays, the atoms return to the Earth, the mind at its subtlest level continues into the next life, and the next, until all learning is complete and Nirvana is achieved. However, Catholic authorities disputed this whole idea and purged any consideration of reincarnation "heresy" by massacres during the Inquisition of the Middle Ages initiated by Pope Innocent III in 1198 A.D. They invoked the teaching of Apostle Paul; "Just as man is destined to die once, and after that to face judgment, so Christ was sacrificed once to take away the sins of many sheeple; and he will appear a second time, not to bear sin, but to bring salvation to those who are waiting for him." (Hebrews 9:27-28) And, he should know, right? Of course, Muslims have a different take on all of this from their holy book, the Koran. They don't believe that God ever needed a son or a concubine because God/Allah is One. All in the will of God the Almighty One, of course.

In Western religions there are varying beliefs in an eternal reward in supernatural Heaven or punishment in Hell for behaving according to a code of conduct…or not. Take the Mormons, for example, who believe in three different heavens each with their own divisions for those appropriately endowed, the telestial kingdom, the terrestrial kingdom, and the celestial kingdom. Brigham Young taught that no one would enter the kingdom without permission from Joseph Smith,

Jr. outrageous as that may seem. In their realm of unreasonable faith, the codes of behaviors usually are delivered by some mysterious man [except for Mary Baker Eddy] granted sacred status by his followers who claims that he got them directly from God, as in Mormonism and Islam, or not God as in Buddhism. He usually is a male form of energy left over from the time when sheeple believed that men planted a seed in women to procreate the species. It was plainly obvious until someone discovered the eggs inside of women. Educated sheeple now believe that we come from fertilized eggs…just like chickens. But, God is assumed to be beyond human understanding so that conveniently makes it a source beyond challenge or even logic. As in, "you better behave or God will send you to Hell." Jesus warned, "I tell you, my friends, do not be afraid of those who kill the body and after that can do no more. But I will show you whom you should fear: Fear him who, after killing the body, has power to throw you into hell. Yes, I tell you, fear him." (Luke 12:5) But, things change. The Catholic Church recently announced that babies who die before they can be baptized no longer go to purgatory, but directly into heaven. If the Pope says so, it must be true.

The Bible is not clear on the matter, to say the least, but we are called back to it in the Western tradition. John 3:16, possibly the most quoted verse in the New Testament, promises everlasting life to those who believe in Jesus Christ. But Jesus implied this was not of their own free will. "... no one can come to me unless the Father has enabled/caused him." (John 6:63-65) And there is its opposite, "There is a judge for the one who rejects me and does not accept my words..." (John 12:48) And..."no man can come to the father except by me." (John 6:6) There are parallel verses in the Koran that display the very same mutually exclusive dichotomy. One theologian says of such religious contradictions, there are no answers, only interpretations. That situation is the reason the Catholic Church claims itself as the one source of scriptural authority as derived from the appointment of Peter and his successors for its foundation. But, Martin Luther and the protestants disagreed, claiming that each believer has individual access to the truth via the Holy Spirit. It seems that you will choose the faith that you must as did Mother Teresa who claimed, "We must take what he gives and give what he takes with a smile." All in the will of God the Almighty One, of course. Think you can handle that?

Perhaps those called Christians look for some resident after-life in heaven to justify their behavior on Earth. If you search the word "heaven" in the Bible the first thing to note is that it occurs 606 times according to the reference, www.biblegateway.com, but nowhere does it say explicitly that anyone is going there. Heaven is mentioned 336 times in the Old Testament, but always as the abode of God and never as a destination of mankind, except for the taking of Elijah "up to heaven in a whirlwind." (2 Kings 2: 11-12) It is first mentioned in the book of Genesis as plural "heavens" and positions them apart from Earth…"In the beginning God created the heavens and the Earth." (Genesis 1:1) Nowadays, science teaches that the universe was initiated from nothing in a "Big Bang" that occurred more than 13.7 billion years ago. Earth was not formed until about four billion years ago. The Bible does not mention that. Then, it shifts to the singular, "Melchizedek blessed Abram, saying, "Blessed be Abram by God Most High, Creator of heaven and Earth." (Genesis 14:18-20) The first mention of heaven as the abode of God is, "Then the LORD said to Moses, Tell the Israelites this: You have seen for yourselves that I have spoken to you from heaven..." (Exodus 20:22) God as Lord of heaven is proclaimed, "Acknowledge and take to heart this day that the LORD is God in heaven above and on the Earth below. There is no other." (Deuteronomy 4:39) Still, no mention of sheeple going there when they die.

The relationship between man and God is throughout the Old Testament one of Earth and heaven. The famous prophecy of Daniel that has occupied scholars for centuries first introduces the coming of a redeemer. "In my vision at night I looked, and there before me was one like a son of man, coming with the clouds of heaven….He was given authority, glory and sovereign power; all peoples, nations and men of every language worshiped him. His dominion is an everlasting dominion that will not pass away, and his kingdom is one that will never be destroyed." (Daniel 7: 13-14) But the prophets also were referred to as Son of Man, as for example Ezekiel. John the Baptist brought a new meaning with his proclamation, "Repent, for the kingdom of heaven/God is near." (Matthew 3:1-2) Pope Benedict XVI, [nee: Joseph Cardinal Ratzinger] says in his "Eschatology" (1988) that heaven is not a place but rather a relationship with Christ that begins with baptism and confession. "One is in heaven when, and to the degree, that one is in Christ. This is why heaven is individual for each and every one. Every one sees God in his own proper way." Perhaps that would include Buddhists and Muslims also as the latter proclaim, there is no god but Allah.

Then Jesus called himself the Son of Man and proclaimed, "For I tell you that unless your righteousness surpasses that of the Pharisees and the teachers of the law, you will certainly not enter the kingdom of heaven." (Matthew 5:20) But, he also cautioned not to look here or there because "...the kingdom of God is within you." (Luke 17:21) He promised his disciples he was going to prepare a place for them where they would be with him, (John 14: 2-3) but he does not say explicitly that everyone who believes will share their abode with him, although John 3:16 claims that is so. However, Jesus taught in parables with secret meanings so that many who are not called would not understand and be redeemed. (Mark 4:11-12) Jesus also threatened sheeple with a fearsome God of judgment; "Fear him who, after killing the body, has power to throw you into hell. Yes, I tell you, fear him." (Luke 12:5) Jesus expands on this theme with the story of a rich man who is cast into hell and pleads for some relief while a poor man resides comfortably with Abraham after they die. (Luke 16:19-31) It is curious that the god of love would use the fear of hell to obtain converts. Jesus never did describe heaven literally. Ten times he used illustrative parables to describe it indirectly..."the kingdom of heaven is like..." Each time he described heaven in terms of personal relationships, not as a place.

In one such parable, Jesus said heaven is like a king who staged a wedding party for his son. When the invited guests failed to come and some even killed his servants, he had his soldiers kill them all and burn their city. Then he sent his servants into the street to collect everyone, the good and bad, to attend the party so his son would not be disappointed. But, one man showed up improperly dressed for a wedding, although the garment normally was supplied by the host, and the king sent him away tied hand and foot, cast into outer darkness. Scholars interpret this wedding parable to describe the Jews who rejected Christ and Gentiles who are invited instead to join the kingdom of heaven, but only if they put on the cloth of Christ. The conclusion stated by Jesus does not seem to fit the facts because he said, "Many are called/invited, but few are chosen." (Matthew 22:1-14) He seems to leave the final choice up to the king. So does the Koran.

In another parable Jesus tells of a wealthy man who left some money with his servants to be invested while he went on a trip, five talents to one, two to another and only one talent to a third. When he returns he reprimands the servant who safeguarded the one talent because he did not invest it like the others to gain more, and the one he had was given to the others while he was cast out. Suppose it had gone down differently, and the servant with five talents bought lottery tickets and lost it all, and the one with two talents invested in the stock market and lost half, while the servant with one talent preserved it safely under his mattress. (Matthew 25: 14-28) But, Jesus also taught, "No one can serve two masters. Either he will hate the one and love the other, or he will be devoted to the one and despise the other. You cannot serve both God and Money." (Matthew 6:24)

In a third parable, Jesus describes an employer who hired workmen for the harvest in a vineyard, some arriving early and working all day and some arriving later in the day, even up to the last hour. Each of the workers was paid the same amount and when the early arrivals complained that they were short changed, he rebuked them, "Take your pay and go. I want to give the man hired last the same as I gave you. Don't I have the right to do what I want with my own money? Or are you envious because I am generous. So the last shall be first and the first shall be last." (Matthew 20:1-16) Note that Jesus does not mention the final destination of any of the characters though. Perhaps the reality of heaven just is too much for mortal minds to absorb.

When he was dying on the cross, Jesus told the repentant convict, "...today you will be with me in paradise." (Luke 23:43) The word "paradise" only appears thrice in the New Testament, and scholars think it is translated, "the place of the righteous dead." According to Catholics, the less than righteous dead go to a temporary place called Purgatory, where they complete their perfection although no scriptures support their claim. This temporary site was not his permanent abode because Jesus rose on the third day. After he allegedly ascended permanently back to heaven, his disciples taught, "He must remain in heaven until the time comes for God to restore everything, as he promised long ago through his holy prophets." (Acts 3:21) Previously, Jesus presented a curious prophecy, "Heaven and Earth will pass away, but my words will never pass away." (Matthew 24:35, Luke 21:33) As for those Mormons and others who think they will be reunited with family members in the afterlife, he said, "When the dead rise, they will neither marry nor be given in marriage; they will be like the angels in heaven." (Mark 12:25) So it appears that families as we know them will not exist in the new heaven. Mormons, take note. Of course, no one knows for sure if he actually said these things or not because scholars say that his words were quoted decades after his death by writers who were not there personally to hear them.

Beyond the four gospels, the whole of Church history rests upon the New Testament writing of those called Saul of Tarsus, Peter, James and John. The other writers of the time were all rejected because their documents did not conform to the letter of Roman Catholic doctrine. It was Apostle Paul who first suggested that some might abide in heaven in a new form of existence, "Now we know that if the earthly tent we live in is destroyed, we have a building from God, an eternal house in heaven, not built by human hands." (2 Corinthians 5:1) "So will it be with the resurrection of the dead. The body that is sown is perishable, it is raised imperishable; it is sown in dishonor, it is raised in glory; it is sown in weakness, it is raised in power; it is sown a natural body, it is raised a spiritual body." (I Corinthians 15:42-45) "I declare to you, brothers, that flesh and blood cannot inherit the kingdom of God, nor does the perishable inherit the imperishable. Listen, I tell you a mystery: We will not all sleep, but we will all be changed in a flash, in the twinkling of an eye, at the last trumpet. For the trumpet will sound, the dead will be raised imperishable, and we will all be changed. For the perishable must clothe itself with the imperishable, and the mortal with immortality. When the perishable has been clothed with the imperishable, and the mortal with immortality, then the saying that is written will come true: Death has been swallowed up in victory." (1 Corinthians 15: 50-54) "For we must all appear before the judgment seat of Christ, that each one may receive what is due him for the things done while in the body, whether good or bad." (2 Corinthians 5:10)

Apostle Paul further explains, "...he made known to us the mystery of his will...to be put into effect when the times will have reached their fulfillment...to bring all things in heaven and on Earth together under one head, even Christ. (Ephesians 1: 3-10) Apostle Paul laid claim to divine revelation not even claimed by Jesus, the Son. "No eye has seen, no ear has heard, no mind has conceived what God has prepared for those who love him, But God has revealed it to us/me by his Spirit." (1Corinthians 2:9-10) But Jesus said, "No one knows about that day or hour, not even the angels in heaven, nor the Son, but only the Father." (Matthew 24:36) Still no mention of where we go when we die. The whole scenario is climaxed by Peter, "The heavens will disappear with a roar; the elements will be destroyed by fire, and the Earth and everything in it will be laid bare…But in keeping with his promise we are looking forward to a new heaven and a new Earth, the home of righteousness." (2 Peter 3:13) Finally it is proclaimed, "Then I saw a new heaven and a new Earth, for the first heaven and the first Earth had passed away, and there was no longer any sea." (Revelation 21:1) But, just who will occupy it and how they will get there is unknown. The Jehovah's Witnesses think that only 144,000 sheeple actually will occupy the new heaven, while the other saved souls will occupy the new Earth. (Revelation 7:1-4, 14: 1-3) If you don't fit in either place, you just sleep away forever. And they use the scriptures to prove it, but trying to make sense of it is impossible.

Perhaps the law of conservation of energy applies and life goes on and on and on like a mobius with no beginning and no ending. The fact is that where we go when we die (if there is any we left) is among the unknowables in life, and the Vatican librarian observed that "even God cannot know the unknowable." But, if God cannot know the unknowable he would not be God, would he? Some sheeple may find a sort of twisted comfort in that logic, but it is normal for sheeple to fear the unknown, especially when it means not knowing where anyone goes after death. Merely dismissing it is not a convenient solution as posed by retired Episcopal Bishop John Spong, "I am simply not concerned with things about which I can know nothing. Predicting the end of the world and awaiting the second coming are the parlor games of literalistic minds."

Awareness of the unknowables leads necessarily to anxiety of indefinite uncertainty, and maturity leads to tolerance for anxiety and uncertainty. Perhaps, if we are so gifted by God, we will approach the ultimate unknowable with the mindset expressed by William Ernest

Henley (1849-1903) in his famous poem titled "Invictus;" (1875) "Beyond this place of wrath and tears looms but the Horror of the shade, And yet the menace of the years finds and shall find me unafraid." C. G. Jung (1879-1961) observed, "One doesn't become enlightened by imagining figures of light, but by making the darkness conscious. The latter procedure, however, is disagreeable, and therefore not popular." Indeed. Long before him, Chinese philosopher Lao Tse taught, "Seeing into darkness is clarity. Knowing how to yield is strength." Apostle Paul seconded that idea by claiming, "...when I am weak then I am strong." (2 Corinthians 12:10) Germanic poet, R.M. Rilke (1875-1926) wrote this advice to a young writer, "Have patience with everything unresolved in your heart and try to love the questions themselves. Don't search for the answers, which could not be given to you now. And the point is, to live everything. Live the questions now. Perhaps then, someday far in the future, you will gradually, without even noticing it, live your way into the answers." Or not.

More sheeple are reporting some form of hallucinations surrounding near death experiences that helps them to feel more comfortable about the afterlife. Actually, this phenomenon may be manifestation of a dying brain for lack of oxygen, like shutting down a computer. After his own near death experience during a heart attack, C.G. Jung explained, "What happens after death is so unspeakably glorious that our imagination and our feelings do not suffice to form even an approximate conception of it." But, not everyone reports pleasant experiences; some are downright horrifying. Some researchers think this experience may be manifestation of oxygen loss to the brain as death approaches, but how it is stored in memory and retrieved is unknown. Astronauts and fighter pilots have reported similar experiences after passing out in their centrifuge training that deprives the brain of oxygen. However, that does not explain those sheeple who report out of body sensing during surgery or trauma when they can see and hear from a perceived position near the ceiling of the room.

Whatever the mind is, it does not seem to be necessary that it be physically located in the body. Since Albert Einstein observed "spooky things at a distance," science has been attempting to uncover secret communications between subatomic elements sans space/time restraints. Psychic and clairvoyant, Edgar Cayce (1877-1945) is claimed to have successfully treated illnesses in sheeple all over the world just through personal correspondence. Tests at the Stanford Research Institute by Dr. Russell Targ seem to show that mind can be located two places at once and that minds can communicate over great distances, maybe even forwards and backwards in time. This phenomenon is consistent with experiments in quantum mechanics. The ability of pets to anticipate the arrival of their owners reinforces this idea. It certainly appears that information is abroad in space/time with no apparent physical medium for transmission, much like television, contrasting with the case of sound waves that require a medium such as air or water for transmission. With radio waves, no medium for transmission seems to be needed as communications with the orbiting space station proves. Such radiated information may not be time or space bound although it is undetectable without the correct equipment. So could it be with the functions of mind. Perhaps new ideas are not created, but merely discovered. King Solomon declared, "Is there anything of which one can say, look, this is something new? It was here already, long ago. It was here before our time...there is nothing new under the Sun." (Ecclesiastes 1:8-10) Think about that.

Not only that, but a growing body of researchers into reincarnation are collecting examples of after death communications reported by survivors of dead loved ones while in a deep hypnotic trance. Among them possibly the most scientific work is that of Victor J. Zammit, a retired lawyer in Australia. (www.victorzammit.com) He claims, "When the objective evidence, near death experiences, out of body experiences, after-death contacts, voices on tape, psychic laboratory experiments, the best mediums, proxy sittings, poltergeists and all of the other evidence contained in this work is seen collectively, the case for survival after death is absolutely stunning and irrefutable." Concepts in philosophy, physics, religion, and paranormal psychology all are being focused upon this question. This effort to contact the dead goes way back into history even before Christ in the Old Testament. The fact still is that although forensics knows how a dead body decays and mortifies, nobody knows what happens to consciousness after death. Nobody knows. Nobody, because no one who has really died has ever actually come back and told us what is out there.

Science and medicine have made gigantic leaps the past century, but metaphysics has been almost stagnant. Clear unambiguous answers to questions about the soul, spirit, and resurrection will have to wait for some future time. After all his words on this subject, C. G. Jung had to conclude, "We know desperately little about the possibilities of continued existence of the individual soul after death, so little that we cannot even conceive how anyone could prove anything at all in this respect...What the myths and premonitions about life after death really mean or what kind of reality lies beyond we certainly do not know. We must hold clearly in mind that there is no possible way for us to attain certainty about things which pass our understanding." But he could not avoid holding out some hope. "As far as we know at all there seems to be no immediate decomposition of the soul. On the contrary. It is just as if the soul detached itself from the body before death actually occurs, sometimes years before." Just as an infant is unwillingly and traumatically disconnected from the security of the umbilical and thrust into a risky and uncertain new form of existence, so too may death be a natural but traumatic transfer from one form of existence into another...or not. We are positioned at death much as the infant in diapers; neither can know the life to come. Just as life for the infant lies in the grand future, so does the immortality of his ancestors and his heirs.

The great and wise King Solomon contemplated this dilemma and wrote before 150 B.C. as follows: "So I reflected on all this and concluded that the righteous and the wise and what they do are in God's hands, but no man knows whether love or hate awaits him. All share a common destiny - the righteous and the wicked, the good and the bad, the clean and the unclean, those who offer sacrifices and those who do not. As it is with the good man, so with the sinner; as it is with those who take oaths, so with those who are afraid to take them. This is the evil in everything that happens under the sun: The same destiny overtakes all. The hearts of men, moreover, are full of evil and there is madness in their hearts while they live, and afterward they join the dead." (Ecclesiastes 9: 1-3)

King Solomon concluded the pursuit of knowledge has its limits because the more one studies the more enigmas are exposed. The evil ones often prosper and the righteous ones often suffer. And after they both are gone, few will ever mark their existence. The wise King acknowledged there were many things he would never know. "For the wise man, like the fool, will not be long remembered and in days to come both will be forgotten...Like the fool, the wise man too must die!" (Ecclesiastes 2:16) His conclusion prevails to this day. More than 2,000 years later, Russian author Alexander Solzhenitsyn (1918-2008) came to a similar conclusion. "Do not pursue what is illusory - property and position: all that is gained at the expense of your nerves decade after decade and can be confiscated in one fell night. Live with a steady superiority over life - don't be afraid of misfortune, and do not yearn after happiness; it is after all, all the same: the bitter doesn't last forever, and the sweet never fills the cup to overflowing." Nevertheless, the wise sage refuses to occupy the seat of a pessimist, but rather commits everything to God the Almighty One and does not rely upon his own limited and faulty understanding.

If we cannot know what happens after we die, perhaps we are not meant to know but rather just to live the life that we have been given as the infant does. It can be the last great adventure to stand by detached and watch it all unfold in your own body at the end, sort of like watching yourself in a movie from the back row of the theater. This, of course, requires detaching the observer from the participant, i.e. the ego/soul from the body. The ultimate detachment from reality may be A Course in Miracles,(1975) claimed to be channeled from Jesus by its scribe. It actually was written by a Jewish-atheist psychology professor, Dr. Helen Schucman who seemed to avoid normal human conflicts by withdrawing into a psychotic world of "spirit" where there is no pain, suffering, guilt, or sin. In a poem titled, "Stillness," she wrote, "My soul is still. It does not know the thoughts my mind imagines. It does not perceive my meaningless endeavors, nor the goals of sin and madness in which I believe...I sleep, and dream of evil and decay and death, of which my soul knows nothing..." Nearing death, she proclaimed, "I know it is true, but I don't believe it." In this statement, she expressed the universal dichotomy in all of us, the duality of spirit and flesh. Her typing partner, Dr. Bill Thetford, explained, "She recognized that if she fully accepted the teachings of the "Course" it was going to mean a very major shift in her perception about absolutely everything, and she felt unprepared to do that." Recall she wrote, "Disobeying God's will is meaningful only to the insane; in truth it is impossible." So her disbelief must be the will of God as there can be no other.

Detaching from dying may involve outgrowing the needy infant within that attached necessarily to its nearest caregiver in order to survive. If infantile care giving is normal, the infant gradually learns to become less and less dependent and learns to self-soothe when needed. Experiments with orphaned baby monkeys showed they would cling to a stuffed mother-surrogate for solace even while taking milk from a wired dummy. Child psychology has known for some time that children deprived of adequate mothers and fathers never develop the ego strength needed to adapt to the social conditions they fill face as adults. Normal care giving is less and less available to human infants so they may not develop fully while the society they enter is getting more complex and challenging. Overcoming this liability is difficult even when it is approached consciously because it requires rewiring primitive brain neurons from their primitive positions. At the end of life, impersonal detachment of the ego/psyche from the body may be the strongest medicine we have to apply when things get out of ego control. If you can do that, watching the dying process in your own body can be quite an interesting growth experience. In the extreme, it converts to dissociation, a well known psychological defense mechanism to protect the psyche from the shock of traumatic experience perceived as personal harm, excruciating loss, or mortal combat.

The wise sage in Taoism avoids the traps of both attachment to the body and aversion of death. He learns that praise and blame, pleasure and sorrow, life and death come and go like the wind. And he rests like a giant tree in the midst of them. The Tao te Ching says, "Whatever is flexible and flowing will tend to grow; whatever is rigid and blocked will whither and die." An African proverb claims, "Smooth seas do not make a skillful sailor." Think about it. Maturity requires that we accept the unknowables in life, weather the challenges, and live with the resulting existential anxiety. This does not mean we are not affected by the ups and downs in life, just that we do not define who we are by them because we become conscious of a self that is not affected by them. But in the end we all are helpless and hopeless about what comes next, no matter what we may believe.

Most of us live and die while leaving no impact. Only rarely does a human life get anchored in history for posterity. Most Homo sapiens disappear without a trace. It is commonly known that Christopher Columbus captained the first expedition to reach central America in 1492 and established the first colony for Spain on Hispaniola (Dominican Republic) on two subsequent trips. It may not be well known that his fourth and last voyage in 1500-1505 ended in disaster and disgrace, when he gave up his dream of reaching Asia by an ocean passage. After surviving the mutiny of his crew, losing all four ships to tropical rot, and being marooned on Jamaica, he had to pay for his own passage back to Spain. He died in 1506 while saying a prayer to God. It was another explorer from Florence named Amerigo Vespucci who would get to see his name inscribed on maps of the "New World." It was Magellan who sailed all the way around South America and found the way to Asia across the Pacific Ocean. The rest is history.

The point is that after you die, things still happen and life goes on, and on with alternating pleasure and pain, suffering and struggle, success and failure, birth and death, as the Buddha discovered. "Birth will end in death, youth will end in old age, meetings will end in separations, gain will end in loss, all things are transient, impermanent. Everything comes to pass and nothing comes to stay. Life begins with breathing in and ends with breathing out." After you are gone things will go on the way they are meant to be. By consciously letting go of all human attachments, you will gain the freedom to move on, even through the tunnel of darkness called death...or not.

Perhaps if we just do the work that is set before us, in the end we may say with St. Paul, "For I am already being poured out like a drink offering, and the time has come for my departure. I have fought the good fight, I have finished the race, I have kept the faith. Now there is in store for me the crown of righteousness, which the Lord, the righteous Judge, will award to me on that day - and not only to me, but also to all who have longed for his appearing." (2 Timothy 4: 6-8) Perhaps the antithesis of St. Paul would be Adolf Hitler who mused, "I go the way fate has pointed me like a person walking in his sleep." And so did all those who followed him to their destruction in Nazi Germany. The interim success of Hitler during WWII was based upon the basic skill of all great politicians: he knew where his sheeple were headed, and he ran around to get in front of them. How could this be unless God willed it so? The ancient sages knew that a certain inner peace, a kind of happy numbness soothes the nerves of the human animal when absorbed in its allotted task. There is no room in the human mind for sorrow and worry that is occupied with other things. For this author, that work has been the preparation of this material with its almost daily revisions for more than ten years. In any case, it seems to be a law of nature that keeping busy with some useful work focused upon the needs of others helps take our minds off of own worries with no solutions.

Someone said to be happy sheeple need something to do, someone to love, and something to look forward to. Unfortunately, eventually you run out of all three, except possibly for loving someone. So we end where we began with the Pope who claimed that it is only by living life fully day by day, sometimes hour by hour, that we prepare for what comes after, if anything. In Theofatalism™, God is the master of your fate so why worry unless, of course, He wills you to? The youthful idealism of Mother Teresa about God's will became practical realism in old age as she proclaimed, "We must give what he takes and take what he gives." And she lost the connection with Jesus as she lamented, "My soul is no longer one with you." Suffering the existential anxiety of indefinite uncertainty about what comes after death is what defines being human. The end.

13. GRIEVING OUR LOSSES.

Living longer means living with losses...many losses. Mark Twain, (1835-1910) [a.k.a. Samuel Clemens] was lecturing in Europe when he got the news that his beloved 24-year-old daughter Olivia Susan Clemens, named for her mother, had died of spinal meningitis. "It is one of the mysteries of our nature that a man, all unprepared, can receive a thunder-stroke like that and still live," he later wrote in his autobiography. "She was full of life, full of activity. Her waking hours were a crowding and hurrying procession of enthusiasms -- joy, sorrow, anger, remorse, storm, sunshine, rain, darkness. They were all there. They came in a moment, and they were gone as quickly. In all things she was intense. In her, this characteristic was not a mere glow, dispensing warmth, but a consuming fire." The beloved daughter he called "Susy" continued to inspire his writing after her death. Clemens and his wife never lived again in the Hartford, CT house where she died.

Losses accumulate throughout the life cycle. They include loss of friends, family members, wealth, health, and meaningful work. If not properly grieved along the way, grief piles up and seriously impairs the immune system by corrupting our ability to cope. Someone said that grief is the price we pay for love, and it comes in proportion to how much we loved what was lost The severest losses are the ones we value the most, the ones that leave the most holes behind. Perhaps the greatest loss is death of a spouse, but there could be preparatory losses along the way that we often overlook. Before we get very old, the realization that life is composed of beginnings and endings begins to sink in. Losses can be casual, like losing a toy or a pet or more severe like losing a beloved family member. Loss and grief are parts of ongoing life but grieving publicly, which is the natural response to loss, is a social taboo in this culture. American anthropologist, Margaret Mead (1901-1978) observed, "When a couple marries they celebrate and when a child is born they jubilate/rejoice, but when someone dies they try to pretend nothing happened." Perhaps the pain is just too great to absorb. When sheeple we have loved enter our hearts they never leave. Consequently, many sheeple carry around pent-up grief from many losses that occur throughout life. Moreover, loss of a loved one makes it impossible to pretend any longer than it will never happen to us. Denial and avoidance of our own mortality no longer are options. Anxiety and depression can set in permanently if not assuaged by appropriate treatment. Eventually, it can be disabling if grief is not appropriately healed, although it can never be totally removed.

Roman Emperor and stoic philosopher Marcus Aurelius (121-180 A.D.) tried to wish away grief by observing, "Loss is nothing else but change, and change is Nature's delight...Time is a sort of river of passing events, and strong is its current; no sooner is a thing brought to sight than it is swept by and another takes its place, and this too will be swept away." One cannot put his foot into the same river twice, according to Greek philosopher Heraclitus. Until losses come to you most sheeple just pretend they don't exist to avoid the impact of grieving. But loss happens, often beginning at a very young age. Favorite toys break, pets die, best friends move away, accidents occur, and sometimes close relatives die before we get very old. Sometimes adults try to help kids adjust quickly and process these losses by buying them a replacement toy or pet. When that doesn't work, the adults feel uncomfortable and admonish the kid to get over it quickly, stop crying, and pretend nothing happened so they can avoid feeling empathy for the survivor. So, we learn to stifle strong feelings and bottle them up in order to protect others from their contagious reactions that many fear can be disabling. American poet, Ella Wheeler Wilcox (1850-1919) observed, "Laugh and the world laughs with you, weep and you weep alone." Although more than two million sheeple die in America each year, many folks reach middle age before they must witness death of a close relative or loved one. Most of them are totally unprepared for the painful shock that it can bring.

When the pain of loss is unbearable, sheeple often avoid its cause or adopt some substitute life style that masks the suffering, including drugs, alcohol, or other risky behaviors. Avoidance and denial are defense mechanisms that protect the ego from fear and they can work for some time, but eventually reality sets in. Such sheeple can live a pseudo life through others to avoid living the painful life they are given until they find courage to work through the loss. A modern example is the "Celebrity Worship Syndrome" or "Mad Idol Disease" now recognized by psychology to be an escape from reality. By stalking the lives of the rich and famous one may avoid looking into the mirror and seeing the reality of what is there, what psychologists call escapism or dissociation. By denying our own condition we hope to keep grief at a safe distance, and it can work up to a point. But, when a celebrity idol dies the reality of death swoops in to remind us that no one is immune from the grief of loss. One moment we can feel secure in our assumptions about life, and the next be thrust into an abyss of uncertainty and suffering far beyond any expectations as though thrashing about like a fish caught upon a hook. In spite of more than four deaths per minute in the U.S., the consequences scarcely are evident until it happens to your family because society hides it from view. Out of sight, out of mind. Maybe.

Sheeple often recoil from the evident grief in others because it opens wounded places in themselves that have not been healed. In fact, neuroscience is proving what the ancients knew from experience; grief is contagious and therefore to be avoided. It seems that human brains are equipped with "mirror neurons" which fire up when they detect suffering or distress in another, even distant relatives or unrelated sheeple. The natural reaction is self preservation, so survivors react either with attempts to fix the problem or to flee from it, the old flight or fight response. Few consider another option, that of calm submission. Consequently, as the late psychiatrist Elisabeth Kubler-Ross observed in her classic book, <u>On Death and Dying</u> (1969), most sheeple are walking around with unresolved grief that prevents them from the full enjoyment of whatever life they have left. They should be helped to process loss in stages to accept reality, from denial, to anger, to bargaining, to depression, to acceptance.

Whatever one thinks happens to the departed after death, for the survivors it is "a fearful piece of brutality," according to C. G. Jung

(1875-1961) who proclaimed after death of his wife, "There is no sense in pretending otherwise. It is brutal not only as a physical event but far more so psychically. A human being is torn away from us and what remains is the icy stillness of death." He might also have said what remains are the holes in our makeup the departed one was filling up for us. A widow described it thus; "Grief is the madness that follows death." It can seem like a flash flood has swooped over the landscape tearing out the basic structures of life and leaving mud, corruption, and debris in its wake.

The one thing that is most important for survivors of traumatic loss seems to be repeatedly describing it to others until it makes some sense. Shakespeare instructed Macbeth, "Give sorrow words; the grief that does not speak knits up the o-er wrought heart and bids it break." It seems that in processing the events and feelings verbally, there comes some kind of accommodation that is difficult to achieve if grief is bottled up in silence or smothered with random activity and substitutes. Unfortunately, the feelings of grief are contagious and many folks just cannot bear catching much trauma. So, you will need to find such resources who can listen, even if it means paying a professional counselor for time to listen until you are finished describing. If you are the friend or relative of a survivor, perhaps you can "lend an ear" as much as possible to help the process along. If there is no opportunity for verbal disclosure, then writing your thoughts about the loss down in a daily journal is a good practice and for some who are prone to pessimism and introversion, maybe even better than talking. If the feelings of grief become so strong there are no words to describe them, nothing remains but to suffer them until they pass. This is when it helps to have friends or a therapist to help carry them in silence.

Sheeple often avoid the losses of others because they trigger sympathetic grief reactions in "mirror neurons" of the brain they would rather prevent. The emotions of mourners may feel contagious and thus to be avoided. The sight of a dead loved one can tear open their fear of mortality and strip away their illusion of immortality with the attendant spiritual crisis that may come with it. When they are caught up in the feelings of irrevocable loss themselves, sheeple often activate the flight response to feeling threatened so they can get on with their lives with little or no disruption. They also may attempt to avoid the feelings by medicating with drugs or alcohol or frantic activities or literally jumping onto some substitute person. But, underneath this façade, grief must get its due and one must submit to mourning or let it pile up until something inside breaks. Smothering it with activities and denial and substitutions merely permits normal reactions to losses to pile up until one day a personal loss may trigger all the pent up grief from all previous losses, and some psycho-physical symptoms appear that can be disabling, even leading to suicide. To avoid its consequences, sheeple must relearn the normal process of grieving their losses. When a close loved one dies, the reaction can be so intense that some sheeple need counseling and even long term therapy to properly recover from loss. Since sheeple won't change until it hurts too much not to, counselors may see clients in deep grief for a personal loss that holds the accumulation of all previous losses improperly grieved.

Grief is said by psychologists to be a normal reaction to loss and, therefore, it is not treated as a mental illness. Perhaps that is a mistake because sheeple sometimes die of grief from a broken heart, or reduced immune defenses that follow a severe loss. Some even commit suicide. Maybe it is all due to the unresolved unfinished business that remains if it was not completed. Hospice educator, Dr. Ira Byock has observed that five most important elements of closure that must be worked through with the dying are; "I forgive you, please forgive me, thank you, I love you, goodbye." If this is not done, the remorse and guilt may last a lifetime or must be treated in therapy afterwards. Grief also has been described as the last great expression of love for the deceased. Such might be the example of Dana Reeve, wife of actor Christopher "Superman" Reeve who was totally paralyzed for nearly ten years after a horseback riding accident. Only nine months after he died she contracted inoperable lung cancer, although she was a nonsmoker, and died in another nine months at age 44. "I'll tell you it's another journey," Dana Reeve said. "And I'm ready to be finished with the journeys."

The impact on a person having experienced traumatic death or terminal violence of a loved one belongs on the level of acute traumatic stress syndrome, occurring immediately after the event, followed by the post-traumatic stress disorder if symptoms of trauma persist beyond a year or so. It matters not the cause; what does matter is the combination and severity of the symptoms of trauma such as memory impairment, difficulty concentrating, irritability and anger, flashbacks and frightening dreams, hyper-arousal, insomnia, loss of interest in formerly pleasurable activities, and disassociative symptoms. The problem with postulating stages and time frames for recovery from loss is that survivors are traumatized even more when they do not see themselves living up to what their social environment apparently considers to be "normal" in a given time period – universal emotional states resolving within a pre-determined, fairly short period of time. Advice dispensed by the uninitiated relatives adds to the trauma of now living in an unfamiliar and extremely distressing emotional dimension, unimaginable to those who have not been there themselves. Advice to focus on others presumed to be "worse off" or on "all the good things in life" may have no effect whatsoever and hence induces even greater distress in the survivor. It is better to have no advice than to do such further damage to the wound that fails to heal.

In spite of thousands of academic studies that show grief to be a serious impact on life - physically, intellectually, emotionally, and spiritually - there still is no standard treatment for grief. The Society on Death Education and Counseling was organized to provide a better understanding among academics about social impacts of grief, but its influence has not spread much beyond the college classroom. Physicians may prescribe a chemical sedative to aid sleep or reduce stress, but each person is left to process the impact of their losses alone and without a road map through the maze. As such, counselors are powerless to help and almost any reaction to grief is considered to be normal, including some pretty bizarre behaviors. Society responds to grieving widowed men and women differently. Women tend to cluster around the widow to offer support and sympathy. If they are sexually active, men may pursue them to help meet their "needs." But, widowed men often are abandoned and avoided, even by close friends and relatives, because they are perceived as a threat to couples and are assumed to have all the coping resources they need. The law of the jungle prevails as single men are perceived, unconsciously or consciously, as threats to committed couples, to be viewed cautiously and defensively. While older widows may stay "married" to their dead spouses, active widowers often either remarry or die within a few years.

Grieving the loss of a close loved one can challenge all previous assumptions about how life should work, as well as what comes after death, and if the loss is untimely or unreasonable, the belief in a loving God can be questioned even by the most devout and faithful. Unless they are given a road map through grief, survivors often heal in ways that leave them permanently scarred or functioning like an amputee with a poorly fitting prosthesis, or none at all. Much as we know it happens, accepting the inevitable endings is difficult for society to implement because ongoing life scarcely stops long enough to attend a funeral. All things in cyclical existence are transient and impermanent, but until it happens to you the realization of permanent loss is only an idea. When inevitable loss comes to your house, things change forever. Letting go and detaching from the past is one of the most excruciating tasks in preparing to reconstruct a new life without the beloved.

A search among religions for some help for mourners turns up very little of much use. Catastrophes happen and wishing their painful impact away with sweet imaginary hopes for a better life to come cannot remove the bitter taste of Gods will in the lives of those left to suffer. The loss of a spouse has been rated as the highest stressor that one can experience, and religion may not offer much support. When British theologian C.S. Lewis (1898-1963) went to the throne of grace for support after the painful untimely death of his wife shortly after they married, he lamented in <u>A Grief Observed</u>, (1963) "...go to Him when your need is desperate, when all other help is vain, and what do you find? A door slammed in your face and a sound of bolting and double bolting on the inside. After that silence, you might as well turn away. The longer you wait the more emphatic the silence will become. There are no lights in the windows. It might be an empty house. Why is He so present a commander in our time of prosperity and so very absent a help in time of trouble?" C.S. Lewis lost the will to live and died within two years.

There is that Bible passage often read at funerals, "Though I walk through the valley of the shadow of death I will fear no evil because you are with me, your rod and your staff they comfort me." (Psalm 23:4) Jesus was quite ambivalent about grief. On one hand he said matter-of-factly, "Blessed are those who mourn for they shall be comforted." (Matthew 5:4) And he instructed, "Ask and it will be given to you;

seek and you will find; knock and the door will be opened to you. For everyone who asks receives; he who seeks finds; and to him who knocks, the door will be opened." (Matthew 7:7-9) But to the disciple who wished to go and bury his father, Jesus retorted, "Follow me and let the dead bury their own dead." (Matthew 8:21-23) That's about it. For the Christian, Pope Benedict XVI, a.k.a. Joseph Cardinal Ratzinger says in his "Eschatology" (1988) that death is nothing less than the ultimate transformation, "The Kingdom of God is found in those persons whom the finger of God has touched and who allowed themselves to be made God's sons and daughters. Clearly such a transformation can only take place through death." Presumably, while they are alive sheeple belong to Satan because Apostle Paul proclaimed the standard belief of his age, "all have sinned." (Romans 3:23)

Although numerous studies show that grief can be disabling for mourners, there are no generally accepted standard therapies for helping mourners to grieve because each situation is assumed to be unique. But, many studies have shown that grief can be a traumatic and serious reaction to loss which can disable mourners if they are not given adequate support. Often, they are ignored soon after the funeral because the pain of mourning is contagious and close family and friends would rather just avoid getting afflicted with it. Failing to find much comfort in scriptures, a grieving widower and a pastoral counselor compiled a book for surviving spouses that now could be the road map for grieving in all types of losses. In Recovery From Loss, (2001) the authors described a process for grieving that is based upon sound psychology as well as the empathy available through spiritual guidance. The model of grief work that they described can be customized to fit each individual mourner according to their specific personality preferences as described by the Myers-Briggs Type Indicator. (Chapter 5) This model is being integrated into some college courses on death and dying. Perhaps it will find its way into mainstream grief counseling and so help to reduce the disabling affects of acute loss. Here is a brief summary of its model for grief.

Sheeple suffering from acute loss must walk through a labyrinth to reach the center of comfort once again. Unlike a maze, which is intended to frustrate and confuse, a labyrinth is an ancient symbol for centering that must be traversed only one way in and one way out. The grief walk requires passing through tasks of 1) acknowledging the loss (overcoming denial), 2) feeling the full impact of loss including the guilt and remorse from any avoidance behavior, 3) developing healthy substitutes for the lost object (emphasis on healthy), 4) detaching from investments in the past and letting go of personal responsibility with forgiveness, and 5) moving forward to reconstruct a new life while integrating the loss. To these tasks the mourner brings the set of resources unique to his personality.

This process is neither easy nor quick because it requires that lifelong patterns in brain neurons must be rewired to accommodate new lifestyles initiated by the loss. The feelings of grief are some of the most intense of all human emotions and they must be suffered alone in isolation if they cannot be conveyed to anyone. If the loss seems to be undeserved or untimely, the feeling of betrayal must be uncovered and dealt with. That effort may require a trial and error approach to see what helps and what hurts. If they don't get professional help, grief can impair the immune system and expose mourners to illness and even death. Many, if not most, sheeple try to avoid the strong feelings of grief and skip ahead by latching onto substitutes before healing is completed. If they skip the work of detaching that involves resolving remorse and guilt, they pile up unresolved losses which can erupt at some time later in various destructive ways, even including suicide.

To each of these tasks mourners bring the whole person that they are; physical, intellectual, emotional, and spiritual. Each person possesses strengths and weaknesses in each of these areas, so the tasks of grief may be customized for the optimum benefits of each survivor based upon their personality profile. When a loss occurs, we are left with the holes in our personality the deceased person or object was filling up for us. When someone enters our hearts and leaves, only memories of wholeness are left. Happiness is having our holes filled. When two sheeple are devoted to filling the holes in each other, that is bliss. And when one of them leaves, that is hell. The normal but unhealthy reaction is to find a temporary substitute quickly to fill up the holes again to feel comfortable, like taking a pill when we feel sick. This could explain why widowed sheeple often marry again, and get divorced again.

A temporary pill always wears off. The healthy way is to identify the holes in our makeup, physical, intellectual, emotional, and spiritual and work on filling them for ourselves so we can bring a more healthy and whole person to any new relationships. However, grief can become complicated by unfinished business with the deceased that may involve unresolved remorse, anger, and guilt from an imperfect relationship. These emotions must be uncovered, resolved, and purged before the tasks of grief can be resumed. Sometimes a professional counselor will be helpful in dealing with such issues. Buddhism speaks of leaning into grief and letting it wash over us until the wounded areas are healed instead of running for cover. That is why it is called grief work. If grief counselors could learn to help their clients work through this model of grief work, perhaps its devastating impact could be softened somewhat.

There is an anonymous poem that might comfort the bereaved:

"Do not stand by my grave and weep
I am not there, I do not sleep
I am a thousand winds that blow
I am a diamond glint on snow
I am sunlight on ripened grain
I am the gentle autumn rain
When you wake in the morning hush;
I am the swift uplifting rush
Of quiet birds in circling flight.
I am the soft starlight at night.
Do not stand at my grave and weep.
I am not there, I do not sleep."

Everyone knows that all beginnings come with endings, but some sheeple learn that lesson only after repeated losses of loved ones and the lifestyles they represent. Even if a broken heart does not lie in your past or present, it probably awaits you in your future, at some place, at some time when you will almost certainly be unprepared. In the words of feminine spiritualist, Jalaja Bonheim: "Make no mistake: those who tell us we can have whatever we want, be whoever we want to be, and have full control of our lives are merely playing into our desire to avoid the discomfort of feeling our vulnerability. True wholeness has nothing to do with getting what we want. Paradoxically, we achieve true wholeness only by embracing our fragility and sometimes our brokenness." Sometimes God must break a heart in order to get inside, and if it seals up he will break it again, and again. There is a saying; to make an omelet one must break some eggs. Some things that are broken cannot be fixed and remain unresolved and unfinished in this life, but perhaps they are contributing to omelets in the sky.

Sometimes neither fight nor flight are appropriate reactions when it is better just to be in the here and now and to suffer when suffering to allow natural healing to occur. If you have an amputation, there may be a prosthesis to help you get around but the lost limb will never grow back again. When a loss is severe enough, basic beliefs may be shattered like Humpty Dumpty who fell off the wall and could not be put back together again. It helps if one has a belief system that works to accompany the losses in life. Such is offered by belief in Theofatalism™. (Chapter 18)

And after all the grief work is done, some sheeple even find the experience of post trauma growth actually is real. Posttraumatic growth is not simply a return to baseline from before a period of suffering; instead it is an experience of improvement that for some sheeple is deeply profound and can take surprising turns into new and unexplored territory. Growth does not occur as a direct result of trauma, rather it is the individual's struggle with the new reality in the aftermath of trauma that is crucial in determining the extent to which posttraumatic growth occurs. Results seen in sheeple who have experienced posttraumatic growth include some of the following changes: greater appreciation of life, changed sense of priorities, warmer, more intimate relationships, greater sense of personal strength, and recognition of new possibilities or path's for one's life and spiritual development. Counselors say that two personality characteristics that may affect the likelihood that sheeple can make positive use of the aftermath of traumatic events that befall them include extraversion (difficult for introverts) and openness to new experience.

Also, optimists may be better able to focus attention and resources on the most important matters, and disengage from uncontrollable or unsolvable problems. The ability to grieve and gradually to accept trauma could also increase the likelihood of growth. It also benefits a person to have supportive others that can aid in post-traumatic growth by providing a way to craft narratives about the changes that have occurred, and by offering perspectives that can be integrated into changes in life schema. These relationships help develop narratives; these narratives of trauma and survival are always important in post-traumatic growth because the development of these life stories force survivors to confront questions of meaning and how answers to those questions can be reconstructed by constructing a different life which accommodates the loss. Without such resources, the personal immune system can be impacted by loss, leading to complicated grief and physical ailments and possibly even death. Those who feel or become isolated and abandoned after major loss can be expected to suffer more, perhaps even to the point of committing suicide or dying prematurely from immune deficiency. So it happened to C.S. Lewis and Dana Reeve, widow of "Superman" Christopher Reeve.

Some things that are broken cannot be fixed. The message from loss seems to be grieve or die. All in the will of God the Almighty One of course. How can anyone feel good inside no matter what happens outside? With God, all things are possible.

14. God is not your friend.

That may come as a shock to some baby boomers and their families. The origin of God in the west seems to be assigned to the writing of Moses in the Old Testament book of Genesis about 1440 B.C. Predating that are Hindu traditions that evolve from translations of Sanskrit words meaning Generator, Operator, and Destroyer. In none of these roles does God consult with mankind before he takes action. [Consider the devastation caused by deep ocean earthquakes followed by awesome tsunami waves that crashed over coastal areas bordering the Indian ocean and the east coast of Japan in recent times, leaving only debris and human catastrophe by the thousands behind. Add to them the destruction in Haiti of a similar earthquake to behold the power and willingness of God to destroy his own creation.]

If you still envision God as he was presented to you in Sunday School, sort of like Santa Claus or General Electric who "brings only good things to life," disappointment, shock, and awe are in your future. There is no shortage of Christian ministers who would try and make suffering into a blessing, as did Jesus who claimed those where "blessed" who suffered. (Matthew 5: 1-12) Although "prosperity preachers" and self-help success writers have been spreading that dogma for centuries, the facts are different if you just look around at the creation of God. In science, theories must fit observable reality to be sustained, but with religion this is not so. For more than two thousand years, sheeple have repeated the "God is love" myth each generation even in the face of overwhelming evidence to the contrary. How many children still are taught this little hymn:

"Jesus loves me, this I know
For the Bible tells me so.
Little ones to him belong,
They are weak but he is strong.
Yes, Jesus loves me,
The Bible tells me so."

Of course, one can rely upon some scriptures that seem to point to this conclusion. In the teaching of Jesus and his apostle, John we have these sayings: "How great is the love the Father has lavished on us, that we should be called children of God! And that is what we are!" (1 John 3: 1) "Whoever does not love does not know God, because God is love." (1 John 4:8) "This is love: not that we loved God, but that he loved us and sent his Son as an atoning sacrifice for our sins." (1 John 4;10) "If you, then, though you are evil, know how to give good gifts to your children, how much more will your Father in heaven give good gifts to those who ask him!" (Matthew 7:11, Luke 11:13) That seems to be a perfect description of a perfectly benevolent Father, very close to Santa Claus. Then, how come this God of love lets Satan loose among his creation to cause so much suffering, as he did with his loyal subject, Job, in the Old Testament.?

But wait, there seems to be a little catch to the story as follows: "I tell you the truth, unless you change and become like little children, you will never enter the kingdom of heaven. Therefore, whoever humbles himself like this child is the greatest in the kingdom of heaven." (Matthew 18:3-4) "Let the little children come to me, and do not hinder them, for the kingdom of heaven belongs to such as these." (Matthew 9:14, Mark 10:14, Luke 18:16) It seems that the love of God is not unconditional after all, for "unless you change and become like little children you will never enter the kingdom of heaven." It seems that simply believing as commanded in John 3:16 is not enough to gain eternal life in heaven. Jesus also said that "no one can enter the kingdom of God unless he is born of water and of the spirit." (John 3:5) However, John the Baptist claimed, "A man can receive only what he has been given from heaven." (John 3:27) And Jesus said, "... no one can come to me unless the Father has enabled/caused him." (John 6:63-65) "By myself, I can do nothing...

but the will of the Father who sent me." (John 5:30) Of course, this is contradicted in John 14:6 where Jesus says, "...no man comes to the Father except by me." Now, what are we supposed to do with that? You see, the Bible seems to be a collection of words and ideas, much like a collection of paints and brushes for an artist, that anyone can use to derive a seemingly infinite variety of pictures about God. We need not stop with Christianity and could include the other world religions in this discussion also. [Victims of the tsunami in Japan practiced mostly Shintoism and Buddhism, and that did not prevent their destruction any more than Christianity prevents a similar disaster predicted for the northern west coast of America that will be much worse than the earthquake that leveled San Francisco in 1906.]

For example, retired Episcopal Bishop, John Spong has written this analysis: "Western religion has regularly and consistently defined God in theistic terms. That is, God is perceived as an external being, supernatural in power, who periodically invades the world in miraculous ways to establish the divine will or to answer our prayers. Eastern religion in general, but Buddhism in particular, does not define God in theistic terms. That has caused some westerners to refer to Buddhism as an "atheist" religion. Well, it is, but only in the sense that "atheist" means "not theist." It does not mean that there is no sense of God in Buddhism. Language is our problem. When I speak about God I embrace the fact that I am only using words as symbols that describe not God, but my experience of God. I experience God as the source of life, the source of love and the ground of being."

This seems to be a restatement of the "God above God" that noted theologian, Paul Tillich (1886-1965) hoped to explain, but few sheeple are able to grasp. Like so many theologians, Tillich tried to reconcile the omnipotent God with human free will and failed. Of this God, he complains; "He deprives me of my subjectivity because he is all-powerful and all-knowing. I revolt and make him into an object, but the revolt fails and becomes desperate. God appears as the invincible tyrant, the being in contrast with whom all other beings are without freedom and subjectivity. This is the God Nietzsche said had to be killed because nobody can tolerate being made into a mere object of absolute knowledge and absolute control." This is precisely why the human ego must be crucified as it will not go voluntarily into calm submission before God the Almighty One.

But, there seems to be a stroke of wisdom buried in those words, "my experience of God." If we experience God as the source of being, then all that is must be the evidence of that source. "All that is" would have to include the stuff we call "bad" as well as the stuff we call "good." Now, obviously, the experience of God, i.e., all that is, varies immensely among the creation. For one thing, there are predators and prey. Thus, the world looks a lot different depending upon your point of reference. The food chain depends upon successful predators, else life would be extinguished in one generation of all species on planet Earth. But for predators to survive they need prey. As for why the various life forms exist at all, that is a mystery with no answer. Apparently, various if not all planets and stars exist without such life as is on Earth so it must not be necessary for the universe to exist to have life as we know it. We are not given to know why. Moving on, we must contend with the observation that creation includes forces of destruction as well as construction.

Natural disasters, such as the earthquakes that destroyed much of Haiti and Japan, plus a tsunami that destroyed much of Sri Lanka and the volcano that destroyed Pompeii and Herculaneum take with them countless lives of sheeple as well as all life forms that lie in the wake of their powers. Wars also take many lives and cause untold suffering, like the more than 56 million souls lost among four dozen countries of Europe during World War II. Or was that just God pruning his creation? Jesus described a Father who pruned the vineyard to increase its fruits. "I am the true vine, and my Father is the gardener. He cuts off every branch in me that bears no fruit, while every branch that does bear fruit he prunes so that it will be even more fruitful." (John 15:1-2) Either way you get pruned. The Koran says much the same. "His is the kingdom of the heavens and the Earth; He gives life and causes death; and He has power over all things." (57:52)

Now, it appears that radical Muslims who take the many commands in the Koran to fight the infidels literally are once again organizing to spread death by suicide bombings in order the receive a "great reward." This war will be different because the enemy does not wear military uniforms or practice traditional battlefield tactics. Nevertheless, they are very effective because a suicidal zealot can kill many sheeple. But, hey, Jesus said, "You will hear of wars and rumors of wars, but do not be alarmed because such things must happen." (Matthew 24:6, Mark 13:7) Now, we can watch them on television. The dead who die quickly may be the lucky ones because survivors must live with broken bodies and broken spirits that can never be put back together again...like it says in this nursery rhyme.

Humpty Dumpty sat on a wall.
Humpty Dumpty had a great fall.
All the king's horses and all the king's men
Could not put Humpty Dumpty together again.

The Rev. Dr. Charles Stanley, leader of the U.S. Southern Baptist Convention, wrote "The Blessings of Brokenness" in 1997 during separation from his wife that led to their divorce in 2000 after 44 years of marriage. He tried gallantly to find the benefits of brokenness, and for some readers he may have succeeded. But to get there he had to go through immense personal suffering and painful demands by God. Among his lamentations are these: "God is at the center of the universe, we are not. He requires that we serve him. He is not our errand boy. He is the Lord God Almighty. We are highly presumptuous when we demand that he do our bidding...We are not going to pray for escape, but for God's grace to be at work in your life so that you can face the situation with courage." [Contrast this with the teaching of Jesus about prayer in Matthew 21:22, "...if you believe, you will receive whatever you ask for in prayer." Are these necessary opposites, or what?] He concluded, "The proper relationship with God is one in which we put ourselves into a position to do his bidding...brokenness is the pruning process God uses to produce inner fruit...When a person is being broken we must not be too quick to come to their aid, to give solace or to attempt to remove the pain. In so doing we are getting in God's way... Rebellion causes us to miss out on the blessing God desires for us." St. Theresa of Lisieux also proclaimed the "joy of suffering" for Jesus as she died of tuberculosis at age 24. She warned, "If you desire to have a place by his side, then drink the chalice he has drunk." (Matthew 20: 20-23) From her childhood she expressed an obsessive desire to become an unknown and insignificant martyr for Jesus, her imaginary "spouse." Her father suffered too. He buried his wife and four children, gave his other five daughters to the Church, then he had two paralyzing strokes and lived his last five years in hospital before he died at age 63. [The ubiquitous crucifix reminds Catholics of the suffering Christ while the empty cross reminds Protestants of the risen Lord, necessary opposites for sure.]

Perhaps Dr. Stanley would agree that all beginnings come with endings and some things which are broken cannot be fixed. Such events as geological destruction are labeled "acts of God" to distinguish from tragedies and disasters that seem to be caused by willful acts of human perpetrators. But other disasters, like the oil spill in the Gulf of Mexico and WWII, are attributed to the mistakes of mankind, willful or unwillful. Perhaps if anyone took notice of some Middle Eastern students who wanted to learn how to fly airliners without taking off or landing, the suicidal attack of 9/11/01 on the World Trade towers may have been prevented. The disasters among human relationships, divorces and such, are attributed to acts driven by the sins of mankind. Why do we make such distinctions if all that is comes from the one source of being?

Some events of destruction such as in wars seem to occur from the instinct of self preservation vested in all forms of life. Whenever a life form is threatened, its natural response is flight or fight. Thus, anyone who prods a venomous snake or invades a nest of hornets or honey bees may expect some harmful consequences, including even death. Similarly, if one tribe of Homo sapiens invades another there could be war. War has led to the invention of weapons of mass destruction that require enormous human and financial capital to produce, unless one chooses to be a suicide bomber. Aircraft carriers and tanks and submarines are no match for one solitary Muslim zealot who thinks he has been promised a reward in heaven for killing infidels who do not accept Allah as their one and only God and Muhammad as his final prophet. "Therefore let those fight in the way of Allah, who sell this world's life for the hereafter; and whoever fights in the way of Allah, then be he slain or be he victorious, We shall grant him a mighty reward." (Koran 4:74) Where do such ideas come from, if not from God, the source of all being? Why do so many sheeple want to let God off the hook, and assume responsibility for actions that would actually make them superior to God? As a child who hurts himself in some accident, they want to rely upon a benevolent Father who is not the cause of their pain and suffering to make it all well again. This attitude was expressed by King David, "God is our refuge and strength, an ever-present help in trouble. Therefore we will not fear, though the Earth give way and the mountains fall into the heart of the sea, though its waters roar and foam and the mountains quake with their surging." (Psalm 46:1-3) That seems to be very comforting in theory, but not so practical when the Earth is removed from under you and buildings collapse onto you and all your family.

It is human nature to fear that which we do not control, and the more you learn about planet Earth the less there is under your control, including the acts of mankind. Fear, not only of the present, but of the hereafter also is the lot of mankind. Prosperity preachers do not often include such scripture in their sermons on health, wealth, and happiness, but they are there. King David wrote, "For as high as the heavens are above the Earth, so great is his love for those who fear him; as far as the east is from the west, so far has he removed our transgressions from us. As a father has compassion on his children, so the Lord has compassion on those who fear him; for he knows how we are formed, he remembers that we are dust. As for man, his days are like grass, he flourishes like a flower of the field; the wind blows over it and it is gone, and its place remembers it no more. But from everlasting to everlasting the Lord's love is with those who fear him." (Psalm 103:11-17). Jesus warned, "I tell you, my friends, do not be afraid of those who kill the body and after that can do no more. But I will show you whom you should fear: Fear him who, after the killing of the body, has power to throw you into hell. Yes, I tell you, fear him." (Luke 12: 4-5)

Jesus is referred to by his apostles and disciples as "teacher" and "master," but never as a friend, although he did proclaim, "Greater love has no man than this, that he lay down his life for his friends." (John 15:13) In his impeccable logic, King Solomon declared, "Two are better than one, because they have a good return for their work: If one falls down, his friend can help him up. But pity the man who falls and has no one to help him up! Also, if two lie down together, they will keep warm. But how can one keep warm alone?" (Ecclesiastes 4:9-11)

So, the next time you feel cold, who is more likely to make you feel warm, God or a friend? Thankfully, God has endowed Homo sapiens with the gifts of compassion and charity to balance indifference and hatred. Both must be necessary to make up the whole. It is probably no accident that the words "love" and "charity" as "the greatest of these" are used in various translations of the scripture in 1 Corinthians 13: 1-13) You might read it sometime in both the King James and the NIV posted at www.biblegateway.com. So, on the one hand God caused the earthquake that destroyed lives and property in Haiti and left millions homeless without the basic necessities of life. And he also sent millions of dollars and thousands of workers to help with the search and rescue and reconstruction for the surviving sufferers, while bulldozing bodies of thousands of anonymous victims into piles of human refuse in shallow graves. How can we accommodate such a god within the scope of human reason?

A definite dichotomy exists between the torturing god and the loving god. The late British theologian, C.S. Lewis (1898- 1963) composed this theodocy while suffering grief from untimely loss of his wife shortly after they married. "Take your choice, tortures occur. If they are unnecessary then there is no God or a bad one. If there is a good God then tortures are necessary." ("A Grief Observed," 1961) He concluded, "Not that I am in much danger of ceasing to believe in God. The real danger is of coming to believe such dreadful things about him. The conclusion I dread is, So this is what God's really like. Deceive yourself no longer... Turn to him in gratitude and praise and you will be welcomed with open arms. But go to him when your need is desperate, when all other help is vain, and what do you get. A door slammed in your face and the sound of bolting and double-bolting on the inside. After that, silence. You may as well turn away." He died soon after.

C.G. Jung pursued the notion that suffering among saints is kin to alchemy in which dross is converted into gold. Perhaps torture is necessary to crucify the human ego and to purify the soul for its ascension, as it was with Jesus on the cross. The energy in good is the same as the energy in evil and the Bible says it all comes from the same source. (Isaiah 45:5-7, Deuteronomy 32:39, Colossians 1:16, I Samuel 18:10) "Shall there be evil/calamity in a city, and the Lord has not done it?" (Amos 3:6) The Koran says the same thing; "No calamity comes, no affliction occurs, except by the decision and preordainment of Allah." (64.11) Both good and evil must be necessary, or it would be different. If there were no evil, how could good be defined or discerned? Where would beautiful and rich be without ugly and poor for comparison?

In spite of such scriptures, Greek orthodox theologian, Philip Sherrard (1922-1995) wrote in Christianity: Lineaments of a Sacred Tradition (1998) "One of the principal means through which we can be induced to submit to diabolic persuasion is by instilling in us the idea that evil is in fact an integral part of our nature, so that in expressing our evil proclivities we are being just as natural and true to ourselves as we are when we express positive qualities of goodness and love... to impute evil to the source of things is to commit one of the most terrible acts of perversion of which the human mind is capable." Poor man, with such a one-sided god. C. G. Jung's greatest contention with Christianity was just this failure to recognize that which is labeled the dark and evil sides of nature are as much a manifestation of God as that which we label "good." Jung himself did not see the challenge of life as being the victory of light over dark but rather accommodation of their coexistence. This argument just goes to illustrate the principle in Theofatalism™ of diametric opposites; for each thought there is an opposite thought. All in God's will of course. AIGWOC...Think you can handle that?

Many examples of diametric opposites exist among Homo sapiens for those with eyes to see. God ordains the irresistible power of reproduction to produce children among parents who cannot or will not provide their basic needs for living and so they die of starvation and neglect. Throughout cities in America, thousands of abandoned children assigned to social networks of temporary and often abusive foster homes literally are kicked into the streets at age 18 with few of the resources they need for success in this competitive society. On the other hand, hundreds of surrogate parents are flocking to adopt a few of the 380,000 orphans from Haiti who were living destitute eating mud pies before the earthquake. Throughout the Earth, millions of God's creatures suffer a life of pain without succor. Why? Perhaps there is an explanation that does not lay the cause in the sin of disobedience by Adam and thereby to all of his heirs through transfer of their genes, as Church dogma dictates. After all, that would totally negate the concept of free will because who would choose to be born in sin condemned to hell if he had any other choice?...Hmmm?

We can take up the scriptures and paint a different picture, one not often heard in churches. Jesus taught, "Do not store up for yourselves treasures on Earth where moth and rust destroy and where thieves break in and steal, but lay up for yourselves treasures in heaven..." (Matthew 6:19-20) He gave no explanation for what were those treasures in heaven, but perhaps there is a clue in what he told a rich young man who had kept all the commandments, "If you want to be perfect, go, sell your possessions and give to the poor, and you will have treasure in heaven. Then come, follow me. When the young man heard this, he went away sad, because he had great wealth." (Matthew 20:21-22) When you contemplate human suffering and wonder where God is in all that, consider that he may be exactly where he was when Jesus was suffering on the cross and lamented through his pain, "My God, my God, why have you forsaken me?" (Matthew 27:46, Mark 15:34) Jesus had no choice in the matter because he came into the world for that express purpose even though in his humanity he felt abandoned by the God he claimed as his Father. So, could it be that we all are in much the same relationship with God the Almighty One? Could it be that we all are born with an express purpose that is impossible to avoid? And that purpose includes suffering as well as joy?

The Rev. Dr. Rick Warren became rich and famous after publishing his book titled, The Purpose Driven Life (2007) He wrote, "It's not about you. The purpose of your [pitiful] life is far greater than your own personal fulfillment, your peace of mind, or even your happiness. It's far greater than your family, your career, or even your wildest dreams and ambitions. If you want to know why you were placed on this planet, you must begin with God. You were born by his purpose and for his purpose... You are alive today because God chose you to be here. You exist for his benefit, his glory, his purpose, and his delight. Bringing enjoyment to God, living for his pleasure, is the first purpose of your life...Because God made you for a reason, he also decided when you would be born and how long you would live. He planned the days of your life in advance, choosing the exact time of your birth and death. The Bible says, You saw me before I was born and scheduled each day of my life before I began to breathe. Every day was recorded in your book! (Psalm 139:16). It is God who directs the lives of his creatures; everyone's life is in his power. (Job 12:10)... God also planned where you'd be born and where you'd live for his purpose. Your race and nationality are no accident. God left no detail to chance. He planned it all for his purpose." It seems that no one needs to search for his purpose in life because he cannot avoid it. Is not this a clear claim for Theofatalism™, although not called by that name? Was Pastor Warren addressing this conclusion just to sheeple in his church, or did that include all the sheeple in the world? And, why did 30 million sheeple buy his book? Perhaps they had to because it was the will of God the Almighty One.

Now, few sheeple ever hear sermons like this in church because such teaching may challenge their concepts about God and even make them so uncomfortable that they leave and take their money with them. Who wants to replace Santa Claus with the cross of Christ? Preachers who have their careers vested in a financially secure income from the voluntary contributions of members would understandably avoid challenging them beyond tolerance for discomfort. If church membership retention and growth is the primary goal, then the reality of the gospel may be lost in desire for fame and fortune. Such was not the ministry of Jesus. Little wonder that few sheeple actually can voluntarily "take up their cross and follow him." Who would do such a thing if they have any other choice? So, the next time someone tells you that the word "gospel" means "good news," consider the source and recall what comedian Bill Cosby said to his errant teenager, "I brought you into this world and I will take you out." And also recall that Jesus said, "Do not call anyone on Earth father because you have one Father and he is in heaven." (Matthew 23:9) If Christ was God, why does the Catholic Church ignore this command? If God is The One, this too must be necessary or it would be different. Get it?

Albert Einstein (1879-1955) thought about God and came to this conclusion: "If this being is omnipotent, then every occurrence, including every human action, every human thought, and every human feeling and aspiration is also His work; how is it possible to think of holding men responsible for their deeds and thoughts before such an almighty Being? In giving out punishment and rewards He would to a certain extent be passing judgment on Himself. How can this be combined with the goodness and righteousness ascribed to Him?" It really is quite simple for those with eyes to see and ears to hear. For the others, it is impossible. Abd-ru-shin [a.k.a.Oskar Ernst Bernhardt, (1875-1941) declared, "All teachings/thoughts were at one time willed by God, precisely adapted to the individual peoples and countries, and formed in complete accord with their actual spiritual maturity and receptivity." In fact, all creation comes from the one source and that source blindfolds many sheeple so they cannot see the truth of it because it would shock them to death. If you think the Bible is the Word of God, consider that it says repeatedly that the creation was "good," (Genesis 1: 4-31) so that must include predator and prey as well as all the various forms of destruction that come with life on planet Earth. It also says that much of what Jesus taught in parables was presented to educate the chosen disciples but to keep others not chosen from understanding and being redeemed. (Matthew 13:10-11, Mark 4: 10-12) Thus, everything must be the will of God or it would be different. This would have to include all the disabling side effects described in the fine print that come with medical drug treatments because all benefits come with burdens. Think you can handle that?

Some sheeple go to great lengths to try and find God. They look in churches and monasteries and among gurus and cult leaders, among others, like children playing hide and seek. They read books and take courses and practice various religious rites and traditions. Some of them renounce the world of senses and thinking to live alone as a recluse in search of God inside themselves. Of all this searching, retired Episcopal Bishop John Spong has written, "No one has seen God, and the deity about whom most of us speak is our own creation. Religious systems try to pretend that God has revealed God to them, but when they describe that God, it is clearly a God in their own image. Throughout history human beings have perceived of God as an animating presence, an Earth mother, the sun, the moon, a tribal chief or shaman, a high priest or guru, and a universal presence. Each image, however, was shaped by human need and human understanding. That is the first thing you should embrace. The God you say you cannot see is a deity of some other human being's creation. As long as you are bound by another's definition, you may well never see God for yourself. I do not believe that any human being can ever know who God is; we can only know how we think we have experienced God. God and my experience of God are not the same thing. That is a crucial difference. We can experience on some level what we cannot ultimately define. What we describe in our words, scriptures, creeds and doctrines is not the reality of God, but our limited human attempt to explain our experiences of that reality. God is not bound to anyone's definition."

However, Apostle Paul admonished the Roman Jews to take a look around because all of nature attests to the creation of God. And God reminded Job that all of creation was his handy work and not that of man. (Romans 1:18:20, Job 38-41) Also, Jesus taught his disciples to pray, "...thy will be done on Earth as it is in Heaven." (Matthew 6:9-11) God being God, how could it be otherwise? Thomas Paine (1737-1809) concluded in his "Age of Reason," (1795) "The creation speaks a universal language, independently of human speech or human language, multiplied and various as they may be. It is an ever-existing original, which every man can read. It cannot be forged; it cannot be counterfeited; it cannot be lost; it cannot be altered; it cannot be suppressed. It does not depend upon the will of man whether it shall be published or not; it publishes itself from one end of the Earth to the other. It preaches to all nations and to all worlds; and this word of God reveals to man all that is necessary for man to know of God." So, if he created it all, just look around at all he created. Some of it stinks pretty badly.

To see God, just look around at his creation. It is one thing to see God in natural beauty or the performance of a great musician or athlete or artist or some evangelical preacher, but what about including land fills, sewage plants, refugee camps, street gangs, prisons, junk yards, mental hospitals, female and male brothels, opium dens, and industrial effluent that pollutes rivers and lakes plus hurricanes, tornadoes, earthquakes, and all the masses of Homo sapiens seemingly abandoned in their misery and suffering, plus the ones who are causing the suffering. Consider all the drug addicts in America who are creating the carnage in Mexico to get their fixes. One would also need to look into diverse religions to see God everywhere. God seems to have many aliases and to wear many costumes. Could you visit a Hindu temple, a Jewish synagogue, a Buddhist shrine, a Catholic cathedral, a Voodoo ritual, a Muslim mosque and an open Bible church, or read both the Bible and the Koran and still say, "Everything is God being God because that is all there is?" Hmmm? And that is only the Homo sapiens. To see God one also needs to look at all the other life forms on the planet both on land and in water, plant and animal included. There also are the geologic processes, both immediate and long term. And beyond this planet one also must look as far as possible out into the vastness of the universe. If there is only one creator, is there not only one possible explanation for all things. The voice of God said as much to Job when they finally met face to face. And Job was overwhelmed, "I know that you can do all things. No purpose of yours can be thwarted and nothing outside your will can succeed." (Job 42:2)

God is a universal construct of human imagination. Even atheists must have a God not to believe in to refute it. The most vocal among atheists are no less fervent in their evangelism than conservative religionists. Each is expressing a form of faith that cannot rationally be proven, God is and God is not, necessary opposites for sure. Indeed, one could speak of a secular fundamentalism that resembles religious fundamentalism of an opposite nature. This may be one of those cases where opposites eventually converge into both/and rather than either/or. Some cultures have many gods, but the common element seems to be acknowledgment that man is the not the master of his fate, although he is given the illusion that he is. This is the necessary opposite complement to belief in humanism which assumes that man is the crown of creation and controls his own destiny as the "captain of his soul," the way William Ernest Henley expressed in his poem, "Invictus." But, who is it that is captain of "his" own soul? How can the soul have an owner? The Bible myth of creation claims that God made man in his own image and likeness. If that is true, then all the evil and brutal forms and criminal behaviors of Homo sapiens are manifestations of God, not just the good and compassionate and lovely parts. In fact, everything in the universe is a manifestation of God in some way to those who believe in creationism and the evolution of a grand divine design. To those who don't, there are only more and more questions with no answers.

King David sings the praises of God, "The Earth is the Lord's, and everything in it, the world, and all who live in it." (Psalm 24:1) But, the prophet sees this power in a different light. "See, the Lord is going to lay waste the Earth and devastate it; he will ruin its face and scatter its inhabitants...The Earth will be completely laid waste and totally plundered. The Lord has spoken this word." (Isaiah 24:1-3) If you look around with clarity, you may conclude that everything is God being God the Almighty One.

When the blindfold comes off and you see God the Almighty One as it is, you may be scared to death. That is why we are given only one small peak at a time. There is a hadith [a saying of the Prophet Muhammad] that tells us: "The world is your friend if it reminds you of God, and it is your enemy if it makes you forget God." But, it takes special eyes to see God the Almighty One everywhere in everything, otherwise the shock would be too great. As Mother Teresa learned serving in the slums of Calcutta, "God does whatever he wants with whoever he wants whenever he wants." But, she concluded, "Heaven will be full of slum people." Think you can handle that?

15. THE DUAL POWERS OF GOD THE ALMIGHTY ONE.

There is a popular religious ballad of uncertain origin titled, "He's got the whole world in his hands." It includes: "He's got the itty bitty baby in his hands...he's got you and me brother in his hands...he's got you and me sister in his hands...the wind and the rain...the Earth and sky... the night and day...the sun and moon...the land and sea...the spring and fall...the rich and poor...He's got the whole world in his hands." What sheeple may not realize is that the hand of the creator that can protect and comfort also can crush and destroy. And does. The evidence is all around, but it takes special eyes to see or the shock would be too great.

Why do many sheeple persist in believing that only good things come from God while all evil things do not? This belief immediately raises the existential question of undeserved suffering among innocents and whether or not God is only just and good or even exists at all. Sheeple may believe their problems result only from their own free will. Maybe not. Why do they believe they control some things among the affairs of mankind but acknowledge that God controls other things in affairs of mankind and nature? And that Satan controls still other things according to the permission of God? This question dates back 2300 years to the dialogues of Epicurus (341-270 B.C.) who queried, "Is God willing to prevent evil, but not able? Then he is not omnipotent. Is he able but not willing? Then he is malevolent and not good. Is he both able and willing? Whence then cometh evil? Of course, if he is neither able nor willing to prevent evil, why call him God?" Indeed.

Christian apologists have tried for centuries unsuccessfully to create a theodocy that accommodates a god that is all powerful and all good with ubiquitous suffering and evil in its creation caused only by unrepentant sinful nature of mankind which they inherited through disobedience of the first man, Adam. (Romans 5:18-19, 1 Corinthians 15: 20-22).Their only solution, which fails basic logic 101, is to give Homo sapiens powers superior to God for disobedience and resistance and to assign them the responsibility for their own suffering which, of course, immediately cancels the omnipotence of their God. One theologian even claimed that since God has perfect foreknowledge of all that will happen, he has no choice but to make it turn out that way. The Bible itself does not support such Christian dogma.

The argument of Apostle Paul that all suffer for the sin of Adam (Romans 5:18-19) does not hold up because; 1) God did not condemn all their descendents to hell for the sins of Adam and Eve, in fact Cain was not punished for killing his brother Abel, 2) Old Testament use of hell merely means sheol, the pit or grave, 3) the Old Testament states that the fathers and sons will be judged for their own behaviors and that only, (Ezekiel 18:19-20) 4) the mention of hell/hades as punishment does not occur until the New Testament, 5) When Jesus healed the man born blind to show the power of God he said neither he or his parents sinned (John 9:3) and; 6) the Kingdom is populated by such as little children so they could not be born as sinners (Luke 18:26). Besides, if everyone is born in sin, there could be no free will.

Internationally famous theologian, The Rev. Dr. Charles Stanley (1932 --) wrote, The Blessings of Brokenness in 1997. This period was during the legal separation requested by his wife, Anna after more than 40 years of marriage that ended in their divorce in 2000. The book reads like his journal of personal dialogue with God to try and find some benefits in the pain, suffering, and threat to his professional career the divorce would bring. His mega-church in Atlanta, GA permitted him to continue his ministry even though the divorce violated limits set by the Southern Baptist Convention. The Rev. Stanley tries very gamely to overcome the compelling question, "Why God allows us to go through hard times..." with the standard arguments offered by the church, i.e., God does not cause bad things but permits them in order to make us into better sheeple. (Other writers have tackled this issue also with similar conclusions.) He claims the traditional use of universal sin as the cause of mankind's distress because the loving God would not intentionally harm his creation for no good purpose. "God will allow us to follow the pathway of sin that we have chosen...God does not strip us of our free will."

Among the desirable personal improvements God desires, Dr. Stanley says we are to bear more fruit, both inner and outer, for the Kingdom of God while presenting God as the gardener depicted in John 15: 1-8 who prunes his creation. The fruits of suffering he lists are love, joy, peace, patience, kindness, goodness, faithfulness, forgiveness, gentleness, and self control. Why we should have to suffer so much pain and loss that often ends in death and abandonment (as it did for Jesus on the cross and many of his disciples during persecution of the early Christians) to gain these benefits he does not explain, except to refer us to the kernel of wheat that must fall to the ground and die in order to produce many more seeds. (John 12:24) He tries to let God off the hook; "I am not saying that God will kill someone you love to get your attention. I don't believe we can ever say that God kills one person to get another to submit to him." But he contradicts himself in saying, "God wants no relationship to be a substitute for our relationship with him. God crushes, breaks, shatters, removes anything from our lives...that... forms a barrier between us and God...brokenness is his way of blessing." As to any choice in the matter that we might have, Dr. Stanley writes, "Brokenness brings us to the place where we realize we have no rights." [Nor control either.] Considering he and his wife never reconciled after their divorce, he should agree: some things that are broken cannot be fixed.

There is a more logical explanation for all the suffering in life that is not so conflicted, but obviously it is not one that sheeple want to believe, yet. God is a duality, just like his creation. God not only is love and creation, but also is anger and destruction, i.e., both/and. The "benevolent father" may have been expressed by comedian, Bill Cosby to his wayward teenager, "I brought you into this world and I'll take you out." Just look around at the creation of God. Did not God create sin so he could practice forgiveness, did he not create pain so he could practice healing, did he not create death so he could practice resurrection? One cannot exist without the other. If this conclusion is so obvious, why do Christians still struggle with the question? Why don't they believe their own source? "I make peace and create evil. I the Lord do all these things." (Isaiah 45:7) "Shall there be evil in a city, and the Lord has not done it?" (Amos 3:6) The Koran says the same thing to Muslims; "No calamity comes, no affliction occurs, except by the decision and preordainment of Allah." (64.11) This would have to include the acts of man as well as the acts of nature. Obviously, God also must create disease and insanity as well as earthquakes and wars. Having seen the whole of creation, one must paraphrase the Queen, "we are not impressed." And those who cannot accept this view of God must be intentionally blinded by him to the obvious truth. Instead of worship, the creator would seem to need a measure of forgiveness for all the harm and suffering endured by the creation. So, it would seem appropriate if not sufficient for him/it to come and suffer death by crucifixion in order to experience what it is like to be human. Surely, if he could have done a better job than this he would have, don't you think? Like his image and likeness of humankind, we must conclude that he did the best he could under the circumstances.

How much more evidence do you need? Read the lament of Job for his unjust treatment by God, "He crushes me with a tempest, and multiplies my wounds without cause; he will not let me get my breath, but fills me with bitterness though I am innocent, my own mouth would condemn me; though I am blameless he would prove me perverse...If I wash myself with soap and cleanse my hands with lye, yet he wilt plunge me into a pit, and my own clothes will abhor me...I loathe my life. It is all one; therefore I say, he destroys both the blameless and the wicked. When disaster brings sudden death he mocks at the calamity of the innocent." (Job 9) Job may have received recompense but his innocent servants and children who were destroyed never were heard of again. He might have appended these words of Saint Teresa of Avila's (1515-1582) that she addressed to God: "If you treat others the way you treat me, it's no wonder you have so few friends." She refers, along with St. Theresa of Lisieux, to Jesus as her "Divine Spouse of Virgins," and presents in her autobiography this dualistic description of an obvious ecstatic but painful encounter with an angel of God. "I saw in his hand a long spear of gold, and at the iron's point there seemed to be a little fire. He appeared to me to be thrusting it at times into my heart, and to pierce my very entrails; when he drew it out, he seemed to draw them out also, and to leave me all on fire with a great love of God. The pain was so great, that it made me moan; and yet so surpassing was the sweetness of this excessive pain, that I could not wish to be rid of it." Sounds like a woman on her honeymoon. Teresa seems to be more woman than saint. During a century when female sexuality was repressed it seems like she found a perfect way to celebrate it...as the bride of Jesus, and the favorite pet of his father, St. Joseph. What is interesting is how the Church interpreted her thinly veiled fantasy experience as spiritual ecstasy and appointed her posthumously the first woman Doctor of the Church in 1970...Hmmm.

Geological tragedies that take human lives and destroy property, like the earthquake in Haiti, flooding of New Orleans, and volcanic burial of Pompeii, commonly are called "acts of God" to separate them from intentional damage to life and property caused by humans. It is very easy to condemn arsonists who set fires intentionally or the violent attack on the World Trade Center by radical Islamic terrorists, but natural disasters often leave sheeple feeling insecure and even abandoned by God. The viral influenza pandemic of 1918 that killed millions worldwide and the current AIDS epidemic are cases in point. Also, as expanding populations of humans invade more wild animal habitats, it is likely that more viruses will be encountered for which humans have no immunity. The largest virus so far was discovered in 2003 by a lab in Marseille and it defies control by conventional treatment. Future pandemics, like the H1N1 swine flu virus, are forecast. The only purpose of a virus seems to be replicating itself by attaching to human cells until they are destroyed. Even a common cold virus can kill sheeple if their immune defenses are overcome. Why should viruses exist in the first place? Actually, it appears that the immune system needs diseases to fight or it turns on itself and creates auto-immune diseases. And, a Reovirus has been discovered that likes to kill cancerous cells in the ovary, breast, prostate, colon, brain, lymphoma and melanoma.

So, once again, burdens and benefits cannot seem to be separated. Geological disasters are continually destroying human habitat and their lives. Hurricane Katrina that devastated New Orleans and the Gulf

Coast and the tsunami that took 250 thousand lives in the Indian Ocean and the earthquake in Haiti left some things broken that cannot ever be fixed. Tornadoes often demolish homes of some sheeple while leaving their neighbors untouched. In the news is the discovery by geologists that the magnetic field of Earth may be poised for a reversal in polarity with unknown consequences, not to mention the unpredictable impact of global climate change. When you perceive all this destruction as the power of God, you will be scared to death unless you can find some benefits. Perhaps they are just the way in which God prunes his creation so it can bear better fruit as described by Jesus...yes, he actually said that. (John 15:1-2)

But, the social and economic affairs of Homo sapiens seem to be taken differently. Then we must invoke free will and assign responsibility to individuals for their actions whether good or bad. But, sometimes things happen that challenge sheeple to look into the face of God that most everyone would rather not see. The genesis of World War II and the Holocaust provides a primary example. Adolf Hitler laid out his scheme very plainly in 1926 with publication of "Mein Kampf," which is still a controversial study in politics of the Third Reich. Unfortunately, no one took it seriously until WWII could not be prevented, although Winston Churchill issued a warning and called it, "the new Koran of faith and war: turgid, verbose, shapeless, but pregnant with its message." Hitler wrote, "While the program of the ordinary political party is nothing but the recipe for cooking up favorable results out of the next general elections, the program of the new philosophy represents a declaration of war against an existing order of things, against present conditions, in short, against the established view of life in general...Any attempt to carry these theories into effect without the aid of a militant organization would be doomed to failure today, as it has failed in the past and must fail in the future...It must not serve the masses but rather dominate them...the best defense is always attack." But all the sheeple were too busy to pay attention, and so 56 million of them died in WWII in Europe and 17 million in Asia. Of these, 405,000 were American warriors. How could this be unless God the Almighty One willed it so to happen? And so it is with all the other fatal political foibles of mankind, the present crusade of radical Islam not excepted.

The U.S. banking debacle of 2008-09 shows how fragile and undependable are the institutions of mankind. All in God's will of course. During its worst bear market of 2008-9, the stock market lost more than eleven trillion dollars. Vanished. Signs of a financial collapse went unheeded by both borrowers and lenders until it finally hurt too much to be ignored. So long as they could resell them to greater fools, banks made more and more loans with no regard to their potential for default. Even the rating agencies, that are funded by the banks, overrated financial instruments that soon were found to be junk. The amount of mortgages in default at this time is estimated to be $2.2 trillion, with the future amount unknown. As many as six million homeowners may be at risk of default because home prices have fallen so badly that perhaps half of them are upside down, owing more than market values. When the Clinton Administration increased the credit risks for home mortgages and credit cards, they had no clue it would come to that. The financial wizards and government officials who caused the problem are some of the most highly educated sheeple on the planet. It seems that they were all relying upon some kind of risk management statistical formula developed by one David X. Li, a mathematician from China. Warnings about the uncertainties in his formula were unheeded because while it worked many investors were making lots of money by trading worthless securities from one fool to a greater fool. But things changed, and no one paid any attention to any of the many warnings. Mr. Li went back to China, leaving the American economy in shambles. In spite of their failures, banking officials retained their jobs and exhorbitant bonuses by manipulating their company boards of directors with no government oversight. How could so many sheeple get it so wrong unless God the Almighty One willed it so? Was David X. Li sent by God from China to destroy the American economy?

As late as a few days before the crash in October 2008 bankers were still maintaining that the fundamentals of the economy were sound. By 2010, banks were being shut down at the highest rate in history and the Federal Deposit Insurance Corp. had a deficit of $20 billion. It seems that common sense is not so common these days. Founder and czar of Berkshire Hathaway, Warren Buffet warned sheeple about corporate deception. He urged investors not to focus on the net income figures that companies report because they are easily manipulated through accounting tricks or by selling investments. He said Berkshire's net income can be particularly misleading because of the large amount of unrealized investment gains or losses the company holds at any given time. He said that regardless of Berkshire's performance, it could easily and legally "cause net income in any given period to be almost any number we would like." The famous trial lawyer, Clarence Darrow (1857-1938) observed, "The law does not pretend to punish everything that is dishonest. That would seriously interfere with business." So, what can you depend on? Don't count on traditional religion.

Quite often, bad things happen to good sheeple. Anicius Boethius was a fifth century Roman patriot who got himself imprisoned and tortured to death while trying to mediate the war between two rivals for the control of Rome. Like Job, from his dungeon he consulted philosophy back to Socrates, Plato, and Aristotle for a solution to his dilemma, asking why a person with such good intentions should suffer so much for his efforts. His conclusion attempts to reconcile the omnipotent God with human free will thus; "Providence is the unchangeable, simple, and unified form of all things which come into and pass out of existence, while Fate is the connection and temporal order of all those things which the divine mind decided to bring into existence. This leads to the conclusion that all things subject to Fate are in turn subject to Providence; therefore, Fate itself is subject to Providence. This same power, this Fate, connects all the actions and fortunes of humanity into an unbreakable chain of causation; these causes have their origin in unchangeable Providence, therefore, these causes, too, must be unchangeable. However, some things subject to Providence are not in turn subject to Fate. So God sees future things that are the result of human free will; these things, then, are necessary, on the condition that they are known by God, but, considered only in themselves, they are still free in their own natures. God sees us from above and knows all things in his eternal present and judges our future free actions, justly distributing rewards and punishments" If that does not satisfy to explain why bad things happen to good sheeple, welcome to a very large group of skeptics.

How can any human action be both free and necessary? That is the challenge for limited human intellects to grasp. But, what about a possible alternative explanation? Suppose the God of Providence does not just permit bad things to happen to good sheeple so they can earn future rewards in some afterlife, but really causes such things to happen for his purpose in this life. After all, was it not God who put the tree of knowledge of good and evil in the Garden in the first place, as the writer of Genesis proclaimed? If suffering was brought into the world by the disobedience of the creatures he created, was that not of his will? The creatures obviously had not the power of their own creation. After all, he is the potter and we are the clay, some for royal use and some for common use, as Apostle Paul described. (Jeremiah 18: 2-6, Romans 9:20-22)

Another writer has explained the suffering story of Job thus: It was God's idea to severely try Job, not Satan's. (Job 1:12) And Satan took strict orders from God as to just how he could try Job. Satan got permission from God at each and every step of this severe trying of Job and destruction of his family and all his servants and cattle. Why do we think God the Almighty One does it differently today? Do we think Satan now has free reign - free will? Do we think that God changes? Nonsense: "For I am the Lord, I change not." (Malachi 3:6). Are not these activities of Satan necessary? Does God use Satan for no good purpose? Then why can't sheeple see that God the Almighty One also created Satan for his very purposes unless, of course, he has blinded them so they cannot see the reality of it. After all, did not Jesus teach in mystical parables so that the Jewish sheeple "may not understand lest they should be converted and their sins be forgiven them." (Mark 4:12) This was written to fulfill a prophecy from Isaiah 6:10. Go ahead, look it up.

What do you do when the foundations of human security are shaken and you realize it is God the Almighty One who is doing the shaking? [First Lady, Laura Bush described in her autobiography, From the Heart, (2010) how she lost faith in God after she ran a stop sign at age 17 and killed an athlete in her high school. "It was the first time that I had prayed to God for something, begged him for something, not the simple childhood wishing on a star but humbly begging for another human life. And it was as if no one heard," she writes. "My begging, to my 17-year-old mind, had made no difference. The only answer was the sound of his mother's sobs on the other side of that thin emergency room curtain."] Sheeple apparently need to believe in a just world so they can go about living with a sense of hope, trust, and confidence. This delusion must be necessary or it would be different. But, where do you go when your past is full of anger, your present is full of disappointment, and your future is full of grief and fear?

Most Christians seem to prefer the idea that "God is love" from the New Testament (I John 4:8) rather than the source of the "evil spirit from God" that plagued king Saul in the Old Testament. (I Samuel 18:10) Also, "God sent an evil spirit between Abimelech and the citizens of Shechem, who acted treacherously against Abimelech. God did this in order that the crime against Jerub-Baal's seventy sons, the shedding of their blood, might be avenged." (Judges 9:22-24) And what of the God who kills Ananias and Sapphira for lying after they withheld some of their wealth from the new Christian cult? (Acts 5:1) Or he who has his angel strike down King Herod because he doesn't properly ascribe praise? (Acts 12:19) Let alone the God who deals out retribution to those who do not know [Him] in the form of eternal destruction? (2 Thessalonians 1:8-9) and the Jesus who, robe dipped in blood, mouth filled with a sharp sword, eyes like a flame, judges and wages war, strike[s] down the nations, rules with a rod of iron, and treads the winepress of the fierce wrath of God? (Revelation 19:11).

After Albert Einstein discovered the laws of physics leading to the atomic bomb he lamented it was like the Earth had been stripped from under his feet and there was no firm ground upon which to stand. So it might be with those who are given to see God the Almighty One as he really is. When your beliefs no longer support your reality, it may seem there is no where to turn for support. You must change either your belief or your reality to regain conformity in order to avoid the discomfort of cognitive dissonance. [Surveys indicate that a third of Russians still believe the sun orbits the earth, sheeple lived with dinosaurs, and nuclear radiation is man made. Many Americans believe that Jesus rose from the dead and eternal hell fire awaits anyone who denies it. But, what has that to do with health, wealth, and happiness in this life?]

Children must give up belief in Santa Claus because they would look ridiculous sitting on his lap every year of their lives. Most everyone makes the transition uneventfully, or do they. St. Theresa of Lisieux (1873-1897) explained her prayers; "I do as a child who has not learned to read, I just tell our Lord all that I want and He understands." This is a woman to took vows of poverty, chastity, obedience, and cloistered contemplation. Jesus declared those who mourn will be comforted. But, where is the comfort for a young widow whose pastor husband dies of cancer leaving her with five small children? Where is the comfort when a father finds his children have all been murdered by his wife, their mother? Where is the comfort for a farmer whose seven children all died in a house fire while he was milking the cows? Where is the comfort for a family whose teenager is killed in a drive-by shooting? Where is the comfort for retirees who find their savings gutted by incompetent banking executives? Where is the comfort for families driven from their homes by impersonal destruction of hurricanes and tornadoes and wild fires? Where is the comfort for those subjected to genocide by their ungodly rulers? Where is the comfort for those orphans whose parents are destroyed by AIDS disease and pestilence? Where is the support for those law abiding young men and women who are compelled to obey their military leaders who demand that they kill anonymous fellow human beings, including women and children, labeled "enemy" in the name of national defense? When you can no longer depend on mother Earth and its creator to protect you, where do you turn for comfort and security? Where do you turn when you discover that the plan of God the Almighty One for your life includes pain and suffering?

If you turn to religion you may choose Christianity or Islam. Nothing could be more opposite. In the former, Jesus taught pacifism; love your enemies, turn the other cheek, give your cloak as well as your coat, carry the burden two miles when you are commanded for one, obey your rulers and masters, and forgive those who wrong you seventy times seventy times, and rejoice in suffering because your reward in Heaven will be great. (Matthew 5:38-48, Luke 6:20-48) Suffering was his thing just as Socrates instructed 400 years earlier, "It is better to suffer an injustice than to commit one." When he prepared to die on the cross Jesus said, "This is why I came," and he forbade his disciples to fight off the Jews who arrested him. (John 18:36) Christianity promotes the absolute separation of church and state; "render unto Caesar the things that are Caesar's and unto God the things that are God's," while Islam demands the total and complete integration of both by force if necessary under the law of Shari'a. In Islam its Messenger, Muhammad said, "I have been commanded [by whom?] to fight people until they confess that there is no god but Allah and that Muhammad is Allah's Messenger." The Koran proclaims again and again those who fight for Allah will receive a "great reward" whether they perish or not, as the case with suicide bombers. [You can now read the intent and plan of Islamic jihad against the West for yourself in publication of the English language magazine, "Inspire," published by Al-Qaeda in the Arabian peninsula.] In contrast, Jesus came as a suffering servant kneeling to wash the feet of his disciples to show the master was not above the slaves. Both Islam and Christianity must be creations of the same Source. Get it?

The first rule of every battle is, "know your enemy." The Muslim manual of practice is the Koran, and it is very specific. The word "fight" appears 64 times in the Koran, all related to converting unbelievers by force and defending their faith by Muslims against invaders. Win or lose, Muslims are promised a great reward in heaven for defending their faith. "Therefore let those fight in the way of Allah, who sell this world's life for the hereafter; and whoever fights in the way of Allah, whether be he slain or be he victorious, We shall grant him a mighty reward." (4:74) The word, "fight" appears 187 times in the Bible, 177 of them in the Old Testament where it is almost always related to attacking some neighbor or fighting off some invader by the Jewish "chosen people." [Fighting for religion is like competing in the Special Olympics. Even if you win, you still are retarded] But in contrast, Jesus only used the word "fight" once and that was to explain that his kingdom was not of this world so he would not fight to avoid crucifixion by his enemies. (John 18:36) If Jesus is the true role model for Christians, not many actually follow him for he was an unconditional nonviolent pacifist who taught a message very similar to Buddhism. "But I tell you who hear me: Love your enemies, do good to those who hate you, bless those who curse you, pray for those who mistreat you." (Luke 6:27-28) The message he preached was rejected in his time and still is being rejected today by many, if not most, Christians. Only Mahatma Gandhi and Martin Luther King, Jr. have successfully implemented his instructions, but both of them were assassinated. We could include all the Buddhist monks of Tibet who were murdered when China invaded in 1959, driving the Dalai Lama into lifetime exile to India. There was apparently a body of Christian writing during the mid-19th century that produced the logic for nonresistance in political affairs based upon teachings of Jesus, but it was totally stifled by the Church and never saw much circulation. Only the Mennonites, the Quakers, and the Church of the Brethren survive among its believers in pacifism.

Instead of fighting unbelievers Jesus taught nothing but compassion and charity, "But I tell you, Do not resist an evil person. If someone strikes you on the right cheek, turn to him the other also. And if someone wants to sue you and take your tunic, let him have your cloak as well. If someone forces you to go one mile, go with him two miles." (Matthew 5:39-41) This is opposite to the law of Old Testament Jews who were taught that justice required "life for life, eye for eye, tooth for tooth, burn for burn, wound for wound, bruise for bruise." (Exodus 21: 23-25) No wonder there is eternal war between Jews and Arabs. Apostle Paul wrote, "I beg you that when I come I may not have to be as bold as I expect to be toward some sheeple who think that we live by the standards of this world. For though we live in the world, we do not wage war as the world does. The weapons we fight with are not the weapons of the world. On the contrary, they have divine power to demolish strongholds." (2 Corinthians 10:2-4) The Jews rejected this message so their temple was demolished and Jerusalem was burned when they rebelled against the Romans in 67-74 A.D, and again in 135 A.D. not to be regained until the United Nations reconstituted Israel in 1947. During this era, Jews lost whatever interest they had in Christ because he gave them no help in routing the Romans. Apostle Paul declared that all governing political authority was to be obeyed by Christians as ordained by God. (Romans 13: 1-7)

Some scholars assume that Islam arose in the seventh century from the descendents of Ishmael, the bastard son of the Jewish patriarch Abraham and his wife's servant, Hagar. Muhammad sought a return to the laws of Moses which the Jews had forsaken and turned toward a secular form of society. (Genesis 17:20) Today there are more than 1.6 billion Muslims and only about 13 million Jews in the world. Very few of them would return to life under the laws of Moses in the Torah. They are practically irrelevant in the present struggle between the two great religions in the world. The dichotomy between passive Christianity and militant Islam could not be more clear by comparing the Koran with the New Testament. So, how can sheeple of the Christian religion be assimilated within military organizations that require obedience to command authority without disobeying Christ by obeying Paul? Presumably, God created both of them, opposite as they may be.

It is more than ironic that the writer of Revelation in the Bible prophesied the ultimate conflict between good and evil would be settled, not by peaceful means in love and mutual forgiveness, but by the bloodiest battle ever known at Armageddon. Neither should it surprise anyone that in the end the twelve tribes of Israel are installed as judges to assure that only the will of God the Almighty One survives thereafter. How convenient is that for the Jews who were under the heel of Rome at the time of its writing? In the end of the story, Satan is confined to chains in hell for eternity and all of his demon servants and their followers are slain while the false prophets are hurled into a lake of fire. (Revelation 19:20-21) If such be the fore-ordained destruction of Satan, why does he persist with his program of deception? The only plausible answer is that he has the notion that the goal of defeating God is just within reach. Now, it is to wonder where he would get such a lame idea from. Indeed, the Bible predicts that the sheeple of God will be removed from Earth preceding a brief period of tribulation, leaving the debauchery of Satan and his demons to gain full sway for a time before the end. But, why would demons reject heaven and choose hell instead, unless God willed it so? Would you choose to be born lost in sin if you had any other choice? How could demons even exist outside of his will? If God is omnipotent and omniscient, then belief in non-existent free will must be part of his creation, along with its potential for both good and evil. After all, it was God who put the tree of knowledge of good and evil in the garden in the first place, was it not. And was it not God who created those good angels and bad demons, including Satan [a.k.a.: Lucifer], during some pre-Earth existence?

The fact is that forces of both creation and destruction are occurring simultaneously all the time in astronomical, geological, animal, and human realms, and it all is the work of God because he said so; "I kill and I make alive, I wound and I heal." (Deuternonomy 32:39) "I bring prosperity and create disaster. I the Lord do all these things." (Isaiah 45:7) Which part of that do you not understand? Either there are two equal and opposing forces at work or a single source produces both forces, and these options are mutually exclusive, one excludes the other. Both the Bible and the Koran lean towards the latter if they are read carefully, i.e. a single source creates both forces. The Bible claims that God created the Earth and everything in it, and it was all "good." That includes earthquakes, volcanoes, hurricanes, floods, disease, etc. that consume human lives. But when sheeple do bad things, many theologians let God off the hook. Daily news reports of physical violence of one Homo sapien against another seem to defy human understanding. The latest form of human violence seems to be the spontaneous sprouting of illegal and clandestine fight clubs that attract amateur fighters into organized brawls in back yards and garages. The spurt in appeal for professional cage fighting is but one step removed from the Roman gladiators who fought to the death. We also face an epidemic of crime by illegal immigrants and drug smugglers flooding across our southern border without adequate deterrence to protect innocent citizens. We can spend hundreds of billions to liberate foreign nations from insane dictators sometimes, but we cannot avoid invasion by illegals across our southern border. All in God's will, of course. AIGWOC. Think you can handle that?

[This growth in violence among humankind may be related to growing lack of mother love for infants. The soul's energy connection with physical life apparently is not fully formed at birth and is not fully accessible during the first few years thereafter. When a baby is born, its brain has just about 50% of the neurological connections it must have as an adult, and this rapid growth must occur in the next two decades. This neurological capacity must be developed by the constant infusion of love from the mother and father if the brain's normal physical growth is to be attained. Should this essential growth fuel be missing during its early months and years, the infant's brain development will likely be curtailed by lack of this essential love energy, causing a variety of serious repercussions. Once the brain neuron patterns are formed, by age ten or so, rewiring them may be impossible.]

Organized street gangs among inner city youth are replacing the missing succor of dysfunctional families in providing a sense of belonging, safety, and mutual aid, including the annihilation of opponents in drive-by shootings. If it were fully disclosed, the amount of criminal behavior probably would shock most sheeple not engaged in it or aware of it. Let's face it; tortures happen, and if they are unnecessary then there is either no God or a mean spirited one. C.S. Lewis concluded: if God is love, then tortures must be necessary. Whether driven by mental illness, disease, or downright evil, Jesus taught that God prunes his creation continually even while he is seeding new ground. (John 15:2) So, perhaps the AIDS pandemic and Muslim suicide bombers are God pruning his creation. Volcanoes in Hawaii have been both creating new lands and destroying existing communities for an estimated 43 million years. Archeologists have uncovered remnants of ancient civilization around the world buried up to 150 feet below the present surface in some cases. Modern archeology uses space satellite mounted ground penetrating radar to uncover ancient architecture hidden under forests and deserts. The shifting and relocation of top soil on Earth seems to be an ongoing process that may cover unimagined secrets from the distant past. In addition, most of the natural resources useful to mankind are found ever deeper under rocks and oceans, making harvesting of coal, oil, iron, gold, silver, and other precious metals expensive and dangerous. Too often, workers are killed or buried alive in mining and drilling disasters while attempting to improve life for the rest of us. What God can create he can also bury. And he does.

Astronomers peering into the heavens report that entire galaxies are being destroyed and reborn on a massive scale beyond human imagination. Closer to home, the God who created the beautiful tulips also created the addiction among humans for beautiful poppies converted into opium and heroin. By the way, how do you think humans ever figured that out? Answer: same way they figured out how to make steel and concrete and personal computers and atomic bombs, i.e., God's will. The sale of poppies sustains the farming economy of Afghanistan, and America may be providing the fertilizer. No one really knows why this should be so, but it is, so it must be necessary or it would be different. Humans are beset by simultaneous forces of reproduction and death all the time, but they are made to emphasize the former and to avoid the latter. Or are they? The rapid growth in violent video games is known to rewire the brains of the players so that their normal conscience restraints are removed and killing others becomes a plausible behavior. Even the U.S. Army uses video war games to help train soldiers more efficiently to kill the enemy. Few sheeple realize this is but an extension of the violent comic books that most soldiers read in camp during WWII.

Entertainment becomes combat training, all in the will of God the Almighty One of course. So it is not surprising to find kids in schools shooting their enemies and young gang members killing each other on the streets. But, how do you rewire the brains of soldiers returning from combat to act peacefully with their neighbors and return to civilian occupations? And how do you erase the damage done to young minds forever rewired for violence by video games? Who imparts compassion and empathy among Homo sapiens so that they will aid each other in time of need and share in their suffering? For that matter, who imparts sociopathic and antisocial behaviors in Homo sapiens if there is only one God? Hmmm?

Anthropologist Margaret Mead observed that .. "when a baby is born people rejoice, and when a couple marries they jubilate, but when someone dies they try to pretend nothing happened." Unless and until tragic events impact their personal lives, few sheeple take much note of the routine traumas which make up the existence of Homo sapiens. Most healthy, wealthy, happy sheeple live in a cloistered palace as did the Buddha [a.k.a.: Siddartha Gautama (565- 483BC)] until they step outside and discover all the suffering and struggle in life, or it comes inside to reveal the true nature of reality. Consequently, when tragedies do occur, sheeple often are pitched into panic and despair if their traditional beliefs about God cannot explain such events. Where do you go when the door to the throne of grace seems to be locked and bolted on the other side, as C.S. Lewis discovered after untimely death of his wife? He said it was like the lights were out inside and nobody was even home. Even the saintly Mother Teresa lost her source of comfort and ceased to prawhen she could not reconcile the poor sheeple living in stinking gutters of Calcutta with te loving Father of the Catholic Church. She wrote to Jesus, "My soul no longer is one with you," and she concluded, "We must take what he gives and give what he takes."

Christians and Jews both seem to be intentionally blinded to the truth of scriptures describing God. How could this be unless God willed it so? Some philosophers and religious leaders will say that God created the universe and that evil exists but that God did not create evil. They cannot see the flaw in this line of reasoning because they are blindfolded by the creator. They want a loving, merciful all-good God, but that is not the description they are given among his creation. Search the scriptures and you find they all point to the two faces of God. In the Bible, which conservative Christians claim is the Word of God, it is written, "I make peace and create evil. I the Lord do all these things." (Isaiah 45:7) "Shall there be evil in a city, and the Lord has not done it?" (Amos 3:6) "Out of the mouth of the most High proceeds not evil and good?" (Lamentations 3:38) "Thus says the Lord; Behold, I frame evil against you, and devise a device against you." (Jeremiah 18:11) [Some scholars prefer the word calamity to evil, but the concept is the same.] Apostle Paul seemed to restate this idea too; "For by him all things were created: things in heaven and on Earth, visible and invisible, whether thrones or powers or rulers or authorities; all things were created by him and for him." (Colossians 1:16) That must include your own pitiful little life. All in God's will of course.

Jesus himself described a Father who pruned the vineyard to increase its fruits. "I am the true vine, and my Father is the gardener. He cuts off every branch in me that bears no fruit, while every branch that does bear fruit he prunes so that it will be even more fruitful." (John 15:1-2) Either way you get pruned. The Koran says much the same. "His is the kingdom of the heavens and the Earth; He gives life and causes death; and He has power over all things." (57:52) [Science thinks a giant asteroid hit the Earth at the Yucatan peninsula about 50 million years ago killing off 95 percent of all life forms. They think this pruning event made it possible for Homo sapiens to eventually replace the dinosaurs. They believe that some such pruning event is likely to occur again in the unpredictable future.] But the God that formed Islam out of the imagination of Muhammad also subverted its idealism (where the penalty for drinking wine is 80 lashes and polygamy is condoned, but adultery merits stoning to death) with the infusion of lust for wealth and power that drove him and the Caliphs who followed him into military conquest and tyranny and terrorism until this very day. It seems that God is continually pruning his creation by pitting one nation against another, one religion against another. Perhaps that is why Islam faded into obscurity after fall of the Ottoman Empire in 1918, but now is rising again towards world conquest through terrorism against Christian nations. Come to think of it, that may be why an estimated 27,000 children die every day of starvation and an infant dies every three seconds for lack of tetanus vaccinations. It may also explain the

60 million souls that were lost during WWII as well as extermination of millions of Jews during the Holocaust. Sometimes it seems that mega-tragedies must occur in order for things to get better and sheeple must die to make room for others. The God who produces new medicines to aid human survival also produces the diseases that require their development as for example, AIDS. Mother Teresa, the saint and Jeffrey Dahmer, the serial killer both were creations of God the Almighty One. And the God who created the pacifism in Christianity also created the brutal torture machines during its Age of Inquisition. Go figure.

Apostle Paul wrote that his generation of Christians was chosen and predestined for that calling before the world was made, (Ephesians 1:4-5), and also that anyone who called upon the name of the Lord would be saved (Romans 10:13). Is this an either/or dichotomy or a both/and dogma that illustrates the dual powers of God to confuse his creation with necessary opposites? Either sheeple are selected for the Kingdom or they have freedom to reject it...or both/and. Perhaps it becomes necessary to transform the nature of God to support reality or to change our view of reality to support God, or both/and. It seems obvious to one who can see clearly. Theologian, scholar, and archaeologist Merrill F. Unger wrote in Unger's Bible Handbook, (1992) "Divine foreordination and human freedom are humanly irreconcilable, but like two parallel lines that meet in infinity, they have their solution in God." [Actually, by definition parallel lines never meet. If two lines were to meet they are not parallel.] It seems obvious: God does whatever he wants to anyone he wants whenever he wants – or not. Accepting this dual image of God as creator and destroyer may require some real changes to your brain neurons. The Old Testament declares, "The fear of the Lord is the beginning of wisdom." (Psalm 111:10; Proverbs 1:7) Jesus admonished his disciples not to worry about things of tomorrow because each day brings its own challenges and besides, God will provide. (Matthew 6: 25-34) Sheeple like to believe that "God is love" and will keep them from all harm. But, Jesus also taught, "Fear him who, after the killing of the body, has power to throw you into hell. Yes, I tell you, fear him." (Luke 12:4-5) Fear can be a powerful motivator such as undergoing serious surgery, even if it is life threatening, to possibly survive a bit longer.

It seems to be very obvious; what God creates he also destroys, from the heavens to the institutions of Homo sapiens individually and collectively. Science tells us that even the Sun and the Earth are destined for destruction...in about 5 billion years. Every beginning comes with an ending and all benefits come with burdens as in the laws of physics where for each action there is an equal and opposite reaction. So, let's stop referring to good and evil things or events and call them what they are...necessary dichotomies. All in God's will of course...AIGWOC.

16. THE POSITIVE POWER IN NEGATIVE THINKING.

There was a book titled, "You Can't Afford A Single Negative Thought" (out of print) which extolled the popular psychology of positive thinking. Many motivational speakers and writers continue making a living from promoting that idea as the pathway to success, health, wealth, and happiness. But, for every thought there is an opposite one. Psychologist Joseph Forgas at the University of New South Wales writes in "Australasian Science," "Whereas positive mood seems to promote creativity, flexibility, cooperation, and reliance on mental shortcuts, negative moods trigger more attentive, careful thinking paying greater attention to the external world," Forgas writes, "Positive mood is not universally desirable: sheeple in negative mood are less prone to judgmental errors, are more resistant to eyewitness distortions and are better at producing high-quality, effective persuasive messages." How come? Forgas also found that sad sheeple were better communicators, especially through written arguments, because "mildly negative mood may actually promote a more concrete, accommodative and ultimately more successful communication style." Dale Carnegie, (1888-1955) consultant to business executives and celebrated self-help trainer got this advice from Willis H. Carrier, developer of air conditioning, "First ask yourself: What is the worst that can happen? Then prepare to accept it." Carnegie explained, "When we have accepted the worst, then we have nothing more to lose and everything to gain." Alcoholics Anonymous has a rule for this situation, "Let go and let God." He will anyway.

Perhaps the notion of "negative capability" attributed to English poet John Keats (1795-1821) deserves a lot more attention in modern psychology. His "being in uncertainty" as a perquisite to "form the man of achievement," i.e., embracing mysteries without any "irritable reaching after fact and reason," has scarcely been explored. Research psychologist, Richard Lazarus (1922-2002) was one of a few who claimed that western medicine actually does more harm than good when it denies suffering sheeple the expression of their legitimate and realistic feelings of despair and depression as though it were some kind of pathology needing to be cured. He declared in Coping with Aging, (2006) "When we refuse to allow suffering sheeple to think negatively about their condition in life we also trivialize their suffering. Those who care about someone sick and dying may pressure them to think positively and maintain a happy demeanor. This often forces the patient to deny what is self evident. Physicians and care givers often are offended by illness they cannot control and feel impotent about their own helplessness. The result of all this well-meaning but often harmful deceit is that those who are suffering cannot feel authentic about their legitimate feelings. They not only face loss of their lives but also loss of their loved ones who are clearly troubled and distancing themselves to protect their own fragile egos." Such behavior only adds shame and guilt and anger to already difficult situations.

Some things hurt like hell and expressing that feeling may be the only rational option. Stifling it only makes the pain worse. This is doubly harmful if it prevents the sufferer from seeking professional support and psychotherapy that could be helpful in navigating the inevitable disasters of life. Sometimes it may be appropriate to "rage against the dying of the light" as in the poem (1951) by Welsh poet, Dylan Thomas (1914-1953) for his dying father that begins, "Do not go gentle into that goodnight. Old age should burn and rave at close of day."

Those who had to clean up the massive oil spill in the Gulf of Mexico and the families mourning the loss of their members lost in the oil rig explosion know what this means in reality. The oil may go away, but their loved ones are lost forever, and the pain will never go away. Testimony by BP executives disclosed that the explosion destroyed both manual and automatic blow out protections, leaving them with no tested options for stopping the spill. There seems to be no limit to the financial liability they faced as a result. BP fired its chief executive, with full benefits of course, but the poor sheeple who lost their fishing grounds have nothing more to lose, except their lives, as one of them committed suicide. Ten years after the Muslim attacks on 9/11/01 surviving family members still feel the sting of loss very acutely as they may for the rest of their lives. Plans to build a mosque near Ground Zero merely renew their distress that has no cure. Although some reconstruction is underway, more than 100,000 sheeple displaced by Hurricane Katrina will never return to their homes in New Orleans. Some things that are broken cannot be fixed.

Things change, and they are not always for the better. Just ask the baby boomer generation of America. They have lived through the most rapid changes in society possibly in human history. If life sucks, it is natural to feel depressed. Fear is a natural reaction to anticipated disaster. If your home is about to be foreclosed and you have no job, you have no pension and your savings are all gone, it is natural to feel stress and anxiety. If your life partner just left you or died, it is natural to feel angry at God and to grieve. To think otherwise is some form of mental illness. Sheeple obviously think differently, maybe even uniquely. For every thought there is an equal and opposite thought. Some may say the glass is half empty while others say it is half full and still others say it is too big or too small. Mental health is a subjective thing. To be happy no matter what, the glass is always full no matter its size if one is living from a place of divine love and compassion, if you truly believe that everything is the will of God the Almighty One. Few sheeple have the goal to live in a state of unconditional charity with no guarantees, as did Mother Teresa who spent her life serving sheeple in the slums of the world. It takes special eyes to see God in the slums, otherwise the shock would be too great. She concluded, "Heaven must be full of slum people."

There is a common notion in psychiatry that automatic negative thoughts, (ANTs) are the cause of much anxiety and depression which should be cured. The cure is to identify such thoughts and counter them with opposing thoughts, as is taught to depressed clients in cognitive behavioral therapy. The underlying assumption is that anxiety and depression are abnormal mental states and must be corrected for mental health. A string of psychiatrists has been promoting this form of therapy during the past 20 years to treat Attention Deficit Disorder, Anxiety, and Depression. One of the most recent is PBS television star, Dr. Daniel G. Amen, who claims, "Your brain controls you, but you can control your brain." He makes no attempt to define who the owner of the brain is or who is the YOU that controls it. Although he is a psychiatrist and neurologist, Dr. Amen advocates natural remedies, including deep breathing, guided imagery, meditation, self-hypnosis, and biofeedback for treating mental disorders that usually are treated with prescription drugs. And, he sells lots of books. So does Dr. Wayne W. Dyer, who is seen on PBS television hawking his some 30 books which interpret the ancient Chinese philosophy of Tao te Ching for modern man. Celebrity preacher, Joel Osteen, also has chosen this niche for his "prosperity preaching" that reaches millions with his motivational books and television lectures masquerading as religious sermons.

The main winners among such thoughts are the authors who profit from selling their books to sheeple who think by reading them life will change for the better. They are blinded to the fact that someone always comes in last, and that the Bible does not promise equal distribution of health, wealth, and happiness but it sells even better than sex; well almost. Although he makes a tidy living preaching the power of positive thinking, Dr. Martin Seligman, was quoted in "Time" magazine saying that about half of us have the genetic predisposition that gives the pleasant state of simply feeling happy no matter what, and the other half of us do not. That other half has the tendency to experience anxiety, worry, and negativity more often, and perhaps more easily, than pleasantly happy feelings. Putting them both together in a both/and theory would likely be most helpful to sheeple, but that would not sell many books. Responding to the marketing potential of positive thinking, Prof. Seligman has launched a new graduate level program at the University of Pennsylvania that educates professionals in the art of positive psychology. He also has been hired by the U.S. Army to help returning soldiers readjust to life at home, after their enslavement in rigid military organizations and slaughter of civilians, with positive thinking.

A couple of books touting pessimism and negative thinking as positive are available, but only a couple. In one of them, "Bright-Sided," (2009) journalist, Barbara Ehrenreich takes on the likes of Seligman and his ilk, which she likens to bait and switch, showing how the hucksters selling health, wealth, and happiness to those who don't have any are distorting the beatitudes of Jesus (blessed are the meek, blessed are those who mourn, etc.) and deluding practical sheeple who, like her, fail to see much benefit in breast cancer. Reading her book reviews shows her critics to be the self righteous and self absorbed success seekers that Seligman finds to be his fans and supporters. All in the will of God the Almighty One, of course.

If behaviors follow feelings which follow thoughts, these experts and prosperity preachers say that it is necessary to change thoughts in order to change behaviors...and it works...sometimes. With this reasoning, if you can think exactly like Tiger Woods, you can be the world's best golfer too. Of course, if you were Tiger Woods, why wouldn't you be happy? Especially with that group of women he had tagging along. Of course, his divorce and golfing decline are expensive burdens he must bear for life.

Motivator and self-made expert, Anthony Robbins says, "If you want to be successful, find someone who has achieved the results you want and copy what they do and you'll achieve the same results...We can change our lives. We can do, have, and be exactly what we wish." Sheeple pay him a lot of money for such "wisdom." That is why they are sheeple and Robbins is very rich. One of these motivators claims, "Achieve Your Goals, Desires and Life Dreams in the Next 90 Days by Using These Five Mind Power Techniques Based on Quantum Physics You Can Learn in The Next 30 Minutes." P.T. Barnum, founder of the traveling circus, observed "there is a new sucker born every minute." Jesus claimed that you can move mountains if you think you can. (Mark 11:23) You don't hear much preaching on this idea. This is the same reasoning that says you have the power to select eternal punishment or salvation, heaven or hell, merely by choosing to believe whether or not Jesus died for your sins. (John 3:16) If you think so you are saved and if you don't think so you are not. Of course, this says nothing for all the sheeple who lived before Christ or for all those who never heard the message of his redemption. There is a flaw in logic here someplace, but many sheeple do not think it is ridiculous at all. Is that stupid, insane, or the will of God the Almighty One?

Obviously, if your body weighs 120 pounds and you are barely five feet tall, it is not likely you can be a NBA basketball star no matter how much you think positively about it. It would be more realistic to seek a different occupation that fits your stature, like race horse jockey. Jesus challenged, "Which of you by worrying can add one hour to your life (or one inch to your stature.)" (Matthew 6:27) And if you live in land-locked Kansas and want to be a champion surfer, it is you who will have to move to the ocean because the ocean sure as hell is not coming to you. Similarly every lottery winner requires millions of losers, and there is no shortage of them. Obviously, free will in this sense comes with conditions attached. In his book, Outliers, the Story of Success, (2008) Malcolm Gladwell shows that over and over again highly successful sheeple seem to be in the right place at the right time to accomplish their achievements.

Founder of Microsoft and richest man in America, Bill Gates has attributed most of his success to plain old luck. Moreover, other sheeple seem to show up just when they are needed to help make it all happen. There is no one formula that works for all but each of Gladwell's subjects did seem to follow a very specific chain of events to success. Change one little link in the chain of events and their stories would be quite different. Each link in the chain of history seems to be inevitable and necessary even if apparently insignificant. However, there does seem to be some secret power of the mind that enables a sugar pill to have the same results as prescription drugs among some medical patients. It is called the "placebo effect" and may account for the miracle faith healings that are described of Jesus from Nazareth in the Bible. During WWI, field surgeons found that substituting salt water for unavailable morphine injections among wounded soldiers without telling them often provided the same pain relief. It turns out, to researchers' surprise, that you can succumb to placebo even when you know you're being fooled. There definitely are some healing effects in the power of belief for some sheeple. You just have to believe the deliverer. Jesus taught that if you can believe it you can have it. (Matthew 21:22, Mark 11:24) But, who it is that controls the believing is unknown.

There are "New Age" books and movies that promote a belief that you create your own reality by controlling the laws of physics with your mind. They call it the Law of Attraction just like the laws of physics.

They offer instant wealth and happiness, but they deliver medieval superstition to many sad gullible sheeple who believe their lies. The sad part is that so many scientists are willing to let the public get their knowledge of physics from celebrity quacks, what one called "quantum flapdoodle." Many popular books make such claims and argue that key developments in twentieth-century physics, such as the uncertainty principle and the butterfly effect, support the notion that God or a universal mind acts upon material reality. There always is an opposite view, and it can pay to look for it. Physicist, Victor J. Stenger examines these faith-based contentions in his carefully reasoned and incisive analysis of popular theories that seek to link spirituality to physics, but fail. Throughout his books titled, <u>God; the Failed Hypothesis</u> (2008) and <u>Quantum Gods</u>, (2009) Stenger provides a useful synopsis of contemporary religious ideas as well as basic but sophisticated physics presented in layperson's terms without complex equations. In his view, the two are mutually exclusive.

Of particular interest is Stenger's discussion of a new-age kind of Deism, which proposes a God who creates a universe with many possible pathways selected by chance, but otherwise does not interfere with the physical world or the lives of humans; a humanistic kind of God for progressives to worship. Although it is possible, says Stenger, to conceive of such a God who plays dice with the universe and leaves no trace of his role as prime mover, such a God is a far cry from traditional religious ideas of God and, in effect, may as well not exist. Stenger argues for the scientific conclusion that science does not need any kind of God to explain the universe. It just popped up spontaneously out of nothing, perhaps through a black hole of a previous universe that died, so therefore God does not exist. He uses phrases including "quantum theology" and "quantum spirituality" to describe those who disagree with him. He claims that the theory of evolution and the Bible are irreconcilable. "We have no empirical fact that requires us to introduce anything beyond matter. No case can be made that we need something more than matter to explain the universe...Either God exists and science is myth or science is right and God is myth. Take your pick." [Stenger leaves unexplained how one mind can communicate with another mind over the latest wireless cell phone circuits with no matter involved at all.]

We can do it all by ourselves, thank you very much. Just give us a little more time, maybe a few centuries, to fill in the gaps.

Jesus challenged such thinking, "Which of you by taking thought can add one cubit unto his stature?" [or by worrying can add a single hour to your life? NIV] (Matthew 6:27, Luke 12:25) On the other hand, recall he said that with faith like a mustard seed, one could move mountains, even cast them into the sea and "nothing will be impossible to you."(Mattthew 17:20, 21:21) But, he never instructed how to have that much faith or where it might be found, hence sheeple need bulldozers and dynamite to move mountains. James, his brother, contradicted with this command, "Whereas you know not what shall be on the morrow. For what is your life? It is even a vapor, which appears for a little time, and then vanishes away. Therefore, you ought to say, if the Lord wills, we shall live and do this or that." (James 4:13-15). So, what shall we do with this apparent contradiction in the Bible? Jesus attributed all that he did to the Father, so this too must be the will of God, confusing as it may be. (John 14:10) But, the Apostle Paul claimed that God was not "the author of confusion."(1 Corinthians 14:33) Since confusion obviously exists in the Bible, it must not be written by God.

Consider, for example that Jesus described the kingdom of god/heaven several times in parables in terms of places and relationships. Eight times he says that one can enter the kingdom of heaven, (Matthew 5:20, 7:21, 18:3, 19:23, 23:13 – Mark 9:47,10:15,10:23) but then he capped them off by saying, "The Kingdom of God does not come with your observation, nor will sheeple say here it is or there it is because the Kingdom of God is within you." (Luke 17:21) How can you enter a place that is within you? Also, compare John 20:9-10 with John 2:22. They both cannot be true. Anyone who cannot see the many contradictions in the Bible must be intentionally blinded by God. It takes special eyes to see this reality, otherwise the shock would be too great. Historian, Acharya S [a.k.a. D. M. Murdock] and other scholars claim the whole Jesus thing is a myth derived from the ancient worship by Egyptians of the Sun God, Osiris. Actually, Jesus did claim that he was the "light of the world," (John 8:12, 9:5) So who you gonna believe? The best we can say is that for every positive thought there appears to be a negative one. If God wants you to be blindfolded to this reality, you will be. All in the will of God the Almighty One of course.

There is a necessary opposing idea to the school of positive thinking; negativity has its place and sheeple require its acceptance and tolerance to be whole. Too much trust can be a bad thing. There is a rare disorder among children who cannot anticipate danger and so are very vulnerable to predators and accidents. Sometimes survival depends upon imagining the worst thing and preparing for it. But, holding two opposing ideas at the same time seems to be daunting for most sheeple. Pioneering psychologist and therapist, Felix Adler (1851-1933) lamented about therapists, "We stand, as it were, on the shore, and see multitudes of our fellow beings struggling in the water, stretching forth their arms, sinking, drowning, and we are powerless to assist them." Since anger, fear, and despair come from feeling powerless, how does one gain power by believing everything is out of their control, but under control of God the Almighty One? Apostle Paul explained, "There was given me a thorn in my flesh, a messenger of Satan, to torment me. Three times I pleaded with the Lord to take it away from me. But he said to me, My grace is sufficient for you, for my power is made perfect in weakness. Therefore I will boast all the more gladly about my weaknesses, so that Christ's power may rest on me. That is why, for Christ's sake, I delight in weaknesses, in insults, in hardships, in persecutions, in difficulties. For when I am weak, [in the flesh] then I am strong [in the spirit.]" (2 Corinthians 12:7-10) He seems to have understood what Jesus meant by teaching, "The spirit gives life...the flesh counts for nothing." (John 6:63) How does one move from contracted faith into such expansive faith? How does one move from fearing life to embracing life no matter what? How can one avoid struggle and suffering when the Buddha observed that all of life is struggle and suffering? These are not rhetorical questions, although answers seem to be just beyond human reach. When Jesus was asked how one could be born again he replied, "For man this is impossible, but all things are possible with God." (Matthew 9:26, Mark 10:27)

Possibly no professional field is more uncertain than treatment for the troubled mind. This is the field of such as psychology, psychiatry, and neurology. One may speak of a psychology of religion, psychology in religion, and religion in psychology. But, religion has scarcely found any place in psychiatry and neurology. Aiding a troubled mind still is mostly a trial and error process, drug therapy notwithstanding. The editor of the "Family Therapy Networker" [a.k.a. "Psychotherapy Networker"] wrote to professional clinical therapists, "Whatever your training, you know less than you once thought you did...The conspiracy that has been set in motion against us is irreversible... we are all doomed to live in a world that is getting more complex and indeterminable all the time...in such a world it is harder than ever to feel certain about what we know." This is not a new idea at all. The sixth century B.C. text of the Chinese "Tao te Ching" says, "The farther you go the less you know. The sage looks at life and smiles and enjoys his ignorance." Neurologist Robert Burton has concluded in <u>On Being Certain</u> (2009), "Despite how certainty feels, it is neither a conscious choice nor even a thought process. Certainty and the state of knowing what we know arise out of involuntary brain mechanisms that, like love or anger, function independently of reason." Some might call that faith. Secretary of Defense Donald Rumsfeld mused, "There are things we know we know. There are known unknowns, some things we know we do not know. But there also are unknown unknowns, that we don't know we don't know." This awareness may be the beginning of wisdom.

This essay is not about the brain that is sick for lack of healthy oxygenated blood or malfunctioning neurons. It is about the normal indefinite uncertainty in life that produces necessary existential anxiety the more closely we approach its ending. Once it becomes conscious, the ubiquitous indefinite uncertainty in life and whatever comes afterward must necessarily make sheeple feel anxious or fearful about the unknown future. It does seem the more we learn, the less we know for sure. Perhaps the endless searches for ultimate truth and meaning are doomed to failure because all of man's reasoning merely is idle speculations about reality. If you don't feel scared and confused, you just don't know what's happening. Things are changing so rapidly long-range planning is useless. Sheeple must change careers several times, because technology and economic shifts are uncontrollable.

The world can seem so complex that no one can figure out what is best to do. If you think you know, better watch out for those inevitable unpredictable unintended consequences. No better example exists than the good intentions of President Clinton to make homes available to lower income sheeple by increasing the insured risk of banks, which led to the loss of eleven trillion dollars of capital invested in the stock market and collapse of the housing business. This illustrates Murphy's Law; if anything can go wrong, it will and its corollary; you can never run out of things that can go wrong. Sheeple have tried to avoid existential anxiety throughout the ages by invoking the option of intuitive knowledge. Chinese philosopher, Chuang-tzu argues, "If you have insight you use your inner eye, your inner ear to pierce to the heart of things and have no need for intellectual knowledge." Western minds that depend upon scientific certainty cannot adopt this mode of thinking and so they suffer anxiety of the unknown. All in the will of God the Almighty One of course.

However, anxiety must exist for a purpose, or it would not be, so there is an opposite side even to the meaning of anxiety, and it comes with benefits in this opinion. The late Rev. Dr. Norman Vincent Peale (1898-1993) pioneered the notion of positive thinking along with his weekly televised sermons from the Marble Collegiate Church in New York City, and many preachers have made a good living from it ever since. But, for every thought there is an equal and opposite thought. For example, a child can be thought of as a book of blank pages to be written one page at time with no assurance of the outcome. Conversely, a child can be thought of as a book that is completely written at conception, with each page to be lived one day at a time just as it is written to the inevitable ending. Whichever thought you prefer is the one you are given by God the Almighty One of course. Everyone wants certainty of health, wealth, and happiness but they obviously are not distributed equally among God's creation. Those who enjoy a seemingly unrestrained line of successes are like a rocket that will eventually fall back to Earth unless they escape the pull of gravity and soar out into space. But, even then, no power is greater than the source of all power. "Though you build your nest as high as the eagle's, from there I will bring you down, declares the Lord." (Jeremiah 49:16, Obadiah 1:4)

If God will pull down the eagle's nest, imagine what he can do to the rest of us. Just ask the survivors of the earthquake that destroyed most of Port au Prince in Haiti in January 2010 and the fishermen on the Gulf coast who lost so much from the accidental oil spill. And recall how the volcanic eruption of Mt. Vesuvius in 79 A.D. destroyed the resort towns of Pompeii and Herculaneum. Consider the glacier volcano in Iceland that shut down air travel all across Europe in April 2010 costing $200 million per day and stranding countless travelers. The god given insatiable demand for oil has led to a massive oil rig explosion in the Gulf of Mexico which threatens the fishing and tourist industries for decades to come. Now, the Arab countries are caught up on a spontaneous revolution to replace dictators who have made nice with the West to sell their oil with who knows what. You may have been taught that God is love, but there is another view. "God is a righteous judge, a God who expresses his wrath every day." (Psalm 7:11) And sometimes, it seems that God just likes to let sheeple know who really is in charge as he did with the horrible example of his faithful servant, Job. In the end, Job had no power to challenge God after losing his family, servants, and all his wealth. While Job was recompensed at the end, none of his innocent servants and children who were destroyed were resurrected. There are Job stories all over creation if you just have eyes to see. So, why should we be so shocked if it happens to us? The answer, of course, is the ego cannot and will not commit suicide so it must be crucified.

Pride and arrogance seem to always precede a fall. Consider the family of the late Joseph and Rose Kennedy of Massachusetts. He made lots of money importing Scotch whiskey during the depression and operating the trade mart in Chicago; then he served as ambassador to Great Britain during WWII. They had nine children; four boys and five girls. One daughter was mentally retarded, another was killed in a plane crash, and their oldest son was killed in combat flying over Germany, another son became President and was assassinated, another son ran for President and also was assassinated, the youngest son, "Teddy" was expelled from Harvard and reinstated and went on to law school and married a stunning blonde model, but his wife was an alcoholic, one of his sons and their daughter had cancer, and the other son had asthma. Teddy enlisted in the Army and washed out of intelligence school, then he was assigned as an embassy guard and discharged at the lowest rank of PFC. He loved sailboat racing, flying, and being a rodeo cowboy, and he almost died in a plane crash that killed the pilot. But, after the loss of his brothers, he picked up the family crest to carry it forward in the U.S. Senate. The Senator was a study in necessary opposites; a loyal family patriarch for his many nieces and nephews, but also a hell raiser and a womanizer, a tireless advocate for the poor and suffering who would compromise with his opponents while blowing insulting cigar smoke in their faces, a faithful Catholic who bought off the clergy to obtain a divorce and who made a final emotional written appeal to the Pope for forgiveness and absolution for his many sins before dying in 2009 of a brain tumor. Perhaps he was so popular because he represented "every man." We may want our leaders to be perfect and immortal, but alas, they are only mortal human beings like the rest of us.

It's like God attacks your highest assumption to remove the naivete and self confidence so you would rely more upon Him alone. One also thinks of the mighty ocean liner "Titanic" that sank at 3:00 a.m. April 15, 1912 after hitting an iceberg on its maiden voyage although it was touted as unsinkable, losing 1,250 lives of some very wealthy sheeple. There was a possible rescue ship, the "Californian," within fifteen miles but it never heard the distress call because its sole telegraph operator was asleep after sending a warning of icebergs that was never acknowledged by the "Titanic.' So it was on 9/11/01 when the monumental symbols of lofty capitalism dominating the skyline in New York City came tumbling down. So it was from the heights of Athens under the rule of Pericles, to the reign of France under Napoleon Bonaparte, to the heights of Nazi Germany under the rule of Adolf Hitler to its fall into history. It seems that empires must rise so that they can fall. So it must also be for the rich and famous individuals as they ultimately must face death and vacate their nests of power for others to occupy. "For the sun rises with scorching heat and withers the plant; its blossom falls and its beauty is destroyed. In the same way, the rich man will fade away even while he goes about his business." (James 1:10-11) One may only wonder about the future of the mighty United States of America with its national bird, the Bald Eagle. God does whatever he wants with whomever he wants whenever he wants.

The banking meltdown and collapse of the stock market of 2008-09 shows how this principle of absolute predeterminism works in real life. The mighty financial wizards who caused it were some of the most well educated graduates of the most famous universities. Subsequent investigations showed that offending banks knew their mortgage loans were fraudulent and still they were passed on as credit worthy investments. And government bank regulating agencies looked the other way. How could this be unless God willed it so? Again on May 6, 2010 the stock market dropped nearly 1,000 points in a few seconds due to some uncontrollable computer crash. A recent record among financial scandals was exposed when a hedge fund run by Bernie Madoff was found to be a gigantic illegal Ponzi fraud that lost $64 billion from seasoned investors who should have known better. Even the Securities and Exchange Commission that is supposed to protect investors ignored repeated alarms and warnings for ten years to let the scheme grow bigger and bigger until it finally collapsed when large investors began to withdraw their principle accounts. In addition, corporations can "cook the books" legally with accounting tricks that make it impossible for individuals to see reality through the numbers. Warren Buffet said so. Hundreds of other frauds continually are in the incipient stage ready to take more unsuspecting victims into their traps. Unregulated capitalism has again disclosed its dark side, and it is not a pleasant sight to see. We now live in a complicated global economy where there inevitably will be large corporations whose failure poses risks to the rest of the economy. Placing them under a class of professional corporate managers whose primary goal is maximizing their personal wealth has been risky from its outset. The entire governments of Greece and Egypt faced near collapse with rioting in the streets by sheeple who could not give up their entitlements for financial restructuring. The U.S. national debt is soaring out of sight. It would take a generation of surplus federal budgets to correct the balance…ain't gonna happen. In the choice between freedom and security, sheeple will choose security every time.

Another issue for Americans is the contrast of national interests with maximizing profits to satisfy capitalism. Outsourcing higher paying jobs to lower paying countries may be good for profits of international corporations but it also lowers the domestic standard of living in the U.S. If unchecked, it could continue until the buying power of domestic workers can no longer afford the credit needed to finance cheap goods produced overseas. More personal bankruptcy and eventual financial collapse are in store if nothing changes. The argument that outsourcing jobs raises the standard of living in less developed countries so they can buy more U.S. goods is hollow if your job has gone overseas and your income with it. When their primary goal is short term stock manipulation, investors can become over-optimistic and bid up the prices of corporate assets above the level that is sustainable based on economic fundamentals. The U.S. has been hemorrhaging dollars overseas for many years with its skewed balance of payments deficit. As asset prices then fall to a sustainable level, investors who purchased inflated assets face ruin. Don't think it can't happen to you. Just check out the home foreclosures in your area. It is hard to see how a reasonable compensation schedule would give failing managers rich bonus payments after it is plain their decisions contributed to the destruction of their company.

Historians may analyze these times and wonder whatever were we thinking. Well, according to Peter A. Ubell, a researcher of medicine and psychology at the Univ. of Michigan, we were sheeple being sheeple. He says in his book, Free Market Madness, (2009) "No matter how much we claim to be rational, everyone is driven by irrational greed, optimism, and ignorance." Think about that. He discovered that items listed on eBay at ridiculously low opening bids often end up at much higher prices than others because early bidders think they can get a bargain. Sheeple have even been induced to pay as much as $28 for a $20 bill in open auctions. Homo sapiens indeed are like sheep, following the leader and hoping for the best. The question is, who drives the leaders? This question can lead to a chronic state of "therapeutic depression" that was explained by the late psychiatrist, M. Scott Peck in his baseline book on therapy, A Road Less Traveled (2003). In medical terms it might be called dysthymia. This malady could be nothing more than a normal reaction to awareness of the negative side of reality. When you realize you don't control your own mind, where do you turn for comfort?

Thinking psychologists are beginning to realize that anxiety of uncertainty can help create "positive pessimism," or the power in negative thinking. Strategic contingency planners in business and government realize if you anticipate the worst-case scenarios, you are more likely to avoid shock and disbelief and disaster when they happen. They invoke Murphy's Law: If anything can go wrong, it will - and its corollary, you can never run out of things that can go wrong. With this attitude, one might be better prepared to live with worst-case outcomes when they are unavoidable...like wars and death. [Perhaps a little more of such planning in the White House could have avoided the messes in

Iraq and Afghanistan and the tragedy in New Orleans after hurricane Katrina or the collapse of banks that provided credit to unqualified debtors. Or not.]

Anxiety also can kick us out of the stupor of unconscious incompetence where we don't know what we don't know, and stimulate us to growth and human development towards conscious incompetence to seek answers in the unknowable. Some of the best leaders and most creative sheeple of history were driven by acute anxiety, including Abraham Lincoln, Winston Churchill, and Vincent van Gogh. From that level of awareness, we can be stimulated to learn what we don't know and to prepare for living the ultimate mystery: what comes after death. In fact, anxiety about an uncertain future that seems threatening may be the power that drives all human development and promotes the survival of the species. When we realize how vulnerable we really are and how fragile and brittle are the institutions of mankind, perhaps then and only then does the blessing of calm submission to life take root.

The "Tao te Ching" proclaims, "The sage would not control the world, he is in harmony with the world." It may be calm submission that has enabled Homo sapiens to survive and adapt to their evolving circumstances by accepting that things change and require a different response. Like the serenity prayer says, "God grant me serenity to accept things I cannot change, courage to change things I can [and should], and wisdom to know the difference." Originated by theologian Reinhold Niebuhr (1892-1971) and adopted by Alcoholics Anonymous, note that it invokes the will of God in the affairs of mankind. The rest of it includes, "...living one day at a time, enjoying one moment at a time, accepting hardships as the pathway to peace, taking this sinful world as it is, not as I would have it that I may be reasonably happy in this life." Let us never forget, as Abraham Lincoln reminded the nation, that both sides in the Civil War prayed to the same God and read the same Bible while they killed each other for opposing goals, "The Almighty has His own purposes."

Uncertainty in life is an opportunity for growth and understanding of sheeple, situations, and ideas including some that make no sense. Some teachers and writers claim you can have anything you want merely by thinking you can based on a "Law of Attraction (LOA)."

This is a manifestation of faith as in..."when you believe it you will have it." One such LOA wag proclaimed, "If you feel negatively about your job, change it. If you feel negatively about your relationship, change it. If you feel negatively about your body, change it. If you feel negatively about your financial situation, change it." Tell that to the thousand of homeless wretches living in tent squalor in Haiti who lost their families in the earthquake that destroyed their domain or the millions of unemployed in the U.S. Others claim that you get what you give based on a "Law of Reciprocity"...so if you want more money just give away all that you have. Since you reap what you sow, what you have is your own creation, although possibly not of your own will. (Galatians 6:6-8, John 4: 36-38) The ultimate power is choosing or rejecting eternal life by accepting or rejecting Jesus as Savior. (John 3:16) Such ideas are sprinkled throughout the teachings of Jesus, but preachers do not often cite them.

But, the Buddha had an opposite thought. If anyone can align their will with what is as the will of God the Almighty One and spend their life maintaining that alignment, it may not matter what is happening in the outside world. For him, happiness is desiring what is and releasing all wishes that things should be different. That seems a bit harsh to tell survivors of natural disasters and family tragedies. Actually any choice you make carries out the will of God the Almighty One as there can be no other. However, doubt is a necessary and unavoidable companion to spiritual seeking. In this process we always are just beginning…with the beginners' mind referred to in Buddhism. The inner alignment is what is important, not external circumstances. Jesus met this place on the cross, "My Father, if it is possible, may this cup be taken from me. Yet not as I will, but as you will." (Matthew 26:39) And Apostle Paul expressed it, "I have been crucified with Christ and I no longer live, but Christ lives in me." (Galatians 2:20) And he admonished, "…who are you, O man, to talk back to God?" (Romans 9:20) Indeed.

A lot of sheeple make money by telling other sheeple they can change the world just by thinking they can, Jesus included. But 2,000 years of history indicates that things change, not by our will, but by the will of God the Almighty One. Could any of the circumstances in the past have been otherwise? Who knows? What about the future? Who knows? You may have heard it said, plan like you may live forever, but live like you will die tomorrow. But, the Apostle James warned not to make any definite plans, "Now listen up you who say, Today or tomorrow we will go to this or that city, spend a year there, carry on business and make money. Why, you do not even know what will happen tomorrow. What is your life? You are a mist that appears for a little while and then vanishes. Instead, you ought to say, If it is the Lord's will, we will live and do this or that." (James 4:13-15) Western cultures emphasize personal effort to right perceived wrongs and to change things more to our liking. But, Buddhist therapist, David Richo has pointed out <u>Five Things We Cannot Change</u> (2005); 1) everything changes and ends, 2) things often do not go according to plan, 3) life is not always fair, 4) pain is a part of life, and 5) sheeple are not always loving and loyal. In his Buddhist philosophy, the only way to avoid suffering in these situations is to accept them instead of attempting to change them; i.e., to align one's goals with the situation because suffering is caused by wanting things to be different. This seems to be the opposite of the practice of cognitive behavioral therapy, developed and documented by the late Aaron T. Beck and David D. Burns, ("Feeling Good," 1999) wherein troubled clients are induced and trained to challenge their thinking and to look at distressing situations from a more constructive viewpoint in order to treat depression. They assume that sheeple who feel depressed can be helped by changing their focus from internal self absorption to external subjective reference, like focusing on the needs of others instead of their own dilemmas. Sounds like the teaching of Jesus about having compassion and charity is more than mythology; it may actually be good for you.

This is not new stuff; first century Roman stoic philosopher, Epictetus observed that events do not disturb men's minds, but their opinions do. In a classic study, head of psychology at Univ. of CA. Berkeley, Prof. Richard S. Lazarus (1922-2002) documented some benefits of denial in the coping process. He demonstrated experimentally that patients who engage in forms of denial - for example, refusing to believe that a serious medical problem exists or to accept that the problem is as severe as it is recover better and more quickly from surgery than patients who do not engage in such denial. Lazarus thus came to believe that false beliefs can have very beneficial consequences to one's health and well-being in threatening situations. The study on denial also documented

Lazarus's claims that an event in itself, taken without consideration of how the person construes that event, does not explain the generation of physical, emotional or physiological states. His work on the benefits of denial has now been replicated by others, and its findings are taken into consideration in health psychology and psychosomatic medicine.

Strip away the illusions about control, and we find the human condition burdened with fear and many other emotions. One checks off the major portions of life clearly beset by fear: infancy, childhood, dreams, religion, war service, competitive careers, illness of all kinds, old age. When we perceive our safety and ego control are threatened, Homo sapiens are hard-wired to respond with flight or fight reactions. If fight is not an option, we tend to flee our fear through action designed to take us toward some secure position that seeks normalcy. This fleeing can take on many forms, all of which involve immersing oneself into things in our day-to-day experience. We therefore escape the threat by doing some diversion, i.e., reading a book, watching a movie or TV, listening to music, playing golf or attending a ball game, etc. Doing some diversion serves as a temporary rest area in our existential fear, but then it returns with greater impact in a rebound effect. A well-known Danish existentialist, Soren Kierkegaard, (1813-1855) believed that the best way to deal with "angst" or existential fear is to learn to face it courageously. In other words, the proper response to anxiety is to stop being anxious about anxiety, accepting it in the belief that it exists for a higher purpose as part of the human condition. Whereas pagan anxiety is expressed most profoundly as fate, and Jewish anxiety as guilt, the anxiety of the true Christian (whom Kierkegaard regarded as practicing the most advanced form of religion) is expressed in the form of suffering. Jesus experienced this fear as he faced the cross and sweat as though drops of blood fell from him. His dread was great enough to produce capillary hemorrhaging as he prayed for deliverance. (Luke 22:44) Throughout the Bible this fundamental, other-worldly fear is depicted as an existential response to the human situation which, if we accept it, will give us otherwise unattainable strength in coping with the fearful situations that arise in the ordinary world. This could indeed be regarded as the basic message of the Psalms and Proverbs: "The fear of the Lord is the beginning of wisdom." (Psalm 111:10; Proverbs 1:7)

But, we must walk through the valley of fear before climbing to this level of faith.

The more we try to reduce or eliminate existential fear, the more we become aware of fear, a form of fear about fear. President Franklin D. Roosevelt (1882-1945) invoked this solution during the Great Depression, "So, first of all, let me assert my firm belief that the only thing we have to fear is fear itself - nameless, unreasoning, unjustified terror which paralyzes needed efforts to convert retreat into advance." Subsequent battles of WWII on sea and land make him look at least a little bit wrong. Fear turns into rage if some reaction is possible and into depression if one feels helpless, as those who lost their homes in New Orleans to hurricane, Katrina. A highly respected Australian expert in treating nervous disorders, Dr. Claire Weekes, (1903-1990) quipped, "Never forget that without fear you are invulnerable." In other words, what you don't know can't harm you. She is among those who claim that by focusing on what we don't want in life, we get more of it. The secret is to focus all our energy on what we do want. But, when unconscious incompetence becomes conscious, fear naturally emerges. She summarized her treatment program from personal experience with midnight panic attacks as follows; facing the feared situation, accepting the feeling of panic and all the related physical symptoms, floating through it, and letting time pass.

In any event, conventional therapy does not help sheeple facing existential anxiety. Neither does religion. The only response offered by Weekes and her subsequent peers is to acknowledge one's helpless condition, accept that condition, keep busy, and wait for deliverance with patience and passive persistence. There are no answers to the fundamental existential questions, where did we come from, why are we here, and where are we going. Only beliefs. C.G. Jung observed... "all the greatest and most important problems in life are fundamentally insoluable...they can never be solved, but only outgrown." All in the will of God the Almighty One of course.

Dale Carnegie (1888-1955) instructed in <u>How to Stop Worryng and Start Living</u>, (1948) if life gives you a lemon, make lemonade. He quoted Santayana's words: "Man is not made to understand life, but to live it." If you can enjoy it, so much the better. If you can't enjoy it, Willam James instructed to act "as if" and you may feel the way you act. That this advice works is seen in the movies whenever costars fall in love. But, what do you do if life gives you a "shit sandwich" as therapist Mary Pipher wondered? Consider the young Marine who returned from Iraq blind with both legs missing. Even though he was honored publicly by President Bush with the Purple Heart medal, his life never will be the same.

After she documented stories of many suffering aging souls encountered in her therapy practice, in Another Country, (1999) Mary Pipher closed her practice to seek inner peace for the broken parts of her own life. The only solution she explained in Seeking Peace, (2007) was the Buddhist practices of acceptance and gratitude inside no matter what happens outside, but she admitted she was "the worst Buddhist on Earth." Even though Marcus Arelius (121-180 A.D.) wrote, "Our lives are what our thoughts make it," to be realistic, you don't have to be happy when bad things happen to good sheeple or good things happen to bad sheeple, and you cannot always prepare for emergencies. When you realize that everything is indefinitely uncertain, rain falls upon the just and unjust, and everybody carries heavy burdens, anxiety and worry are the natural human responses. Sometimes screaming in the dark is the only logical response. Nevertheless David Richo (above) says, "Our tears are precious, necessary, and part of what makes us such enduring creatures." The challenge is to stay steadfastly in the here and now of reality, however unsavory.

The paradox is that going further into despair is what grants access to hope, going fully into the pain grants access to healing, going fully into the dark opens into light even when it may be on the other side of life. An unconditionally embraced predicament becomes the threshold to whatever comes next." [Even if that light at the end of the tunnel is an oncoming train?] Families who are unemployed being evicted from their homes with their belongings set upon the sidewalk could have problems accepting this concept. Try to imagine what it must be like for animals being led to slaughter or one who is innocent sentenced for life in solitary confinement, even one on death row awaiting execution for years, or the old one in a nursing home going deaf and blind, then go look in a mirror. Perhaps you should visit the killing room in a modern slaughter house to appreciate the sacrifice made of animals for your food supply, or volunteer for helping the disabled addicts in a drug rehab facility or help to clean up a nursing home. Then try to practice the acceptance of here and now that Richo claims is so enduring. Perpetrator of the greatest fraudulent financial Ponzi scheme in history, Bernie Madoff, sits in a high security cell with no windows under suicide watch serving a life sentence where he can only remember what it was like to live like a billionaire in his New York penthouse while it lasted for more than twenty years. Even he cannot explain why he did it, except that he could. He could not even attend the funeral of his oldest son who hanged himself, leaving a wife and small child alone. There are some things worse than death.

Sheeple who feel powerless and fearful often seek out some form of professional therapy to gain more control over their lives, because that is what the human ego wants more than anything, control. Counselors, therapists, psychologists, and psychiatrists have responded with an endless string of theoretical approaches. There is cognitive behavioral therapy, rational emotive therapy, ego therapy, reality therapy, family systems therapy, existential therapy, gestalt therapy, psychoanalytic therapy, person centered therapy, feminist therapy, Jungian therapy, Adlerian therapy, hypnotic regression therapy, and more. There is also Reike, Rolfing, Body Therapy, Massage Therapy, and Tapping Therapy. Sheeple must reach the point where it hurts too much not to change in order to benefit from such professional interventions. All of them help some sheeple some times, but none of them help everyone all the time because the ego always resists losing its control. By suspending the ego, the Chinese Taoist wrote, "The sage has no ambitions, therefore he can never fail. He who never fails always succeeds. And he who always succeeds is all powerful." A wise old woman declared, "If you never expect anything, you will never be disappointed." Neurologist Robert Burton claims that to be healthy we need to learn to cope with anxieties and to tolerate the contradictory aspects of human biology, including the fundamental conflicts in our minds. Since absolute certainty is not possible, we must live with the anxiety of indefinite uncertainty. When all is said and done, the best we can say is that some things happen some times. How and if they are connected by some undiscovered form of energy in a formless spirit world will be for future investigators to explain. The positive power in accepting absolute predeterminism, i.e. God's will, can help you feel good inside no matter what happens outside.

17. Come on home.

"Home" is a very interesting word. It is the symbol of many different things for different sheeple at various stages of life. Home can be here and now or it can be then and there from someplace in the immediate or distant past. It can be a location on a map or a specific dwelling place at a specific address. It can exist in the present or it can be something only in memory. The memory can be pleasant and comforting or it can be troublesome and painful. It can include members of the immediate family or not. It can provide the launch of a successful long life and career or it can be the stagnant cesspool of a life lost to suffering and untimely and sometimes violent death. Home can be a something or a somewhere for good or bad. Thanks to a sinking economy, 44 million Americans now live in three-generation households much like in Europe, Asia, and Africa for centuries. But, underlying all these different possible definitions and descriptions that are unique to individuals, there is something that is universal and fundamental to the human condition about "home." Swiss psychiatrist, C.G. Jung (1875-1961) called such human universals "archetypes," so let's explore the archetype of home a little more.

Some species of life on Earth are born with the full ability to look out for themselves with no help from their parents. Presumably, their instincts for self development are so far developed that home does not mean much to them, if anything at all. However, many species are born more or less dependent upon one or both parents, and sometimes the larger community, to assure protection from predators and the elements as well as provide food for sustenance until they are mature enough to take care of themselves. The higher level primates, if they can be so called, seem to need some education into the ways of their species beyond the mere instincts of self preservation. The highest primates of all, if they can be so called, are Homo sapiens. They are born totally dependent and vulnerable and will die during infancy if they are not sustained by care giving adults. They are born with bodies and minds that are mostly undeveloped except for the instinct of sucking to obtain liquid food from some provider. Most often, these are the immediate parents. The mother normally provides the infant with food and the father provides the means for obtaining shelter and safety. By the way, it is the father who determines the sex of the child, whether male or female. So, if the sexual orientation is ambiguous, look to the father as the source. These roles comprise the Jungian archetype of "family." If these roles are not performed well enough, the child grows up with a faulty home life and can be harmful to themselves and their peers. Where infants feel secure and comfortable, they can gradually emerge into mature humans over a couple decades of education and social development. Nevertheless, deviations are the norm and no such thing as "normal" can be defined. But, "abnormal" and "dysfunctional" can be discerned when they are encountered. Homo sapiens are distributed about the Earth in a wide variety of cultures and social organizations, often related to the local area climate and natural resources that first sustained their lives. The study of the variety in lifestyles among Homo sapiens is called "anthropology."

Everyone seems to have some desire to know their family roots. Some sheeple find the study of their genealogy quite interesting. Making up a family history tree can be very enlightening and helps to fit one into the longer history of things. The ancestry of modern Homo sapiens has been traced by genetic research back to a location in north central Africa, from which they migrated north then east and west to populate the planet. The discovery in China of tantalizing fossils of human jawbones raises the possibility that Homo sapiens arrived in eastern Asia far earlier than first supposed. The principal discovery of a mandible (jaw bone) about 100,000 years old is unmistakably Homo sapien, Chinese scientists contend. Until now it has been thought the earliest that members of our species left Africa was around 50,000 years ago. It is approximately in that time period the earliest evidence indicates they entered Europe, and it had been assumed the same timing applied to entry into Asia. These new finds revive the controversy surrounding two contending hypotheses of human evolution, the multi regional versus African origin.

So, whether Homo sapiens sprang from a singular location or appeared simultaneously in many places likely will never be known for sure. That being the case, how can one account for the universal archetype of "home" that seems to be hardwired into the brain neurons of all Homo sapiens. One approach is to invoke theories of evolution. In biology, evolution is the process by which populations of organisms acquire and pass on novel traits from generation to generation, affecting the overall makeup of the population and even leading to the emergence of new species. The development of the modern theory of evolution began with the introduction of the concept of natural selection in a joint 1858 paper by Charles Darwin and Alfred Russel Wallace. This theory achieved a wider readership in Darwin's 1859 book, "The Origin of Species." Science now postulates that, instead of being created in their present form by God, humankind actually evolved from original single-cell creatures several billion years ago to multi-cell organisms to complex life forms which eventually became Homo sapiens. Darwin and Wallace proposed that evolution occurs because a heritable trait that increases an individual's chance of successfully reproducing will become more common from one generation to the next, and likewise a heritable trait that decreases an individual's chance of reproducing will become rarer. [Of course, this theory infuriates the simple-minded folk who believe the Earth is about 6,000 years old and all the humans today are offspring of the first man and woman, Adam and Eve, who were created by God from dust and animated by his breath of life.]

In the 1930s, scientists combined Darwinian natural selection with the theory of heredity to create the modern synthesis, now one of the fundamental scientific theories of biology. In the modern synthesis, "evolution" is defined as a change in the frequency of alleles (several forms of a gene responsible for hereditary variations) within a population from one generation to the next. This change may be caused by different mechanisms, including natural selection, genetic drift, or changes in population social structure. Now, a lot of discussion goes on about whether we are the product of our home environments or merely the result of our genetic inheritance. Studies done among identical twins who were separated at birth and raised in different environments show they are more alike than different. While it seems that genes do play a dominant function in how sheeple turn out, it does appear that genes can be modified by their environments. Still, environments are created by sheeple with functioning genes, so which is dominant may never be proven. Somewhere in that process of evolution, the concept of home was formed and began its journey through the centuries.

Of course, creationists don't like the theory of evolution and prefer to believe that sheeple sprang full grown from the dust of the Earth by a source they call God. By taking the creation myth described in the Bible book of Genesis literally, and working backwards from the genealogy of Jesus listed in the Gospel of Luke, chapter three, they even concluded that it was possible to calculate the precise timing. If you take it literally, as many sheeple do, creation of mankind occurred at nightfall the evening before Sunday, October 23, 4,004 B.C. according to some conservative Bible scholars based upon assumptions published in 1654 by Anglican Archbishop James Ussher (1581-1656) of Armagh, now in Ireland. So, if "home" defines the precise location of our birth origin, the description of the Garden called Eden and its relation to the creator may serve to support the origin of that heritable place in brain neurons or genes that harbors the archetype. Never mind that science claims the Earth was formed from swirling space dust collected by gravity slightly more than four billion years ago. It may be that "home" is hardwired into our brains from the ancestral experience of the first man, Adam, and his helpmate, Eve. We must note, however, that the woman came from the man and the man came from the Earth with life from the breath of God the Father. What is most interesting is that "home" exists as a universal concept, what C.G. Jung called an archetype, among all sheeple on Earth, and not just the segment that aligns with the Judeo-Christian heritage of western religions. Home exists among Asian cultures as well where it predates the Bible by thousands of years. So, no matter which culture one investigates, one finds faith-based comfort in the concept of home whether invested in a personal God, many gods, or family gods.

Science and religion seem to be inherently mutually exclusive, so the more is learned about the cosmos the less appears to be the need for religion. It is amazing how sheeple come to believe in myths Take one example, for example. Although he was assassinated in Illinois for promoting polygamy, the leadership of Joseph Smith, Jr. was accepted by a group of followers that has grown into the international Church of Jesus Christ of Latter-Day Saints after they migrated further to Salt Lake City, UT in 1847 led by his chief apostle, Brigham Young. Young also was a polygamist who sired 56 children and married some 50 women, which bordered upon white slavery. Brigham Young, (1801-1877) designated leader of the Mormon church wrote, "No man or woman in this dispensation will ever enter into the celestial kingdom of God without the consent of Joseph Smith...every man and woman must have the certificate of Joseph Smith, Junior, as a passport to their entrance into the mansion where God and Christ are...Joseph Smith reigns there as supreme a being in his sphere, capacity, and calling, as God does in heaven. Many will exclaim - Oh, that is very disagreeable! It is preposterous! We cannot bear the thought! But it is true." And they believed him, too. How could this be unless God willed it so?

So long as Utah was governed as a polygamous theocracy, it was denied statehood by the Federal government. Although the church officially disavowed polygamy to gain statehood in 1896, it is still on the church books as a revelation from God to Joseph Smith, Jr. and some Mormons still practice it. Mormons emphasize traditional family roles and perform ritual celestial marriages that are sealed for all eternity, which leaves no room for any alternative living arrangements under penalty of excommunication. (Jesus claimed that in heaven there will be neither marriage nor giving in marriage because souls will be like the angels, presumably asexual.)The Mormon Church also excluded blacks as agents of the devil until 1978 when its leaders received a new revelation and changed its position after blacks in Africa spontaneously accepted the faith. A unique Mormon temple ritual is baptism for the dead, including Jews, when they are recommended by members. Things change, and the Mormon Church continues to grow, cult though it may be.

Here is another example. Catholics are told to believe that the bread and wine served at the Eucharist service during mass miraculously become the body and blood of Christ. And the nuns are imagined to take Jesus as their loving spouse. How all this happens is just called a mystery. Others believe eternal punishment in hell awaits all who do not accept Christ as savior. And the Muslims think that their prophet, Muhammad had the last word from God/Allah which tells them how to live in order to obtain a "great reward." Is this the best that the omnipotent all knowing all being God the Almighty One could really do with this creation? How much education does it take to obtain liberation from religious beliefs that conflict with reality? There are many highly educated sheeple with Ph.D. degrees in science attending churches, temples, synagogues, and mosques every week.

Possibly the greatest scientist of all time, Albert Einstein (1879-1955) showed how difficult it is for the human mind to accommodate both science and religion. He never seemed to complete such reconciliation for himself. He wrote in a letter a year before his death in 1954, "The word God is for me nothing more than the expression and product of human weaknesses, the Bible a collection of honorable but still primitive legends which are nevertheless pretty childish. The religion of the future will be a cosmic religion. It should transcend a personal god and avoid dogmas and theology. Covering both the natural and the spiritual, it should be based on a sense arising from the experience of all things, natural and spiritual, as a meaningful unity." But, he cleaved that unity in two by writing, "I believe in Spinoza's God, who reveals Himself in the lawful harmony of the world, not in a God Who concerns Himself with the fate and the doings of mankind."

Einstein distinguished three styles which usually are intermixed in actual religion. The first is motivated by fear and poor understanding of causality, and hence invents supernatural beings, heaven and hell. The second is social and moral, motivated by desire for mutual love and social support. Einstein noted that both have an anthropomorphic concept of God. The third style, which Einstein deemed most mature, is motivated by a deep sense of awe and mystery. Einstein saw science as an antagonist of the first two styles of religion, but as a partner of the third style. Still, he argued that conflicts between science and religion "have all sprung from fatal errors." And "a legitimate conflict between science and religion cannot exist." So, must true believers forever believe, and nonbelievers be forever skeptical, with no possible middle ground? It seems that everyone must believe in something, even if it is atheism. Will all religions ever merge into the One Source from which they all seem to come? Should that be a reasonable goal for Homo sapiens? Perhaps that day has come. You can get the full story of Theofatalism™ in Lessons from Sedona and the complete text that describes five awesome principles of reality, Voices of Sedona. They may be ordered from www.IUniverse.com, as well as the Amazon and local Barnes & Nobles book stores.]

Let's take it from another angle, that of the four elements or functions of personality proposed by C. G. Jung (1875-1961). In his model the necessary functions of human personality are two mutually exclusive forms of perception, sensing (S) or intuition (N), which are opposed by two mutually exclusive forms of judging, thinking (T) or feeling (F). These functions are ranked in a particular order of preference by individual makeup and also come in two "attitudes," either introverted or extraverted. When you put all the options together you get 16 different possible combinations of rankings. What is most significant is that everyone has a dominant function among the four that is either introverted (held inside) or extraverted (exposed to others). Thus, one is said to be an "introverted sensor" or an "extraverted thinker" etc., etc. Jung's theory of personality was modeled by the very popular Myers-Briggs Type Indicator (MBTI) a trade mark of Consulting Psychologists Press or CPI, Inc. Let's consider how each one of the four dominant persuasions might conceptualize "Home."

For the sensor, home may be defined by a structure or residence, a street address, a high school, or some other physical traits. It may include memories of sensory activities that took place there, eating, playing, working, and maintaining. It may recall weather patterns and seasonal variations in appearance from spring flowers to wintry blizzards. For the thinker, home may present logical connections between the past and the present. It may offer explanations for the way things are based on the way things were, which could be either pleasant or unpleasant. For the dominant feeler, home may be expressed in terms of relationships with parents, adults, siblings, and peers during the earliest memories. These memories can color and impact the present relationships also as they are projected upon others in terms of the role models from the past. For those with dominant intuition, home may represent a place of meaning and spiritual significance, possibly a place of comfort or fear depending upon the inferences drawn from the experience. The intuitive may impart a spiritual significance to home that transcends time and place, maybe including the concept of heaven. Since a dominant function of personality does not close off completely access to the other functions, everyone likely will experience home as some combination of these four preferences, either introverted or extraverted according to Jung.

According to attachment theory that was first labeled by psychologist John Bowlby, (1907-1990) the trappings of home provide needed support to enable a child to explore the unknown beyond comfort limits. Without a firm base attached in parents or other symbols of security a child is reluctant to take risks that may threaten its feeling of safety. But taking risks is necessary for human growth, and that includes the aging baby boomers. The main function of home may be to help facilitate the growth that makes it possible to leave home and to develop one's own lifestyle and to create a new home for the next generation. However, attachment can be too much of a good thing and if it crosses a certain line the individual may be reluctant to leave, ever. Practically everyone knows somebody with a child who exhibits such attachment hunger who never really grew up and prefers to continue living at home to forego normal adult relationships. Such a child may be helped along with some "tough love" that induces him to step out on his own in spite of the "attachment hunger" and "homesickness" that may accompany the departure, even temporarily. Leaving home for the first time to enter college or depart for military duty are typical break points when attachment is stressed and future risks are accepted for growth...or not.

All benefits come with burdens and all beginnings come with endings in normal life. A comfortable balance must be attained between attachment to infantile care givers and independence if mature adult relationships are to become possible. Nevertheless, the comfort and security of home is never forgotten and often leaves a void in life that cannot be fulfilled any way except by returning to one's roots now and then for the renewal that it provides. Poet laureate Robert Frost observed, "Home is the place where, whenever you go there, they have to take you in." One thing about going home - sheeple tend to remember you as you were and not as you are. Even Jesus could perform no miracles in his hometown because his neighbors recalled him as the carpenter's son. (Mark 6:3-5) Sometimes, a mature independent lifestyle is not achieved in one step and several return cycles are needed for the launch to be completed.

Another interesting aspect of home invokes two different models of human life. One has it beginning at conception and terminating at death in a very linear fashion. What comes after depends upon one's religious exposure. For many there follows immediately a day of judgment followed by some forms of reward and punishment for behavior that conforms or deviates from religious dogma. For Catholics, there follows the possibility of a second chance for purification in an intermediate state, called Purgatory, that can be influenced by prayers from living relatives. For those believing in reincarnation, life is more like a mobius, i.e., a continuous circular process of repeated birth and death which affords the opportunity of growth and development towards an ideal state, called Nirvana, after which no further needs exist for rebirths on Earth. What happens after that is unspecified.

Towards the end of life, it is natural to renew the image of home and the relatives and friends who may no longer be alive to sustain it and may have been temporarily forgotten. Going back to a home town and a house now occupied by strangers may induce a feeling of abandonment and insecurity that requires some solution. The solution may be found in looking forward rather than backward. In his popular song, "This Ole House," composer Carl Stuart Hamblen recorded in 1954 such a transition from past to future. "...ain't gonna need this house no longer, ain't gonna need this house no more...ain't got time to fix the shingles, ain't got time to fix the floor...ain't got time to oil the hinges or to mingle window panes...ain't gonna need this house no longer, I'm getting ready to meet the saints." When the end of life nears, going back home no longer may be an option. The time may come to look for a new beginning in whatever may come after the ending.

The human infant that is kept warm and dry and clean and is fed when hungry and provided a safe place to sleep as needed may be the happiest creature on Earth. Little wonder that they can be seen smiling so happily so often. Unfortunately by the age of two or so, the Id that demands "just do it" and the super ego that demands "just say no" must begin to be moderated by the ego that balances the dichotomy in accord with the social standards of the family. As such, the ego conducts a necessary role in successful integration and participation of the individual in the culture. Trouble comes as the ego knows no limits and tries to control everyone in contact with it. In the end the cycle must be completed as the ego must "let go and let God" as the twelve-step programs proclaim. It must once again trust in a higher power than itself to walk into the great indefinite uncertainty of what comes after life.

Jesus declared, "Unless you change and become like little children you will never enter the kingdom of Heaven." (Matthew 18:3) The inner child gets submerged in the living of life, but it still resides in the memory recesses of brain neurons. Recovering the dependency, trust, and humility of a child may require crucifying the ego through pain and suffering before one can achieve the calm submission that presages the final homecoming. One may think of himself as the prodigal son who squandered his inheritance in wild living but was welcomed back home by a loving father who celebrated his return to the family after it was all gone. (Luke 15:11-32) In his recounting the story as applied to his own life, author Henri Nouwen proclaims in The Return of the Prodigal Son – A Story of Homecoming, (1994) "Home is the center of my being where I can hear the voice that says: You are my Beloved, on you my favor rests - the same voice that gave life to the first Adam and spoke to Jesus, the second Adam; the same voice that speaks to all children of God and sets them free to live in the midst of a dark world while remaining in the light. I have heard that voice. It has spoken to me in the past and continues to speak to me now. It is the never-interrupted voice of love speaking from eternity and giving life and love whenever it is heard. When I hear that voice, I know that I am home with God and have nothing to fear."

It seems that home can be perceived at least three ways. For those with memories of pain, suffering, and trauma, home may be a place that they are glad to be from. They may have no desire to return and see no benefits in sustaining any family relationships. For others who must roam the Earth seeking fame and fortune, or for necessities of life, home may always stimulate a yearning for the place and family they are from, with all its many variations in relationships. For those with the necessary spiritual awareness, home may be reference to some eternal relationship that is beyond words and cannot be bound by the senses.

This realm was described by Helen Schucman, scribe of A Course in Miracles (1975) in one of her poems titled, "Song to Myself."

"I cannot be replaced, I am unique
In God's creation, I am held so dear
By Him that it is madness to believe
That I could suffer pain or loss of fear.
Holy am I; in sinlessness complete,
In Wisdom infinite, in love secure,
In patience perfect and in faithfulness
Beyond all thought of sin and wholly pure.
Who can conceive of suffering for me?
Surely the mind that thought it is insane.
I never left my Father's house. What need
Have I to journey back to him again?"

The only reasonable explanation worthy of belief for what drives many sheeple to seek a savior to save them from their sins and avoid everlasting punishment in hell is that something must be happening at some unconscious level that is beyond the control of the individual consciousness. It is as though God, who created the illusion of free will and the consequences of it, also embedded in his creation the feeling of a guilty conscience in addition to the perception of disobedience. Since this is natural state of mankind there may be no need to go home because we never left. C. G. Jung discovered that, "Whoever reflects upon himself is bound to strike upon the frontiers of the unconscious which contains what above all else he needs to know." Elsewhere he claimed, "I do not need to believe. I know, because I have been touched by something that sheeple call God. This is the name by which I designate all things which cross my willful path violently and recklessly, all things which upset my subjective views and plans and intentions and change the course of my life for better or worse. In accordance with tradition I call the power of fate in this positive as well as negative aspect as much as it is beyond my control, God. Although my experience can be good or evil, I know the superior will is based upon a foundation that transcends human imagination." Jung expressed that "something" in his psychology of religion, which is nothing less than the universal struggle between perceptions of right and wrong. Thus, it seems that no matter how we perceive of home, we can assume that we are right at the place we must be like an indispensable piece of a cosmic jig saw puzzle, and we are one invisible link in the visible chain of history, insignificant but indispensable, that comprises the individual and collective destiny of Homo sapiens. All in the will of God the Almighty One, of course. Feel good inside no matter what happens outside.

18. THE PRINCIPLES OF THEOFATALISM™.

Leon Trotsky (1879-1940) observed, "Life is not an easy matter. You cannot live through it without falling into frustration and cynicism unless you have before you a great idea which raises you above all kinds of perfidy and baseness." Only you can decide if the burdens are worth the benefits of this new great idea. But, beware of the burdens that come with new knowledge. Voltaire (1694-1778) [a.k.a. Francois Marie Arouet] wrote, "It is dangerous to be right in matters on which the established authorities are wrong." Most sheeple prefer to be wrong with the support of a group than to be correct all by themselves. You may find yourself out on a very long limb all alone. Those who are called to further knowledge must be able to live without social approval. The trouble with making new discoveries is that they destroy our confidence in the establishment. But you will be in some very good company. Every major change in human beliefs originally began as a heresy, and the originator usually was condemned for his efforts. Sometimes a belief becomes so strong that suggesting it might be wrong is nearly impossible. Apostle Paul wrote, "Do not deceive yourselves. If any one of you thinks he is wise by the standards of this age, he should become a fool so that he may become wise. For the wisdom of this world is foolishness in God's sight." (1 Corinthians 3:18-19) It was Arthur Schopenhauer (1788-1860) who stipulated that new truth goes through three stages. First it is ridiculed, then it is opposed, and finally it is accepted as self-evident. Perhaps this work will have to survive the first two in order to achieve the latter, if it ever does.

The history of science is full of discoveries that went unnoticed because the establishment did not recognize the author until some time later when another one got the attention with the same message. For example, a French astronomer named Ole Roemer predicted in 1676 that light traveled at a finite speed when everyone thought it was instantaneous, but it took 50 years for anyone to agree with him. And Vesto Melvin Slipher actually discovered that the universe is expanding at increasing velocity, using the Clark telescope at the Lowell observatory in Flagstaff, AZ, but it was Edwin P. Hubble who became famous for it after repeating the same discovery from the Mount Wilson observatory in Pasadena, CA. Many discoveries have been made several times before they actually were perceived, and often legacy beliefs linger long after they are obsolete. In surveys reported by Newsweek of March 2007, 48 percent of U.S. respondents claimed they believe that God created man as is about 6,000 years ago. How long will it take for belief in this creator to die off? Must we wait for evolution to finally surpass the remnants of Paleolithic man that still occupies our brains? Most new discoveries mean change and that means threats to some and opportunities to others. Sir Winston Churchill (1874-1965) observed, "Men occasionally stumble over the truth, but most of them pick themselves up and hurry off as if nothing happened." Perhaps you will not be one of them. Or, maybe you will. All in the will of God the Almighty One of course.

Someone once said be careful what you pray for because you might be surprised at what you get. Athenian philosopher, Socrates, (469-399 B.C.) observed, "Life contains but two tragedies. One is not to get your heart's desire, and the other is to get it." Here is the result of one search for inner peace and serenity among the ubiquitous suffering and struggle - plus insanity - in the world.

When we have nowhere else to turn and we stand naked without any barriers to the universe, the stark helplessness we feel may be the first step towards acquiring true wisdom. Aging does not guarantee wisdom automatically. Some baby boomers have much further to go than others in their journey to maturity. Some are still infants, some are in kindergarten, some in grade school, some in high school, some in college and some are beyond in the school of life no matter their physical age. Apostle Paul spoke of this as he led the Christian flock from its infantile beginnings. This is solid food, not milk, so you may not yet be ready for it. (1 Corinthians 3:1-9) Most sheeple get to a certain maturity level and stay there the rest of their lives. Continuous growth throughout life is possible but it comes with increasing pain and requires continuous stretching beyond the zone of comfort, and so it is avoided by most everyone. If you are reading this, you are one of a very small number of advanced souls who is ready to advance even further. The journey is like school, stepping up from one grade to another to another, each step taken with trepidation and only the hope for some benefits to come. Wherever you may be in the spiritual climb, this is the place to begin the rest of your journey...or not.

Trust in God the Almighty One occurs when we have nowhere else to turn and no longer have any need for control. Abraham Lincoln (1809-1865) said, "Many times I have been driven to my knees because there was nowhere else to go." Modern churches have replaced their fundamental purpose, preparing sheeple to suffer and die, with running a tax-exempt social clubs for sheeple who think they are immortal. This human trait could help explain why so many sheeple flock to celebrity preachers who promise health, wealth, and happiness in troubled times if you just join up with their flock and donate more than you can afford to their cause. The alternative offered here is walking into a labyrinth where you cannot go wrong and where there are no mistakes. There could be dangerous choices and even lethal consequences but no mistakes. "Even though I walk through the valley of the shadow of death, I will fear no evil, for you are with me; your rod and your staff, they comfort me. (Psalm 23:4)

One blogger observed that most sheeple accept their parent's prejudices, society's morals, their culture's traditions, their generation's aesthetics, the politics of their economic class, and whichever religion got to them first. We were given a name, taught a language and religious views without our permission. Most sheeple stick to these teachings and remain programmed throughout their lives, never considering that they have been molded by outside forces beyond their control. Seldom, if ever, does the average person ask, "Why? Why do I believe this? Is it true? What is the evidence that supports it? What is the evidence against it? Can it be refuted? What do others believe? Why doesn't everyone believe as I do?" The fool never asks these questions, never examines his experiences with a critical eye and so despite all the experiences of a lifetime he has gained no greater wisdom with age. He does not seek answers because he just accepts the answers he's been given. He does not seek knowledge because he believes that he already knows.

Unconscious incompetence is the ruin of Homo sapiens. But conscious incompetence is the beginning of wisdom. Learning begins when you realize what you don't know can harm you. However wisdom, for all its value, cannot be taught, only experienced in daily living because it is a process and not a goal. If traditional organized religion and your inherited belief system no longer meet your needs for spiritual comfort and serenity, here is one option for thinking sheeple who need a new kind of faith for the modern world. You must be ready to face the uncertainty of reality as it is really is or you would not be reading this. If we resist reality, life becomes an endless series of disappointments, frustrations, and sorrows, with nothing but fear ahead. A wise Buddhist teacher observed, "Facing the bluntness of reality is the highest form of sanity and enlightenment. It proceeds through various stages of unmasking until we reach the point of seeing the world directly without our projections. There may be a sense of being lost or exposed, a sense of vulnerability...that is simply a sign that the ego is losing its grip but it is not a threat." It actually may be a step towards personal freedom. So, read on. This is what you came for. The ability to see God in everything opens new spiritual awareness that transcends church dogma and prepares one to live fully in the reality of here and now. If the student is ready, the teacher has come.

Principles are never created, only discovered. These principles of Theofatalism™ may be a new model for evolution of consciousness. They were developed fully in the book, <u>Voices of Sedona</u>, by the author. Without these principles, life is so unreasonably ridiculous as to be absurd. But they will help only if you ponder and review them, and apply them to your life and the events all about you over time long enough and consistently to rewire the neuron patterns in your brain. If applied routinely and daily in every situation, you will develop new appreciation for struggle and suffering because they are required for growth. Much stress and the pain of grief also would be alleviated, and the enjoyment of life would be enhanced far beyond normal expectations by applying them continually. But it takes persistent practice to make them a natural reaction to the stress and anxiety of life, because the evolution of faith takes a lifetime to complete and maybe more. So, the earlier in life you begin to learn and apply these principles the better able you will be to grow through the inevitable issues in aging. It is not too late for baby boomers to begin now. But, no matter how far you go you will always be at the beginning of the rest of your life. Remember that your mind is like a parachute; it only works when it is open. Recall the words of Sir Francis Bacon, founder of the scientific method, (1561- 1626) "Read not to contradict and confute, nor to believe and take for granted, but to weigh and consider."

Like gravity, Theofatalism™ exists whether you believe in it or not and it certainly does not need your permission. Whether your organized social religion is Hindu, Buddhism, Jewish, Muslim or Christian, or some other including Atheism, this virtual Church embraces them all. Everyone is a member and no one can ever live outside of it. It has no treasury, no buildings, and no clergy. It is pure soul. The universe and all it contains is its sanctuary, and its central theme is "God always wins." Everyone is a member and no one can leave or be expelled. Theofatalism™ says that we all are on the pathway of life...exactly where we need to be here and now just like walking the Chartres Labyrinth. All the ageless arguments about the existence - or not - of gods in philosophy and religions considered, in this view God the Almighty One is "that which makes all things happen." This definition arises from the law of physics that says a body at rest tends to remain at rest unless some external force is applied to it. It also arises from the various laws of thermodynamics that avoid a specific definition of energy because it only exists as a mathematical abstraction. Still, it is assumed that nothing happens of itself without some force or cause behind it. The definition of "all things" refers to everything from the smallest subatomic particle to the largest interstellar galaxy, in all the universes however many there may be, with the lives of Homo sapiens barely discernable among them when seen from the satellites orbiting in space. Considering all the happenings in the universe, it is the ultimate hubris for Homo sapiens to think they are anything special. Of course, hubris also must have a cause, that which is called God the Almighty One. However, its essence is the universal energy or Theos, not the god of mythology but the one that created the mythology.

The symbol of Theofatalism™ is the labyrinth tiled into the Cathedral of Our Lady of Chartres in France. With its roots in ancient mythology the design reappears throughout history in different forms. Unlike its opposite maze, which is a primitive symbol of chaos intended to confuse and frustrate, the labyrinth provides a clear and undistorted pathway to the center, which contains its distinctive central feature of the Lotus blossom. The Lotus blossom symbolizes the inseparability of cause and effect, the provision and reality, and the source and manifestation of enlightenment. Many churches are using the Chartres Labyrinth to provide a walk of comfort and serenity for seekers of inner peace as the symbolic walk of life. The practice of labyrinth walking integrates the body with the mind and the mind with the spirit. It can be perceived as a sacred pilgrimage to the center Source after meandering about in reversing directions. There are three stages to walking a labyrinth: 1) releasing control by the ego on the way in by walking the pathway set before you, 2) receiving sublime energy in the center, and 3) returning to serve as you follow the path back out of the labyrinth. At its most basic level the labyrinth is a metaphor for the journey to the center of your deepest self and back out into the world with a greater acceptance of who you really are. If life is a school this may be what you came to learn. As in walking the labyrinth, there are only two rules to follow in application of the Principles of Theofatalism to life: begin and continue.

1. Absolute Predeterminism: Everything is happening as it must or it would be different. The divine will of God the Almighty One cannot be disobeyed. It is the utmost arrogance and ignorance to assume that the creature can disobey the creator. Disobeying God's will is imagined only by the insane because it is impossible. God's will be done, and that includes the arrogance and ignorance to assume otherwise. Everything that is or is not must be as it is or is not and everything must go as it goes, or it would be different. That includes both belief and disbelief in this principle. God creates atheists too. Everything is happening exactly as it was meant to be throughout the universe, from the smallest subatomic particle to the largest and remotest galaxies. Each form of life on planet Earth is a small but necessary element of the whole. Individual choices are driven by unseen forces incomprehensible to our conscious

minds. The "I Am" that we are merely watches the mind/body as it manifests the will of God the Almighty One as there can be no other. [We cannot know what it is that we are outside of a body because that would be like spinning around fast enough to see your own back. Psychology calls it the "self" but words cannot describe what cannot be seen. Some things really are impossible.] This principle presumes a superior source called God the Almighty One that controls the will of Homo sapiens no less than all other forms of matter in the universe. We must make decisions, and we are affected by their consequences through cause and effect, but the choices all were predetermined at the time of creation, which occurs outside of time/space. The greatest challenge sheeple face in life may be letting go of the wishful dream that things should be different. If they could be, they would be. You are right where you are supposed to be here and now. And so is everyone else... believe it or not. Of course, this principle exposes belief in free will as a necessary illusion. But, that belief in illusion too must be necessary or it would be different as nothing can happen outside the will of God the Almighty One. So, this work will either be discovered and become widely distributed or it will not. All in God's will of course. AIGWOC. Get it? Think you can handle that?

2. Necessary Opposites: Famous physicist, Albert Einstein (1879-1955) said there are only two ways to live, believing everything is a miracle or nothing is a miracle. For every action there is an equal and opposite reaction. As in physics so it is in human thoughts and actions. All beginnings come with endings, some just take longer than others. Human beings either think they are a little lower than angels or a little higher than apes. Saints are one and imbeciles are the other, except that apes do some things better than humans and imbeciles are all too plentiful. The creation myth of the Bible and the Darwinian theory of evolution seem to be incompatible, either/or ideas. Charles Darwin (1809-1882) observed that everything is continually changing and life forms must either adapt or die out. He noted that supplies of food never keep up with demand of geometric growth in consuming populations, making it necessary for individuals to compete for scarce resources, thus his law of "survival of the fittest." If God the Almighty One is the what, evolution is the how. Unfortunately, among human societies it seems that reproduction is not always based upon fitness to compete,

so many sheeple suffer from lack of resources to support health, wealth, and happiness. There is no law against being stupid and no restraint against the sexuality of stupid sheeple. But, creationists say all it takes is the voice of God to change things, so he must want things the way they are, opposites and all. Some sheeple find it curious that Lincoln and Darwin share the same birthday. Both were called to interpret death so that life could prevail, one with the pen and one with the bayonet and bullet.

Indeed, Charles Darwin set off a civil war in western religion that forced Christians to choose whether they believed the Bible was the inerrant and infallible Word of God or merely the best attempts by its writers to describe their understanding of God that must be interpreted for modern times with aid of the Holy Spirit. The former became fundamentalists and the latter became the reformed modernists and progressives. This split reached its zenith in the trial of John Scopes in Tennessee for his attempt to teach evolution in the public schools that was sponsored by the American Civil Liberties Union. This court debate reached across the whole country and set up the battleground engaged to this day. Scopes lost his case but his lawyer, Clarence Darrow launched the modernist movement. Its opponents included the evangelical likes of Dwight L. Moody, Amy S. McPherson, Billy Sunday, and Billy Graham, and Jerry Falwell, all great fundamentalist orators. It was like the religious energy aligned with opposing north and south poles of a magnet. It is interesting that during the same time period, politics was separating into the Democrats and Republicans, the former being the modernists and the latter aligned with the fundamentalists.

Perhaps, all energy of the universe is distributed about a neutral center like the air in a balloon, with equal power invested in opposing forces manifested in life events as well as laws of physics. A magnet must have both north and south poles to be complete. Physics now assumes that both matter and anti-matter are necessary to sustain the universe. The opposite ideas, God the Almighty One is and God the Almighty One is not, must both exist in order to have the center. For every action, there is an equal and opposite reaction in nature, and so in thought. The idea that everything sensible is changing, and everything is impermanent must be balanced with an idea that permanence in some form also exists, so sheeple invented the ideas of immortality, heaven, hell, and eternity. Even the concept of Christ is balanced with the necessary anti-Christ. Jesus said that he was come to bring life, and that more abundantly. But he also said he came to bring a sword that would put family members against each other. You could look it up.

The necessity of opposites to make up the whole was expressed by Greek philosopher, Heraclitus (535-475 B.C. who took as a first principle the notion that, "Opposites all are the same." The corollary would be all units are composed of opposites. If apparently contradictory expressions in the world religions can in fact carry some meaning, then they must do so by depending on the "logic of paradox," i.e., two seemingly mutually exclusive things that coexist. However, it was Georg Wilhelm Friedrich Hegel (1770-1831) who developed a system of higher logical thought he called dialectical reasoning, thesis-antithesis-synthesis, that could accommodate the necessary opposites.

Since Homo sapiens manifest energy in thoughts and behaviors, they, and all material and spiritual forms, must conform to this principle of necessary opposites. Inner peace and serenity can be found by spending time in the central null, but realistically we must exist for life in some place and time distributed throughout the universe, as with the air molecules within a balloon. Sometimes this is a happy-healthy-wealthy place, and sometimes it is tragic and painful. When all possible nuclear forces are applied to all sub-atomic events, the result in energy is neutral as they cancel each other out. Every atom is in perfect balance with equal and opposite forces among electrons and protons until some intervention unbalances them. Sheeple create necessary polar opposites by labeling events with value-driven adjectives. There must be predators and prey, peacemakers and warmongers, creators and terminators, up and down, in and out, sweet and sour, joy and sorrow, or it would be different…believe it or not. The task in Jungian psychology, as in Buddhism, is to function while holding the opposites, both/and rather than either/or, because they are necessary to have the peaceful center that lies between them. This is the most difficult challenge to Western thought because it threatens the very existence of ego driven desire for power and control based upon either/or. But, maturity requires that either/or must give way to both/and. In no case is this more important than the dichotomy of simultaneous fear and love of God.

3. Unconscious Decisions: All behavior is driven from unconscious forces that select options with more valuable benefits than burdens. Sheeple all basically take in information and make decisions about it. All decisions, though predetermined choices, employ the ranking of benefits and burdens and the values one ascribes to them, even though unconsciously. Stress from conflicts and ambiguity in making decisions are reduced by consciously listing all benefits and burdens for each choice and placing a value on them. All options among choices are selected because the benefits are worth more than the burdens, even though they may be unconscious and seem to be unreasonable or even insane to a rational observer. Behavior can be changed only by changing the benefit/burden ratio of individual decision making in our value system. For example, presumably one who is driven by a compulsion to wash his hands uncontrollably may be induced to stop if the pain of some punishment exceeds the pleasure in washing. Since most of this process normally is unconscious and beyond conscious control, we can never be fully aware of our deepest drives and motives.

C. G. Jung concluded, "Man's task is to become conscious of the contents that press upward from the unconscious. Whoever looks outside, dreams; whoever looks inside, awakes." Roman Emperor and stoic Marcus Aurelius concluded, "He who lives in harmony with himself lives in harmony with the universe." This phrase implies existence of a subject and object which are beyond consciousness. As these drives and motives (between he and himself) become conscious, perhaps new contents arise in the unconscious to take their places. They operate through a process, although unknown, as dependable as the rotation of the Earth and its orbit around the Sun...until they cease. Science may one day discover the secret to this process lies in the unimaginable complexity of our genes or something even more complex, like morphic energy or maybe even a soul created by God. One may liken this idea to an iceberg, with much more under water than above. The top must go where the bottom takes it. Whatever their source, we can assume inevitable decisions and consequences that are not accidents or mistakes rule human life. There may be no mistakes, only choices and consequences. Believe it, or not.

4. Indefinite Uncertainty: Life does not grant us certainty, only options and unknown probabilities. The past is irrevocable, but nothing

about the future can be forecast with accuracy, especially those things that we think we know for sure. Realization of that reality is a stressful situation, and stress is known to cause clogged arteries and ulcers, and other nasty ways of reducing life expectancy. When the world we depended upon from a life time assumption of "do this - get that" no longer works, where can we turn for comfort? That famous American philosopher and baseball star, Yogi Berra once said, "Making predictions is hard, especially when it is about the future." That awareness makes humankind feel anxious necessarily. Existential anxiety is a fundamental, unavoidable, human response resulting from the awareness of universal uncertainty in the human condition. Tolerance for uncertainty is an element of wisdom that is not popular among sheeple who are given to think they have free will and control of their own lives. Sheeple in a state of unconscious incompetence cannot be anxious because they don't know what they don't know. When incompetence becomes conscious, tension begins to demand either competence or return to unconsciousness. When things are out of our control we desperately want them to return to "normal." This awareness commonly is called "the existential predicament" and the "normalcy syndrome." Thinkers have wrestled with it since the dawn of consciousness, whatever that is.

To be anxious is to be human, because it is a normal reaction to the awareness of indefinite uncertainty. Everyone questions eventually where they came from, why they are here, and where they are going without finding any substantial answers. Anxiety is the feeling they get from thinking about it too much. It might even be argued that anyone who knows what is happening and does not feel anxious is practicing denial or is mentally deficient. To have peace of mind is to be less than human or even possibly mentally unhealthy. If you are not scared and confused you just don't know what's happening. Suffering to some extent or other is part of the human experience because no one can know what is coming next. Here and now is all we have for sure and that is a conjunction of past and future that moves through time instant by instant. Life is unpredictable and that is about all one can say about it. Absolute answers may exist only beyond infinity; among sheeple there are only transient interpretations of inaccurate perceptions. But, there is an opposite idea of course. Some explorers claim the greatest opportunities for joy, purpose, and personal growth don't happen when we're clinging to security. They happen when we explore what's novel, and when we live in the moment and embrace uncertainty. Life events last longer and we can extract more pleasure and meaning from them when we are open to new experiences and relish the unknown instead of resisting it, so they say. Perhaps it is just this trait of curiosity that enables mankind to survive the shocks of life and to adapt to changing situations. But, it comes with anxiety of indefinite uncertainty.

Although there are apparent causes and effects in science, no one can tell which sources the other. No one can step into the same river or situation twice, and in the realm of spirit, there is imagined no beginning or ending; just a continuous flow of now like the roundabout called a mobius. Everything comes to pass; nothing comes to stay. Human understanding is affected by inevitably imperfect perception and judgment that is scientifically unpredictable with absolute accuracy. Undeveloped sheeple seek avoidance of uncomfortable existential anxiety in transient relations with other sheeple, things, and ideas or pills and drugs. But human nature requires living in an unavoidable state of existential anxiety about the unknown future, instant by instant, including the uncertain application of the other principles in this set. Maturity may be surrendering the need for answers to unanswerable questions and accepting the stimulant of anxiety that creates new discovery. The anxiety of indefinite uncertainty calls sheeple out of unconscious incompetence into conscious incompetence to work through discomfort toward painful growth and development physically, intellectually, emotionally, and spiritually. Supporting each other in that divine process may be the greatest form of human service…believe it or not.

5. Immaculate Immanence: God works a very specific plan for each material element and sentient being that forms a unique and necessary part of the whole universe. Most of human life is like attempting to assemble a jigsaw puzzle without the picture on the box. At first it seems impossible, but the closer to the end you get the easier it gets. As you see the pattern form, the individual pieces are easier to fit into their one and only spot. The best way to begin is by laying down the four corner pieces of human personality, sensing/physical, thinking/intellectual, feeling/emotional, and intuition/spiritual, and from there to build up

the pieces in all directions. Only when you are finished does the way all the pieces fit together, each one in its only possible unique place in time and space, actions and consequences, become apparent. In the large jigsaw puzzle in the sky, each individual sentient being may be only one small insignificant piece, but a necessary piece or we would not be here.

[Jigsaw puzzles were originally created by painting a picture on a flat, rectangular piece of wood, and then cutting that picture into small pieces with a jigsaw, hence the name. John Spilsbury, a London mapmaker and engraver, is credited with commercializing jigsaw puzzles around 1766 as an educational aid for children of the wealthy. Jigsaw puzzles have since come to be made primarily on cardboard, but you can find many virtual jigsaw puzzles as free shareware on the Internet. Jigsaw puzzle enthusiasts in the Great Depression discovered what many in our own time are rediscovering - that working on a jigsaw puzzle is a great way to reduce stress. Go ahead, amuse yourself.]

"Immaculate" means without flaw or error…pure, innocent, and sinless. And "immanence" means operating within, inherent...present throughout the universe. Of course, this idea comes with several questions. For example; do we get to choose our puzzle for this life before birth? Does God give us a puzzle with a definite beginning and ending and no options? Does God create our puzzle piece by piece as we go for his own enjoyment? Do we create the puzzle as we go as co-creators with God? Are we all necessary pieces in the puzzle of life for each other? Whether we choose the puzzle of life before birth for its growth benefits or whether it is given to us as part of a universal plan we cannot know. Whatever belief you choose about this, it is the one you are given, like entering a labyrinth that has no options but the path just ahead. But, it is that environment in which we live and move and have our being, immaculate immanence, ImIm. Taken together, these are the principles of Theofatalism™. This is the stuff of God.

19. Give thanks in all things.

The sages discovered that if you expect nothing you will never be disappointed and if you desire nothing you will always be content. To this wisdom Apostle Paul instructed, "...give thanks in all circumstances for this is the will of God for you..." (1 Thessalonians 5:18) Can you give thanks for the cross you bear in hopes it will lead to some form of resurrection? The original English colonists we call Pilgrims celebrated days of thanksgiving as part of their religion. But these were days of prayer, not days of feasting. Our national holiday really stems from the feast held in the autumn of 1621 by the Pilgrims and the Wampanoag and their leader or "Massasoit" called Ousamequin, to celebrate the colony's first successful harvest. Ten months after their arrival at Plymouth, in Massachusetts, they had erected seven houses, a common meeting place, and three storehouses for supplies and food from the first harvest. They had much to be thankful for. However, the roots of our holiday are far older, and they stem from suffering and not blessings.

Apostle Paul was the official organizer for Christianity, as you know, along with Simon Peter of course. He claimed that he was called by Jesus himself to preach his message to all the gentiles of that age even though he was not one of the original apostles. Sometimes it is difficult to separate his own ideas from those of Christ since we have much more of his writings than teachings by the apostles themselves and nothing directly from Jesus himself. One such situation lies in his instruction to "give thanks in all things," as one instance among several throughout his writing that met all cares of living with thanksgiving. (1 Thessalonians 5:18, Philippians 4:6, I Timothy 4:4) If you are like a fish caught on a hook, anger and fear are the only reasonable human reactions, followed by frantic instinctive attempts to break free. But, the religious propose another option. Many bad things happen to good sheeple and good things happen to bad sheeple, so everyone looks for a plausible explanation. Christians claim that man has no one to blame but himself for his own sin brought suffering into the world. "...just as sin entered the world through one man and death through sin, in this way death came to all men because all sinned." (Romans 5:12) Other scriptures dispute this claim, but they seldom are taught among mainstream churches. Was it not God himself who placed the tree of knowledge of good and evil in the Garden? Why is it practically impossible for sheeple to blame God for the pain and suffering in life? Jesus said that a man was born blind just so that God could show his power to heal him when the time was right to show off his will to do so. (John 9:3) But, what of all those sheeple who are broken that God never heals?

Tolerating and even accepting evil things as from God seems to be illogical and unreasonable. Consider the story of Job in the Old Testament. You recall that God enabled Satan to kill off all his herds, and then his servants plus all his children, and finally covered him with humiliating and painful boils. His wife finally exclaimed, "Why don't you just curse God and die?" But, he replied, "You are talking like a foolish woman. Shall we accept good from God and not trouble? Though he slay me yet will I trust in him." Job 2: 8-10, Job 13:15) Although scripture states that Job was restored to his previous health, wealth, and happiness, it does not claim that his servants, cattle, or children ever were resurrected. Scholars think the happy ending was added at some later time to avoid leaving him stranded and abandoned by an unjust God, the Almighty One. Mother Teresa, the saint of slums in Calcutta, also repeatedly instructed to "Take what he gives and give what he takes with a big smile."

The Dalai Lama, head of Buddhism, gave a similar instruction as follows: "Let us retire and be thankful, for if we didn't learn a lot today, at least we learned a little, and if we didn't learn a little, at least we didn't get sick, and if we got sick, at least we didn't die; and if we died, well who knows; so, let us be thankful." That was after the Chinese invaded his homeland of Tibet and demolished the Buddhist temples and killed the monks and drove him into exile for life in India after 1959. The Buddhist way is to detach and accept one's circumstances, maybe to the point of a mental illness, what psychiatrists call dissociation. If I am not in my body, then none of its pain can affect me. Under extreme threats, this is a normal defensive reaction. Another is to avoid sheeple who are worse off because it makes one feel so bad due to the "mirror neurons" recently discovered in human brains that help motivate charity for the poor and disabled. Still another is to focus energy on getting what we want while denying energy to that which we do not want.

University of Nevada Professor, Steven Hayes argues from the Buddhist school that happiness is not a normal state of being because pain is inevitable and working through it is better than attempting to avoid it. As such, happiness is a byproduct of living which is distributed unevenly, and not its central goal. Consider that things are never so bad they cannot get worse. He has created "acceptance - commitment therapy" to help sheeple do as he says to build up tolerance for pain. Psychologist and theologian, Dr. Tom Stevens says that thinking you are entitled to more than you have leads to feeling deprived and resentful. (<u>You Can Choose to Be Happy</u>, 1998) He got that right! "Some people spend much of their lives feeling like victims. What a waste!" Says he. If you learn to view every moment and everything you receive as gifts to appreciate and be grateful for; then you will be happy. He said so. Hope for the best, be prepared for the worst, expect something in between, and be grateful for all that you receive. Seers and sages claim that each situation, no matter how bad, contains something that can be appreciated, and finding it can be the path to inner peace. There is even a new response to post trauma shock called post trauma growth being applied to war veterans and others who have suffered a disabling impact to the survival instinct.

It seems that having a positive attitude is helpful to some of those whose world has been shaken by threats to life and limb. [The Rev. Robert Schuller built an international ministry from the Crystal Cathedral in Orange, CA by repeating his mantra, "The attitude of gratitude." However, the whole thing spun out of control and went bankrupt in 2010 leaving $50 million of unpaid debts. The Rev. Schuller has not been preaching much lately.] Moreover, finding something to sincerely thank sheeple for who have harmed you seems to create a peaceful environment in which to work or play, although it likely won't provide restitution. Jesus instructed, "You have heard that it was said, Love your neighbor and hate your enemy. But I tell you: love your enemies and pray for those who persecute you, that you may be sons of your Father in heaven. He causes his sun to rise on the evil and the good, and sends rain on the righteous and the unrighteous...Give to everyone who asks you, and if anyone takes what belongs to you, do not demand it back." (Matthew 5: 43-45, Luke 6:30))

The price for happiness seems to be relinquishing all desires that things should be different and giving up painful memories of the past to focus on the now and future of life. Memory that is required for the accumulation of learning also stores the pain and suffering of the past. It must be necessary or it would be different. If things could be different they would be, and you have no control over the will of God the Almighty One. That may be the supreme lesson for human egos to learn. The ego that will not commit suicide must be crucified. Trust in God occurs when we have nowhere else to turn, when we release the need for control. Like the hymn by John Sammis says, "...simply trust and obey, for there's no other way." This calls for calm submission, like the relationship between a pet dog and its master. But, this is not in the nature of normal human ego, so it must be crucified to give up its incessant demand for control; "Not my will," as Jesus declared.

Saul, persecuter of Christians had to suffer blindness for three days before he could be converted into Apostle Paul. "This man is my chosen instrument to carry my name before the Gentiles and their kings and before the people of Israel. I will show him how much he must suffer for my name." (Acts 9:15-16) In his deepest suffering and loss Job, the servant of God, seemed to overcome his self righteousness as he exclaimed, "Though he slay me, yet will I trust in him." (Job 13:15) Although it is said that God made restitution to Job, none of his cattle and servants and sons and daughters that were lost were resurrected. St. Theresa of Lisieux (1873-1897) expressed her willingness to suffer in this prayer; "My God, I choose everything, I will not be a Saint by halves, I am not afraid of suffering for Thee, I only fear one thing, and that is to do my own will. Accept the offering of my will, for I choose all that Thou willest. Thou hast given me, O Lord, delight in all Thou dost. For what joy can be greater than to suffer for Thy Love? I know

I shall never recover from this sickness, [tuberculosis] and yet I am at peace. For years I have not belonged to myself, I have surrendered myself wholly to Jesus, and He is free to do with me whatsoever He pleases. O my God! from how much disquiet do we free ourselves by the vow of obedience!" Note that she died at age 24.

There is an opposing view, of course. [There is always an opposing view]. There is no progress unless one becomes irresistably discontent with what is, although many sheeple won't change until it hurts too much not to. The price for growth seems to be solving problems that contain hidden opportunities. There is a saying; think the way you want to be and soon you will act the way you think, act the way you want to be and soon you will think the way you act. That is the way they train soldiers to kill other soldiers. On the battlefield, anger and fear are powerful motivators. Admittedly, the Dalai Lama still is waiting for the Chinese to abandon their invasion and occupation of his homeland in Tibet, but who knows, maybe it is better this way. But, the bones buried in common graves of a million dead soldiers and civilians killed in the thwarted Russian campaign attempted by Napoleon Bonaparte in 1812 may have a different view of the matter. So may all the victims made homeless and those killed by the earthquake that decimated the struggling nation of Haiti.

The scriptures seem to say that everything is the will of God the Almighty One, and the only appropriate human response is thankfulness, no matter what happens. Paying back evil with evil, like the "eye for an eye" treatment of the Old Testament, does not appear to be a part of authentic Christian philosophy but it is the foundation of Shari-a law in Islam.

[Islam is not just a religion but a secular way of life also. Its dogma divides behaviors into five categories: obligatory, recommended, neutral, discouraged, and forbidden. Penalties for violations are often stark and barbaric by modern western standards, but rely upon the laws of Moses for authority, i.e., death by stoning for a woman guilty of adultery and amputation of hands as punishment for theft. Jews no longer enforce the laws of Moses in the Torah, but radical Muslims would impose those very laws on secular society by violent means because the Koran demands it. It appears that the gap between enlightened and primitive societies is getting wider and wider. But, the ubiquitous presence of cell phones and the Internet may be changing that.]

The Bible declares we should be anxious for nothing, prayerful for everything, and thankful for anything. "Do not be anxious for anything, but in everything by prayer and petition, with thanksgiving, present your requests before God. (Philippians 4:5-6) You don't often hear this message from church leaders because it is a curious idea for Western thinkers to accept. Yet, it is the hallmark of Apostle Paul as he attempted to soothe the pain of suffering Christians being persecuted in Rome; "And we know that in all things God works for the good of those who love him, who have been called according to his purpose. For those God foreknew he also predestined to be conformed to the likeness of his Son, that he might be the firstborn among many brothers." (Romans 8:28-29) Unfortunately, he leaves little hope for those who are not "predestined" and not called "according to his purpose." Apparently, they must look out for themselves. Unless, of course, we all are included in his statement, which would include the criminal as well as the saint.

If you have been blessed with health, wealth, and happiness, giving thanks and smiling all the time might be a reasonable response to the Almighty. After all, nothing comes of itself without the necessary participation of many other contributors over whom you have no control. For sellers to be successful there must be buyers. Homo sapiens are competitive, greedy, and aggressive at their core, but we also are a care-taking, empathetic and forgiving species, and emotions like compassion, gratitude, mirth, love and awe have wired into our nervous systems the path to social well-being. Individuals who are highly successful will admit that it took many others to help make it happen, if they are honest. Only pride, arrogance, and hubris would attribute it all to their own hard work. But, many sheeple work hard with little at the end of life to show for it. In fact, results often are not proportional to effort at all. The winner of a race scarcely works much harder than the one who comes in second, or even last for that matter. The owner who enjoys the benefits of a building scarcely works as hard as those who built it but never occupy it. Many times the one who starts something new is upstaged by others who get all the credit and the rewards because life often is not fair. In the U.S. one of the worst labels one can earn is "loser." Legendary football coach, the late Vince Lombardi (1913-1970) said, "If winning isn't important, why do they keep score...winning isn't everything, it's the only thing."

[Sports fans may know that bicycle racer Lance Armstrong won the Tour de France seven times, but no one knows who came in second. Would competitive sports be as interesting without the scoreboard and the playoffs? In fact, some would suggest that the will to compete and to win is a basic part of human nature that is thwarted by government entitlements which prevents winners and losers. Carried into war, this human need for competition could include the body counts in mass graves at the end of battles. This is not a gender issue as competitive sports for women now will prove. In fact, women in military combat roles now are no longer the exception including snipers, fighter pilots, astronauts, and submarine crews.]

Americans love competition in various forms to establish rank among peers. There is even a national competition for bed making among the hotel custodial staffs each year, believe it or not. Many TV shows popularize the selection of a winner at the expense of many losers. Coming in second scarcely matters at all in many sit-coms. Take the lottery for example. For one to win, many must lose. It is difficult to be thankful for coming in second much less last. This emphasis on winners seems to be opposite to the teaching of Jesus who said, "The last shall be first and the first shall be last" in his kingdom. (Matthew 20:16) He also dismissed the self righteous hypocrites; "I tell you the truth; the tax collectors and the prostitutes are entering the kingdom of God ahead of you." (Matthew 21:31) You don't hear many preachers using that text for their sermons, especially if the healthy, wealthy, and happy ones are in the congregation. They know who pays their salaries.

Apostle Paul also instructed his readers to come before God with thanksgiving before asking for any special favors. This notion seems to be opposite to the voice of Jesus who said that God knows what you need, so don't be anxious about tomorrow because God will provide as he sees fit, or not. (Matthew 6:30, Philippians 4:6,) In fact, Jesus admonished everyone to avoid flaunting their blessings in public; "Do not your alms before men to be seen of them, otherwise you have no reward of your Father which is in heaven." (Matthew 6:1) "All such boasting is evil." (James 4:14-16) Anyway, what kind of wishy-washy

God would it be who could be persuaded by prayers and supplications or sacrifices to change his plan and reward anyone who asked for their pleasures to be met? Research attempting to determine whether prayer for others helps, even for strangers who do not know they are being prayed for, has not proved that it improves convalescence after serious medical treatments. But it seems to help some sheeple sometimes. This research may indicate something about morphic energy resonance between the subjects at a distance, as proposed by British biologist, Rupert Sheldrake, and should be expanded. Perhaps prayer transfers healing energy from healthy sources to unhealthy receptors in ways not presently understood. While miracles may happen, most sheeple who find their prayers unanswered may be challenging the will of God the Almighty One…and losing. Mother Teresa referred to all the poor outcasts living in slums of the world as God's people, and she said, "Heaven will be full of them." He must have loved the poor and rejected ones because he made so many more of them than the healthy, wealthy, and happy ones...and continues doing so.

Indeed, how often among Homo sapiens are their basic needs left unmet by their creator and their governing authorities. In addition to wars and blatant genocide, including the annihilation of natives by the invaders of North America after the fifteenth century and the human slavery they employed to help some of them get rich, there also come other forms of devastation such as Hurricane Katrina that destroyed most of the homes and lifestyles of the Gulf Coast. If you are one still living in a FEMA trailer several years later with no hope of rebuilding your home, it might be difficult to find something to be thankful for, as Paul ordered, or to smile as Mother Teresa instructed. The mentally ill living in prisons with no hope of treatment can scarcely be thankful, and their smile is more like a grimace. What about the veterans returning from combat in Iraq with missing limbs and destroyed lives? Or the millions routed from their homes by foreclosures resulting from the banking meltdown of 2008? Or the father who returns home from work and finds that his wife has drowned their four children in the bathtub? Or the grossly disabled woman who was attacked by a pet chimpanzee owned by her friend and lost her face and both of her hands. Or, the sheeple who lost their meager retirement investments in the great recession of 2008-09. Lawrence Summers, then director of the White

House council of economic advisors, declared the stock market was revalued same as 1967 when corrected for inflation. Or, the rich ones who lost their booty to the fraudulent Ponzi scheme of Bernie Madoff. For him to succeed, many greedy investors had to help make it happen. Or, the U.S. Marine who returned from Iraq blind and missing both legs. Or the families of 13 soldiers murdered at Fort Hood, Texas by Maj. Nidal Hasan, psychiatrist and Muslim. Being thankful in acute suffering seems to go against human nature…which was formed in the image of God the Almighty One according to the account of creation in Genesis.

By the way, Jesus did not abolish slavery or wars or poverty or disease and suffering or…well, you get the picture. As to him conquering death, well that remains to be seen. Even the Apostle Paul had his doubts as he wrote, "God, the blessed and only Ruler, the King of kings and Lord of lords, who alone is immortal and who lives in unapproachable light, whom no one has seen or can see. To him be honor and might forever." (I Timothy 6:16) After all, the prophesy of being buried "three days and three nights" in death to prove his divinity was not literally fulfilled as Jesus was only buried for two nights and two days, from Friday evening until Sunday morning. (Matthew 12:39-41, Matthew 28:1) The whole basis of Christianity, the resurrection, may be based on a fallacy. And his alleged appearances after resurrection to 500 sheeple made no impression upon secular historians or the leaders of Rome at all until 325 A.D. Thousands of loyal Christians were slaughtered meantime. Pontus Pilate, the Roman governor at Jerusalem was on thin ice with Caesar, and any slight hint of social upheaval among the Jews would certainly be high on his list of priorities. There is no Roman historical account of any resurrection, although first-century Jewish historian Flavius Josephus (37 – 100 A.D.) apparently mentioned it briefly as hearsay. None of the Gospel writers [who are anonymous] were eyewitnesses, and neurology experiments now prove that memory is highly subjective and becomes less reliable as time passes from the event.

Saul of Tarsus, who claimed he was called by Jesus to proclaim him to Gentiles, is assumed to have been beheaded in Rome for treason against the state for preaching Jesus was some kind of king. But he admonished the church at Rome, "Everyone must submit himself to the governing authorities, for there is no authority except that which God has established. The authorities that exist have been established by God." (Romans 13:1-7) Thus was born the "divine right of kings." If so, then how come the Jews rebelled against Rome which destroyed the temple and dispersed them among the gentiles for 2,000 years. In addition to Israel (5.7 million) and the U.S., (6.5 million) Jews live in 48 different countries. Were they justly punished for disobedience to God? Historians claim that thousands of Jews were killed by the sword in the revolt of 66-74 A.D., and the Jewish temple cult died with the Roman destruction of the Temple in 70 A.D. by Titus, eldest son of Emperor Vespasian and the mass suicide/slaughter of Zealot Jews by Roman soldiers at the siege of their mountaintop fortress called Masada where the remaining 960 holdouts remained until 73 A.D. Jews could no longer buy forgiveness for their sins by sending the appropriate sacrifice to the priestly nobility in Jerusalem.

Rabbinical Judaism replaced the temple cult. Instead of one world center in Jerusalem, the center of Jewish religious life shifted to the synagogues in each Jewish community, where it exists to this day. And for three hundred years, Christian Jews were fed to the lions and crucified for their beliefs. So what is there really for Christians and Jews to be thankful for or to smile about? Really. If Jesus could not save his own sheeple what more can we expect from his benevolence if God wills us so to suffer – more or less? Perhaps neither blame nor praise are appropriate, for the impersonal will of God the Almighty One always wins. "I make peace and create evil. I the Lord do all these things." (Isaiah 45:7) "Shall there be evil in a city, and the Lord has not done it?" (Amos 3:6) The Koran says the same thing; "No calamity comes, no affliction occurs, except by the decision and preordainment of Allah." (64.11) This would have to include the acts of man as well as the acts of nature. Obviously, God also must create disease and insanity. Why is not for us to know. Mother Teresa wrote these words to U.S. President G.H.W. Bush and Iraq President Saddam Hussein in January, 1991 on the eve of the Gulf War; "I come to you with tears in my eyes and God's love in my heart to plead to you for the poor and those who will become poor if the war that we all dread and fear happens. I beg you [both] with my whole heart to work for, to labor for God's peace and to be reconciled with one another." We all know how that turned out. Give thanks in all things, yes indeed.

Perhaps there are appropriate times to be thankful, and maybe not. Perhaps some are called to greatness and some are not. Perhaps a healthy mental attitude has space for outrage and hatred, anger and fear, for a god that would demolish its own creation willy-nilly whether by earthquakes, fires, droughts, hurricanes, tornadoes, or disease, wars, murders, and economic depressions, etc. Perhaps "freedom is having nothing left to lose...nothin ain't worth nothin but its free" as the lyrics in "Me and Bobby McGee" by Kris Kristofferson declare. Perhaps it is true; if you are not scared and confused you don't know what is happening. Attempting to be thankful when being outraged if outcast, and destitute of health, wealth, and happiness would be more appropriate may be an idea whose time has come. But that is not the Christian way. The Bible instructs, "If it is possible, as far as it depends on you, live at peace with everyone. Do not take revenge, my friends, but leave room for God's wrath, for it is written: It is mine to avenge; I will repay, says the Lord. (Deuteronomy 32:35) On the contrary: "If your enemy is hungry, feed him; if he is thirsty, give him something to drink. In doing this, you will heap burning coals on his head." (Proverbs 25:21-22, Romans 12:18-20) It seems that Maj. Nidal Hasan, the U.S. army psychiatrist and Muslim terrorist who killed 13 soldiers and wounded 29 others at Fort Hood, TX on November 5, 2009 thought otherwise. For him, commands in the Holy Koran to fight for the way of Allah won over his sworn allegiance to the U.S. Constitution. The grieving families of all those murdered may find it difficult to "give thanks in all things." All in God's will of course...AIGWOC.

The Realm of the Real is the place of our essential fragmentation, vulnerability, and death. It's the place where every disaster leaves us wounded and helpless. It's our wretched human reality in each pitiful life. To most conscious sheeple, it's a terrifying place, and so most everyone will do most anything to hide this reality from their own awareness. In fact, that's the function of a psychological symptom: to hide a horrifying reality behind mental and physical manifestations such as anxiety, insomnia, lethargy, nightmares, depressed mood, and so on. And protesting to God in anger and disobedience about any suffering that afflicts us, and about how unfair it all seems, only serves to sustain the illusion that we - not God - should be in control of our lives.

Psychologically, then, when you encounter the real world, you experience a trauma. Or, more precisely stated, you experience a trauma if you encounter the real with nothing but symptoms and defenses from the ego or imaginary realm. On the other hand, if, when you encounter the real, you have the trust and patience to place yourself totally in God's protection with the trust of a child, in calm submission as claimed by Jesus, "Into your hands, Lord, I commit my spirit," then perhaps a new possibility may open. New Age preacher, Joel Osteen has observed, "It is not happening to you, it is happening for you. Just remember that as you suffer and struggle through life." Perhaps there is a small kernel of truth there because all benefits seem to come with burdens and all burdens may have unseen benefits. The U.S. Declaration of Independence claims that among the inalienable rights of mankind are life, liberty, and pursuit of happiness. The founders did not include a peaceful and comfortable dying in the list. But Jesus warned not to lay up treasures on Earth but rather treasures in Heaven. He proclaimed, "The man who loves his life will lose it, but the man who hates his life in this world will keep it for eternal life." (John 12:25) He also proclaimed, "The spirit gives life, the flesh counts for nothing." (John 6:63)

In the end it may be necessary to crucify the ego that is so useful in life (to modify the id that says "just do it" and the superego that says "just say no,") in order to prepare for the life to come where there is no further need or role of ego to perform and humankind will become "just like the angels." (Matthew 22:30) Perhaps the only prayer that is appropriate is not "Please let me avoid going through this," but rather "Please help me to grow through this." That kind of belief would include acknowledging that it rains upon the just and the unjust, what goes up comes down, and every bell curve has a bottom side. As with poet Robert Frost, we must acknowledge that "it is hard to get into this world and hard to get out and what lies in between doesn't make much sense." Neither does all Gospel seed fall upon fertile ground to produce abundant harvest...some is blown away by wind, some falls upon rocks, and some gets eaten by the birds. (Mark 4: 3-8) And so it is with this work as well. AIGWOC...all in God's will of course.

St. Theresa of Lisieux (1873-1897) declared, "Jesus does not demand great actions from us but simply surrender and gratitude." If the New Testament presents the truth about Jesus and the plan of redemption for mankind, why does not all of it fall upon fertile ground? How come there are so many different religions, often fighting for their own supremacy? If we are expected by the Savior to have the trust and faith of a child, why are we given reason to challenge scriptural religious teachings that make no sense? It does seem that we see reality only through a dark glass of distortion and must tolerate the existential anxiety of indefinite uncertainty until such day that all will be made clear...or not. But, hey, things are never so bad they cannot get worse. Think you can handle that...with thanksgiving?

20. OF JUNKYARDS, GARBAGE DUMPS, CEMETERIES, AND ENTROPY.

Everything that man makes eventually returns to its natural state...including man. Garbage disposal is a big business. Every year, eleven million tons of refuse is discarded in the United States, three million from New York City alone. Whatever is consumed or used up eventually ends up in a garbage dump, sewage plant or a junkyard, or a cemetery unless it lies untended or flows into the ocean. Whatever is discarded eventually returns to its original natural state no matter how long it takes. All matter in the universe comes in solids, liquids, and gases. Changing from one state to another and sustaining it requires application of energy. Without energy, matter always reverts to its natural state. The measure of energy it takes to retard this process is called entropy. Mankind also must absorb energy from water, sun, oxygen, and food in order to live so long as possible until they die, from dust unto dust. Entropy is a measure of the amount of energy it takes to prevent all this from happening. You know if you own a car or house that it takes repairs and maintenance to keep its original condition. Concrete and steel are two examples of this principle in action. Eventually corrosion, rust, and decay take their toll of bridges and buildings and the elements reclaim their own. The U.S. Navy employs "cathodic protection," through electro-magnetic fields to retard the tendency of the ocean to return steel in the hull of its ships to its natural state by the corrosion process of oxidation seen in rust. The familiar "Ziebart" franchise locations throughout the country attempt to retard the rusting of automobiles caused by contact with corrosive materials, including coarse salt used to melt ice in winter road maintenance. Concrete used in building structures often is reinforced by bars of steel inserted throughout, but this too is destined for eventual demolition and recycling. So it is with human bodies also.

If it is not retarded, all organic materials go through a chemical process of decomposition. The concept of entropy is central to the second law of thermodynamics, which deals with physical processes and whether they occur spontaneously. Spontaneous changes tend to smooth out differences in temperature, pressure, density, and chemical potential that may exist in a system until stasis is reached. Entropy is a measure of how far this smoothing-out process has progressed. Left alone, a cup of hot or cold water will eventually assume the temperature of the surrounding area. One must charge one side or other of the equilibrium with energy to keep it unbalanced. The concept of entropy has been adapted in various fields of study, including information theory, psychodynamics, thermo-economics, and evolution. In astrophysics, time no longer is considered a constant. In theory, as time slows down and approaches zero, space may expand to infinity, and vice versa. The energy in the universe is measured in terms of heat liberated by molecular reactions as scaled into calories. If some form of energy from an external source is not continually imparted to keep time running, some scientists suggest the universe may eventually come to a standstill and be locked up in a frozen single mass. This may be the condition inside of black holes, although there is no theory yet to explain how that works. But, since energy itself can neither be created nor destroyed, and Albert Einstein provided the relationship between matter and energy, the material content of Earth appears to be a constant even though Homo sapiens have learned how to change the form of materials temporarily by application of energetic forces. Do you see where this is going yet?

All the above means simply is that material elements that undergo a change from their natural state always endeavor to return to their natural state or equilibrium. Everything that happens is no more than the disturbance of a perpetual state of rest which is forever attempting to re-establish itself. In physics, a body at rest tends to stay at rest. Since all man-made materials originate in natural states of Earth, they naturally want to return to their original homes, and they will not deviate from that state without imposition of some external force. Application of such a force requires that energy must be converted from its static to its dynamic state. In human terms, bodies are made from energy in the sperm and egg, but they die if they are not given energy from food and water and air. One can live without food for up to a month but lack of water will kill the body by dehydration in a few days to a week. The main organs, heart, lung, kidney, liver, will live a few hours disconnected from the body if refrigerated, but the brain will die in less than ten minutes without being fed oxygenated blood. [Hearts have been restarted up to 45 minutes after stoppage but brain damage was never recovered.]

The bodies of Homo sapiens are aggregated into families, cultures, and nations. If nations did not use so much force to preserve their artificial sovereignty and geographic boundaries, it might be interesting to see how long it would take for them to unify into a homogeneous world like the origin from which they came. Nevertheless, all earthen materials return eventually to their original state. From dust to dust as it were. That is why there are junkyards and garbage dumps, as well as cemeteries and crematoriums. Sometimes the process of recycling is accelerated by insertion of destructive energy that may be called "acts of God," even though they are implemented by mankind. Examples are wars, criminality, and accidents, for example plus diseases and geological disasters. Some things that are broken cannot be fixed. Take the case of the woman who was attacked by a domestic chimpanzee and lost both eyes, much of her face, and both hands. Words like healing and recovery are meaningless to her. So it is for many sheeple living with irrevocable losses.

But what about cemeteries? The unsolved mystery is the source of the energy that creates and sustains life, the conversion of inanimate to animate. Sometimes called the "vital force," it is the greatest of mysteries. Human bodies that begin with union of microscopic sperm and egg are composed of a few naturally occurring materials, mostly water and a few minerals, and they too adhere to the law of entropy. God admonished man in Genesis 3:19 "…from dust that art and to dust thou shall return." In fact, all forms of life including plant, animal, and human are composed of the very same earthen materials packaged in their own unique ways temporarily as depicted in chemical formulas. It seems that the cycle of birth and death among Homo sapiens is related somehow to all other earthen cycles. Perhaps the law of conservation of energy applies here as it does with all matter. If energy can neither be created nor destroyed as the first law of physics claims, then perhaps life merely is recycled from one discarded container into a new one. This idea could be expressed by a model called a "*mobius*" a model with a mysterious property. It was discovered independently by German mathematicians August Ferdinand Mobius and Johan Benedict Listing in 1858, and mathematical formulas developed in 2007 have verified its property. [A mobius can be made easily by taking a paper strip about six inches long and half inch wide and giving it a half-twist, and then gluing the ends of the strip together to form a single strip. Although you begin with a two-sided linear strip, the resulting mobius strip has only one edge and one side with no beginning or ending. Try it.] If you travel around an edge or a surface of a mobius, you always end up where you started. The mobius construct is used to create a continuous audio/video recording tape. Perhaps it also models the continuum between life and death, imagination and insanity, much like the Chinese symbol of Yin and Yang which merges opposites into unity. So, is life more like a linear strip with a definite beginning and ending or like a mobius that has neither?

Modern physics assumes there is a beginning and ending to space and time so perhaps discovery of the mobius was God's way of showing sheeple there is more to be learned about a continuum beyond space-time than we have yet thought possible. Of this possibility, C. G. Jung observed, along with Albert Einstein that, "Beginning and end are unavoidable aspects of all processes. Yet, on close examination it is extremely difficult to see where one process begins and another ends since beginnings and endings merge into each other and form an individual continuum. We may establish that an individual consciousness has come to an end, but whether this means that a continuity of psychic process is also interrupted remains doubtful. The fact that we are unable to imagine a form of existence without space and time by no means proves that such an existence is in itself impossible. There are paranormal experiences all the time that seem to prove otherwise. So we are not entitled to conclude from the apparent quality of our perception that there is no form of existence without space and time. It is not only permissible to doubt the absolute limits of space-time perception, it even is imperative to do so. The possibility that the psyche/soul touches on a form of existence outside time and space presents a scientific question that merits serious investigation for a long time to come." Another useful related model of investigation for this concept is the labyrinth as opposed to a maze. The labyrinth has only one destination and one pathway to it as well as one path to its origin. On the other hand, a maze is a puzzle with no easy solutions in which one can get hopelessly lost while looking for the exit. So, is life depicted by a mobius, a labyrinth, a maze, or elements of them all?

The social institutions of Homo sapiens all exist under the rule of entropy. Marriages, for example, must constantly be energized to overcome the natural tendency of sheeple to be sexually promiscuous. Without that energy, couples drift into boredom and that leads to infidelity and divorce. Gardens must be weeded constantly to keep out the natural growth of weeds, insects, and pests that destroy crops. All relationships are the same; begin, end, and recycle. Buildings and bridges must be maintained to keep them from rotting and falling down. Even churches must be supported and energized for growth or they will stagnate and die. That is why most church leaders teach only what sheeple will pay for by their donations.

Governments must be energized by public taxes or by military force or they will degenerate into anarchy. Perhaps a primary role of government is to maintain a structure for the rule of law so that sheeple will not fall to their lowest common denominator, that of anarchy, which appears to happen when there is inadequate law enforcement. The cost of maintaining law and order in a society may be a form of entropy, i.e., the energy needed to keep the society from self-destructing. So also may be the cost of educating the next generation to replace the retiring population of baby boomers. When this boundary is breeched, social unrest and civil wars may occur or invaders may take over. Such was the end of the imperial Roman Empire, the Ottoman Empire, the British Empire, etc.

Human bodies must be nurtured by food and rest for energy to keep them from rotting from the inside out, eaten up by bacteria and parasites. When the biological process of converting food into energy declines, the cells die and the organism decays. So, also the Bible claims that the soul must be nurtured and protected from invasion by demons that are evil and harmful to spirit personalities, hence the ongoing entropy of spiritual warfare against principalities described by Apostle Paul. "Put on the whole armor of God, that you may be able to stand against the wiles of the devil. We wrestle not against flesh and blood, but against principalities, against powers, against the rulers of the darkness of this world, against spiritual wickedness in high places." (Ephesians 6:11-13) Apostle Paul saw human life of the individual as a linear construct, from birth to death to judgment, (Hebrews 9:27) but perhaps life in general is more like a mobius with no beginning or ending...or is it merely a very small part of the solar system, all destined to wind down like a gigantic clock and eventually to disappear in a giant "poof" of cosmic disintegration when the Earth, all the planets, and the Sun implode to whatever end there is for only God the Almighty One to know.

Is life like a maze or a labyrinth…a linear strip from birth to death, or a mobius of never ending reincarnations? Pierre Teilhard de Chardin said we actually are spirits having a human experience. Modern science says there could be an infinite number of universes to accommodate all possible options...amazing. Where could such a thought come from? Are life and death merely transitions from dust to dust, one state of entropy to another, all seeking equilibrium? If energy is not expressed in some material form of tension between creation and decay, good and evil, where is it? Since it can neither be created nor destroyed, does energy exist outside of space and time or does it have finite limits that will eventually be concluded? What does all this have to do with life and death, wars and rumors of wars? Or the new heaven and the new Earth the Bible predicts are to replace what now exists? Why even think about it?

21. Words, More Words, Beyond Words.

Tobias S. Gibson (1776-1804) said, "Great people talk about ideas, average people talk about things, and small people talk about other people." No matter what they talk about, sheeple all must use words to convey their thoughts. We may take the use of words for granted, but only a little investigation reveals some very deep illusions and misconceptions. The use of words as symbols of thoughts is called semantics. The study of words is called philology. When it is applied to different cultures it is linguistics. No one actually knows how many languages there are as some of them are yet to be discovered and many have no written form. In western English there are estimated to be more than one million words, although most sheeple use less than 2,500. The first real language seems to be Sanskrit, found in ancient India. The invention of symbols or characters to make up words, called alphabets, is lost in history. The earliest known form of cuneiform writing is dated to about 3,000 B.C. and attributed to Sumerians in southern Mesopotamia. The Bible says that various languages were invoked by God to scramble the communications between sheeple who were building a tower to heaven so they could not share knowledge and become gods. The gods were not happy with the ability of mankind to share their discoveries without limitation so various languages were assigned to the different tribes to add more than a little confusion and prevent the completion of the tower called Babel. (Genesis 11: 1-5)

Now, there are thousands of different languages among Homo sapiens, each with its own set of symbols and numbers and rules of grammar. The first pure alphabet emerged around 2500 B.C. to represent the language of Semitic workers in Egypt during the Middle Bronze Age, and was derived from the alphabetic principles of the Egyptian hieroglyphs, pictorials that showed the lives of the pharaohs on walls and in tombs. Most alphabets in the world today either descend directly from this development, or were inspired by its design. Some languages use symbols for word combinations instead of letters, as in Asian cultures, China, Japan, and Korea. One thing common to all of them seems to be the way words are strung together into sentences to convey messages. Another is that words can be grouped into descriptive functions including nouns, pronouns, verbs, adverbs, adjectives, etc. Further, there are rules of grammar about how all this should be done. Words are learned as sounds long before they take any kind of visual form in the mind of a child. Attribution of meaning to words seems to be one of the instinctive abilities of Homo sapiens, but obviously that meaning is subjective and unique to each individual learning it. [Some words are politically and socially more sensitive, thus powerful, than others. For example, the 'N" word in "The Adventures of Huckleberry Finn" (1885) by Mark Twain was so offensive to some school boards that the classic was edited and reissued in 2010 with the offensive word changed to "slave" throughout.]

The acquisition of word meaning is one of the fundamental issues in the study of mind and what separates humankind from the other animals. Children, like Helen Keller, who are born sans sight and hearing are little more than instinctive animals until they get the notion that the touch of fingers in their palms conveys meaning. Once she understood hand language, Helen Keller (1880-1968) became the first deaf/blind person to earn a college degree (at Radcliffe college) and a world famous writer and speaker about the contemporary issues of her time. Researchers are studying, in addition, how exposure to words shapes the brain of a child and affects his perception of the world and vice versa. There is a distinct cultural indoctrination that undoubtedly goes on in each social area where children are taught and otherwise pick up through their experience certain rules and standards as to how things are, how life works, by the use of words. What each kid takes away from that experience creates the filter through which everyone interprets reality. Learning the meaning of "banana" is far different from that of "stockbroker." Words are added to personal vocabulary all through life, whether in a random fashion or by some divine design is unknowable.

The restriction of email messages to 140 characters called "tweets" by Twitter undoubtedly is changing word usage even now. Inner city ghetto children obviously have a different view of the world from those in affluent and rural areas. If parents do not care if a child says "goed" instead of "went" or "aks" instead of "ask," guess what. Consider how "negro" was replaced with "black" to create and sustain a social dichotomy that presages racial strife. Words classified as profanity are politically incorrect and are not used in public by upper class sheeple. What children hear at home and in the streets trumps what they hear in school; this is a fact. To complicate matters, some different words have common meanings (synonyms) and some words have opposite meanings (antonyms), and maybe the most confusing are words called homonyms that sound alike but have different meanings (passed-past, mail-male, capital-capitol, principle-principal, weight-wait, here - hear for example.) Consider explaining this to a foreign student, "I have to spend some capital to go to the capital to see the capitol." Some words have different meanings related to their context of usage; "patient," for example which can be noun or verb. "Sit here and be patient while I go see my patient."

Moreover, the meaning of words changes with time and the social standards of culture. This poses a challenge for Bible scholars who wish to discern the actual meaning the writers meant to convey in their original Greek language as it was compiled from the Hebrew version of the Old Testament and the Aramaic as spoken by Jesus. The Roman version was translated into Latin where it stayed until Martin Luther made his translation into German and from there to the other various languages. Therefore, the original meaning and context of the "Word of God" is clouded in mystery and misunderstanding. Words are used to compose sentences and they are used to communicate concepts, ideas, opinions, observations, etc. all of which are unique to the source, but they are translated and interpreted differently by the receiver. New thoughts and concepts often require that new words must be created to provide adequate symbols. New English language words are being created all the time. "Tweet," for example.

Trying to translate words from one language to another cannot be exact, so that understanding between sheeple is indefinitely uncertain. There is no such thing as word for word translation from one language to another. For example, one might think that "white house" rendered as "casa blanca" in Spanish indicates the word for "house" in Spanish is "blanca," if you did not know that in Spanish the order of adjectives and nouns is reversed. Thus, "casa blanca" literally is "house white." That is, the words of one language do not perfectly correspond to the words of another language. As words are used in different contexts and with different shades of meaning, a decision has to be made on which English word or phrase is the best to use in each case of translation. Little wonder that sheeple have such difficulty understanding and accepting their differing cultures.

The Bible is a prime case in point. Originals in Hebrew and Aramaic languages were translated into Greek and then into Latin before German by Martin Luther and then to English. Almost all common Greek or Hebrew words can be translated into more than one English word at different places in the Bible. The Greek word "agape" is translated both as "charity" and "love" in many places. Charity is an interesting case in the King James Bible because the 1 Corinthians 13 passage, which uses charity 9 times, was translated using the word love in Tyndale's New Testament of 1526 - 85 years before the King James translation. It is tempting to assume that love is expressed in charity or that charity is an expression of love. In either case it is interpreted as unconditional giving, but for many scholars they are not the same. When C.G. Jung (1875-1961) was asked if he believed in God he replied, "I don't have to believe...I know." You could do some homework trying to figure out what he meant. This all gets very complicated as the meaning of words can only be explained by using other words. American English now contains more than one million separate words, and a new one is being added every 98 minutes. Some researchers claim that American high school graduates are exposed to about 45,000 words, but most sheeple get by with fewer than 1,000 words in their daily communications. Talking is taken for granted by both sexes, but it seems that women use talking more to help each other while men use talking to teach

each other. Cross gender confusion abounds because of this difference, according to Deborah Tannen in her classic work, You Just Don't Understand. (1991, 2001) She claims that a six year old girl has more words in common with a teenage girl than with a six year old boy.

Words often are used for power and control. There is a dialogue in Through the Looking Glass (2001) by Lewis Carroll as follows: "When I use a word," Humpty Dumpty said, in a rather scornful tone, "it means just what I choose it to mean – neither more nor less." "The question is," said Alice, "whether you can make words mean so many different things." "The question is," said Humpty Dumpty, "which is to be the master – that's all." Indeed. Words actually are symbols of thoughts which are...well, incomprehensible. Consider the various ways that various Supreme Courts have interpreted words in the U.S. Constitution. One example is the way it overturned a Federal law prohibiting images of dog fights on the Internet. By a vote of 8-1 it concluded the law went too far in prohibiting free speech, even though dog fighting is illegal. It is not unusual for the Court to use words to overturn rulings of lesser courts and even to reprimand legislatures for their use of words. Judges still are debating a precise meaning for Amendment 2 which states, "...the right to keep and bear arms shall not be infringed."

It's all about dominance and submission. Isn't that the basis of wars? Adolf Hitler (1889-1945) mastered the art of propaganda and used it relentlessly during WWII to support his goals. He commented about its success during WWI in Mein Kampf, (1926) "Once the basic ideas and methods of execution [of propaganda] were recognized as correct, they were applied throughout the whole war without the slightest change. At first the claims of the propaganda were so impudent that people thought it insane; later, it got on peoples' nerves; and in the end, it was believed. Propaganda is no more than a weapon, though a frightful one in the hand of an expert." Presently, Sec. Hilary Clinton has complained to Congress that we are losing the international war of words needed to influence hearts and minds among youth in the Muslim nations who hate our way of life.

Nowhere is this more obvious than in the wordy deliberations of the U.S. Congress which often/usually result in unintended consequences. When ambiguity reigns in the public press, as it usually does, the solution to a public need cannot be legislated until there is a consensus on the problem that goes to an issue that is followed by a national policy. Another obvious, although seldom recognized, example is the necessity of words from the pulpits of churches to keep the faithful coming back each week with their monetary donations. Experience shows that without the weekly doses of oratory from the pulpit, the lambs soon forget they need a shepherd and move on without him, seldom cracking the "good book" on their own volition. Little wonder the Vatican recommends daily mass for the faithful, to keep them faithful. Actually, the use of words by hypnotists and practitioners of neurolinguistic programming (NLP) to reprogram the mind shows how powerful they are. Words create an involuntary reaction. For example, compare "vomit" with "rose." That is why advertisers often use the word "save" when they really mean "buy."

Words grouped into sentences seem to be the glue that holds social groups together, limited by various languages. The optimum size of tribal groups without mass communications seems to be about 150 sheeple. Communicating with a common language enables sheeple to bond together for support and defense, as well as to distinguish their tribe from another. As the ability to disseminate words from invention of the printing press expanded, so did the size of social groups until now there are nations that occupy entire continents. But, in a multicultural nation like the U.S, regional differences in use of words and dialects distinguish subsets of the culture from each other. This is seen dramatically in the Canadian province of Quebec that is more French than English. Someone said that great sheeple talk about ideas, average sheeple talk about things, and little sheeple talk about other sheeple. Some have used this form of covert conversational hypnosis over the Internet for illegal purposes and to create support for political ideologies. The Internet is a neutral mass medium of communicating words that can have monumental impact, for good and ill. Since the advent of television and now iPhone-text marketing, sheeple are spending more and more of their discretionary time listening and watching the purveyors of information contaminate their reasoning ability without realizing it is being stolen from them.

[Much of the product marketing on the Internet actually is done by independent sellers fronting for undisclosed suppliers. Their product claims usually are nothing more than just that, claims, and their guarantees are nothing but web site promises. After they get your money the results are indefinitely uncertain. Some of the worst offenders are the resellers of dietary supplements sold to substitute for FDA approved drugs. The Internet is totally unregulated and the scammers want to keep it that way. So, buyers beware.]

Studies of the brain indicate that sheeple are more inclined to recognize words visually than they are random color patterns. Thus, if the word "blue" is presented in a red color, and observers are asked to identify its color, most sheeple will say blue. Pick up any commercial magazine and you will likely see images in advertisements overwhelming words. Check an older magazine in the library and you will see this change in print. The meaning of words changes with time and the social context, so there is no absolute definition of anything, except by the use of other words which change with time and context. For example, 1+1 = 2 only in the Arabic number system, while in the binary system of computers 1+1= 10. Sometimes new words are invented to convey new thoughts. So it is delusional to assume that words mean the same things to everyone. A thing is just a thing…it is we who give it a label and attach meaning and value to it. Gravity would still be the same even if we called it peanuts or ice cream. But some things are different. One of the most common confusions in use of words is substituting "feel" for "think"…as in I feel that …whatever. Soon as you see or hear the word "feel" followed by the word "that" or "like" you know the person is making this confusion between thinking and feeling. It is very common among writers and can be seen and heard all the time. Women are more likely to use the word – feel – while men prefer – think-. There-in lies much of the gender wars. So if the word "feel" is substituted for the word "think" both words lose their meaning. Since words with variable meanings are used in scriptures made sacred there is little wonder that translations become interpretations, the reason why there is no end to arguments about the meaning of sacred texts.

When you attempt to translate ancient words into modern usage, the original meaning is totally obscured. In just one example, the original Hebrew word "nphish" is translated into at least forty-four different English words in the Kings James Bible, although its original meaning might have been "spirit." A list of the Biblical occurrences of "psuche," thought to be the Greek word for "soul," in many different forms also proves the point. The Greek word for "will," as in the will of God the Almighty One, is translated into at least ten different words in the King James Bible. There are at least eleven different Hebrew words that were all translated as "word' in the Old Testament. So, who knows what the original text really meant to the writer, as; "In the beginning was the Word and the Word was with God and the Word was God?" (John 1:1) Also, throughout the Kings James Bible, God and the Holy Spirit are referred to as "he" and "him," while in the earliest and more accurate translations the words "it" and "itself" were used. British philologist, John Allegro, (1923-1988) studied the words in the Dead Sea Scrolls and suggested that they indicated the story of Jesus in the Bible was an extension of the "Teacher of Righteousness" who was a central figure among the Essenes of the first century, possibly a shaman who used a psychedelic mushroom in his incantations; The Sacred Mushroom and the Cross. (1970).

[Allegro's linguistic clues criss-cross different cultures and lead into many-layered webs of association. They led him to believe that a fertility myth based on using the sacred mushroom, amanita muscaria, as a gateway to divine understanding, was at the root of many religions, including Christianity. The mushroom was seen as a symbol of God on Earth and in its life he saw the culmination of the act of procreation by God. But because mushroom lore was secret, he reasoned that the myth had to be written down in the form of codes hidden in folk tales, which became the New Testament. "This is the basic origin of the stories of the New Testament. They were a literary device to spread the rites of mushroom worship to the faithful…The stories of the Gospels and Acts were a deliberate hoax. Through studying Sumerian cuneiform texts which go back to 3500 B.C., we can trace the proper names and words used in the Bible back to their original meanings."]

Allegro was soundly criticized by Catholic authorities for his suggestions and isolated by his peers; he did not live to see the full presentation of the Dead Sea Scrolls. Nothing seems to be more confusing than attempts to discuss concepts of religion, spirituality and such in words. [A case in point could be use of the word "sheeple" for "people" in this text. Although Jesus referred to the relationship between him and his followers as that of a shepherd and his sheep, not everyone likes it.] As a result of such confusion, each one interprets scripture to suit his inclination, according to his given system of theology and contemporary use of words; one might even say his faith. "Now faith is being sure of what we hope for and certain of what we do not see. (Hebrews 11:1-3) One might ask where does such faith come from? Is it something that is taught or does it just come naturally? Abd-ru-shin [a.k.a. Oskar Bernhardt (1875-1941)] claimed that it comes from God; "All teachings were at one time will by God, precisely adapted to the individual peoples and countries and formed in complete accord with their actual spiritual maturity and receptivity."

Some concepts are unexplainable in words. *Just try to describe a bicycle to someone verbally without using a picture of it. "Spirit" and "soul" also come with much ambiguity.* When Job laments, "My soul is weary of my life," who is the possessor of soul and life speaking? (Job 10:1) Try explaining what "my self" means. Conscious, unconscious, and subconscious mind also lack clear definitions, as does the Jungian concept of personal wholeness. Words cannot explain such things. In fact, the very existence of mind can only be inferred from actions, sort of like assuming the existence of an invisible planet in space by observing the wobble of its star from the pull of its gravity in orbit. Trying to steer sheeple into new thoughts became too much for St.Thomas a Kempis (1380-1471). He concluded, "It is more profitable to leave everyone to his way of thinking than to give way to contentious discourses."

The Bible says that there was a time when all sheeple spoke the same language, estimated beginning some 40,000 years ago according to anthropology. The earliest written language seems to date back to 4,000 B.C. in the land of Sumeria, presently southern Iraq. From there languages spread throughout both east and west. They got cocky and tried to build a tower all the way up to Heaven to see what it was like. But God stopped them and confused their languages lest "...nothing will be restrained from which they imagined to do. Therefore, the name of it is called Babel and the sheeple were scattered abroad upon the Earth." (Genesis 11:4-9). The master has spoken and it is so. But that is not the end of the story. Sheeple eventually learned how to translate from one language to another, and to communicate instantly via the Internet, so it appears that God had to then confound their understanding by continually creating new words and even whole new belief systems to keep them ignorant of his reality.

Not only are nationalities and cultures separated by languages, but within societies the use of words varies within groups and according to education and preferred usage. Some words evoke emotions that many sheeple would rather not feel, so they use milder substitutes, like "passing over" instead of "dying." Some words evoke actions, like the retail store with the marque that says "Buy, Buy, Baby." To make it even more interesting every society seems to have words that are acceptable and unacceptable. Some words are socially taboo for this reason. Dirty words are used in states of emotional arousal and distress when the socially approved versions will not suffice to convey the full meaning among sheeple with insufficient vocabulary. The meanings of words also changes with time and social standards. During the Victorian era of sexual repression in English literature words like "leg," "thigh," and "breast" were not used in public. So we got "dark meat" and "light meat" instead. Santa now is being instructed to go "HA HA HA" because the more traditional "HO HO HO" has degraded the historical profession of prostitutes. Words of praise can make sheeple feel pride in themselves and motivate them to extraordinary behavior, while words of criticism demean sheeple and make them feel like losers. Relationships are greatly enhanced if sheeple include praise, empathy, attention, and approval in conversations. Also, new words are continually being created as existing words fail to express the latest developments in human endeavors. "Astronaut" did not exist before the space program invented it. Now there is "website" and "twitter" and "tweet" and "texting" and "sexting" made possible by wireless personal cell phones. It goes on and on.

You may never have realized it, but the meaning of words is controlled primarily by the receiver of them and not the sender. Humpty Dumpty was wrong. Every word we utter activates what neuroscientists call networks of association - these are interconnected sets of thoughts, memories and emotions stacked up in every life, what Apostle Paul referred to as seeing "through a glass darkly." As such, words have unique meanings to every person. Proof of this is in the response that you get. As the brain ages it becomes less able to organize all the words that it has compiled and eventually mental disorders, such as Alzheimers disease and dementia, make communications all but impossible. Now, overlay this situation with the need for translations between languages to engage in commerce and political negotiations and the confusion among Homo sapiens becomes all but insurmountable. For example, there is no ham in hamburgers; they are all beef. How would you explain a "hot dog" or "bicycle" to someone who never saw one? In addition, as one progresses through evolution of consciousness words become less and less able to convey the meaning of spiritual matters. Perhaps the ancient Chinese knew this principle when they said, "The tao that can be expressed is not the eternal Tao." And, "the one who knows does not speak and the one who speaks does not know." But even misdirected silent meditation has no merit according to this ancient Buddhist saying; "Sitting peacefully on a cushion day and night, rejecting life and death in hopes of realizing enlightenment, is all like a monkey grasping at the moon reflected in the water."

It should be pointed out to all Sunday School classes that an actual Word of God does not exist. Only man's feeble attempts to recover the scattered and often mistranslated fragments of writing by ancient scribes and prophets in Hebrew, Greek, and Latin are available. The Nicene Creed, or Symbol of Faith of the Catholic Church, was written by the First Ecumenical Council at Nicaea in 325 C.E., with the third paragraph and following added by the first Council of Constantinople in 381 C.E. The final version was accepted by the Church in the year 1014 C.E., and that revision has been part of Catholic doctrine ever since. However, this led to the Great Schism in 1053 CE and to this day, the Eastern Orthodox Churches do not accept the Creed and raise this as one of many reasons that prevent their re-unification with the Roman Catholic Church. All translations of sacred scriptures contain variations of contemporary interpretation; the venerated King James Version of the Bible probably is the most objectionable. For example, the word "love" that is favored in most translations of First Corinthians, chapter 13, is entered as "charity" in the King James Version. As such, charity has come to mean unconditional love. But, the intention of the original Hebrew writer is lost.

In part to standardize these variations, The New International Version® (NIV) is a completely new translation of the Holy Bible made by more than 100 scholars working directly from the best available

Hebrew, Aramaic, and Greek texts. It took 10 years to complete the NIV translation. The process started in 1968 and was finished in 1978. This does not include more than 10 years of planning before 1968. The work was sponsored by the International Bible Society. But, there are some "King James Only" believers who claim any deviation from that translation is a work of the Devil. It's challenging to fit your personal perspective of the cosmos into someone else's definition of how things should be. Therefore, arguments about the meaning of scripture will go on forever, all in the will of God the Almighty One of course. If there is any truth at all, it probably cannot be put into words. Things are just as they are. It is we who give them names and assign them a value. With nothing to prove the truth of scriptures, sheeple are left to live with indefinite uncertainty about the sacred. It is impossible to define spirituality because faith beliefs defy words. If you aren't content with dogmatic religious thinking, go explore metaphysics for yourself and then change your worldview if necessary...or not. And think about the role of words as you enter the polling booth next time to cast your vote for your favorite candidate because you cannot possibly know the outcome of your choice from campaign rhetoric. It is beyond words.

The words that we all live by, and die by, must come from some place or other. Perhaps we all are given to believe what we believe by the words that we are given. They all seem to come from someplace, perhaps from God. Abd-ru-shin [a.k.a. Oskar Bernhardt (1875-1941)] concluded, "All teachings/words were at one time willed by God, precisely adapted to the individual peoples and countries and formed in complete accord with their actual spiritual maturity and receptivity." If you think God ever gets it wrong, that's because you are a mere human who lacks God's perfect knowledge. Tragedy and brutality, such as cancer and the Holocaust, are attributed to human sinful free will but that, too, must be the will of God the Almighty One and reflects the nature of God since he made man in his own image. Parents of the infants who were killed by order of King Herod in his attempt to remove Jesus, "king of the Jews," must have been stunned by the evil power of his words.

When you are hurting very badly sometimes words are not very helpful but they may be all we have to offer. C.S. Lewis tried to reconcile human suffering with these words: "Tortures occur. If they are unnecessary then there is no God, or a bad one. If there is a good God, then these tortures are necessary. For no even moderately good Being could possibly inflict or permit them if they were not." "As for God, his way is perfect." (2 Samuel 22:31). Mother Teresa concluded we must take what he gives and give what he takes. On the one hand there was Parmenides in the dialogues of Plato who believed God was unchangeable being, known only by reason and unaffected by emotion. Change, to Parmenides, was just an illusion of the senses. Everything that might happen is foreknown by God the Almighty One, and in a world where only one mind exists the foreknown has in effect already happened and no different action is possible. The view of Parmenides was widely accepted in western Christianity and endures to this day.

Heraclitus, on the other hand, believed God was eternal becoming and that change was the only constant in life. This alternate view of Heraclitus became a bridge for many later views of God. Some things, like orgasms, just are beyond words. Poet laureate, T.S. Eliot (1888-1965) wrote for the speaker in "The Lovesong of J. Alfred Prufrock," "It is impossible to say just what I mean!"...as though the tongues of both writer and character were paralyzed by their consciousness. Prufrock's vision is incommunicable. The Calvinist declares, "So it must be concluded that while the turbulent state of the world deprives us of judgment, God, by the pure light of his own righteousness and wisdom, regulates these very commotions in the most exact order and directs them to their proper end."

In their deepest sense, words are symbols for thoughts that are symbols of meanings that cannot be conveyed except by the use of other words. There are some words used to describe ideas beyond words. "Nothing," for example can only be defined with words that mean something. Therefore, some philosophers claim that "nothing"cannot exist. A Course in Miracles (1975) proclaims, "Only the Word of God has any meaning because it symbolizes that which has no human symbols at all...there are many who must be reached through words, being as yet unable to hear in silence...The teacher of God must learn to use words in a new way. Gradually he learns how to let his words be chosen for him by ceasing to decide for himself what he will say." Jesus instructed his disciples, "When you are brought before synagogues, rulers and authorities, do not worry about how you will defend yourselves or what you will say, for the Holy Spirit will teach you at that time what you should say." (Luke 12:11-12) But, he remained silent when Pontius Pilate, the Roman governor asked him, "What is truth?" Recall the Taoist sage wrote, "The one who speaks does not know and the one who knows does not speak." Odd, isn't it, that Jesus first chose his disciples, then taught them his wisdom, set them before adversaries, and finally disallowed them to speak for themselves. All in the will of God the Almighty One of course.

However, there is always an opposite thought and Adolf Hitler had an opposite idea as he explained in his autobiography, Mein Kampf, (1926) "For let it be said to all our present-day fops and knights of the pen: the greatest revolutions in this world have never been directed by a goose-quill! No, to the pen it has always been reserved to provide their theoretical foundations. But the power which has always started the greatest religious and political avalanches in history rolling has from time immemorial been the magic power of the spoken word, and that alone. Particularly, the broad masses of the people can be moved only by the power of speech. And all great movements are popular movements, volcanic eruptions of human passions and emotional sentiments, stirred either by the cruel Goddess of Distress or by the firebrand of the word hurled among the masses; they are not the lemonade-like outpourings of literary aesthetes and drawing room heroes. Only a storm of hot passion can turn the destinies of peoples, and he alone can arouse passion who bears it within himself. It alone gives its chosen one the words which like hammer blows can open the gates to the heart of a people. But the man whom passion fails and whose lips are sealed- he has not been chosen by Heaven to proclaim its will. Therefore, let the writer remain by his ink-well, engaging in theoretical activity, if his intelligence and ability are equal to it; for leadership he is neither born nor chosen." Thanks to his passionate oratory, some 56 million sheeple lost their lives in Europe during WWII. [Another 17 million sheeple were killed in Asia during the war with Japan.] Nevertheless, Hitler acknowledged he was self-educated by reading many books and pamphlets, although he never quoted any of his sources. And it remains that the pen of Thomas Paine was singularly powerful toward inciting the American Revolution against the British crown when his hand-distributed pamphlets were the only practical means of public communications.

For all his powerful oratory, Hitler ended his life in utter failure and disgrace taking his sheeple with him. Some say his interim success was not due to his oratory but, rather because he was merely the voice of the German culture during his time chosen by God for that role. How else can one explain his rise from obscurity to infamy unless it was the will of God the Almighty One?. Perhaps, though, Hitler was right, because both Jesus and Muhammad relied upon oratory for the communication of their messages, as do the most successful evangelists among the various religions as well as politicians [which actually means "many tongues"]. In contrast, the oratory of Paul and Barnabas seems to have been the primary form of persuasion that spread Christianity from the Jews to the Gentiles as described in the book of Acts. Muslims rely primarily upon the oratory of their local imams to interpret teachings of the Koran. But, that was before the Internet. The political success of President Obama may support the power of oratory, but the power of Internet written communications definitely helped to get his campaign words to the voters. All in the will of God the Almighty One of course.

Some things just are beyond words. Mark Twain (1835-1910) [a.k.a. Samuel Clemens] observed, "Anyone who lifts a cat by the tail learns something words cannot convey." It is more than interesting that none of the twelve astronauts who walked on the moon ever found words satisfactory to convey their experience. Especially for Edgar Mitchell, it was a mystical journey. After his view of Earth from space he organized the Institute of Noetic Science to explore the intuitive nature of mankind. Bishop John Spong expressed this experience thus: "Mysticism is to me primarily coming to terms with the limitations of words. That seems to be harder to do in religious circles than anywhere else. Words are always symbols or pointers. They are not the truth or the essence they seek to describe. They are always human, always time bound and always time warped. When any human experience is reduced to words, it is always distorted by time, place, one's level of knowledge, one's time in history and one's culturally conditioned language. Nowhere is that more clear than when we try to frame who or what God is in the vehicle of human words. A horse cannot communicate to another horse what it means to be a human being, for a horse cannot escape its horse nature. A human being can never tell another human being what it means to be God, because human beings can never escape the limits of our human nature. Perhaps that is why all human images of God look very much like a great big human being. I doubt if Humpty Dumpty ever sat on a great wall only to fall and be shattered in such a way that all the king's horses and all the king's men could not put Humpty Dumpty together again. I do think it is literally true, however, that some human actions have irrevocable consequences, which can never be overcome, so this nursery rhyme points to truth that mere words cannot capture. Much of the religious language of both the Bible and the church liturgy is this kind of communication. The deeper I experience the reality and presence of God, the less my words seem like adequate vehicles to express that truth. Then words cease and one enters the experience of wordless wonder."

The hope for some afterlife fails to find words sufficient for explanation. The prolific science fiction writer, Isaac Asimov, (1920-1992) interviewed for Bill Moyers' series on PBS, "A World of Ideas," questioned the traditional religious picture of our fate after death: "When I die I won't go to heaven or hell, there will just be nothingness." Asimov's naturalistically based skepticism about heaven or hell is common among secular humanists because there is no evidence for such realms, but he commits an equally common fallacy in his blithe assumption about nothingness, namely that it could be. By substituting nothingness for heaven and hell, Asimov implies that it awaits us after death. Indeed the word itself, with the suffix "ness," conjures up the strange notion of "that stuff which does not exist." In using it we may start to think, in a rather casual, unreflective way, that there exists something that doesn't exist, but of course this is not a little contradictory. We must simply see that nothingness doesn't exist, period. We have no word for something that does not exist. We say the deceased "are" dead, a being verb.

Of this gnosis, knowing without words, St. Teresa of Avila (1515-1582) wrote, "Though perfectly formed, the words are not heard with the bodily ear; yet they are understood much more clearly than if they were so heard, and, however determined one's resistance, it is impossible to fail to hear them. For when, on the natural plane, we do not wish to hear, we can close our ears, or attend to something else, with the result that, although we may hear, we do not understand. But when God talks in this way to the soul, there is no such remedy: I have to listen, whether I like it or not, and my understanding has to devote itself so completely to what God wishes me to understand that whether I want to listen or not makes no difference. For, as He who is all-powerful wills us to understand, we have to do what He wills; and He reveals Himself as our true Lord." A Course in Miracles (1975) which is claimed to be channeled from Jesus to its scribe, Dr. Helen Schucman (1909-1981) declares: "We say God is; and then we cease to speak for in that knowledge words are meaningless. God does not understand words, [as if God had some limitations] for they were made by separated minds to keep them in the illusion of separation. Let us not forget that words are but symbols of symbols. They are thus twice removed from reality." It is more than a little curious that the "Course" requires three volumes of words to reach that conclusion. Sometimes it is better to keep your mouth shut and be thought a fool than to open it and remove all doubt.

Words contain information and science now claims that information, like energy, can neither be created nor destroyed. This idea means that all the thoughts of all mankind ever put into words may be drifting about someplace beyond time and space. As such, information is not created, only discovered. If there is any immortality, perhaps it exists in the immortal energy of words. As he was dying St. Thomas Aquinas, (1225- 1274) who probably wrote the basis for Catholic dogma said, "I can do no more. Such secrets have been revealed to me that all I have written now appears to be of little value." As it is said in Taoism, the one who speaks does not know, and the one who knows does not speak. Ultimately, truth may be beyond words. Feel good inside no matter what happens outside. Enough said.

SUMMARY

This collection of essays focuses on some metaphysical issues that baby boomers may contend with as they get older and encounter the many challenges of aging. They were selected by inspiration from among the complete set of essays by the author that was compiled from metaphorical encounters during trips to Sedona, AZ published in Lessons from Sedona. Although "metaphysics" has become so broad a word that a definition is difficult, it may said to be a branch of philosophy dealing with matters for which rational logic runs into a dead end. Consider the effectiveness of placebos in medical treatments, for example, for which there is no scientific explanation. It also contends with the wholeness of being human in terms of the physical, intellectual, emotional, and spiritual quadrants of life. Life itself is an enigma that has little to no specific definition. The use of words for such a discussion has limitations because their meaning is in the mind of the receiver more than the sender. And everyone sees what they perceive through a unique filter based upon experience and genetics over which they have no control. As such, some things are beyond words. Perhaps that is why new words are being created continuously.

Like words, ideas are not static and cannot be contained within time and space. Nevertheless, one hopes that reading these essays will stimulate thinking among the baby boomers as they might not have been motivated before. Moreover, they may also enable those who must contend with the existential crisis that marks the end of control to reconcile courage and surrender in measures that equal calm submission to the inevitable suffering that presages death. This may be the only way to feel good inside no matter what happens outside. Traditional belief systems often avoid contending with the challenges that mankind encounters when coping with the terminal years on Earth. They may be impotent and irrelevant to the reality of issues in aging. When the dependable "do this-get that" assumptions no longer work mental health requires that some new and different system of thought must tackle the existential anxiety of mankind. For this author, the solution he found is described in the principles of Theofatalism™ and applying them to the affairs of Homo sapiens. All in God's will of course, as there can be no other...AIGWOC.

Only one thing is certain, what's done is done, as was described in the poetry of Omar Khayyam (1048-1131): "The moving finger writes; and, having writ, Moves on: nor all thy piety nor wit shall lure it back to cancel half a line, Nor all thy tears wash out a word of it." No one can change the past, but perhaps there is some hope for the future. Maybe this could be it; delivered with love and pity for all those sheeple who did not ask to be born and will have to suffer the many disappointments, losses, and painful struggles in order to live as long as they must.

If you wish to continue this dialogue with the author, email him at lewtag@aol.com.

Appendix
Start a Discussion and Support Group.

Anthropologist, Margaret Mead (1901-1978) observed, "Never doubt that a few thoughtful, committed people can change the world." The flight crews of the suicide flights that attacked America on 9/11/01 certainly proved that. Support groups can be convened by average sheeple to deal with a wide variety of life issues. All you need to do is invite a group of sheeple who want to work together on common issues in managing stressful living amongst struggle and suffering. Merely having a mutual interest in helping each other can produce effective results. Perhaps you are called to get such a group started in your neighborhood among families dealing with issues in the aging of America.

A few basic ground rules of operation can help make group discussion a very effective growth experience.

[Note: This is not professional therapy for clients seeking counseling for mental or emotional distress. Anyone seeking such treatment should be referred to competent professionals or local government agencies for appropriate services.]

1. Choose a quiet meeting place without distractions and make it a regularly scheduled event that is convenient in the weekly calendar of activities. Sometimes churches or other public facility managers will make such a place available for weekly meetings at a convenient time for

the participants. Homes are suitable meeting places if a quiet room big enough is available. Avoid refreshments until after the meeting.

2. Open each meeting with a short restatement of its purpose, e.g., healing the stress of life with the Principles of Theofatalism™. Select the essay for discussion and print out a copy for the participants who may not have the book. Read the selected essay and ask for discussion that relates it to current experience and understanding of the members.

3. Start and end each meeting precisely at the agreed-upon times. Keep the sessions to two hours or less. Give each newcomer a few minutes to share his/her background and objective for joining the group. Then have those in the group who volunteer to do so give a short summary of their backgrounds to the newcomer.

4. Use first names only, following with the first letter of the last name, unless participants specifically decide to share their full names. Exchange telephone numbers or e-mails and encourage members to call each other between meetings to share further. Often close friendships are developed this way.

5. During the meeting, members may focus discussion on one of these essays. Other members may then comment on the way the same material has affected their lives and offer feedback to the originator if permission is asked and received. However avoid crosstalk between members and specific responses directed to one who has just spoken. Such crosstalk can be harmful to the healing process and creates a codependent environment, especially if it involves judging or advising by unqualified speakers. You want to create a safe place where sheeple can be free to express their thoughts and feelings without being judged, rejected, or ill-advised. Each member should share only his or her own experience, thoughts, feelings, strength, despair, or hope.

6. If it is part of the agreement, take a collection at each meeting to compensate the space provider for snacks and compile a central account for occasional group socials, publicity, and the like. Members might be chosen to keep the records, make plans, and safeguard any financial resources. However, no formal organization is needed or recommended.

7. Encourage expressions of negative and positive feelings alike, complete with profanity and tears or laughing and hugging if a person wants to make such a disclosure. Let all expressions of emotion be OK

without judging them. Do not deny or prevent expression of any strong emotions or belittle tears and rages. Have some soft tissues handy.

8. Alternate leadership of the group regularly, so no one person becomes a teacher or takes on responsibility for fixing broken members of the class. Each person must be free to work out his or her own healing in relation to God. Leaders should not display fear, tension, nervousness, or insecurity around the group. They should be detached, but interested facilitators during their period of service.

9. Encourage everyone to leave the group when their work is well along, so they can transition to spiritual evolution on their own, and make room for others. Support groups should not become a lifetime crutch or substitute for self-reliance, but they often can provide the baseline for launching lifelong evolution of growth in consciousness.

10. If the group grows beyond ten to twelve members, consider starting a second group. Participation may be attenuated if too many sheeple prevent adequate time for sharing. Caution: If any member of the group seems uncontrollably disruptive or misbehaves to the point of alarming or threatening other members, that person should be carefully, but seriously, invited to leave and encouraged to get professional help. If there is evidence of actual mental disorder, insist that the person see competent medical professionals.

When the worst kinds of things happen, many cannot reconcile reality with their traditional assumptions alone. That may be more or less difficult for you to do, depending on how you are made. The secret to growth is in expecting that benefits of your new life will far exceed the burdens of giving up your old life. Some sheeple seem to accept the benefits of growth more easily, while others resist giving up the familiar burdens; in other words, they hang onto legacy behavior and beliefs because it hurts too much to give them up. C. G. Jung observed that all growth is painful, so if you are not hurting you are not growing. Learning means change and that always is fearful, but it can be exciting too. Many are called to walk alone, but it helps to have partners in your walk through the suffering growth of life.

Personality plays a role in group participation. It may be that extraverts, who respond to events, sheeple, and things outside themselves, will be less able to give up their externally driven stimulants, while introverts, who respond more to ideas, concepts, and information from inside themselves, are less prone to being controlled by events outside themselves. However, extraverts may feel more comfortable sharing their thoughts in groups than introverts. Extraverts must speak to know what they are thinking, and introverts must think to know what to say. It is said that if you don't know what an extravert is thinking, you haven't listened, and if you don't know what an introvert is thinking, you haven't asked.

All growth is painful and scary, as we must let go of familiar discomfort to move into uncertain futures. In comfort there is no growth. The psyche/soul must grow or decline, like an airplane that must fly faster than its stall speed or it will crash. A soul that is not growing is dying. The continuous process of discovery can always benefit from renewal through group therapy. One who learned this lesson said, "It is like spring cleaning. You get to dust off everything and sort through stuff. You get to throw a lot of junk away." Another said it is like weeding your garden: "once is never enough." The Dutch have a saying, "We grow too soon old and too late smart." Perhaps these essays will provide a little way of offsetting that truth with some challenges for baby boomers that could help before it is too late to avoid the shock.